# Getting Good Crops

*The Civilization of the American Indian Series*

# Getting Good Crops

## Economic and Diplomatic Survival Strategies of the Montana Bitterroot Salish Indians, 1870–1891

ROBERT J. BIGART

UNIVERSITY OF OKLAHOMA PRESS : NORMAN

Publication of this book is made possible through the generosity of Edith Kinney Gaylord.

*Library of Congress Cataloging-in-Publication Data*

Bigart, Robert.
Getting good crops : economic and diplomatic survival strategies of the Montana Bitterroot Salish Indians, 1870–1891 / Robert J. Bigart.
p. cm. — (The civilization of the American Indian series ; v. 266)
Includes bibliographical references and index.
ISBN 978-0-8061-4133-6 (hardcover : alk. paper)
1. Salish Indians—Montana—Bitterroot River Valley—History—19th century. 2. Salish Indians—Wars—Montana—Bitterroot River Valley—History—19th century. 3. Whites—Montana—Bitterroot River Valley—Relations with Indians—History—19th century. 4. Whites—Montana—Bitterroot River Valley—History—19th century. 5. Bitterroot River Valley (Mont.)—History—19th century. I. Title.
E99.S2B54 2010
978.6'89—dc22

2010008794

*Getting Good Crops: Economic and Diplomatic Survival Strategies of the Montana Bitterroot Salish Indians, 1870–1891* is Volume 266 in The Civilization of the American Indian Series.

The paper in this book meets the guidelines for permanence and durability of the Committee on Production Guidelines for Book Longevity of the Council on Library Resources, Inc. ∞



1 2 3 4 5 6 7 8 9 10

*Dedicated with thanks to those who have supported and encouraged my research over the years:*

*Tony Kuzniewski*
*John Ewers*
*Ross Toole*
*Clarence Woodcock*
*Jerry Slater*
*Joe McDonald*

Everything was going along fine. We were making a good living and learning the White man's way. Then [James A.] Garfield came to see us. He came to visit my father, for Charlot was the head man among the Salish. Garfield told my father that we would have to move out of the Bitterroot and go to the Jocko.

"I am doing some farming," my father said. "I am getting good crops and my people and I are living here as the agents and priests taught us to do. I am not going to move."

—related by Martin Charlo to J. Verne Dusenberry, 1939

# Contents

# Illustrations

# Figures

# Preface

This book is the outgrowth of some forty years of research. I first tried to come to terms with the topic in my bachelor's degree honors thesis at Harvard College in 1969. Moving from high school in Arlee, Montana, on the Flathead Indian Reservation, to college at Cambridge, Massachusetts, emphasized how different life in Arlee was from the experiences of most of my college classmates. I came to appreciate that Arlee was a special place, and I wanted to learn more about what made it unique.

In the 1960s and 1970s many academics were arguing that Indian culture had been lost, replaced by a culture of poverty. What I saw around me on the Flathead Reservation, however, was a changed but still distinctively Indian community. That community had wrestled over the years with many problems, but it also possessed a rich social and family fabric that had managed to survive the changes and challenges.

Over the years of research I have been blessed with the support and encouragement of many older scholars. At Harvard College, Tony Kuzniewski directed my senior honors thesis; at the Smithsonian Institution, Dr. John Ewers made it possible for me to explore the National Archives and the Library of Congress; at the University of Montana, Professor K. Ross Toole supported graduate research; and at Salish Kootenai College, President Joe McDonald and Vice President Jerry Slater have encouraged my research and writing. Needless to say, I have imposed on a multitude of librarians and archivists over the years. Any full listing of those who contributed to this work would include hundreds of names. I am grateful to them all for their generous assistance.

I would like to thank those who have taken the time to read and comment on earlier versions of this manuscript. This book has benefited greatly from their suggestions. Special thanks are due to Professor David Moore, University of Montana, Missoula; Joseph McDonald, president of Salish Kootenai College, Pablo, Montana; Richard T. Malouf, Twin Falls, Idaho; Professor James M. Scott, University of Montana, Missoula; Professor Ronald Trosper, the University of British Columbia, Victoria; Margaret Kingsland, Missoula, Montana; and Thompson Smith of the Salish–Pend d'Oreille Culture Committee, St. Ignatius, Montana. Of course, only the author is responsible for any errors of fact or interpretation.

This book contains my best attempt to make sense of the evidence I have had access to, but it's impossible to know what future researchers will be able to uncover. Therefore, I reserve the right to change my mind as new evidence and/or better arguments become available in the future.

The title, *Getting Good Crops*, is taken from the words of Chief Charlo describing Salish farming in the 1870s, as related by his son, Martin Charlo, in the 1930s and recorded by J. Verne Dusenberry, *Samples of Pend d'Oreille Oral Literature and Salish Narratives.*

Robert J. Bigart
Salish Kootenai College
Pablo, Montana

# Bitterroot Salish Political and Economic Survival Strategies, 1870–1891

| | 1870 | 71 | 72 | 73 | 74 | 75 | 76 | 77 | 78 | 79 | 80 | 81 | 82 | 83 | 84 | 85 | 86 | 87 | 88 | 89 | 90 | 91 |
|---|---|---|---|---|---|---|---|---|---|---|---|---|---|---|---|---|---|---|---|---|---|---|
| **Political Strategies** | | | | | | | | | | | | | | | | | | | | | | |
| Salish wars with Plains tribes on Great Plains hunts, 1870–84 | ■ | ■ | ■ | ■ | ■ | ■ | ■ | ■ | ■ | ■ | ■ | ■ | ■ | ■ | ■ | | | | | | | |
| Cultivation of white allies and peaceful relations with whites on buffalo hunts, 1870–83 | ■ | ■ | ■ | ■ | ■ | ■ | ■ | ■ | ■ | ■ | ■ | ■ | ■ | ■ | | | | | | | | |
| Keeping peace with whites in the Bitterroot Valley, 1870–91 | ■ | ■ | ■ | ■ | ■ | ■ | ■ | ■ | ■ | ■ | ■ | ■ | ■ | ■ | ■ | ■ | ■ | ■ | ■ | ■ | ■ | ■ |
| White campaign for Missoula army post, 1871–77 | | ■ | ■ | ■ | ■ | ■ | ■ | ■ | | | | | | | | | | | | | | |
| Decline of buffalo and other wild game, 1875–91 | | | | | | ■ | ■ | ■ | ■ | ■ | ■ | ■ | ■ | ■ | ■ | ■ | ■ | ■ | ■ | ■ | ■ | ■ |
| Garfield visit confirms white title to Bitterroot farms, 1872 | | | ■ | | | | | | | | | | | | | | | | | | | |
| Missoula County attempts to tax Bitterroot Salish, 1874–77 | | | | | ■ | ■ | ■ | ■ | | | | | | | | | | | | | | |
| Protection of whites by Salish during the Nez Perce War, 1877 | | | | | | | | ■ | | | | | | | | | | | | | | |
| Last buffalo hunt, 1883 | | | | | | | | | | | | | | ■ | | | | | | | | |
| **Economic Strategies** | | | | | | | | | | | | | | | | | | | | | | |
| Salish farms used as secondary economic resource, 1870–83 | ■ | ■ | ■ | ■ | ■ | ■ | ■ | ■ | ■ | ■ | ■ | ■ | ■ | ■ | | | | | | | | |
| Crash of wild game populations in western Montana, 1875–91 | | | | | | ■ | ■ | ■ | ■ | ■ | ■ | ■ | ■ | ■ | ■ | ■ | ■ | ■ | ■ | ■ | ■ | ■ |
| Last buffalo hunt, 1883 | | | | | | | | | | | | | | ■ | | | | | | | | |
| Expansion of Salish farms to replace buffalo and other game, 1883–89 | | | | | | | | | | | | | | ■ | ■ | ■ | ■ | ■ | ■ | ■ | | |
| U.S. government agricultural aid, 1885–86 | | | | | | | | | | | | | | | | ■ | ■ | | | | | |
| Severe drought, 1889 | | | | | | | | | | | | | | | | | | | | ■ | | |
| Bungled removal of the Salish to the reservation, 1889–91 | | | | | | | | | | | | | | | | | | | | ■ | ■ | ■ |

# Getting Good Crops

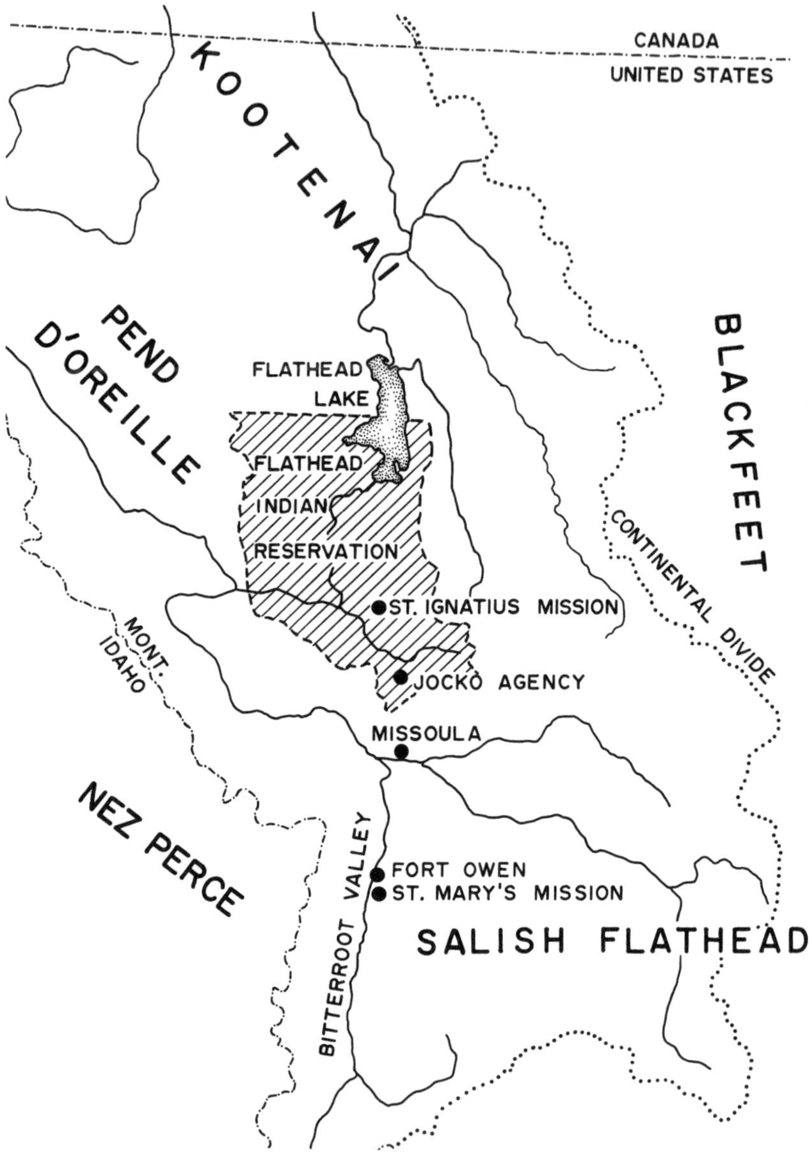


Western Montana, including the Indian tribal territories, the Bitterroot Valley, and the Flathead Indian Reservation. Map by Marcia Bakry, Smithsonian Institution, Washington, D.C., 1973.

# Introduction

## Survival Strategies of the Montana Bitterroot Salish Indians, 1870–1891

### Questions and Methods

In the nineteenth century the Bitterroot Salish were a small, Salish language–speaking Indian tribe living in the northern Rocky Mountains with an economy based on a seasonal round of hunting and gathering. Semiannual buffalo hunts were the foundation of the Salish economy and diplomacy. The Salish and their allies from west of the Continental Divide—including primarily the Nez Perce, Pend d'Oreille, Kootenai, Coeur d'Alene, and Spokane Indians—fought with the Blackfeet Confederation, Sioux, and other Plains tribes for the right to hunt buffalo in central Montana.

The nineteenth century presented the Salish leadership with a host of new challenges related to the invasion of white people into the northern Rocky Mountains. Whites were military allies for the Salish against the Blackfeet, but also avaricious competitors for land, game, and grazing resources. Aspects of Western technology were attractive to the Salish, but the lifeways of western Montana whites probably seemed less moral and less satisfying to them than traditional Salish culture.

This book explores the survival and coping strategies developed by the Bitterroot Salish Indians in the late nineteenth century. How did the Salish survive into the twentieth century despite (1) a catastrophic military struggle with the Blackfeet and other Plains tribes over buffalo hunting rights, (2) mallpox and other new diseases that decimated their population, and (3) an invasion of white people competing for and destroying resources?

Most histories of the Salish people are actually histories of white people dealing with the Salish. What the government and white people did to the Salish is important, but it is only one part of the tribe's history. The history of the Bitterroot Salish is the story of the local situation they faced, and how the tribal community changed and coped over time. The historical evidence does suggest that the small size of the Bitterroot Salish tribe and the longevity of nineteenth-century Salish chiefs facilitated focus and stability in dealing with the crises they faced. The Salish community numbered only about five hundred people during the second half of the nineteenth century and had just two senior chiefs over the seven decades between 1842 and 1910. Somehow, despite all the challenges thrown at them, the Salish have survived into the twenty-first century as a changed but distinctively Indian community. The survival of the Salish involves physical and cultural aspects. Physical survival resulted from protecting and nurturing their children and actively replacing war casualties. Cultural survival involved accepting innovations as additions to their culture rather than substitutions. For example, the Salish accepted the power of Christianity as a supplement to their traditional religious beliefs; they developed farms but maintained the buffalo hunts until the wild buffalo were gone; they built log cabins but used tepees most of the year. This distinctive combination of adaptability and conservatism has influenced the survival strategies of the Salish Indian people for over two hundred years.

## *Overview*

The introduction to the book outlines the methodological problems of attempting to reconstruct tribal history from indirect evidence and compares the experiences of the Salish to those of other Native American tribes in the 1870s and 1880s.

Chapter 1 surveys the ecological and strategic origins of Salish survival strategies in the pre-1870 period.

Intertribal diplomacy between 1870 and 1883 is explored in chapters 2 and 3, which examine the evidence available about Salish diplomacy on the buffalo hunts and their fight with many Plains tribes for access to the buffalo while trying to keep the peace with Montana whites.

Chapter 4 describes Salish efforts to keep peace with whites during the Nez Perce War of 1877 despite: (1) a campaign by Missoula business leaders to attract a U.S. Army post and its spending to western Montana,

(2) an attempt by Missoula County to tax Bitterroot Salish farms and herds, (3) efforts by the *Weekly Missoulian* and Flathead Indian agent Charles S. Medary to stoke white fears after the 1876 defeat of Gen. George Armstrong Custer, and (4) the white hysteria surrounding the 1877 Nez Perce War and its aftermath of violence in 1878.

Chapter 5 focuses on the efforts of Salish leaders to manage tribal relations with the U.S. government between 1869 and 1884. Tribal leaders nimbly worked to avoid conflict with the whites while preserving their right to a Bitterroot Valley Salish community.

Chapters 6 and 7 are the crux of the volume. These chapters describe the Salish people's efforts to manage their relations with white Bitterroot residents. Chapter 6 examines the surviving evidence of Salish-white cooperation and friendly relations in the Bitterroot Valley between 1870 and 1891, while chapter 7 details Salish-white friction and the efforts of Salish leaders to control the situation.

Maintaining economic independence after the loss of the buffalo in the mid-1880s forced the Bitterroot Salish leaders to work to expand their farms and herds in the valley. Chapter 8 examines the resource constraints the Salish faced in the 1880s and their efforts to grow their farming operations. The record 1889 drought halted Salish agricultural development and set the stage for the wrenching decision to move to the Jocko Reservation.

Chapter 9 details the negotiations between Charlo and Gen. Henry B. Carrington as the Salish leaders wrestled with a strategy to preserve the tribe despite the economic devastation of 1889. Government bungling delayed the removal until 1891, further impoverishing the Salish and leaving a bitter legacy of unfulfilled promises.

### *Methodology and Problems with the Sources*

My reading of the sources suggested two hypotheses that could be tested using the historical evidence. These proposals were that between 1870 and 1891 the Salish pursued a policy of (1) keeping the peace with the white settlers to avoid a two-front war, and (2) expanding their farms and herds to protect and diversify their economic base after the extermination of the plains buffalo herds in the early 1880s. I then searched the historical sources for evidence describing specific events that either supported or opposed these hypotheses. Conclusions or general statements in the sources that did not include specific incidents were avoided. Most of this volume presents the concrete evidence found about Salish diplomacy and economics between 1870 and 1891; I have tried to sketch out why I believe the evidence indicates that the Salish were following a set of strategies to protect the interests of the tribe and ensure its survival. I evaluated the evidence available according to my best judgment and then assembled it like the few surviving pieces of a mosaic to see what the evidence might say about my hypotheses. The chapters that follow present the evidence in detail so that readers can consider the argument and decide for themselves how convincing it is.

Chapter 4, which deals with the Nez Perce War and the Missoula campaign to secure a U.S. Army post, is the only chapter based on white attitudes and interpretations of Salish motives. Understanding the propaganda war carried out by the *Weekly Missoulian* and some Missoula boosters will enable readers to put the white inflammatory statements and the actions of the Salish into context. This chapter explores the economic and ideological motivations behind the hostility of some white Missoulians towards the Salish. Missoula newspapers during the 1870s contained frequent allegations of Salish perfidy and hostility toward white settlers, but few, if any, descriptions of specific incidents to justify such conclusions. During the 1870s almost all of the more detailed references describe peaceful interactions between the races. During the Nez Perce War of 1877, Chief Adolph even traveled to Missoula to reassure its residents of the Salish's peaceful intentions. In 1878 a series of clashes and murders across the state were first blamed on the Salish. It soon turned out, however, that they had been carried out by a band of hostile Nez Perce returning to Idaho.

Since the bulk of the historical sources available to researchers in 2010 were written or recorded by white people more than a century ago, serious problems with bias and prejudice must be confronted by the twenty-first-century scholar. The surviving written and oral sources are largely clouded by either the fog of cultural differences or the passage of time. Even those few Indian statements that are available have, in most cases, been recorded, and edited, in English, by white men. Some of the written sources available in 2010 reflect the Salish viewpoint, but almost all include the opinions of the nineteenth-century white authors. Since the historical sources written by white witnesses in the nineteenth century include both descriptions of concrete historical incidents and the writers' prejudices, we might be able to separate the two elements. When divested of the white writers' value judgments, the concrete historical incidents could form patterns that indicate the aims and strategies of the Indian people involved.

Numerous sources describe the results of Bitterroot Salish strategies, but none specifically spell out Salish policies and goals. For example, we have detailed evidence of Salish raids and battles with the Plains Indians and cooperation with the white settlers. This pattern illustrates Salish diplomacy to avoid a two-front war, but we have no leadership meeting minutes laying out the strategy. I hope that the evidence which follows will enable readers to evaluate the argument that the Salish deliberately worked to minimize conflict and promote tribal survival.

A special complication in any history is that the incidents described in the sources are not a random sample of events. Since history relies heavily on written records, literate observers have a distinct advantage. In addition, some written records were more likely to survive than others. Official bureaucratic records and newspapers are much more accessible to researchers than personal papers or letters sent out of state. The historian can be seduced into the trap of assuming that the disparate volume of surviving records reflects the importance of those sources. The many federal records preserved by the National Archives and the extensive writings of the missionaries can make it hard to find the voices of other white actors and the Indian actors in the story. The reservation agent might have been lucid and may even have believed in the official government policy, but that is no reason to assume that he knew everything that was going on or that he was necessarily honest with his superiors in Washington. The government did influence events, but it did not control all of the players and was not a party to many local social, economic, and political developments that had considerable impact on the Salish people. Similarly, many missionaries were misled into interpreting the interest of the Salish in Christian teachings and spiritual power as a desire to replace their Native culture with a European lifeway. Period newspapers provide volumes of opinions, ideology, rumor, and boosterism in addition to concrete observations and description. Much of the research for this book has involved struggling to find new sources to help balance the historical record, and to develop more discriminating ways to use the federal and newspaper sources that are so readily available.

Somehow, despite the cultural differences, competition over economic resources, and occasional injections of alcohol, the Bitterroot Salish and their white neighbors were able to keep the peace and maintain friendly interactions over the time span covered by this volume. I believe that the evidence presented in the following chapters indicates that the Salish set goals, developed plans, and worked to implement their strategies; and that their white neighbors pursued positive relations with the Salish despite the differences between the communities.

### *Personal Names, Indian Speeches, and Oral Histories*

The historical documents used in this study include many variant spellings of personal names, especially those of Indians. I have chosen to standardize the spelling of the Indian names that appear repeatedly in the text, but most other names are kept as they are spelled in the source being discussed. When the common spelling or form of the name is significantly different from that given in the source, the more frequent spelling or version of the name is given in brackets following the name as used in the source. The spellings of the following names have been standardized in the text: Dominic, Kizer, Lamoose, Lumprey, Matte, Michelle, Minesinger, Moiese, Ninepipe, Sapiel, Silverthorne, and Vanderburg. Individual Salish who could not be identified are referred to using only the name found in the source.

Another problem with the evidence is using English versions of Indian speeches. The surviving speeches have been translated and edited by the white recorders, and the speakers' words and ideas were probably altered significantly by this process. Salish oratory was in Salish, not English. It seems reasonable to assume that the broad ideas contained in most of the speeches are accurate, but the speeches must be carefully compared to other available sources.

Salish oral traditions recorded in recent years avoid most of the cultural problems associated with nineteenth-century records of Salish speeches. The Salish–Pend d'Oreille Culture Committee at St. Ignatius has an especially valuable collection of interviews with Salish elders who died many years ago, but the collection cannot be used by researchers until their tribal history is published. After a century in oral form, the stories may not always be as detailed as we could wish, and they could have changed over time, but oral traditions are one of the best sources for learning the Salish perspective on events.

### *Social Boundaries*

The terms "Salish" or "Bitterroot Salish" are used in the text to refer to the tribal community based in the Bitterroot Valley of western Montana during the nineteenth century. "Flathead" is used to refer to the Indian reservation in the Lower Flathead River valley north of the Bitterroot inhabited by the Pend d'Oreille (or Upper Kalispel) Indians, the Kootenai Indians, and, after 1873, a portion of the Bitterroot Salish tribe under Chief Arlee. Many of the historical sources use "Flathead" when talking about the Bitterroot Salish Indian tribe or band.

Who was a Salish Indian in late nineteenth-century western Montana? The tribal leaders kept no official enrollment. Many white men and Indians from other tribes had married into the Salish tribe, and their children identified with their relations on both sides. Some Indians from other tribes settled with the Salish for a few months, a few years, or even permanently. For the purpose of this volume, the Bitterroot Salish band includes all the Indian people of Salish descent living in the Bitterroot Valley and other Indians or mixed-bloods who lived in the Bitterroot and took part in Salish social or economic activities. Those Indian people who left the Bitterroot Valley for the Jocko Reservation after 1872, such as Chief Arlee's family, were still considered part of the Salish tribe, but were no longer politically and economically part of the Bitterroot Salish under Charlo.

For this discussion, all the non-Indian people who invaded western Montana and competed with the Salish for land and other resources are considered white people. The social categories of Indian and white and Salish and non-Salish were used widely in the nineteenth century. The categories were problematic biologically and socially, but they are used in this volume because they were loosely valid in nineteenth-century western Montana society.

Most of the evidence used in this book identifies the Indian people involved as being Flathead or Salish, but there is no way to be sure the tribal designations were accurate in all cases. The problem is especially important in situations where the Salish were away from the Bitterroot Valley and on the buffalo hunt. I have worked hard to carefully evaluate the contexts and sources for the references, but cannot guarantee that every tribal identification used is correct. Most of the sources, however, have enough detail to allow confidence that the people being discussed were part of the Bitterroot Salish Indian community.

## *Internal Salish Politics*

One casualty of the paucity of Indian-oriented sources is an almost total lack of documentation of the relationship between the community and its leaders in developing policy. Salish leaders traditionally led by consensus, not autocracy. They were spokesmen who relayed policy decisions to outsiders, but those policies were the result of many long and torturous community meetings and debates. Certainly the Salish community valued the wisdom and judgment of its leaders, but decisions required the involvement and consent of the entire community. The historical records contain only a few hints of this behind-the-scenes process. One of the reasons Charlo gave in 1872 for not signing the agreement with James A. Garfield was that he wanted to "see my people" before making such a commitment. In 1884 Chief Charlo requested that the Salish delegation to Washington, D.C., be enlarged so that all the factions in the community could be represented. Gen. Henry B. Carrington recorded that in 1891 Charlo's agreement to move to the Jocko Valley before the Salish lands in the Bitterroot were sold followed a long community meeting and prayers. Charlo made the speech acceding to the move only after the entire Salish community had reached a painful and torturous consensus. Consent does not always imply harmony, and Vanderburg's refusal to join the rest of the Salish at the benediction service held immediately following the arrival of the Salish at the Jocko Agency may have been a symptom of residual wounds over the removal decision. Other stresses in the community reflected the tensions between young men seeking horses and war honors, and the older leaders who worried more about protecting Salish lives and resources. Given the limits of the historical sources, this volume cannot explore the details of the internal politics of the Salish community as they wrestled to cope with the catastrophic events of the late nineteenth century.

## *Previous Historical Studies*

Earlier historians of the nineteenth-century Bitterroot Salish seem to have missed some of the most important questions. For example, the 1805 meeting between the Salish and the Lewis and Clark Expedition generated some valuable historical sources but was really a minor event from the Salish perspective. Treatments of the Salish and the white missionaries recorded Salish adulation and adoption of Christian customs, but they failed to consider the discordance of vision between the Salish and the missionaries. Unlike the missionaries, the Salish seem to have viewed the exchange as adding Christian power to Salish life, not the rejection of traditional Salish lifeways. Many historians have discussed Charlo's "forged" signature on the

1872 Garfield agreement while ignoring the more important story of how Salish diplomacy defused an escalating crisis of white military hysteria that could have exploded and destroyed the tribe.

Previous studies of the nineteenth-century struggle by Salish leaders to preserve an independent Salish community in the Bitterroot Valley have similar problems. Because of the biases in the sources, almost all the earlier treatments of late nineteenth-century Salish history present the Salish as being acted on—not as actors. Most of the writers do not explore the possibility that Salish leaders had strategies and plans that they struggled to implement to further the tribe's interests and goals. Most describe Charlo as motivated by personal character defects such as pride and an inability to adjust to changing times. They did not see Charlo as a leader in a consensus-based polity with ideas and plans to promote the goals chosen by the Salish community. The six studies of late nineteenth-century Bitterroot Salish history discussed below illustrate these problems.

One of the earliest studies of the Salish in the Bitterroot is Seth K. Humphrey's *The Indian Dispossessed* (44–72). Humphrey opposed nineteenth-century federal Indian policy but saw Charlo as a pathetic and helpless figure with a "childlike faith" (65) that the government would keep its promises. In the end, Humphrey says, Charlo was "embittered, broken in spirit, with little faith in the white man and his ways" (71). Humphrey described the Bitterroot Salish as "Charlos and his heroic band. Charlos—an ignorant, unknown Indian" (71).

The best-known missionary history of the Bitterroot Salish is by Lawrence B. Palladino, S.J.: *Indian and White in the Northwest: A History of Catholicity in Montana, 1831 to 1891* (second edition). Palladino saw the impasse over removal as resulting from a combination of government bungling and Charlo's rigid personality. Charlo had no plans or strategies, his "exasperation and bitterness . . . , in turn, made him the more obstinate, and the more suspicious of the Government and all its agents" (88). According to Palladino, Charlo's character defects made him unable to adjust or change, even when the tribe's best interests were at risk (89).

A 1960 article by Michael Harrison in *Montana, the Magazine of Western History*, "Chief Charlot's Battle with Bureaucracy," emphasizes the 1872 signature controversy and the wrongs done to Charlo. Harrison views Charlo as a passive subject acted on by events—not an actor.

Helen Addison Howard's popular treatment of Charlo's story in *Northwest Trail Blazers* (175–202) portrays him as motivated by stubbornness and pride. According to Howard, the forged mark on the 1872 Garfield agreement "embittered Charlot to the end of his days, made him stubborn and distrustful. . . . Charlot faced the intrusion of his ancestral homeland with resignation" (188). Her interpretation emphasized the personal animus between Charlo and Arlee (191) and claimed Charlo's character defects blinded him to the poverty and suffering of the Salish people: "As the years passed Charlot seemed deaf to the plaintive cries of hungry papooses" (193). She asserted that Charlo's actions were dictated by vanity rather than strategy: "It must have cost Charlot untold mental anguish to capitulate [in 1889]. For years the old chief had fought a continuous struggle with his own spirit—his stubborn pride pitted against his tribal loyalty" (200).

In John Fahey's *The Flathead Indians,* Charlo is described as "a sympathetic figure" (234, referring to an 1883 newspaper account) who was unable to change his mind in 1889 (249). According to Fahey, Charlo "recognized the [changing] situation but found no way to insert himself into the process of governance by bureaucracy. He simply resisted" (xi). In other words, Charlo was just too stubborn to adjust to the changing circumstances, and he became a victim, not an actor, in events. Fahey acknowledges the problems with his sources:

> The flaw in my dependence on contemporary [white] accounts is common to studies of Indian peoples—no Indian version exists. But I do not feel secure, and I don't think you would, with an inferential history—a mirror history, if you will, in which the story is deduced by reversing or reading from the back accounts by men of an alien culture. Therefore, I have used the letters, journals, diaries, and reports available, recognizing their shortcoming." (x)

A 1975 PhD dissertation by Ellsworth H. Brown continued the tradition of seeing Charlo as motivated by obstinacy and arrogance, not strategy. Brown's dissertation, "The History of the Flathead Indians in the Nineteenth Century," emphasizes the importance of Charlo's personal feud with Chief Arlee (271–72) in Charlo's refusal to move to Jocko: "The government had recognized that Charlot would not suffer the embarrassment of living under Arlee's rule when it offered to restore the head chieftainship to him in 1884. Charlo's pride precluded acceptance of the offer, and it is questionable whether he would ever have removed had Arlee not died" [in 1889] (374).

These histories of the Bitterroot Salish in the late nineteenth century tell only part of the story. Charlo was headstrong and proud, but I believe the evidence indicates he was also a thoughtful, capable leader who consciously developed strategies to support goals that were important to the tribal community. The Salish were finally forced to move to Jocko in 1891, but they continued their struggle to survive physically and to preserve valuable parts of Salish culture in the twentieth century. As a case study, the experience of the Bitterroot Salish during the late nineteenth century has interesting parallels with the histories of other Indian tribes during the same period.

## Contrasting and Comparable Experiences of Other Indian Tribes

The use of Bitterroot Salish history between 1870 and 1891 as a case study in the broader Native American ordeal is both useful and problematic. Comparing and contrasting the experiences of different tribes can test hypotheses, but in history the experiments cannot be truly replicated. The situation confronting each tribe was in some ways unique. Despite this limitation, it is useful to examine the experiences of different tribes for commonalities.

Many recent studies of American Indian tribes during the late nineteenth century have described a process of change aimed at limited accommodation with Euro-American society. The massive resource loss that affected most western Indian tribes during the late nineteenth century forced dramatic economic changes on them. However, the tribes actively tried to manage the change in order to preserve valuable aspects of their traditional lifeways and survive as distinctively Native communities. Many tribes found leaders who were skilled at mediating between the tribe and white power brokers. The massive economic damage resulting from the loss of land, the buffalo, and other resources limited the maneuvering room available to tribal leaders, but the struggle was not to become like white people, but to survive as an Indian community. The Indian people were actors in the drama, despite the overbearing military and economic power of the white authorities.

Two case studies of Salish allies during the intertribal wars on the plains—the Nez Perce and Crow Indians—illustrate both parallels with and differences from the Salish experience. The Crows during the late nineteenth century have been studied by Frederick E. Hoxie in *Parading Through History: The Making of the Crow Nation in America, 1805–1935*. The Crow allied with the Salish and the whites in a long and bloody struggle against the Sioux, Blackfeet, and other Plains tribes over buffalo hunting rights. Crow experiences in diplomacy and alliance closely paralleled those of the Salish, but the Crows bore the brunt of the late nineteenth-century attacks by the expanding Sioux Nation. During the 1880s the Crows developed leaders who could appear "friendly while resisting the white man's demands" (119, 122–25). Compared to the Bitterroot Salish, the Crows had the advantage of a larger population—2,456 in 1887 (131)—and the minimal protection from white competition provided by an officially recognized reservation. The Crows had the disadvantage of relying on government rations, which hobbled their independence, and they lacked the rudimentary agricultural infrastructure the Salish had available in the Bitterroot Valley when the buffalo herds were killed off in the late 1870s. In the 1880s, when the Crows established their first farms, they worked hard to incorporate traditional residence patterns and cooperative work arrangements into the new agricultural economy (130).

The Nez Perces were linked to the Bitterroot Salish both by alliance and intermarriage. The Nez Perces fought and traveled with the Salish on the plains, but their homeland was far enough west to be safe from Blackfeet raiding parties. A 2002 Ph.D. dissertation by Elizabeth Jean James, "Forging an Indigenous Future: The Nez Perces, 1893–1934," describes the struggle to ameliorate some of the negative consequences of coerced allotment in the 1890s. Unlike the Bitterroot Salish, the Nez Perces had an official reservation, but the Nez Perces were selected for early allotment, and the process began in 1889. After initial resistance, the tribe acquiesced, but tribal members attempted to co-opt the process by selecting tracts in different topographies to enable them to continue their seasonal round of farming, gathering, grazing, and hunting. Families also tried to keep traditional residence patterns intact (35–44). According to James, the Nez Perces used "the Dawes Act to formally recognize existing systems of land use, whether related to older subsistence patterns, family connections, or more recent agricultural developments" (44). In 1893 the Nez Perces opposed selling the so-called "surplus" reservation land to white settlers, but finally succumbed to the blandishments and threats of a government commission that would not accept "no" for an answer (46–54).

Alexandra Harmon found similar strategies among the Indian peoples around Puget Sound, Washington. *Indians in the Making: Ethnic Relations and Indian Identities around Puget Sound* (112–19), studied a group of tribal communities, but even at that level, tribal strategies to counter Office of Indian Affairs coercion were obvious. Since many of the Puget Sound Indians did not live on reservations, they were able to take part in proscribed activities such as potlatches. Harmon also found local agents were obliged to rely on traditional leaders to help police the population at the very time that government agents were competing with the chiefs for influence. A final irony was when off-reservation white employers helped their Indian workers avoid forced relocation to the reservation.

The story of the Ojibwa, or Anishinaabe, Indians of the White Earth Reservation in Minnesota was told by Melissa L. Meyer in *The White Earth Tragedy: Ethnicity and Dispossession at a Minnesota Anishinaabe Reservation, 1889–1920*. The population of White Earth—1,427 in 1876 (49)—was considerably larger than that of the Bitterroot Salish and expanded even more in the 1890s with immigrants from other Ojibwa reservations (56–63). The White Earth Reservation had a faction of mixed-bloods who concentrated political and economic power in their hands (101–107). Unfortunately, the Ojibwa controlled very valuable timberlands, and the reservation mixed-blood power brokers allied themselves with off-reservation economic interests to exploit tribal assets for private benefit (155–59). The consequent factional conflict consumed the tribe during the entire twentieth century (159–72). In this case, the tribal leaders working to protect the interests of the community had to fight other tribal members rather than concentrate on dealing with outside forces.

A dramatic counterpoint to the White Earth experience is provided by the Menominee Indians of nearby Wisconsin. In *The Struggle for Self-Determination: History of the Menominee Indians Since 1854*, historian David R. M. Beck describes a community that was able to unite to protect tribal interests despite internal factions and disagreements (13–15, 25–26). The Menominee numbered considerably more than the Bitterroot Salish—1,522 in 1874 (29)—and had a formally recognized reservation, but they were surrounded by white capitalists who wanted reservation timber. The nineteenth-century Menominee found the leadership and cohesion to fight off multiple attempts by their white neighbors to force the tribe to sell their timberlands. Tribal leaders made repeated trips to Washington, D.C., to plead for personnel changes and policy modifications, and even lobbied Congress to defend tribal interests (13–14).

Loretta Fowler examines the survival strategies of the Southern Cheyenne and Southern Arapaho Indians in Oklahoma in *Tribal Sovereignty and the Historical Imagination: Cheyenne-Arapaho Politics* (3–47). Compared to the Bitterroot Salish, the Cheyennes and Arapahos had the advantages of a larger population—2,142 and 1,578 in 1873 (6)—and an official reservation. The Cheyennes and Arapahos did not begin to engage in agriculture until the late 1870s (18). The tribes soon developed cattle herds, but they had to compete with white cattlemen who were leasing tribal grazing land (19). Contract freighting for the government in the late 1870s helped some bands survive after the loss of the buffalo herds (13). The tribal leaders during the 1870s and 1880s were skilled as intermediaries struggling to protect Indian interests (19–25). The chiefs promoted peace and cooperation with agency efforts to expand farming and cattle ranching (24–25). Farming involved sharing of food and cooperative work patterns (33). Chiefs supported schools but tried to limit government interference in traditional religious and social gatherings (40). According to Fowler, "The Cheyennes and Arapahos initially had considerable success adapting the institutions imposed by the federal government to their own cultural understandings and social organization, for the federal agent on the reservation had only a limited ability to coerce compliance" (42).

The experiences of the Comanche Indians during the 1870s and 1880s are relayed by Morris W. Foster in *Being Comanche: A Social History of an American Indian Community* (75–99). The Comanche population was larger (1,564 in 1888 [88]) than that of the Bitterroot Salish and more dependent on government aid after the buffalo were gone. Comanches relied on rations (79–80) and treaty annuities (82), which made them particularly vulnerable to government pressure. In response to their economic crisis of the 1870s, the Comanches developed cattle herds, freighted for the government agency, and began cooperative farming operations (80–81). Quanah Parker, the best-known Comanche chief in the late nineteenth century, skillfully maintained peace with the whites and obtained continued economic support from the federal government (85–86). But Quanah was also a leader in the new peyote religion which the Comanches were using to preserve their community life and many traditional Comanche beliefs: "The innovation of peyote gatherings during the reservation period maintained many prereservation Comanche beliefs in a new context" (93).

These case studies of American Indian experiences during the 1870s and 1880s illustrate the active efforts of tribal leaders to cope with massive economic dislocation and government policies of coerced culture change.

The tribes found leaders who were skilled at dealing with white authority figures and committed to the survival of their tribal communities.

The absence of direct evidence to document Bitterroot Salish survival strategies between 1870 and 1891 is unfortunate. Readers must examine the indirect evidence offered below and decide if they find the argument convincing. The discussion assumes that unless there is evidence to the contrary, the Salish leaders were rational and intelligent. The historical evidence that has survived is consistent with an interpretation of deliberate Salish efforts to manage military risk and cope with devastating economic dislocations. During the 1870s and 1880s the Bitterroot Salish competed with other Indian tribes for resources and were the victims of the political and economic policies of Montana whites, but they were also players in the historical drama as they fought to survive and cope with change.

CHAPTER 1

# Strategic Seeds

## Pre-1870 Origins of Salish Survival Strategies

Indian history before white contact was not static and unchanging, as is sometimes assumed. Details are vague, but archaeology indicates that even before 1750, the ancestors of the Salish spent centuries adjusting to climate changes, new technologies, and population movements.[1] Historic evidence is available to document dramatic military, technological, and disease challenges confronted by the Salish during the last half of the eighteenth century. During this period, the Salish had to adjust to (1) the introduction of horses, (2) the increasing military prowess of the Blackfeet and their allies on the northwestern Great Plains, (3) the race to secure guns and ammunition supplies, and (4) the devastation of two major smallpox epidemics. Long before the 1870–1891 period studied in this volume, the Salish people and their leaders were coping with, and developing survival strategies to meet, dramatic and catastrophic challenges to Salish survival.

In August of 1870, Charlo succeeded his late father, Victor, as head chief of the Bitterroot Salish tribe. Under Charlo's leadership, between 1870 and 1891, the Bitterroot Salish fought the Plains tribes for the right to hunt buffalo on the east side of the Continental Divide while struggling to keep peace with whites invading the northern Rocky Mountains. In this twenty-one-year period, the Salish confronted cataclysmic economic adjustments as the escalating white population in western Montana increased competition for hunting, gathering, and grazing resources. The survival strategies followed by the Salish between 1870 and 1891 relied on an informal alliance with Montana whites, the Nez Perces, and other western tribes, while expanding Salish farms to preserve their economic independence. The diplomatic strategy of cultivating alliances with the western tribes and white settlers was well developed by 1870. The economic changes involved with developing farms and herds of cattle and horses began slowly during the first half of the nineteenth century.

## The Bitterroot Salish in the Eighteenth Century

During the early eighteenth century, the Salish and their allies—the Kootenais, Snakes, and Crows—dominated the northwestern plains. By the end of the century, however, the Blackfeet Confederation and its allies had driven the Salish-Kootenai-Snake coalition west of the Continental Divide. This military catastrophe was an important source of the dogged determination of the Salish to continue their seasonal buffalo hunts on the plains and ally with the white fur traders in the nineteenth century.

Elderly Salish informants interviewed by ethnographer James A. Teit in the 1920s indicated that the introduction of the horse early in the mid-eighteenth century ended a period of relative peace.[2] In the winter of 1787–88, Saukamappee, a Cree who had been adopted into the Piegan tribe, told fur trader David Thompson that the Kootenai, Salish, and Snake Indians had recently been driven out of the northwestern plains by the Piegans and their allies.[3] Historian Theodore Binnema has recently organized the evidence describing the eighteenth-century confrontation between the "Southern Coalition," made up of the Salish, Kootenai, Shoshoni or Snake, and Crow tribes, and the "Northern Coalition" of the Blackfeet Confederation and the Cree, Assiniboine, and Gros Ventre Indians. The Salish and the Piegans became the frontier tribes on the opposite sides of the boundary that separated the horse-rich Rocky Mountain tribes from the gun-rich Plains tribes. The Salish obtained horses before the northern Plains tribes, and the sheltered Rocky Mountain valleys enabled the Salish horse herds to multiply faster than the Blackfeet herds on the open plains. At the same time the Salish confronted serious supply problems in the arms race to secure guns and ammunition. The Salish and their allies traded with the Crows and, through them, the Missouri River tribes for a few guns, but they failed to find reliable sources of guns and ammunition during the eighteenth century. Horses offered a natural increase, but guns required regular replacement and ammunition, available only from white traders.[4]

In the 1930s an elderly, but unidentified, Salish warrior described to anthropologist Harry Holbert Turney-High how the Salish obtained their first horses in the eighteenth century. According to this source, the Salish first saw horses while scouting a Shoshoni camp and planning an attack to avenge the murder of two Salish families. The Salish war party attacked the Shoshoni camp, stole the camp's herd of horses, and drove the horses north to the Salish homeland.[5] The Salish soon learned how to ride the horses and use them to transport goods. The horses revolutionized Salish life by increasing mobility and material wealth, but they also spawned more conflict with neighboring tribes. Horses allowed the Salish to expand their buffalo hunts, allowing them to travel farther onto the plains, kill more buffalo, and bring larger cargoes of dried meat and hides west of the divide.[6]

Salish horse herds quickly grew in size and quality. In September 1805, when explorers Meriwether Lewis and William Clark met the Salish in Ross' Hole, they traded seven of their horses for fresh Salish horses and purchased eleven others. Clark wrote in his diary that "those people [the Salish] possess ellegant horses."[7] Additional testimony to the quality of Salish horses was supplied in 1853 by "The White Man's Hare," a Blackfeet warrior. He told Washington territorial governor Isaac I. Stevens that he was so impressed with Salish hoses that "he stole the first Flathead [Salish] horse he came across—it was sure to be a good one."[8]

In the nineteenth century, U.S. Army lieutenant James H. Bradley calculated the average number of horses per lodge for some major Montana Indians tribes in 1830: Crows, 15; Piegans, 10; Blackfeet and Bloods, 5; Gros Ventres, 5; Flatheads and Nez Perces, 50; and Assiniboines, 2. Bradley did conclude that the horses raised on the plains were hardier than those raised west of the divide.[9]

As the growing Salish horse herds enticed Plains war parties, the Salish fell behind in an arms race with the Plains tribes. During the eighteenth century the Plains tribes had access to British traders to secure guns and ammunition, whereas the Salish could obtain guns only indirectly through trade with other tribes who had access to fur traders. Guns available through Indian middlemen were often in poor repair and usually lacked ammunition supplies. No descriptions of the impact of firearms on a nineteenth-century Salish–Blackfeet battle have survived in the literature, but during the winter of 1787–88, Saukamappee described to David Thompson the impact of guns on a recent battle between the Piegan and Snake Indians. The traditional pre-horse Plains battles, according to

Saukamappee, involved both ambushes of small hunting parties and larger, almost formal set battles between tribes. The larger battles involved the opposing tribes facing each other across the battlefield, sheltered behind facing rows of large shields. The shields protected the fighters from arrows, and only a few warriors were injured when an arrow caught an exposed part of the body. When night fell, the battle usually ended with minimal losses. When the Piegans introduced guns into their battle line, any Snake warrior who briefly exposed himself to shoot an arrow could be killed by the Piegan gunmen lying in wait. According to Saukamappee, the guns caused "consternation and dismay," and the Snake battle line was soon depleted by casualties and desertions.[10] Presumably, after the Blackfeet obtained guns, their battles with the Salish had similar outcomes. In 1809 Alexander Henry, a British fur trader, observed that the northern Indians easily stole horses from the Snake and Salish Indians, "who have vast numbers of horses and who appear to be a defenseless race. Having no Fire Arms, they easily fall a prey to the Slave Indians, who are tolerably well provided in arms and ammunition."[11]

During the summer of 1810 the Salish shocked the Piegans by inflicting sixteen casualties with their newly acquired guns. Henry reported that in October the Piegans established a camp along the trade route across the northern Rocky Mountains to keep the traders from moving more supplies to the tribes west of the mountains. Henry noted that after the western tribes obtained firearms and ammunition, they became "a formidable enemy" for the Plains tribes: "The first severe check the Peagans ever received from the nations on the west side of the Mountains inhabiting the waters of the Columbia was in the Summer of 1810, when they met the Flat Heads &c while on their march to the Plains in search of Buffalo. . . . At last the Peagans were obliged to retreat, leaving sixteen of their principal Warriors dead upon the field of battle. The defeat sustained by the Peagans has tended much to exasperate that nation against us as being the cause of strengthening their enemies in the manner we have done, by supplying them with arms and ammunition."[12]

The newly armed Salish and Pend d'Oreilles proved such dangerous enemies that during the fall of 1811 the Piegans sent a peace delegation to the Pend d'Oreilles and Salish, who then called a council of the western tribes to consider the offer. Many of the Salish and their allies were concerned because the offer of peace came only from the Piegans. Peace with them would still leave the western tribes open to attacks from other Plains tribes. The limited peace offer was thus rejected, and the council concluded that since the Salish and their allies were "now as well armed" as the Plains tribes, and "while we had no Guns, nor iron heads for our arrows, we had to yield to them, and we were called cowards. We must therefore show ourselves on their lands, as they have been seen on our grounds, and for which purpose we are ready."[13]

About 1780 a severe smallpox epidemic devastated the Salish, their allies, and enemy tribes. In the 1840s Salish elders told Father Gregory Mengarini, S.J., at St. Mary's Mission of an outbreak of disease about seventy years earlier that produced red or black pustules over the entire body. Those with red pustules died in a few days, while those with black pustules died almost immediately. Mengarini did not know how many Salish were killed, but he calculated that the population was about four thousand before the 1780 smallpox epidemic, compared to only about five hundred in 1848.[14] Reminiscences of Nez Perce elders in the late 1830s indicated that the 1780 smallpox epidemic first appeared among the Nez Perce and Salish buffalo hunters on the plains. According to the Nez Perces, after smallpox hit the hunting parties, "Only here & there one survived the disease." From the plains the disease swept westward across the Rocky Mountains.[15]

In the 1930s Zephire Lumprey, a Salish elder, told anthropologist Claude Schaeffer how Ctemú, or "Grizzly-Bear with Its Head Pointed Upward," survived the 1780 smallpox epidemic. Ctemú was about fifteen years old in 1780, and the only survivor from his camp in the Bitterroot Valley. A bear spirit spoke to him and helped him find other Salish survivors camped near Drummond. Ctemú was the Salish head chief in 1840 when Father Pierre De Smet, S.J., came to western Montana.[16]

The sources indicate the Salish suffered massive population losses during the 1780 smallpox epidemic. Historian Robert Thomas Boyd estimated that the Plateau tribes lost more than a third of their pre-1780 population.[17] The disruption in Salish economic, social, and religious life resulting from the epidemic would have been staggering. The deaths also greatly reduced Salish military strength; however, since the same epidemic killed many Salish enemies, it is not known how it affected the military balance between the Salish and the Plains tribes.

In 1800 and 1801 smallpox again spread to the Salish. This time they contracted the disease from the Crows. Michel Revais, a Pend d'Oreille elder and interpreter, told ethnographer James A. Teit that another 50 percent of the Salish population died in the 1800 epidemic.[18]

The eighteenth century was a period of military turmoil and change for the Salish. The exciting and explosive growth in travel and transport that came with the horse, the struggle to open up supply lines for guns and ammunition, the loss of more than a third of the population to smallpox, and the loss of their plains villages to the Blackfeet and their allies must have tested the Salish to the limit. By century's end, the Salish had survived as a people, and their leaders had developed strategies of alliance and flexibility that they would continue to use in the nineteenth century.

## Survival Challenges in the Nineteenth Century

Between 1800 and 1870 the Salish were pushed ever closer to the brink in their military struggle with the Plains tribes, but they tenaciously refused to give up their plains buffalo hunting trips. In the nineteenth century new white actors entered this military drama and became allies of the Salish. The white fur traders offered the Salish reliable access to guns and ammunition, and additional manpower in their struggle with the Blackfeet.

Two letters written on April 21, 1810, by beleaguered white fur traders at the Three Forks of the Missouri indicate the value of the alliance to the American traders. After outlining the American losses to Blackfeet attacks, Reuben Lewis wrote his brother Meriwether that the Americans were sending an emissary to the Salish: "he takes with him a few goods & an invitation to come to this place to trade, & perhaps if they should come into this Country it would be the means of keeping the Blackfeet out & inable us to bouy the Beaver if not to ketch it."[19] Similar sentiments were expressed on the same day by Pierre Menard, another leader of the American party: "I hope between now and then to see the Snake and Flathead Indians. My plan is to induce them to stay here, if possible, and make war upon the Blackfeet so that we may take some prisoners and send back one with propositions of peace. . . ."[20] The informal alliance between the white fur traders and the Salish was necessitated by their common enemies: the Blackfeet, other Plains tribes, and sometimes the Shoshoni Indians. The alliance was mutually beneficial and became a bedrock of Salish military strategy in the nineteenth century.

According to McDonald family traditions, a battle occurred in 1812 on the plains between the Salish and Blackfeet in which Finan McDonald, a fur trader, played a heroic role on the side of the Salish. Six feet, four inches tall, with long red hair and a beard, Finan advanced alone on a surrounded

Blackfeet party and systematically shot two of their warriors. They were the only Blackfeet casualties in that battle.[21]

The whites were valuable military allies for the Salish, but the pursuit of profit led the whites to also sell guns and ammunition to the Blackfeet. During the 1855 negotiations for the Hellgate Treaty, Big Canoe, a Pend d'Oreille chief, expressed frustration at continued white arms sales to the Blackfeet: "You white man don't be afraid, you can see it—the Blackfeet, your own powder and ball shooting at us and you white man. Now I and you, you white man, both die with your own powder and ball. I think so when I think about it—stop that, quit giving them powder and ball."[22]

The historical record for the 1860s includes both expressions of white appreciation of Salish assistance and descriptions of some specific incidents of Salish military cooperation with whites. On June 17, 1861, Granville Stuart, a white miner on Gold Creek, recorded that the Salish had recovered some horses recently stolen by the Blackfeet from white men in Deer Lodge. Stuart was pleased when the "Flatheads (honest fellows) brought them over the mountains . . . and delivered them to their [white] owners." Three days later Stuart rejoiced when a Salish war party displayed the scalp of a Bannack horse thief.[23] In 1863 six Salish warriors escorted John D. Brown and his small party of white prospectors to the safety of Fort Benton.[24] On April 30, 1863, Emily R. Meredith, a white resident of Bannack, wrote to her father that a party of Salish were camped nearby, and "If this crazy [white] populace treat them well, they will be as good as a company of soldiers for their friendship for the whites is reliable, and they are mortal enemies of the Snakes and Bannocks."[25] In the midst of simmering hostilities between the Blackfeet tribes and Montana whites in 1865, the *Montana Post* of Virginia City assured its readers that when hostilities broke out, the Bitterroot Salish, Pend d'Oreilles, and Kootenais would join the whites against the Blackfeet.[26] In March 1866 a party of whites and Salish outside of Helena encountered four Blackfeet butchering a stolen ox and killed three of them.[27] That same month Michael Ogden, a mixed-blood trader, and three other Salish in the Musselshell Valley joined eight white men in attacking a Blackfeet camp to recapture cattle and mules that they had stolen from the whites.[28] In July 1868 the *Helena Weekly Herald* made note of a party of Salish Indians visiting town on the way to a buffalo hunt in the Yellowstone. The writer waxed eloquent in warning: "Look out, Mr. Flatheads, for your glossy ringlets; for the peace commission pets, the Sioux and Crow's [*sic*], are hovering in that locality, and might wish to raise your *har*, as a memento of Auld Lang Syne."[29]

The intertribal war was not a total war. The conflict was opportunistic and sporadic, and did not necessarily involve all members of an opposing tribe. A good example was the friendship between the Salish and the Little Robes band of the Piegans. The Little Robes were friendlier to the Salish than were other Piegan bands. Father Nicolas Point left a pictorial record of "Friendly Trade Between the Blackfeet and Flathead" in the 1840s. The Blackfeet in the drawing, presumably Little Robes, are trading guns, pipes, decorated skin clothing, and other items to the Salish.[30] The Little Robes were even reported to have furnished the Salish with ammunition used to fight other Blackfeet.[31] One of the chiefs of the Little Robes, Nicholas, and his family were baptized at St. Mary's on Christmas Day 1841 while on a peaceful visit to the Salish camp.[32] There were, however, periods of conflict between the Little Robes and the Salish. In 1848 Charles Larpenteur, a fur trader, recorded a fight between the Little Robes and the Salish that resulted in deaths on both sides and stolen horses.[33] By July 1860 the hostilities had been resolved, and John Mullins, a U.S. Army officer, encountered several Salish traveling with the Little Robes in the Judith River country.[34] The Little Robes' military capability was severely limited after a disastrous battle with the Crows in 1845.[35] Military conflict on the plains was fluid, with alternating periods of peace and war.

A demographic consequence of the intertribal wars was a high death rate among young Salish men. In the 1850s Washington territorial governor Isaac I. Stevens estimated that the population of the Bitterroot Salish was 350 individuals in about sixty lodges. But Stevens reported that many of the lodges were "only inhabited by old women and their daughters." At a council with Stevens at Fort Owen, the Salish pointed out six or seven orphan boys whose fathers had been killed by the Blackfeet in the previous two or three years. Stevens found that the Salish had been "almost exterminated by the Blackfeet." Adopting members of other tribes and encouraging them to marry Salish widows had cushioned the war losses, but Stevens wrote in the mid-1850s that "the mass of the [Salish] nation consist of Pend d'Oreilles, Spokanes, Nez Perces, and Iroquois."[36]

Marriages of Salish women to white fur traders helped secure the informal Salish-white military alliance, but some of the families moved away from the northern Rocky Mountains and the Bitterroot Valley. A famous example was James Bridger, a white fur trader who was married to a daughter of Insula, a Salish chief, between approximately 1835 and 1846. Bridger traveled and fought with the Salish at times in the 1830s, but he later established Fort Bridger in the Green River area of southwestern Wyoming. Insula's daughter died at the fort in 1846 from the bite of a mad wolf. Insula's grandchildren went to school in St. Louis and the Whitman Mission in Walla Walla Valley. His grandson, Felix Bridger, served in the Civil War, but there is no record of the children returning to the Bitterroot Valley to visit their Salish relatives.[37] Even before 1870, the Bitterroot Salish were under enormous military and demographic pressure.

## Spiritual Warfare: Religious Renewal among the Nineteenth-Century Salish

The Salish reached out to allied tribes and whites for guns and manpower, but warfare was also a spiritual struggle. In the eighteenth century a Salish cultural hero and prophet, Shining Shirt, foretold the coming of white-skinned men with new spiritual teachings and power.[38] In the early nineteenth century, Catholic Iroquois Indians settled in western Montana and married into the Salish tribe. The Salish were receptive to their stories about the powers and teachings of Christianity. In the 1830s four fabled Salish–Nez Perce–Iroquois "delegations" to St. Louis reflected Salish interest in learning more about the spiritual powers of the white men.[39] Apparently, during the 1830s the Salish also received religious teachings and dances from other sources. On Sunday, May 5, 1833, Nathaniel J. Wyeth, an American fur trader, witnessed a "new great man no[w] getting up in the [Salish] Camp" whose "followers are now dancing to their own vocal music" on a flat area nearby. Wyeth did not learn the details of the new teaching, but he compared the gatherings to the religious revivals that were then common in his native New England.[40] The 1830s seem to have been a time of widespread religious ferment across the Columbia Plateau.[41]

St. Mary's Mission in the Bitterroot Valley, founded by Jesuit priests in 1841, was consecrated by the vision and prophecy of a dying Salish girl named Mary.[42] But while both the Salish and the missionaries saw the advent of Christianity among the Salish as providential, each had a different understanding of the consequences of the new spiritual powers.

To the Jesuits, Salish acceptance of Christian practices implied agreeing to European social values and lifeways. Father Pierre De Smet, S.J., was greeted with joy and adoration, but his paradigm was the coercive theocratic "reductions," or communities, earlier Jesuits had established among the

Indians of Paraguay in the seventeenth and eighteenth centuries.[43] The reductions were agricultural communities manned by Indians but heavily influenced by the Church and missionary priests.[44] In his first exhortation to the Salish in 1840, De Smet urged the Salish to give up their hunting and gathering economy and establish a European agricultural community. He set daily schedules of spiritual exercises and abolished gambling as an unchristian means of acquiring wealth.[45] After establishing St. Mary's Mission, De Smet wrestled with pressing Salish marriages into the rigid mold of Roman Catholic canon law.[46] Forcing young Salish children to be clothed to nineteenth-century European standards, however, had to wait until a later date.[47] Imposing European rules governing "civilized" conflict on intertribal warfare confounded the missionaries for most of the 1840s.[48] The struggle of the priests to remake Salish culture must have been almost as mystifying to the Salish as the priests' efforts to explain scholastic Christian theology in the Salish language.

More immediate benefits of Christian spiritual powers were demonstrated on the battlefield. Shortly before De Smet's arrival in 1840, seventy Salish warriors—fortified with Christian prayers—triumphed over a thousand Blackfeet. Later Insula, or Little Chief, led a war party against the Bannacks and invoked Christian prayer to triumph over a Bannack force ten times the size of Insula's party.[49] In 1842 the Pend d'Oreilles were able to defeat a Blackfeet war party at least thirty strong and kill almost all of them. Not one Pend d'Oreille was killed in the battle. A few years later, in 1846, the Salish, allied with the Little Robes Blackfeet, Pend d'Oreilles, and Nez Perces, defeated the Crow Indians with the aid of their new Christian powers. Ten Crows were killed, but only one of the Salish alliance died: a Nez Perce warrior who had failed to make the sign of the cross at the beginning of the battle.[50] Both the missionaries and, apparently, the Salish attributed these victories to the new Christian spiritual powers.

The priests, however, could not restrain themselves from interfering in Salish military decisions. Father Gregory Mengarini's efforts to apply European concepts to the Salish-Blackfeet warfare on the bison range contributed to growing Salish resentment during the 1840s. On one or two occasions Mengarini pressured the Salish to release captive Blackfeet warriors. In another case, when Mengarini feared to intervene, Chief Victor had a Blackfeet captive executed. Mengarini pressured the Salish to abandon the battlefield in one incident when a Blackfeet force was near defeat and forced the Salish to give up a saddle and two Blackfeet women captives after the battle. By 1846, when Mengarini insisted on accompanying a Salish buffalo hunt, his pack was loaded on a wild horse and lost in a river crossing in an unsuccessful attempt to force the missionary to return to St. Mary's.[51]

As already noted, Nicholas, the chief of the Little Robes band of Blackfeet, and his family were baptized at St. Mary's on Christmas Day in 1841.[52] By 1846, the other Blackfeet were asking whether "the medicine of the Black-robes is stronger than theirs."[53] Incomprehensibly, the priests proposed giving the new spiritual powers to the hostile Blackfeet. The Little Robes had friendly relations with the Salish, but in the 1840s a reasonable and logical Salish thinker would probably have seen the spread of Christian power to the hostile Blackfeet as treason. In 1846, when the tribes met on the plains, Salish chief Victor made a speech outlining his desire for peace. De Smet left Father Nicolas Point at Fort Lewis during the winter of 1846 and 1847 to teach the Piegan Blackfeet the secrets of Christianity.[54]

The dissonance resulting from the priests' efforts to reform Salish culture and the imprudent interference by Father Mengarini in Salish military efforts melded with Salish reluctance to share spiritual powers with the Blackfeet.[55] The resulting friction aggregated into a rupture between the Salish and the priests, forcing the closure of St. Mary's Mission in 1850. Some of the Salish lamented the closure and followed the missionaries as far as the junction of the Jocko and Flathead rivers.[56] According to one report, Chief Victor later traveled to Oregon with an unsuccessful request for Father Mengarini to return to the Bitterroot Valley and reopen St. Mary's.[57]

Christian prayers and ritual continued, and in 1853 John Mullan, a U.S. Army explorer, visited a Salish camp, where "They [the Salish] received him in a friendly manner, and astonished him by having prayers on his arrival, as well as in the morning and evening. The whole tribe being assembled in the chief's lodge."[58] That same year George Suckley, an army surgeon, found the Salish "professedly Roman Catholic," but he noted that "they still keep up their aboriginal mode of dress, and many of their old customs." Suckley commented that the Salish "still remember the good teachings of the missionaries."[59] In 1857 Father Joseph Menetrey, S.J., visited the Salish and deplored the prevalence of gambling, but he noted that the Salish chiefs had "never deviated from the path traced out for them by our Fathers."[60] The closing of St. Mary's in 1850 represented a discordance of vision between the Salish and the priests, not a rejection of Christianity or its spiritual power. St. Mary's Mission reopened in 1866 but never did become the nucleus of a theocratic agricultural community. It was, however, an important center of Salish spiritual and community life in the Bitterroot Valley.[61]

## Promises, Promises, Promises: The 1855 Hellgate Treaty Sets the Stage for Land Conflict

The informal alliance between the Salish and the white fur traders and trappers against the Blackfeet and other Plains tribes was context for the 1855 treaty between the Salish and the U.S. government. The Salish appreciated government efforts to secure peace between the Salish and the Plains tribes, but they were surprised and troubled by discussion of land cessions. Different understandings of the Bitterroot Valley provisions of the treaty set the stage for the Salish negotiations with government agents between 1869 and 1891. The treaty put Salish land claims in direct conflict with the efforts of white settlers in the Bitterroot to secure title to their farms, and complicated Salish efforts to maintain peaceful relations with Bitterroot whites. A modus vivendi reached in 1872 defused much of the unease: Bitterroot whites received official title to their lands, and the U.S. government recognized Salish title to farms in the valley.

According to several members of Isaac Stevens's railroad exploration party, the Salish were interested in establishing peace with the Plains tribes in the 1850s. Intertribal peace—with secure plains buffalo hunting rights—would have had obvious appeal to Salish leaders struggling to protect tribal welfare. On October 11, 1853, Lt. Andrew Donelson interviewed Samide, a Salish man camped on Horse Plains. According to Elwood Evans's notes, Samide expressed a "Kindly disposition to the whites—great dread of Blackfeet. . . . [The Salish would] willingly join in peace with Blackfeet and welcome them as friends—none but can say— I lost a Father, son, Brother or Mother From Fort Benton to St Marys village—the road is strewn with the bones of our deceased relatives—We love peace and will keep it but it is pleasant to fight and kill our enemies."[62] In November 1853 another member of Stevens's expedition, John Mullan, informed the Salish chiefs of the intertribal peace council at Fort Benton that Stevens was planning for the summer of 1854. According to Mullan, the Salish chiefs "received the intelligence of the council with much joy & exaltation and they now look forward to the coming summer as a period from which they are to date a new & happy period in their nations [*sic*] history."[63]

Stevens used Indian interest in peace to secure the attendance of the Bitterroot Salish, Upper Pend d'Oreille, and Lower Kootenai Indians at the treaty council grounds west of Missoula on July 7, 1855. When the council commenced, however, the Indian leaders were surprised to learn that Stevens wanted to talk about land cessions rather than intertribal peace. The Salish chief, Victor, complained at the opening of the council that "The Blackfeet have troubled us very much."[64] Big Canoe, a Pend d'Oreille chief, questioned Stevens about why a treaty was needed between the Bitterroot Salish/ Pend d'Oreilles and the whites: "Talk about treaty, where did I kill you? when did you kill me? What is the reason we are talking about treaties; that is what I said, we are friends, you are not my enemy." Big Canoe pleaded for the whites to stop trading ammunition with the Blackfeet: "Sometimes my people get mad when the Blackfeet kill us."[65] Stevens, however, would not discuss intertribal peace on the plains until later, at the Fort Benton council, which included the Blackfeet and representatives of the western tribes.[66]

Ignoring Indian sensibilities, Stevens pushed ahead at the Flathead council to force the issue of Indian land cessions in exchange for annuities and white recognition of Indian title to one limited reservation. Alexander, chief of the Pend d'Oreille, and Victor, the Bitterroot Salish chief, upset Stevens's master plan and timetable by refusing to agree on a common reservation. Stevens's arrogance and bigotry surfaced in his frustration. Since Victor refused to accede to Stevens's pressure to move to the Jocko or Flathead Valley reservation, Stevens suggested Victor was "an old woman" and "dumb as a dog."[67] Victor walked out of the council. The negotiations resumed a few days later, after Stevens had regained his composure. Victor complained that Stevens "gave me a very small place; then I thought, here they are giving away my land."[68] Stevens was finally able to cobble together a compromise that promised the tribes a reservation in the Flathead Valley and provided for a possible second reservation in the Bitterroot Valley for the Salish.[69]

Article 11 was added to the previously prepared treaty to have the Bitterroot Valley "carefully surveyed and examined, and if it shall prove, in the judgment of the President, to be better adapted to the wants of the Flathead tribe than the general reservation provided for in this treaty, then such portions of it as may be necessary shall be set apart as a separate reservation for the said tribe." The treaty also specifically provided that "No portion of the Bitter Root Valley, above the Loo-lo Fork, shall be opened to [white] settlement until such examination is had and the decision of the President made known."[70]

Questions surrounding translation cloud the negotiations for the 1855 Hellgate Treaty. One of the principal translators was Benjamin Kizer, a half-blood Shawnee. According to Stevens, Kizer spoke English "quite well," was "exceedingly reliable" as an interpreter, and "remarkable" as a hunter and guide.[71] Father Adrian Hoecken, S.J., who attended the council as an observer, was much less impressed by Kizer's abilities as a translator. Hoecken complained in an August 1, 1855, report to his superior, Father Joseph Joset: "What a ridiculous tragi-comedy the whole council proved. It would take too long to write it all down—ah well! Not a tenth of it was actually understood by either party, for Ben Kyser speaks Flathead very badly and is no better at translating into English. A treaty has been made—or so they will say." Hoecken wrote that Chief Alexander called Stevens "two-faced and a treacherous Blackfoot." Hoecken also commented about how illogical it was to the Indians to make a treaty with the whites when they had never been at war with them.[72]

Political problems in Washington, D.C., delayed ratification of the Hellgate Treaty for almost four years, and it was not approved until April 18, 1859.[73] In contrast, the treaty with the Blackfeet, which was negotiated three months after the Hellgate Treaty, was officially proclaimed on April 25, 1856.[74] The Blackfeet were getting annuities under their treaty—despite their failure to keep the peace with the western tribes—while the Salish and Kootenai had not received any payment for their lands. In April 1857 John Owen wrote that the Salish complained that they were being treated like dogs. It had been two years since the Hellgate Treaty, and the government had still not responded, while "The Same year Some moons later a treaty was made with the Blackfeet which was responded to immediately by their great Father in the Shape of Blankets, Guns, Groceries &c. Why Should the Blackfeet Stand so much better with the Great Father than we who have never shed the blood of a white man."[75] In September 1857, R. H. Lansdale, the former Flathead Indian agent, complained about the failure of Congress to approve the Hellgate Treaty when the treaty with the Blackfeet had been ratified at once. Lansdale declared the policy "wrong and reprehensible." To the Salish the policy was "a glaring exemplification of the insane policy of [the government] rewarding enemies and punishing friends."[76]

After the Hellgate Treaty was formally ratified in 1859, the bungling efforts of the government to implement the treaty provisions left the Salish very skeptical of future government promises. Problems developed with almost every promise the government had made in 1855: (1) to protect Indian use of both the Jocko Reservation and the provisional Bitterroot Reservation; (2) to pay annuities for land cessions; (3) to erect and staff mechanics' shops, mills, a hospital, and a school to serve tribal members; and (4) to pay salaries to the head chiefs and establish farms and houses for them. During the treaty negotiations, Stevens also made a verbal promise to the Salish to provide military protection from the Blackfeet, but this promise was not included in the final document.

Between 1870 and 1891, it was Article 11 that was particularly pregnant with difficulties for the Bitterroot Salish. Stevens expected to comply with the article by having Flathead agent R. H. Lansdale make a cursory evaluation of the two potential reservations and then recommend that the Bitterroot Salish move to the Flathead Valley. Stevens's instructions to Lansdale, dated September 7, 1855, were not in agreement with the treaty, which provided that the Upper Pend d'Oreille and Lower Kootenai Indians would have a reservation in the Flathead River valley, while the Bitterroot Salish would, at the president's discretion, either have a separate reservation in the Bitterroot Valley or join the other tribes in the Flathead Valley. Stevens's instructions to Lansdale, however, asked him to consider whether the Bitterroot Valley or the Flathead Valley Reservation would be the best location for those three tribes combined with the Lower Pend d'Oreille and Coeur d'Alene Indians. Stevens's preferred conclusion was made obvious by his assertion that "weight must be given to the fact that a large majority of the Indians prefer the Flathead River reservation."[77] A few weeks later, after riding around the Bitterroot and Flathead valleys, Lansdale obediently concluded that "the northern district is preferable."[78] Stevens was apparently going to consider Lansdale's report as fulfilling the treaty provision for having the Bitterroot Valley "carefully surveyed and examined." The delay in ratification of the treaty and the federal government's distraction with the Civil War aborted any use of Lansdale's report to fulfill the terms of Article 11. The unwillingness of the government to keep its promise to exclude white settlers from the Bitterroot until the question was settled created a cloud over Salish title to the valley.

Stevens's verbal promise during the negotiations—to provide white soldiers to protect the Salish from Blackfeet attacks—was not included in the written document, and yet, to the Salish, this offer of military aid was probably the most important pledge the government had made. In the

English-language transcript of the negotiations, on July 11, 1855, Stevens promised military protection so long as the Salish were on the reservation. We do not have the Salish translation of Stevens's speech, so we cannot tell if the caveat to the promise was explained to the Salish: "You have asked to be protected from the Blackfeet; you *shall* be protected from the Blackfeet, but you must do your part. Go there [to the reservation] and the government will protect you."[79] The Salish had been frustrated before by Stevens's propensity to promise more than he could deliver. In September 1853, Stevens had met at Fort Benton with a group of Piegan and other Blackfeet chiefs from both sides of the forty-ninth parallel to try to establish intertribal peace on the buffalo grounds. The Blackfeet chiefs promised Stevens they would "meet them [the Salish and Nez Perce] in council, and desired to live on terms of peace with them." They also promised to "cease to send war parties into the Flathead country before the council was held" and to encourage their tribesmen to do likewise.[80] Only two months after Stevens obtained the promise of peace from the Blackfeet chiefs, John Mullan reported that the Blackfeet had "kept their promise most faithlessly."[81] The impotence of Stevens's repeated promises to arrange peace with the Blackfeet was accentuated by events following the Hellgate Treaty. Stevens could not even protect the Salish representatives who attended the Blackfeet treaty council held October 1855 at the mouth of the Judith River. Four Salish horses were stolen by northern Blackfeet while the owners were visiting Governor Stevens at Fort Benton shortly before the council began. These horses were retrieved from Canada by the Americans and returned to their owners.[82] Three weeks after that council concluded, Piegan and Blood warriors stole twenty-two horses from Francois Saxa [Lamoose], a Salish farmer and interpreter, before he even made it back to the Bitterroot Valley. Saxa's horses were never returned.[83]

The 1855 Hellgate Treaty obligated the government to provide $120,000 over twenty years to compensate the Salish and Kootenais for the off-reservation land ceded to the U.S. government. The first year $36,000 was promised, with $6,000 each of the next four years, $5,000 a year for years six through ten, $4,000 a year for years eleven through fifteen, and $3,000 a year for the final five years. The money was to cover the cost of moving off-reservation tribal members to the reservation, establishing farms and houses there, and other things the president "may deem necessary."[84] It is impossible to make an accurate accounting from the surviving documents, but there is evidence that a substantial portion of the money that the government appropriated for treaty expenses was consumed by graft and incompetence, and provided little benefit to the Salish and Kootenai tribes.

On May 25, 1860, Flathead agent John Owen complained that a large portion of the $36,000 for the first year was being wasted on consumables such as coffee, rice, hard bread, blankets, shawls, and flannel instead of livestock, agricultural equipment, guns, ammunition, and metal cookware. According to Owen, the hard bread was particularly inappropriate. Owen fumed, "The Flatheads are not a barbarous people. They know very well that the lands they sold were not to be paid for in hardbread & the likes. Assist them in producing a change in their herd of horses by purchasing them some American breed mares, & a few hundred heifers. . . . Their advancement in the scale of social life is not promoted by the shipment of trash."[85] After months of expensive bungling and disputes over paperwork, on November 29, 1860, Owen finally reported that he had the first annuity shipment in his warehouse at Fort Owen. He found that the blankets were "inferior," and the shawls and flannels were "miserable flimsey things of no earthly use." The coffee was "mouldy & musty" and reportedly had been salvaged after sinking in the Missouri River. Owen concluded that "I have no hesitation in saying I could have purchased the same bill in Portland for one third less money."[86] Apparently Owen spent most of the remaining annuity money on cattle, which he distributed to tribal members.[87] The treaty committed the government to pay all transportation expenses for delivering the annuity goods to western Montana, but Owen received no funds to pay for freighting the goods from Fort Benton to the Bitterroot Valley. Consequently, he had to sell a portion of the annuity goods to cover the freight expense. In 1863, Flathead agent Charles Hutchins calculated that the government owed the Salish and Kootenai $12,000 to reimburse the freight on the 1860 annuities.[88]

Congress had failed to appropriate money to pay for the 1861 treaty obligations, and the 1862 annuities were lost when the boat carrying them, the *Chippewa*, burned on the Missouri River.[89] By 1866, Flathead agent Augustus Chapman calculated that the government owed the Salish and Kootenai tribes a total of $30,793.50 to correct for duplicate charges, annuity goods sold to pay for transportation, annuity goods sold for agency purposes, and Flathead annuity goods given to the Snake Indians.[90] In 1868 the bales of blankets sent for annuities were tampered with during transport, and 113 pairs of blankets were missing.[91] By August 1868, Salish chief Adolph complained that they had received annuities for only five of the eight years the treaty had been in force.[92] An honest accounting of the annuity payments due under the Hellgate Treaty may not be possible from the surviving documents, but it is obvious that the Salish and Kootenai were shortchanged, and that tribal leaders understood they had been cheated.

The 1855 treaty obligated the government to establish, equip, and staff a blacksmith shop, a tin and gun shop, a carpenter shop, a wagon and plow maker's shop, a sawmill, and a flour mill to serve tribal members. In addition, the government was to provide two farming instructors, erect a hospital, employ a physician, and establish a school. [93] The historical record indicates that the services actually provided were of minimal use to tribal members. The shops and mills at the agency were either dysfunctional or used to supply material and services for agency operations. In 1868, special Indian agent W. J. Cullen found the blacksmith shop had no iron, and the carpenter shop had no nails.[94] Alvin Galbreath, the new Flathead agent in 1869, reported that the carpenter, blacksmith, and gunsmith tools at the agency were incomplete and inadequate.[95] The agency farm seems to have been operated mainly to provide subsistence for the agent and agency employees.[96]

Treaty positions at the agency were political patronage jobs and not filled by skilled craftsmen. Wages were not paid regularly, and in 1868 the agency employees had not been paid for a year.[97] Some of the employees on the payroll did not even exist but drew salary money that the agent theoretically used to provide subsistence for the real employees.[98] Other employees, who were at least real people, were relatives of the agent. Agent Augustus Chapman's brother-in-law was agency farmer in 1867,[99] and in 1872 agent Charles Jones had two employees whose last names were "Jones."[100] Congressman James Garfield described some of Jones's employees in 1872 as "mere boys, whose chief functions seemed to be to sign the payroll and draw their pay."[101] The agency clerical staff seems to have been paid with funds appropriated under the treaty for service positions. Charles Schafft, the longtime Flathead Agency clerk, was officially the head farmer, despite having lost both legs below the knees. He was reported to be an excellent clerk, but his disability raises questions about his proficiency operating a horse-drawn plow.[102] In 1872, when James Garfield promised to build twenty houses in the Jocko Valley for the Bitterroot Salish under Chief Arlee, he directed that employees hired under the 1855 treaty be used to saw the lumber and build the houses.[103]

The agency physician could have been selected based on technical expertise, but the surviving evidence suggests political patronage was more important. In 1870 the agency physician, a Democrat, was replaced with a Republican doctor who, it was charged, was rarely able to see patients outside of Missoula. According to agent Charles Jones, even agency employees went to another physician in Missoula rather than use the services of the Republican agency doctor.[104]

Governor Stevens's promise to provide the services of a series of shops and mills was a charade, but even when the agency had competent services to provide, its location in the Jocko Valley limited their use. Most of the tribal members lived in the Flathead Valley to the north or the Bitterroot Valley to the south. Transporting lumber, grain, or flour over the primitive roads of the time was a challenge. Agent Charles Hutchins commented in 1865 that since the agency sawmill was in the Jocko Valley, it was "located where it can never be of the slightest utility to the Indians of these tribes."[105] Most tribal members probably patronized the mills and shops at St. Ignatius Mission or in the Bitterroot Valley. Bitterroot Salish farmers who needed plows sharpened or grain ground, or hunters who needed guns repaired were rarely able to use agency services.

The 1855 treaty also obligated the government to build and operate a hospital and vocational school, but neither promise was kept. The government paid the St. Ignatius Mission the money appropriated for teachers' salaries, but it never built a hospital or school.[106] In August 1868 Salish chief Adolph included the promised school and hospital in a list of broken promises from the Hellgate Treaty.[107]

The treaty provided for salaries, farms, and houses for the Bitterroot Salish, Pend d'Oreille, and Kootenai head chiefs, but only sporadic salary money seems to have been paid to the chiefs. In 1868 the chiefs were so irritated with the erratic payments that agent W. J. McCormick had to sell agency lumber to get funds to pay them after they refused to help the agent track down horses stolen from white miners until they were paid.[108] In 1869 agent Alvin Galbreath wrote to the Office of Indian Affairs about the failure of the government to provide houses and farms for the chiefs.[109] This promise was apparently never fulfilled.

Thus ends the litany of promises made by Governor Isaac Stevens in 1855 that the government either failed to fulfill or fulfilled only partially. Unfortunately for the government, the Salish and Kootenais had no problem remembering what Stevens had offered. In August 1868 Salish chief Ambrose summarized his frustration about the promises the United States had made: "The provisions of the Treaty which we made with Govr Stevens long ago have never been complied with. Not one half of what was promised us has ever been received by us."[110] This legacy of frustration and broken promises from 1855 made the Salish very skeptical when later government negotiators tried to sway them with glib promises of future benefits. Avoiding a two-front war and maintaining access to weapons and other goods traded by the whites continued to offer the Salish leaders the best path to Salish survival, but the whites could be incomprehensible and frustrating allies.

## Economic Expansion: Cattle Ranching and Farms

The century and a half between 1720 and 1870 was a period of economic as well as military-political change for the Bitterroot Salish Indians. The acquisition of horses and access to European goods through the fur trade had obvious economic as well as military consequences. The horse expanded the hunting and trading range of the Salish and greatly increased the volume of meat, trade goods, and household items that could be moved by a family. The fur traders offered metal tools and craft supplies as well as guns and ammunition. Traders also provided a new outlet for furs, dried meat, and leather goods. But while the fur trade expanded and enriched the Salish economy, it also left them vulnerable to economic changes in Europe, half a world away.

Farming was first introduced in the Bitterroot Valley by the Jesuit missionaries at St. Mary's Mission. De Smet's first trip after founding St. Mary's was in the fall of 1841 to Fort Colville for provisions and seeds.[111] While the Salish did not prove willing to give up their traditional hunting and gathering activities, they did add farming to their annual economic cycle. According to Father Palladino, the seed obtained from Fort Colville consisted of potatoes, wheat, and oats. Brother William Claessens, S.J., who was responsible for the farm, remembered later that "Indians could be seen day after day perched on the fence for hours waiting for the seed to come to life again." The yield in 1842 was bountiful, and the missionaries were able to share their first crop with the entire Salish camp. According to Father Palladino, "The Indians became very fond of potatoes, green corn, peas, beans, turnips, and carrots. But they had no use for greens, and especially disliked onions. The latter made their eyes water, while they thought the former good only for horses."[112]

Salish farming expanded slowly in the second half of the nineteenth century because seed and agricultural equipment were very limited. The parallel agricultural enterprise of cattle ranching, however, exploded in the 1850s. A group of white and mixed-blood trappers and traders, many of whom later married into the Salish tribe, spent summers on the immigrant road south of Montana trading with white migrants for poor and sore-footed cattle. The cattle were then wintered in the Bitterroot or other nearby valleys and traded to the Salish for horses. The Salish horses were finally driven to the immigrant road to trade for more worn-out cattle. Joseph Lumprey, William Rodgers, Ben and James Delaware, Ben Kizer, and Gabriel Prudhomme were among those involved in the trade who married into the Salish.[113] On January 14, 1851, Prudhomme purchased two sets of branding irons at Fort Owen for twelve dollars.[114] Caleb Irvine also took part in the this trade between 1851 and 1856.[115]

### *Iroquois and White Farms and Ranches*

Early in the nineteenth century, parties of Iroquois Indians came west during the fur trade, and one group settled among the Bitterroot Salish.[116] The Iroquois married into the tribe, and some took up ranching and farming. In 1850 and 1853 Iroquois Aeneas, or Ignace, sold yokes of steers to John Owen.[117] In 1862 Owen butchered a six-hundred-pound beef belonging to Aeneas's wife, and in 1852 he purchased sixteen pounds of beef from Iroquois Peter.[118] Two years later Peter visited Owen's camp while out hunting his missing cattle.[119] In 1855 Peter sold oxen to Owen.[120] Charles Lamoose, half Iroquois, settled his account at Fort Owen in 1853 with a cow and an eight-month-old heifer.[121]

In the 1850s the Iroquois also had farms. In 1853 Aeneas paid Owen to grind three and a half bushels of wheat.[122] George Suckley, a medical doctor with Isaac Stevens's railroad exploration, described Iroquois Peter's Bitterroot Valley farm in 1853: "Pierre farms, raises cattle, horses, potatoes, wheat, & a few vegetables, butter, eggs &c &c." Suckley added that Peter herded his cattle much more closely than did the other Indian ranchers.[123] In 1858 Frederick H. Burr, an early white settler in the Bitterroot, traded a plow to one of the Iroquois Lamooses for a horse.[124]

The white men who married into the Salish developed some early farms in the Bitterroot to support their families. For example, Joseph Lumprey paid Owen in 1853 for grinding wheat. That same year Lumprey sold a steer to Owen, and in 1854 he sold another steer to Lt. John Mullan. Six years later, in 1860, Lumprey sold Owen fourteen pounds of beef.[125] Thomas W.

Harris, a white farmer in the Bitterroot, visited Lumprey's farm in May 1860 and noted that Lumprey's wheat "looks much worse than mine. he says the Indian wheat looks still worse than his."[126]

The farms operated in the Bitterroot by the Iroquois and whites introduced the Salish to agricultural technology, and some Salish found seasonal employment on these farms. On May 17, 1856, Owen's horse Jennie was sick, and Owen sent for Palchina, a Salish chief, "to act a Veterinary Surgeon he being the best one I know of." Unfortunately, Palchina could not diagnose Jennie's illness.[127] Later that same month, Owen let Palchina use three of Owen's horses on the buffalo hunt in exchange for "breaking them & getting them gentle."[128] In his diary, Thomas Harris recorded hiring Salish women to dig potatoes in fall 1864, 1867, and 1868.[129] In October 1866, Owen hired "Some Ind women" to dig potatoes.[130] The Bitterroot Salish had access to a variety of sources in the 1850s and 1860s to learn skills needed for farming and raising cattle, and to acquire seed, breeding stock, and agricultural equipment.

### *Government Agricultural Aid*

Some assistance and equipment for developing Bitterroot Salish farms came from the Flathead Indian Agency during the 1850s and 1860s. Agent John Owen, in particular, used agency funds to hire white men to help plow and fence the Indian fields. In September 1858, Owen informed Chief Victor that the government had authorized him to spend $1,000 for presents for the Salish. Victor asked that half of the money be used for "ammunition and tobacco that we much need, the other half open us a field with and get us a plow we will sow wheat and have flour to eat as Buffalo are growing scarce." Owen used the money as requested and also hired a white blacksmith to keep the plow in order and mend and repair Salish traps, guns, kettles, and axes. When not doing blacksmith work, the smith was to make rails for Salish fields and assist them in plowing and tending the crops.[131] During the 1859 growing season Owen made arrangements for some of the Salish farmers to grow grain in his own enclosed field.[132] In August Owen reported that "I Encouraged Some of the Indians here last Spring in Sowing Wheat & I am happy to State to you that they are highly Elated With the prospect of a plentiful harvest. There is Now under fence & in Wheat & potatoes in the Valley over one hundred Acres all of which promises a bountiful Yield."[133] Shortly before September 6, 1860, Owen spent $10,990 for heifers and stock cattle, and $2,420 for forty-four head of beef cattle for the combined Salish and Kootenai tribes. At the same time $5,736 was allocated for transportation of "Seed Wheat Tools &c" from Portland to the Jocko Valley.[134] Owen later mentioned purchasing three hundred head of cattle for the Salish and Kootenai.[135] While many of these cattle, seed, and tools must have gone to the tribes on the Jocko Reservation, a portion would have gone to the Bitterroot Salish. Between May 7 and 15, 1862, Thomas Harris, John Silverthorne, and another white man named Thornton were hired to plow and sow wheat for Bitterroot Salish farmers. Harris's May 9, 1862, diary entry mentions Salish farmers sowing wheat along with the white men helping them.[136] On July 9, 1862, Harris noted that Francois Lamoose (or Saxa) and a white man named John Chatfield had returned from the Jocko Reservation with fifty head of cattle for Salish ranchers.[137] Even after turning the Flathead Agency over to Charles Hutchins in 1862, Owen had a cabin built near Fort Owen for Chief Victor, who was too sick to go on the plains buffalo hunt. Owen promised Victor he would prepare a field for the chief to grow wheat.[138] A few years later, in 1865, Owen noted that Victor and the Bitterroot Salish had left for Jocko to get plows and agricultural supplies.[139] Government agricultural aid during the 1850s and 1860s was sporadic and limited, but it must have been useful as the Salish slowly expanded their farming and ranching operations.

### *Early Salish Farms and Ranches*

Records have survived relating to a number of Salish cattle herds and small farms in the 1850s and 1860s. The evidence is anecdotal, not systematic, but suggests that by 1870 most Salish extended families had a herd of cattle and horses, and a small farm. Almost all the Salish farms were seasonal enterprises, planted in the spring before the traditional root crops ripened and harvested after the summer buffalo hunt was completed. Most seem to have been small—probably just five to fifteen acres, or even only a vegetable garden.

The correspondence of members of Isaac I. Stevens's railroad exploring expedition describes Salish cattle and agriculture in 1853 and 1854. On December 24, 1853, the *Oregon Spectator* at Oregon City carried an article about the railroad exploration and described the Bitterroot Valley, which the Salish "have filled with cattle, and raised wheat and potatoes for their own use."[140] As with most of the railroad exploring references that follow, the author does not distinguish between herds and farms owned by the Salish and those owned by the Iroquois and white men who had married into the tribe. Lt. Rufus Saxton visited the Bitterroot Valley on August 28, 1853, and noted that the Salish had "a considerable village of log-cabins around Fort Owen, and own a large number of cattle. . . . I saw a considerable quantity of wheat, just harvested. They have also eggs, milk, potatoes, &c."[141] Dr. George Suckley, also with Stevens, visited the Bitterroot in September 1853 and recorded that the Salish "raise some wheat and potatoes, but depend principally on the chase for subsistence. They have quite a large number of cattle; these they corral at night to prevent them from being killed by the Blackfeet. The latter Indians do not steal cattle as they do horses, but kill them out of malice."[142] In his diary for September 29, 1853, Suckley noted that the Salish free-ranged their cattle during winter and did not feed them hay.[143] Abiel W. Tinkham, an engineer with the expedition, visited the Bitterroot in November 1853 and observed a "multitude of horses and cattle owned by the Indians and half-breeds, in the most thriving condition."[144] Another member of the Stevens's expedition, George Gibbs, estimated that in 1853 the Salish had one thousand head of cattle.[145] In 1854 Lt. John Mullan, also of the Stevens' expedition, paid unidentified Indians at Fort Owen $160 for six small steers.[146]

Other sources allow us to identify Salish cattle owners and farmers as distinct from the Iroquois, white men, and other Indians who married into the tribe. On January 13, 1855, Owen paid Elecsu—unidentified but probably Indian—twenty-five dollars for a steer killed by Lt. John Mullan that had been thought to belong to Pasha, a Salish man.[147] In his diary in February 1856 Owen recorded killing a small steer belonging to Moiese, the Salish chief.[148] Frederick Burr, a white Bitterroot farmer, noted in his diary for February 1857 "Edwards & Palchina 18 heads oxen," which probably refers to the purchase of cattle from two Salish subchiefs.[149] On July 9, 1857, Owen noted the arrival of some of the Salish, "I believe for the purpose of hunting up their cattle & mark[ing] the young calves."[150] In 1858 the Salish stock owners branded their cattle on March 5.[151]

By 1859 the Salish were protesting expanded white settlement in the Bitterroot because they had "large bands of Animals and Say there is Not More pasturage than they would like to have for themselves."[152] Ambrose, a Salish chief, sold some cattle to whoever was keeping John Owen's diary on May 22, 1860.[153] In October 1860 Owen killed a beef belonging to Indian Sanprobrill.[154] A few months later, Owen told of finding two young steers belonging to Chief Victor. The next day, one of Owen's employees butchered the steers, which yielded 1,100 pounds of "fine fat Beef."[155] In February 1862 Thomas Harris killed a two-year-old steer belonging to Chief Victor.[156] Presumably range stock were slaughtered as needed for domestic use in the Bitterroot and the absent owner compensated later.

The winter of 1861–62 was unusually cold and snowy, and winter losses of Indian-owned range cattle in the Bitterroot were heavy. On February 6, 1862, Joseph Lumprey reported to Owen that "Stock fast falling off in flesh and some dying. The Indian Cows now Calving nearly all perish the Calves certain & in some instances both Mother and offspring."[157] About a month later, on March 7, 1862, Harris recorded that "The Indians say there is over two hundred head of cattle already dead on burnt fork [Creek] and they are still dyeing every day."[158] Owen sent Harris and some other employees to drive the Indian stock to bare, south-facing hillsides: "It is quite a job the Stock are So poor and Weak that it is hard & difficult to Move them particularly when they come into the Crusted Snow He thinks he got out some 500 head to day."[159] In July, Moiese and Francois Eneas [Lamoose] traveled from the Bitterroot to the Jocko Valley for "some cattle" to replace a portion of the Indian losses that winter.[160] Harris bought a beef from an unnamed Bitterroot Indian on May 5, 1862, and when butchered it was "still very poor no tallow or fat."[161]

Harris and Owen record other purchases of Salish cattle for meat. On March 24, 1862, Owen "Found a Young Steer belonging to Chief Ambrose which I have Butchered for Beef."[162] Two months later Harris purchased a two-year-old heifer from Palchina for $16.75 in merchandise.[163] That December 24, Owen butchered a young steer he had purchased from Chief Victor, who had visited Fort Owen a few days earlier.[164] Harris sold a steer in 1863 to a Mr. Clark, who also purchased cattle from Joseph Lumprey and "the Indians" to sell at the mining camps.[165] The next year Harris purchased a cow and a yearling heifer from "Peer Abraham Indian."[166] A month later Harris bought a two-year-old steer from Chief Arlee.[167] On September 24, 1867, Ninepipe, a Salish farmer, sold Owen a quarter of fresh beef.[168] The next year Owen hired a yoke of oxen from Indian Felix for eight days at $2.50 per day.[169] The evidence indicates that by 1870 many Bitterroot Indian families had herds of beef cattle as well as horses. The cattle were free-ranged during the winter, but new calves required branding each year. The stock seems to have been sold, traded, or butchered by the Salish cattlemen as needed through the year.

There is also substantial evidence during the later 1850s and the 1860s of Salish farmers raising grain. On March 10 and 11, 1858, Owen ground Indian wheat in his flour mill but did not mention the names of the Indian farmers or the amount of the wheat.[170] Owen reported to the superintendent of Indian Affairs that "several" Bitterroot Salish farmers had harvested between ten and forty bushels of wheat each during 1859.[171] Harris wrote in his diary on June 14, 1860, that "the Indians wheat it looks well tho I saw none that looked any better then mine."[172] A year later Harris felt his wheat was the best in the Bitterroot, but "Indian wheat looks bad."[173] In Harris's diary for the 1860–61 period are several pages of accounts. One page lists the amount of money Harris owed Victor, Moiese, and Ninepipe, among other Indians. Harris owed Ninepipe $25 for "five Bushes," which may mean five bushels of wheat. Another page has a list of "Wheat bought of Indians." Harris bought 3 ¾ bushels of wheat from Chief Arlee for $18 in merchandise at the store. Moiese sold 6 ¼ bushels for $31.50; Victor, 6 bushels for $30.00; Sarele, 6 bushels for $30.00; and two unnamed Indian women, 1 ½ bushels each for $7.50 per woman.[174] On April 30, 1862, Harris wrote that "to day the Indians moved up to their fields to commence Plowing."[175] According to Flathead agent Charles Hutchins, the Bitterroot Salish harvested two thousand bushels of wheat in 1862.[176]

In May 1863 Harris was "grinding wheat until noon for the Indians."[177] Agent Hutchins reported to the commissioner of Indian Affairs in 1863 that the Salish "have very creditable farms, but their operations in this branch are necessarily restricted for want of agricultural implements; they have but few ploughs among them, and for such implements as they do possess they are not at all indebted to the government."[178] Hutchins estimated that in 1864 the Bitterroot Salish harvested about 2,500 bushels of wheat as well as other products. He figured about forty of the one hundred Salish families remained year-round on their Bitterroot farms and did not go on the buffalo hunts. Some of the better-off Salish farmers had log houses, cows, work cattle, and a few agricultural implements.[179] Chiefs Victor and Moiese left the Bitterroot for the buffalo hunt on May 18, 1865, but Moiese surprised Owen by returning a day later "having concluded Not to go to Buffaloe but Stay home & look after his Crop."[180]

There were also setbacks for Salish farms. In 1865 Agent Hutchins reported that Indian and white farms in western Montana had suffered from bad weather, grasshoppers, and crickets. He expected no more than one-fourth of a crop.[181] In September 1865, however, one Salish farmer,

Ninepipe, brought fifteen bushels of wheat to Owen's mill for grinding. Owen's miller declared it "the best & cleanest Wheat he had recd Since the Mill Started."[182] In 1866 the Salish crops were successful, and the new Flathead agent, Augustus Chapman, pronounced them "excellent, and could not be better."[183] Between September 13 and 26, 1866, and again on June 10, 1867, Owen's mill was busy grinding Indian grain, which must have come from the 1866 crop.[184] In May 1867 the new Flathead agent, John Wells, had to postpone a council at Fort Owen because many of the Bitterroot Salish were plowing and sowing their fields.[185] Unfortunately, their 1867 crop was lost to grasshoppers, and Wells requested funds to subsist the Salish through the winter.[186] Ninepipe may have been more fortunate than most of the other Salish farmers, and on July 3, 1868, he brought fifty bushels of "good Wheat," possibly from his 1867 crop, to be ground at Fort Owen.[187] Fortunately, in 1868 the Bitterroot grain crop was bountiful. In his diary, Owen mentioned grinding Salish wheat from September 11 through 28, 1868.[188] On September 16, Owen mentioned that the Salish planned on "leaving for Buffalo So Soon as they get their Wheat ground."[189] Owen calculated on September 18 that he had already ground five hundred bushels of grain for Indian farmers.[190] In 1868 the miller told special Indian agent W. J. Cullen "that the wheat raised by the [Bitterroot] Indians was of better quality and better cleaned than that grown by their white neighbors."[191] On June 1, 1869, when the Salish left for their summer buffalo hunt, the bitterroot had been harvested and stored, and the Salish planned to return to harvest their wheat crop in early fall.[192]

Several records indicate that during the early 1860s some of the Salish farmers had surplus potatoes to sell to the whites. Charles A. Cunningham, a lawyer and gold miner, recalled going to Fort Owen in January 1864 to purchase seed potatoes from an unnamed Indian.[193] In December 1864, R. W. Nicol, a white immigrant to the Bitterroot, could not purchase flour in the valley but found "plenty of potatoes" for sale for six dollars a bushel. With one or two exceptions the potatoes were raised by Indians, mixed-bloods, and white men married to Indians.[194]

The Salish pattern of integrating farming into their seasonal round and keeping most of their farms small was highlighted at the end of the 1860s. Bitterroot whites argued that these Salish accommodations meant they were not maximizing the agricultural potential of the valley. A few Salish farmers, such as Ninepipe, apparently had larger operations, but in 1869 many Salish farms must have been limited to a garden and five to fifteen acres of wheat.

Plows and other equipment were probably shared between farms. During busy periods, such as plowing, planting, and harvesting, most Salish farmers likely relied on temporary help from relatives who did not themselves farm. A petition by Bitterroot whites on March 7, 1868, asserted there were only about twenty Salish farms in the valley averaging about ten acres each under cultivation.[195] On August 22, 1868, a letter from one Stevensville white claimed that because of the small size of many Salish farms, the Salish had only a total of 250 to 300 acres under cultivation; however, this estimate did not include the farms of Indians from other tribes who had married into the Salish.[196] In 1869 Father Joseph Giorda at St. Mary's Mission gave Alfred Sully, the superintendent of Indian Affairs in Montana, a list of fifty-one Bitterroot Salish farmers.[197] Father Giorda's list was probably much more accurate than the number used in the 1868 petition by Bitterroot white farmers.

Ironically, the Salish tradition of generosity and hospitality induced the Salish to assist the newly arrived white immigrants by sharing cattle, plows, and other assets. John A. Simms, a white man, spent the winter of 1865–66 at Fort Owen and listened to local whites who wanted to see the Salish moved from the Bitterroot Valley. Simms observed that "Many of the Indians being thrifty farmers the settlers were willing to recognize the Material advantage they had derived from the use of their Cattle, Ploughs &c when they [the whites] first settled in the Country."[198]

Hunting and gathering were still the most important parts of the Salish economy in 1869, but farming and ranching had grown in significance.[199] In 1868 Flathead agent W. J. McCormick listed wheat, oats, barley, potatoes, cattle, and horses as the principal products of the Salish farmers and ranchers.[200] The Salish readily accepted agriculture as a supplement to their traditional economy, but their intense dedication to continuing their buffalo hunts emphasized their determination to also maintain their traditional economic activities. Some years provided generous harvests, but in other years, such as 1869, the crops failed miserably.[201] Equipment shortages were dramatized in August 1868 by Chief Adolph, who showed special Indian agent W. J. Cullen his hands and said: "Look at these; they are my tools; I scratch the ground with my nails." Witnesses corroborated Adolph's story that he had put in a crop that year with his bare hands.[202]

When Charlo became chief of the Bitterroot Salish in 1870, he inherited a legacy of survival strategies developed over a century. Maintaining peace with the white men was one of the foundations of Salish diplomacy and military planning. This strategy had enabled the Salish to survive a century of warfare with the Blackfeet, other Plains tribes, and occasionally the Shoshoni. Farming and cattle and horse ranching greatly diversified the Salish economy. Between 1870 and 1891 the basic diplomatic and economic strategies developed in the years before 1870 needed to be applied to changing conditions. Maintaining the alliance with Montana whites became increasingly difficult as their population in the Bitterroot Valley and the rest of Montana exploded during the 1870s and 1880s. The economic dislocation involved with using farms and ranching income to replace the buffalo hunts far exceeded the changes needed to add agriculture as a supplement to the traditional Salish hunting-gathering economy.

CHAPTER 2

# Dancing with Death

## Bitterroot Salish Diplomacy and Military Struggle on the Buffalo Grounds, 1870–1883

On August 7, 1870, the Bitterroot Salish Indians gathered on the banks of the Bitterroot River for a feast in honor of their recently deceased chief, Victor. He had sometimes been a controversial leader, as when he signed the strange treaty in 1855 with the impetuous and arrogant Isaac Stevens, governor of Washington Territory—a treaty that the white men insisted on despite the long history of friendship and military alliance between the whites and the Bitterroot Salish. The policy of Victor and the other Salish leaders had been to gain spiritual power from the white man's God while maintaining their alliances with the other western Indians such as the Pend d'Oreilles, Nez Perces, Spokanes, Coeur d'Alenes, and the white trappers and traders. The white allies were especially important because they controlled the tribe's access to guns and ammunition. Under Victor many Salish widows from the Plains Indian wars married white men or men from other tribes. These new tribal "in-laws" became either allies or tribal members. Death feasts had become a much too frequent part of Salish life, but the Salish refused to give up their semiannual hunts of plains buffalo, which were fiercely contested by their Blackfeet, Sioux, and (sometimes) Crow enemies.

Victor was about eighty-five years old when he died on the return from a buffalo hunt in the Yellowstone Valley. The death feast consisted of dried buffalo meat, dried salmon, many kinds of berries, four beeves, bitterroot, and camas. Many speeches praised the fallen leader. One was given by

Michelle, who only two years before had become chief of the Pend d'Oreille tribe. The personal loss felt by Victor's forty-year-old son, Charlo, or Little-Claw-of-a-Grizzly Bear, must have been compounded by his realization of the trials facing the small tribe and its leaders. After the feast, the leading men of the tribe unanimously selected Charlo as the new chief.[1]

One of the most challenging problems facing Charlo and the other Salish leaders was maintaining the delicate diplomatic dance that preserved the Salish alliance with the whites and the western tribes in the contest with the Plains tribes. This chapter examines the diplomatic position of the Salish in the Bitterroot Valley and the course of their conflict with the Sioux, Crows, and Blackfeet between 1870 and 1891. Evidence about the Salish who lived on the Flathead Reservation between 1873 and 1891 will be avoided, but not all of the sources make it possible to differentiate between the two groups.

Intertribal conflict on the northern Great Plains had driven the Salish villages west of the Continental Divide into the Bitterroot Valley. The Salish continued semiannual buffalo hunts on the plains, but these had to be organized as military operations in the face of opposition from the Blackfeet and other Plains tribes. Most of the Salish hunting parties combined with Nez Perces, Pend d'Oreilles, and other allies for better defense.

## The Impact of Intertribal Warfare on the Bitterroot Salish Population

The northern Great Plains tribes had adopted forms of warfare that minimized their losses, but when small camps were caught off guard, or were heavily outnumbered, significant losses could result.[2] In addition, most of the Plains tribes were much larger than the Salish and their allies combined. In 1855 the governor of Washington Territory, Isaac Stevens, estimated the Bitterroot Salish had only about 350 warriors. At that time the Piegans, Bloods, Blackfeet, Gros Ventres, Assiniboines, and Crees could field 4,275 warriors.[3]

Since the priests residing with the Salish regularly recorded the deaths that occurred during the plains buffalo hunting trips, the St. Mary's *Liber Mortuorum*, or *Book of Deaths*, is probably an almost complete record of Bitterroot Salish mortality between 1867 and 1890. The entries distinguish between those who died violent deaths or were killed, and those who died of disease or natural causes. Most of the violent deaths were of men and occurred in the first half of the 1867 to 1890 period covered by the St. Mary's records. During the first half of the period (1867–78) forty-nine Indian males and two Indian females suffered violent deaths compared to eleven males and one female during the 1879–90 span. Between 1867 and 1878, 18 percent of all Salish deaths, and 35 percent of all Salish male deaths, were the result of violence.

Most of the entries for violent deaths identify who committed the murder. Six or seven Salish were killed by whites between 1867 and 1890. Five were killed by the Blackfeet, four before 1870. Conflicts with the Crows resulted in the deaths of seven Salish warriors. The Sioux killed twenty-two Salish between 1867 and 1890, eighteen of whom died in one day: July 11, 1871. A few other Salish between 1867 and 1890 were killed by unidentified horse thieves, drunken Salish, unidentified hostile men, and a male bear. Sixty-three Salish men and women met violent deaths between 1866 and 1890.

The entries in the *Liber Mortuorum* provide further evidence of the impact of war losses on Bitterroot Salish population. Since almost all those killed in battle were men, many more Indian women lived to old age. The *Liber Mortuorum* records forty-seven deaths of Bitterroot Salish between 1867 and 1890 who were sixty years of age or older, or classified as "old" or "an elder." Almost two-thirds (64 percent) of those who died at an advanced age during this period were women. Thirty elderly deaths were female, and only seventeen were male.[4]

Figure 2.1 outlines the age and sex distribution of the Bitterroot Salish population in the 1886 Office of Indian Affairs census. Two trends stand out from the data: (1) an under-representation of young females, and (2) proportionately more older women than older men. No reason was found for the smaller number of young women, but the absence of older men was probably the result of intertribal warfare, which had ended only a few years before the census was taken.

Most of the war losses occurred before 1880, but the effects were still obvious in 1886. Figure 2.2 shows the number of widows as a percentage of the female population, and the number of widowers as a percentage of the male population among the Bitterroot Salish in 1886 and 1887, the Flathead Reservation in 1887, and the United States in 1890. The United States had an unusually large number of widows in 1890 as a result of the Civil War, which had ended twenty-five years earlier. The Bitterroot Salish and the Flathead Reservation had even more widows, proportionately, than the post–Civil War United States. The number of widows in the 1886 and 1887 censuses of the Bitterroot Salish reflects the tremendous human

**Figure 2.1.** Bitterroot Salish Indian Band, 1886, by age and sex

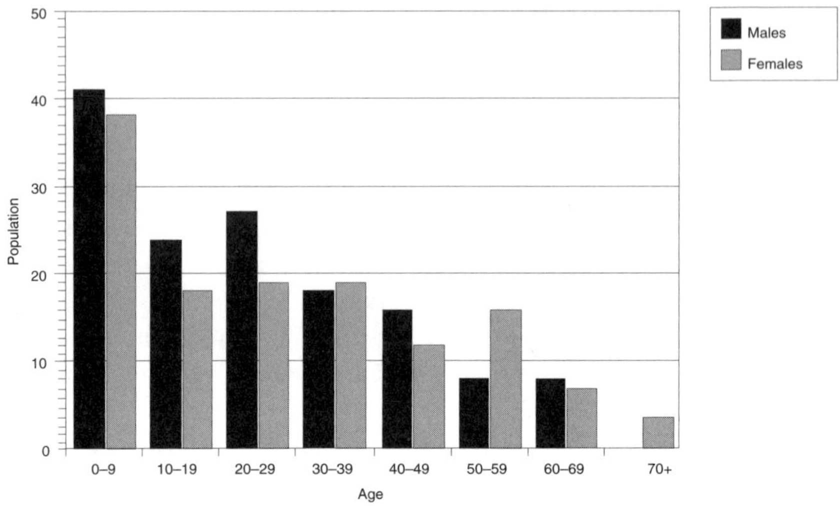


*Source:* Calculated from the 1886 Office of Indian Affairs census, National Archives microfilm M595, r. 107, fr. 83–91.

**Figure 2.2.** Percentages of females identified as widows and males as widowers among the Bitterroot Salish (1886 and 1887), on the Flathead Reservation (1887), and in the United States (1890)

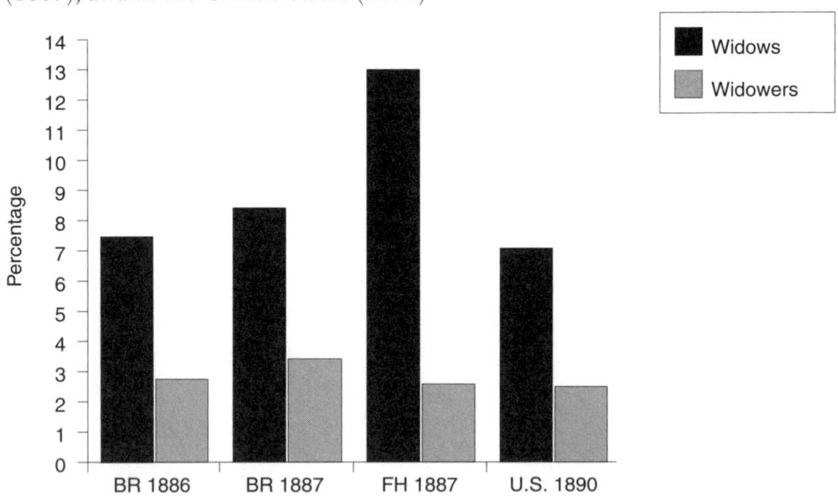


*Source:* Calculated from National Archives microfilm M595, r. 107, fr. 83–91, 94–159, and 160–71; U.S. Census Division, *Abstract of the Eleventh Census*, pp. 58–61. The 1886 Flathead Reservation census could not be used because one page is missing from the National Archives copy.

cost of intertribal warfare, which also forced many Salish women to marry outside the tribe.

The Bitterroot Salish were able to maintain their population during the 1870s despite the war losses. Between 1867 and 1880 the parish records of St. Mary's Mission recorded 323 Indian births compared to 304 Indian deaths. Office of Indian Affairs censuses in 1886 and 1887 indicate that despite having comparatively fewer women of childbearing age (fifteen to forty-nine years), the Bitterroot Salish had proportionately more children under five years of age than did the Flathead Reservation in 1887 or the entire United States in 1890.[5]

Nevertheless, the historic evidence suggests that intertribal warfare and horse raiding resulted in continuing and substantial loss of Salish life during the 1870s and early 1880s. None of the tribes was always an enemy. The military situation confronting the Salish was fluid, but the evidence presented below suggests that the accumulated casualties and property losses were serious.

### *Bitterroot Salish versus the Sioux*

One frequent Salish enemy during the late nineteenth century was the Sioux. The best documented battle between the two tribes was in early July 1871 on the Musselshell. The Sioux were led by Sitting Bull, who two days earlier had had a vision of an approaching battle. Sitting Bull's strategy was to send a small party of young warriors to attack the Salish camp and retreat. Seeing only a small war party, the Salish pursued them into an ambush by the main Sioux war party. The Salish attacked the Sioux but were forced to retreat in the face of superior numbers. White Bull, Sitting Bull's nephew, later recounted one incident during the battle: "This Flat Head had wounded 3 Soo [Sioux] when they surrounded him. I was so mad I got off my horse & ran at him—just [as] I got near him he drew & shot an arrow at me but missed me & I drew my pistol and knocked him down & jumped on him cutting his face. then I scalped him & he got up & ran around before he dropped dead."[6]

The fight was called off by the Sioux chief Flying By, but Sitting Bull and some of the younger Sioux warriors remained behind and attacked a party of Salish searching for bodies. One of the Salish shot Sitting Bull in the forearm before the Sioux broke off the battle.[7]

In this battle the Salish lost eighteen warriors, a serious setback for the small Salish fighting force. Two young men were lost, and sixteen heads of families. In August two funeral feasts were held in the Bitterroot Valley, one near St. Mary's Mission at Stevensville and the other on Burnt Fork, two miles above Stevensville.[8]

One Salish warrior, John Kizer, carried a wrought-iron arrowhead in his neck from an 1871 horse-stealing expedition against the Sioux. Dr. L. S. Tesson, the Flathead Agency doctor, removed the arrowhead in 1874 shortly before Kizer was scheduled to testify in a federal alcohol case. After the operation Kizer rushed back to the Bitterroot Valley without giving his testimony.[9] He died in the Bitterroot on June 16, 1874, about six weeks after the operation.[10]

Sioux-Salish warfare continued between 1871 and 1876, but the surviving sources provide little detail. In March 1872 a Deer Lodge newspaper reported that several hundred Bitterroot Salish, Pend d'Oreille, and Nez Perce warriors remained on the plains to fight the Sioux, and the Salish had already captured fifty Sioux horses and some Sioux scalps.[11] A year later, in March 1873, Flathead agent Daniel Shanahan claimed two Salish had been killed by the Sioux during that winter's hunt.[12] By 1875, the commandant at Fort Ellis, near Bozeman, reported that the Crows and all the western Indians, including the Salish, were fighting the Sioux under Sitting Bull.[13] About this time, the Nez Perces who lived in the Bitterroot with the Salish lost thirty horses to Sioux and Blackfeet raiders on the plains. The Nez Perces chased the thieves and killed a Blackfeet and a Sioux.[14]

In January 1875, the Sioux stole Joseph Barnaby's horses while the Salish were camped along the Musselshell River. Barnaby set off with Antoine Arlee and another Salish named Felix to get his horses back. After several days' travel they came to the camp of white men who were cutting firewood for the Missouri River steamboats. The whites were friendly and cooked a good meal for them. The Salish said they were after Sioux horses, and the whites volunteered to help them in any way they could. After several more days, the three Salish reached a Sioux camp and stole a large herd of horses. Antoine Arlee feared Sioux pursuit and rode ahead, but he finally returned to help Felix and Barnaby. Being considered a coward would have been worse than possibly being killed by the Sioux. The three Salish again reached the Missouri River camp of the white woodcutters. Barnaby asked for food they could eat while they traveled. When the Sioux chasing the Salish reached the white camp, the whites gave them misleading information about the Salish war party and slowly prepared a meal for the Sioux.

The Sioux ate and continued after Barnaby and his party but soon returned home, saying the Salish were too far ahead to be overtaken.[15]

During the spring of 1876, Col. John Gibbon made several efforts to get Pend d'Oreille or Bitterroot Salish scouts to accompany him to the Yellowstone Valley to fight the Sioux, but he could only promise them rations, a share of any plunder, and the possibility of soldier pay. The Pend d'Oreilles and Salish did not accompany Gibbon to the Yellowstone during that eventful summer.[16] The Salish contest with the Sioux and other Plains tribes was seriously hampered by the decision of the federal government in 1877 to forbid the sale of arms and ammunition to all Indians in Montana as a result of the Nez Perce War. The white control of Salish access to arms and ammunition had always been a problem, and in 1877 it threatened the ability of the Salish to defend themselves against Sioux attacks.[17] Before the Salish returned from the plains to the Bitterroot in spring 1879, Sioux horse raiders stole 160 Salish horses. No Salish casualties were mentioned.[18] In spring 1879 the Salish buffalo hunters were in the Judith Basin and came across a seven-person Sioux war party. Two of the Sioux were killed in the ensuing fight. That spring the Salish held a scalp dance near Missoula to celebrate the victory, and it was attended by a number of white Missoula residents. On their arrival in Missoula the Salish warriors rode down Main Street and up Front Street displaying a Sioux scalp, shooting off blank cartridges, and shouting for joy.[19] During July and November 1879 reports reached Helena that some of the Salish avoided going very far east in fear of Sioux retaliation.[20]

In April 1880 the main band of Bitterroot Salish returned from the winter hunt on the plains with reports suggesting several different fights with the Sioux that spring. John X. Beidler, the famous vigilante and Montana lawman, used sign language to learn about an early February 1880 Sioux raid on the Salish horse herds. In this case, forty Sioux had raided the Salish camp. In the ensuing battle one Sioux was killed and one Salish was wounded. The Sioux retreated without a single Salish pony.[21] Charlemagne, a Nez Perce youth hunting with the Salish during the 1879–80 winter hunt, mentioned several fights with Sioux war parties. He reported that a Nez Perce hunting with the Salish was wounded, but the Salish captured sixty head of horses from the Sioux.[22] A letter published in a Helena newspaper told of a Sioux horse raid that netted seventy-five head of horses from white men in the Sweet Grass Valley and a hundred head from the Salish.[23] One of these Sioux raids may have been the one led by Yellow Eagle on a Salish camp in the Musselshell about 1880. Yellow Eagle's party stole about forty head from a Salish camp. The Sioux thought the Indians in the camp were Crows, but learned later that they were Salish. After traveling two days, the Salish caught up with the Sioux and killed and mutilated two of them. One Salish was killed and another wounded in the fight.[24]

After 1880, attacks on the Salish by the Sioux fade from the record, probably because the collapsing buffalo herds and the expanding white military pressure on the plains reduced Salish-Sioux contact. The sources do not identify which Sioux bands fought with the Salish on the plains, and no incidents of peaceful Salish-Sioux dealings were found. The Salish-Sioux warfare may not have lasted as long as the Sioux-Crow or Crow-Blackfeet competition, but fights with the Sioux were a dangerous part of Salish buffalo hunts on the plains.

### *Crows and Salish: Friends, Traders, and Enemies*

The relationship between the Crows and Salish during the 1870s and 1880s was more complex and contradictory than that with the Sioux. Trade between the Crow and Salish was important, but it was punctuated with frequent horse raids and occasional revenge battles. The Salish-Crow horse raids and other contacts lapsed during the turmoil of the Sioux wars with the white, Blackfeet, and Crows from 1875 through 1878. The raids ceased for good with the end of Bitterroot Salish buffalo hunts in 1883.

Relations with the Crows occupied Chief Victor during his last days. During the winter of 1869–70, Victor discovered eight horses in the Salish camp that belonged to the Crows. The horses had been stolen by some young Salish warriors. Victor had the thieves tied up and flogged in the presence of the Salish tribe. He sent word to the Crows through the Flathead and Crow Indian agents about the punishment and promised to return the stolen horses as soon as possible.[25] The conflict between the efforts of tribal elders working to keep the peace and of young warriors eager for honors and property appears frequently in Salish-Crow affairs.

On February 22, 1870, the Crows killed seven Salish and Pend d'Oreille horse raiders in the Musselshell Valley. The Salish and Pend d'Oreilles stole the Crow horses before dawn, but they were overtaken and killed. Later that day the Crows exhibited the fresh scalps and a hand to Charles M. Lee, a white gunsmith living nearby.[26]

The importance of trade in the Salish-Crow relationship is illustrated by the story of Pi-Lu'-Ye-Kin, or Albert Thomas Moore, a Nez Perce youth who lived in the Bitterroot Valley with the Salish during the 1870s. Pi-Lu'-Ye-Kin's mother often visited their Nez Perce relatives in Idaho and traded dried buffalo meat from the plains for camas and other edible roots gathered in Idaho and Oregon. The roots were, in turn, used as trading material with the Crows when his mother was on the plains. His mother had an especially close relationship with one Crow woman. Pi-Lu'-Ye-Kin learned the Crow language and sign language while on plains hunting and trading trips with the Salish.[27] Paul Antoine, a Salish elder in the 1930s, remembered that the Crow Indians would trade with the Salish for camas and bitterroot when the tribes met on the plains. The Salish man would direct the prospective buyer to his wife, who would make the bargain and sell the roots as she pleased. The Crows traded buffalo robes, parfleche bags, clothing, and other articles.[28]

In contrast to the incidents of peaceful trade, Little Martin, a Pend d'Oreille warrior, told of a battle between the Salish and Crows on the plains probably during the 1870s. A Crow war party attacked the Salish camp. While the battle raged outside the camp, the Salish women prepared fresh horses for the fighters and got ready to go to battle themselves if required. In the midst of battle, Little Martin was chased by two Crow warriors whom he shot. While retreating to the Salish camp, he shot another Crow. Just as he rejoined the Salish fighters, his horse stumbled and threw him. Little Martin did not tell how the battle turned out.[29]

Two Leggings, a Crow warrior, described a battle between the Salish and Crows near the Little Rockies. After discovering several Salish buffalo hunters, Two Leggings had returned to the Crow camp for reinforcements. More Crow warriors joined them before they attacked the Salish hunters. One of the Crows, Hunts the Enemy, used a long-legged sorrel horse in the battle that had been previously stolen from the Salish. Two Leggings was shot in the left arm by one of the Salish men. As the Salish man and Two Leggings continued to shoot at each other, they made insulting signs, calling each other "women." The Salish man was struck, and Two Leggings started to scalp him but stopped to help load the body of a dead Crow onto a horse. Two Leggings never got a chance to scalp the fallen Salish, but did make it back to the Crow camp. In addition to the one Crow killed, three Salish died that day.[30]

In the 1930s Martine Vanderburg described the Salish custom of naming their dogs after specific war honors. Her father had a dog whose name was the

Salish word for "pitiful pleading." When her father was about to kill a Crow warrior, the Crow had pleaded very pitifully for his life. He was then killed by another Salish warrior. Martine's uncle killed a Crow warrior who was a fine-looking young man and named one of his dogs "good-looking young man." Antoine Ninepipe had a dog named "a legging dropped to the ankle" to commemorate his own bravery and calmness under fire when the Crows had attacked the Salish camp. In the midst of the confusion, Antoine had stopped a Salish lady and calmly helped her tie up her leggings. In the excitement, she had not realized that her leggings were slipping immodestly.[31]

Big Sam, a Salish warrior and leader, wore a white robe at the 1910 Arlee celebration that was painted with accounts of his war honors, including thefts of horses from the Crows and Blackfeet, and the capture of Crow thieves who had stolen horses from the whites. Big Sam then returned the horses to their white owners.[32] An interesting mirror image to Big Sam's return of horses to the whites was the adventure of a Crow warrior in 1871. The Crow was captured by whites near Helena with five horses belonging to white men near Lincoln Gulch. He claimed the horses had been stolen by the Salish and that he had taken them from the Salish in order to return them to their white owners. Helena whites put him in jail for stealing horses while he appealed to the Crow Indian agent as a character witness.[33]

The fluidity of Salish-Crow relations was again indicated during the winter of 1871–72. A letter from Camp Baker, near White Sulphur Springs, and a Helena newspaper report that winter indicated that the Crows and a combined Salish–Pend d'Oreille band were living in neighboring camps in the upper Musselshell–Judith Basin area. Late that winter a few of the young Salish and Pend d'Oreille warriors stole sixty head of Crow horses. The next day the Crows appeared at the Salish camp in war paint; ample Salish/Pend d'Oreille apologies were made, and the stolen animals were returned. Two nights later the Salish and Pend d'Oreille thieves stole seven more Crow horses and quickly left the area.[34]

The story of a Salish horse raid on a Crow camp on the plains during the early 1870s was recorded by anthropologist Claude Schaeffer. Three Salish men—Peter Sinatsi ("One Ear-ring") [Pierre Snatse], Peter Tekaepens ("Hair behind the Ear") [Pierre Chkakaepe], and Isaac—headed for the Crow camps on the Bighorn River. The Salish started from the spring buffalo camp on the plains and after three days reached a small Crow camp with one tepee and about thirty horses. Peter Sinatsi, the leader of the Salish party, went into the camp during the night, cut the horse pickets, stole a pair of moccasins from inside the tepee, and then proudly announced to the sleeping Crows that their horses were gone. The Salish did not realize there was a larger Crow camp only four miles away. The next morning about thirty mounted Crow warriors caught up with the Salish and the stolen horses. In the battle that followed, the Salish lost the stolen horses but were able to escape. Peter Sinatsi repeatedly charged the Crows to slow their attack. Peter Tekaepens fought well but became crippled with leg cramps. Isaac ran off some distance and waited there. One Crow warrior was killed. The three Salish returned to their tribe unharmed but without the Crow horses. Isaac, however, was taunted and laughed at as a coward by the other Salish.[35]

In November 1872 the Crows killed two Salish men who had gone to the Crow village to eat and smoke. According to Chief Arlee, the Crows shook hands with them and then killed them. One was a brother of Ninepipe and the other was Pascal. Arlee's testimony suggested that Pascal was the son of a Salish chief, but the burial record at St. Mary's identifies him as a Kalispel.[36]

During the winter of 1872–73 an incident resulted in the killing of a Salish man by Crows, who hid the body in a well at the Crow Agency near present-day Livingston. According to a white man adopted into the Crow tribe, Thomas H. Leforge, a band of Salish was leaving after a pleasant visit with the Crows. As they left, the young Salish men rounded up and stole some of the Crow horses. Flathead Charley, a mixed-blood Salish, and some of the older Salish men returned the horses when they learned of the theft. They also brought apologies and mollifying gifts of blankets and robes. Unfortunately, when a hot-headed Crow man, Little Iron, discovered one of his horses among the stolen animals, he killed Flathead Charley in a fit of rage, and the other Salish peacemakers raced away. Flathead Charley's body was thrown into an abandoned well at the old Crow Agency. War between the tribes was avoided, but the Crows always after held Little Iron in contempt.[37] Chief Arlee described this murder differently. According to Arlee, when he was near the Crow Agency, he sent a messenger to warn the Crows of a Blackfeet war party in the neighborhood. The Crows killed the messenger and threw his body into the well at the agency. The messenger was Chawl-paw-paw-tcheel (Charles Palpalshi). The young man who accompanied the messenger was Baptiste Marengo's cousin, and he received multiple gunshot wounds as he fled on his horse. Arlee claimed that the Crows had accused the Salish of stealing Crow horses that were actually stolen by the Blackfeet, so the messenger was killed for nothing.[38] According to the *Liber Mortuorum* at St. Mary's, the Salish man killed by the Crows in this incident was named "Charles (Palpalshi)" and was buried at the Crow Agency.[39]

In May 1873, Maj. S. B. Switzer, of Fort Ellis near Bozeman, reported that parties of Salish and Bannacks were hunting with the Crow Indians.[40] Later that same year, on August 15, 1873, the Crow chief named Blackfoot complained that while the Crow were negotiating with a U.S. government commission, Crow horses were stolen by a Salish war party. U.S. Army troops made an effort to catch the raiders and return the horses.[41] Further evidence of Salish-Crow conflict in 1873 is in an army report from Fort Ellis claiming that during September 1873 a party of nineteen Salish Indians under Antoine Arlee was secretly lurking near the white settlements around the border of the Crow reservation. They were attempting to steal Crow horses and get Crow scalps in revenge for a Salish killed by the Crows in 1872. That same month, Father Jerome D'Aste at St. Mary's Mission complained that while Chief Arlee was at the Jocko Agency, his son went on a stealing expedition and left his crop in the Bitterroot uncut.[42]

To add to the confusing Crow-Salish relationship, about 1873 a Salish warrior was killed by the Cheyenne Indians while trying to steal their horses on the Little Big Horn. According to Wooden Leg, a Cheyenne warrior, the Cheyennes thought he might have been staying with the Crows.[43] During December 1873, Chief Arlee had a series of complaints about the Crows. He said that they had stolen many Salish horses, but he promised he would return any Crow horses stolen by his warriors in the future. The Salish tried being peaceful with the Crows. In summer 1873, however, the Crows killed a Salish chief, Cow-ackan, Arlee's father-in-law. The Crows had also killed a Salish man named One Night while he was peacefully trapping near Heart Mountain. During the fall of 1873 the Crows stole thirty-one horses and a jackass from a Salish hunting party on the Little Blackfoot. Arlee was disgusted because the government was furnishing guns and ammunition to the Crow and Blackfeet Indians but not to the Salish.[44]

That winter, in January 1874, the commander of Fort Ellis reported that the Crows were at war with the Sioux, Blackfeet, Pend d'Oreilles, and recently also the Salish.[45] The *Liber Mortuorum* at St. Mary's listed two Salish men who were killed by the Crows that winter, Francis Henry and Andreas.[46] On February 8, 1874, a letter from Judith Basin reported the Salish theft of twenty-six horses from the Crows.[47] Several sources during the fall of 1874 spoke of hostility between the Salish and the Crows. The Bozeman newspaper in August reported that the Salish stole horses from the River Crows as the Salish began their fall hunt.[48] Flathead agent Peter Whaley visited the Bitterroot Salish and claimed in September 1874 that the Salish feared going to the buffalo country as a result of thefts committed against the Crows and Blackfeet.[49] An October 1874 article in a Helena newspaper referred to imminent warfare between the Salish and Crows during the upcoming buffalo hunt.[50]

Salish-Crow hostilities seem to have lapsed during the Sioux-white wars of the late 1870s, possibly because both tribes took advantage of the opportunity to attack the Sioux while they were on the defensive. In spring of 1879 Salish warriors stole a number of horses from a Crow camp, but according to a newspaper report, the Salish chief compelled them to return the stolen property.[51]

A well-documented theft of Crow horses in 1881 resulted in the death of Antoine Arlee, son of Chief Arlee. John R. Barrows, a white trader in the Musselshell Valley, reported that two Pend d'Oreille Indians had been with the Salish camp hunting buffalo in the Musselshell during the winter of 1880–81. The two Pend d'Oreilles went on a successful expedition to steal horses from a Crow camp in the Yellowstone Valley. The Salish, however, insisted that the stolen horses be returned. The horses were left with the Barrows family, who were to notify the Crow agent and return the horses. After getting drunk, the two Pend d'Oreilles returned to reclaim the Crow horses. In the ensuing fight between the Salish and Pend d'Oreilles, Antoine Arlee was killed, and the Pend d'Oreilles fled. The murder was reported in the Deer Lodge newspaper in April 1881, and in June of that year Chief Arlee traveled to the Musselshell to his son's grave. One of the newspaper stories indicated that while some of the Salish in this camp were from the Jocko Agency, many were Bitterroot Salish.[52]

On August 7, 1881, Father Jerome D'Aste learned that little Stephen (Chechen) was killed by the Crows while on a horse-stealing expedition.[53] The *Liber Mortuorum* explained that while Stephen was guarding some horses that the Salish had stolen from the Crows the day before, "unfriendly" men attacked and killed him.[54] The next spring, in March 1882, the Crows stole fifty-five horses from a Salish camp in the Musselshell. Before the theft, the Crows stopped at the home of Mr. Hall, a white man in the area, and told him they were planning to steal horses from the Salish camp. Mr. Hall sent a messenger to warn the Salish, but he failed to find their camp.[55]

During spring 1883, Otto Maerdian, a white farmer in the upper Musselshell Valley, wrote home about the theft of 150 horses from his white neighbors. The Salish were blamed because a large number of Crow horses were stolen at the same time. Seven Crow lodges and soldiers from Fort Ellis near Bozeman passed the Maerdian homestead searching for the Salish party thought to have the missing horses.[56]

One last battle over Crow horses took place on the Shields River in the upper Yellowstone Valley in November 1883. According to the newspaper reports, a Salish party stole Crow horses from near the Crow Agency on the Little Big Horn River and drove them west. The Crows caught up with the horses on the Shields River near Livingston, and two Salish and one Crow were wounded or killed before the horses were recovered. The Crows were led by Plenty-Coups.[57]

In April 1884, Frank Eneas and Peaille, two Bitterroot Salish, were murdered near Bozeman as they returned from a friendly visit to the Crows. They had been arrested in Bozeman on suspicion of stealing horses from Gallatin Valley whites but were released. The murderers were thought to be white men.[58]

The conflict between the Salish and Crow Indians during the 1870s and 1880s was punctuated by trade and friendly visits, and it did not approach the intensity of the Salish conflict with the Sioux Indians during the nineteenth century. Trade between the Salish and Crows seems to have been especially important. Many of the incidents of Crow-Salish conflict involved efforts by Salish leaders to avoid war and keep the peace with apologies and gifts after young warriors had stolen Crow horses. The Salish and Crows shared a common and numerous enemy in the Sioux.

### *The Blackfeet: Traditional Enemies, Occasional Friends*

The history of Salish-Blackfeet conflict dates back to the eighteenth century, when the Blackfeet drove the Salish villages from the western Great Plains. The ensuing warfare was long and bloody but punctuated with occasional truces and friendly visits. In fact, the Small Robes, or Little Robes, band of Blackfeet gave the Salish ammunition and other military aid while the Salish fought the other Blackfeet bands.[59] During the first half of the nineteenth century, Blackfeet raids penetrated deep into the northern Rocky Mountains. These raids were part of the reason St. Mary's Mission was closed in 1850. By the 1870s and 1880s Salish-Blackfeet conflict was much less intense due to Blackfeet losses to white troops in the Baker Massacre of

1870 and the increasing intensity of the Blackfeet conflict with the Sioux and Crow Indians.[60]

Charlo and the other Salish leaders arranged a peace treaty with the Blackfeet early in the winter of 1870–71 with the assistance of Blackfeet agent Michael M. McCauley, who had been the Flathead Indian agent between 1868 and 1869.[61] According to a Blackfeet winter count kept by Big-brave, a Blackfeet named Black-cheek was killed by the Salish in early 1870.[62] During the winter of 1870–71, after the peace treaty, a large party of Pend d'Oreilles and Salish hunted buffalo with the Piegans in Blackfeet country. The buffalo hunt was very successful, but the Salish and Pend d'Oreilles lost about half of their horses due to the severe winter weather.[63]

In 1871, however, Big Pierre led an unsuccessful Salish war party walking back from a raid on a Gros Ventres camp on the plains. When they got near Blackfeet country, Big Pierre and Three Heads stole three Blackfeet horses so the returning survivors could ride to the Bitterroot Valley.[64] Big Pierre and Three Heads were Pend d'Oreilles, but the story recorded by anthropologist Claude Schaeffer suggests that they lived in the Bitterroot Valley in 1871.[65]

As the 1870s unfolded, Salish-Blackfeet hostilities resumed. The *Liber Mortuorum* at St. Mary's recorded the death of Dominic, a Nez Perce married to a Salish woman, during the winter of 1873–74 while he was stealing horses from the Blackfeet.[66]

Joseph Lamoose, a prominent Salish warrior who fought the Blackfeet in the 1870s, reminisced in 1903 that "Many years ago we used to fight our enemies towards Three Forks and other places where there were lots of buffalo. I thought I was a great man so if I saw an enemy with a good costume or clothes I would go after him and take everything from him. One time I killed a Blackfoot. As he laid there I scalped him, and pulled off his britch cloth. I cut off his penis and threw it to the other boys."[67]

Another Salish warrior in the Salish-Blackfeet warfare of the 1870s was Sam Resurrection, who was also active in the fight against allotment in the twentieth century. Resurrection was in his late teenage years in the middle 1870s, and years later he described his first coup to anthropologist Harry Holbert Turney-High. The Salish were camped near the site of Browning, hunting buffalo. One morning some of the camp's horses were stolen, and Resurrection and his friends chased after the thieves. The thieves turned out to be three Blackfeet whom the Salish overtook by traveling night and day. Resurrection described what happened when they overtook the Blackfeet:

> We were able to surprise these Blackfoot. Two of them succeeded in galloping away, but I got quite close to the third before he realized his fix. I galloped close to him, and the Blackfoot took his bow from the case and strung it. Because he was in such a hurry he did a poor job and the bowstring slipped off. This gave me a chance which I took, galloping up to count *coup* on the enemy. . . .
>
> The chief then said, "Let us not kill him, but let us punish him by leaving him here in the winter storm naked so that he will freeze," and we did that. All those who had counted *coup* on the Blackfoot then notched their sticks. That was the first time I ever counted *coup*, and that is what this feather stands for.[68]

As mentioned above, another eyewitness account of Salish-Blackfeet conflict was given by Pi-Lu'-Ye-Kin, a Nez Perce living in the Bitterroot Valley with the Salish in the 1870s. Pi-Lu'-Ye-Kin remembered hunting with the Salish when the Sioux and Blackfeet on the plains stole thirty horses from his family. While recovering the horses, the Nez Perces killed a Blackfeet and a Sioux.[69]

Yet another battle was described by White Calf, a Blackfeet warrior who took part in a war party led by Mad Wolf. They entered Salish territory west of the Continental Divide, and Mad Wolf and the other Blackfeet fought off the Salish, killing a number of them. Mad Wolf fought so bravely and killed so many Salish that the Salish ran off in fear.[70] At least that was White Calf's version of the battle.

No details have survived, but Big Sam, a Salish warrior in the 1870s, gained some of his war honors by stealing Blackfeet horses. In the 1910 celebration at Arlee, he wore a robe painted with pictures of his exploits.[71]

In counterpoint to these hostile interactions, James Willard Schultz took part in an 1877 Christmas dinner at the Blackfeet lodge of Hugh Monroe, a white trader who had married a Blackfeet woman and lived with the Blackfeet. The menu included stewed dried camas roots traded from the Salish.[72]

The delicate balance between Salish-Blackfeet cooperation and conflict is illustrated by the story of Charlemagne, a young Nez Perce who in 1880 was with Charlo's band on the plains, where Charlemagne spent some time visiting a Blackfeet camp in the Judith Basin. Salish-Blackfeet relations were rocky, and the visit almost resulted in conflict. The Blackfeet were angry about the arrest of one tribal member and the hanging of another by white men. The Blackfeet stole two horses from two white men camped nearby in the Judith Basin. The Salish wanted the Blackfeet to return the horses, and armed conflict between the tribes over the matter was only barely avoided.[73]

More evidence of Salish-Blackfeet fighting was given in an 1880 newspaper report of the Salish theft of sixteen horses from a Piegan camp on the plains.[74] In March of 1881 a Piegan camp in the Sweetgrass area complained that the Salish had stolen fifteen head of their horses.[75] Bear Chief, a Piegan warrior, told of a Blackfeet war party in 1882 that ran into a Flathead war party on the plains. After a brief battle, the Flatheads stole the Blackfeet horses.[76]

In a January 1883 incident on the Musselshell, the Salish captured a Piegan Indian and sixteen head of horses the Piegans had stolen from white men. The Salish debated the fate of the captive and the stolen horses. White sheepherders in the area refused to take custody of the captive and the stolen horses. The Salish finally decided to take the Piegan's gun, ammunition, and clothing and set him free to find his way home. The stolen horses were still a problem, but two other white men arrived and claimed them.[77]

Mountain Chief described "a fierce fight" with the Salish in the Sweet Grass Hills during the mid-1880s. He recalled that "Many on each side were killed, but the Flatheads lost the most horses and men."[78] Mountain Chief also stole ten Salish horses that had been hobbled.[79] In 1885 a Salish raiding party stole an unspecified number of horses from a Piegan camp on the Marias River, according to Bear Chief. The Piegans found four Salish horses, but were unable to catch up with the Salish raiders or the missing Piegan horses.[80]

A number of undated war reminiscences by Blackfeet warriors born after the late 1840s probably record incidents from the late 1870s and early 1880s. Black Bear (born 1847) shot up a camp of Salish Indians while they slept. Wolf Eagle (born 1851) told of a battle between mounted Salish and Piegan warriors on foot in which he shot the leader of the Salish in the back. Wolf Eagle also stole twenty-three Salish horses from a corral and another group of eight Salish horses.[81] Chief Crow (born 1855) captured two Salish horses and two Salish warriors, whom he took alive to his lodge. Bear Head (born 1856) stole the same Salish horse twice.[82] Bear Chief (born 1856) killed five Salish Indians in a pit.[83] Boy Chief (born 1857) took three horses and saddles from the Salish in a fierce battle.[84] Big Moon (born 1859) and a Piegan party attacked and massacred a group of Salish and their horses in a fort.[85] Finally, Green Grass Bull (born 1860) was captured in a fight with a Salish Indian and taken to the Salish camp. After he pulled the Salish chief off a horse, the Salish let him go free.[86]

The surviving evidence suggests that Salish-Blackfeet warfare during the 1870s was much less intense than Salish-Sioux warfare during the same period. As with the Crows, much of the conflict centered around horse stealing. Even at this lower intensity, there was occasional loss of Salish life and property, which added to the cost of intertribal conflict for the Salish.

The danger of intertribal warfare for the Salish was accented during Charlo's last hunt in the plains buffalo country in 1883. In July of that year a band of thieves had stolen all of the camp's horses. Sources disagree on whether the thieves were Indian or white. Charlo had no horses left when he returned to the Bitterroot. Several other tribal members gave him five or six head to begin a new herd.[87]

The intertribal warfare during the 1870s and 1880s underscored the importance of the Salish alliance with the white settlers in western Montana. The war losses to the Sioux, Crows, and Blackfeet made maintaining peace with the whites critical to Salish survival. A two-front war in which the Salish fought the white settlers in addition to the Plains tribes could have quickly destroyed them. The efforts of Charlo and the other Salish to preserve the military alliance with the whites indicated that they appreciated the danger the tribe faced and made the strategic choices required to ensure the survival of the Salish people.

CHAPTER 3

# Prickly Allies

## Salish Efforts on the Buffalo Hunt to Preserve Their Military Alliance with the Whites, 1870–1883

At daybreak on July 28, 1875, ten soldiers led by Lt. W. H. Nelson and thirty white volunteers surrounded an Indian camp on Deep Creek near Townsend, Montana. Reports had reached surrounding white settlements the day before of a party of forty hostile Indians pursuing white travelers and killing two white men. Fortunately, rather than just opening fire, the soldiers and white volunteers demanded that the Indians surrender. They did—and then invited the soldiers and volunteers to join them for a breakfast of antelope. The supposed "hostiles" turned out to be a Salish hunting party of five men, two women, and three children. Dr. Bembrick, a white man on his way home from tending his cattle herd, was camped with them.[1]

The ability of Salish hunting parties to defend themselves would have restrained most hot-headed and outlaw whites, but the incident on Deep Creek that July morning dramatized how vigilant the Salish people and their leaders had to be to avoid conflict with white settlers. Only a few incidents have survived in the historical record describing the efforts of the Salish to keep peace with the white settlers during the buffalo hunts. The evidence below outlines the absence of conflict between the Salish and white settlers outside of the Bitterroot Valley, but as such it is only indirect evidence. The absence of conflict between white people and the Salish on the buffalo hunt could have been an accident rather than a planned development. However, the preponderance of peaceful relations, despite the pressures pushing towards conflict, argues that those relations were more than likely the consequence of a deliberate policy on the part of the Salish than a historical accident.

The incidents recorded here are not a random sample of occurrences in the nineteenth century. Since almost all of the records used were written, the voices of white and Indian people who could not write are missing. Most of the incidents of Salish-white interaction documented below were friendly rather than hostile, but we cannot prove that the preponderance of friendly contacts represents the real world of nineteenth-century Montana. We know, however, that enough friction occurred between the Salish and white communities to indicate that active and deliberate efforts on both sides were needed to keep the peace.

Both the local army commanders and Indian agents were concerned with avoiding accidental conflict with the peaceful Indian tribes. In 1873 Maj. S. B. Switzer of Fort Ellis, near Bozeman, complained several times to his superiors of the danger of a war breaking out from a mistaken attack on a party of friendly Indians. In 1874 James Wright, the Crow Indian agent, warned the commissioner of Indian Affairs of the danger.[2]

According to a newspaper report in July 1877, white stockmen in the Shields River valley ran into a party of about thirty Indians and stampeded home. A few days later, they learned the Indians had been Salish hunters accompanied by women and children.[3] In July 1878 the George Norton family was picking berries on Deep Creek and encountered a party of Indians. Mrs. Norton screamed, and Mr. Norton ran for his gun, but the Indians disappeared before any conflict broke out. The Indians were later identified as peaceful Salish, but violence could have resulted from the contact.[4]

An example of how easily the whites blamed the Salish for thefts committed by others can be seen in accounts from the White Sulphur Springs area in May and June of 1878. Several thefts of white-owned horses, a shooting incident, and the murder of a white man by unidentified Indians resulted in charges that Salish Indians camped nearby were responsible. One resident even identified a dead raider as a Salish man.[5] A correspondent from Camp Baker came to the opposite conclusion, as the dead Indian appeared to not have "been at home for a very long time." In addition, the post trader's clerk at Camp Baker, Mr. Bryan, who for years had had extensive dealings with the Salish hunters, did not recognize the dead Indian as being Salish.[6]

The raids in central Montana during the summer of 1878 were probably the work of a band of refugee Nez Perces returning from Canada. This band left a trail of conflict across the territory before the army caught up with them in the Clearwater Valley in Idaho. Other parties of Nez Perce refugees probably passed unnoticed through Montana that summer, but this band hit a nerve with Montana whites. Early on the morning of July 12, 1878, a group of Nez Perces arrived at the cabin of three white miners on Rock Creek. They did not realize the Indians were Nez Perces. According to the report of a white survivor, the Indians asked for food, and the miners got up and began preparing breakfast. The Indians laughed and talked pleasantly, and some were proficient in English. They professed to be friendly until they began shooting and killing the miners without warning or provocation. Two of the three miners in that cabin and another man in a neighboring cabin were killed. No Nez Perce descriptions of the incident were found. The story of J. H. Jones, the surviving miner, was recorded by two white residents of nearby Philipsburg and published in a Deer Lodge newspaper. The writers added fulminations about the dangers of trusting "friendly" Indians.[7]

After leaving Rock Creek, the Nez Perce party was involved in several cases of theft and attacks on white settlers in the upper Bitterroot Valley.[8] A party of nine white and Salish men rode up the valley to warn the settlers of the approach of the hostile Nez Perces. One of those delivering the warnings was Francois Lamoose, a Bitterroot Salish farmer of Salish-Iroquois blood.[9] A party of soldiers from Fort Missoula took up the chase, accompanied by white and Salish volunteers. The Salish volunteers included Francois Lamoose, Narcisse, Louis Vanderburg, and Martin Charlo. They followed the Nez Perces out of the Bitterroot Valley and into the headwaters of the Clearwater Valley in Idaho, where the white and Indian volunteers decided to give up the pursuit. Shortly after the volunteers left to return home, the soldiers encountered the fleeing Nez Perces. In the battle that followed six Nez Perces died, and three were wounded.[10]

Duncan McDonald, a Flathead Reservation cultural broker and leader of Nez Perce and Scottish descent, wrote an article for the *New North-West*, the Deer Lodge newspaper, pointing out the unfairness of blaming all Indian people for the actions of a few. McDonald waited until the Nez Perce murderers from Rock Creek had been captured and white emotions had cooled. He pointed out that killing all Indians because some were hostile would be unjust and would force the peaceful Indians of western Montana into war. He suggested that such a policy was as foolish as killing a Frenchman in revenge for a murder committed by an Italian. In 1877 the Salish in the Bitterroot Valley had proved their friendship and reliability during the Nez Perce War (discussed further in chapter 4), so how could the Philipsburg writers justify killing a Salish in response to a murder committed by a Nez Perce? The *New North-West* editorial accompanying McDonald's letter countered that few whites could distinguish Indians of different tribes, but now that emotions had calmed, friendly Indians were traveling safely through western Montana.[11]

One of the Philipsburg correspondents, "Sand Bar," replied to McDonald that most white people could not discern an Indian's tribe from his appearance: "No one would willingly kill a Flathead for a Nez Perces, but how is one to know?" The writer reported that "Jones, the survivor of the Rock creek four, states that every year he fed Indians, cooked for them, and that they always stole as much as they ate. 'But,' said he, 'I let them go. When they woke us up that morning I opened the door as I often did, and when they sat down and said they were hungry I cooked for them. And now,' continued Mr. J., 'I am going to stay there, and if any Indian comes to that door, friendly or hostile, he'll catch h-ll[.]'"[12]

Whether or not Jones's account of the murders was accurate, it was widely publicized among Montana whites. Where emotions ran so high, it must have taken hard work and vigilance on the part of the Salish community and responsible white people to avoid conflict. The fact that Salish hunting parties were alert and armed probably deterred most hot-headed whites from violence, but the Salish leaders also tried to limit tribal access to alcohol and avoid situations that could spawn violence. It must have been exasperating for the Salish as they tried to make sense of and predict the strange behavior of many white men.

About the same time that the Philipsburg murders took place, in the summer of 1878, a small party of Salish stayed in the Camp Baker area of central Montana to hunt until Charlo and the rest of the Bitterroot Salish returned in the fall. Among them was a one-eyed Salish man known as Azack [Isaac]. Some of the local whites had identified Azack as the Indian killed during the recent raid, but Azack was still very much alive. Lt. Col. C. C. Gilbert at Camp Baker insisted that Azack and the Salish return to the Bitterroot because they were at risk of being attacked by local whites who might mistake them for the hostile Nez Perces who had carried out the recent attacks in the area.[13] Fortunately, despite the white hysteria across Montana during the summer of 1878, no Salish appear to have been killed in response to the conflict that followed this Nez Perce band across the territory.

The aftermath of the January 1883 incident on the Musselshell, when the Salish captured a Piegan warrior with sixteen white-owned horses, further illustrates Salish efforts to avoid conflict with the whites. The Salish tried to turn the captive and the stolen horses over to white sheepherders in the neighborhood, but the whites refused to accept them. The Salish finally released the Piegan—without his gun, horse, or clothing—to find his own way home. The Salish left descriptions of the sixteen horses with the white sheepherders in hopes that their owners would be identified. When two white men arrived at the Salish camp and claimed the horses, the Salish were happy to unload the stolen property before they could be accused of theft. Given that the white men took the horses and rode away in the opposite direction of the white settlements, the true owners probably never saw their horses again, but the Salish were able to avoid friction with the settlers.[14]

## Salish-White Cooperation in Late Nineteenth-Century Montana

### *Salish-White Commerce*

The Helena newspapers made frequent references to the importance of Salish trade. They reported at least fourteen Salish visits to the city to buy supplies and trade horses and furs between 1870 and 1883, when the buffalo hunts ended. Instead of discussing each reference to Salish trade at Helena, only a few highlights will be considered. For instance, in July 1871, the *Helena Daily Herald* mentioned that a Salish party was in town trading furs, robes, and other items for coffee and various necessities of life. A few months later another party of about a hundred Salish men with their women, children, and ponies were on Main Street trading and trafficking with Helena merchants.[15]

Again in the fall of 1872 a large group of Salish and Pend d'Oreille Indians were in Helena trading horses for money, flour, and other provisions. According to the *Rocky Mountain Gazette* report, "They hold their ponies rather high, not taking a less price for [an] ordinary one than $25. They exhibited a good deal of tact and judgment in trade, and the common belief that the whites cheat the Indians, does not hold good with these."[16]

In March 1873 numerous Salish were in Deer Lodge selling furs. Two months later thirty Salish lodges were camped near Helena, and a Helena reporter observed one Salish trying to sell a pony for $2.50 that the writer felt was old and played out.[17] That fall the *Helena Daily Herald* noted that Salish and Pend d'Oreilles were in town, "bartering ponies, buying blankets, and in one way and another supplying themselves with second-hand creature comforts." Salish cooks made use of the viscera from the slaughterhouse, and Salish families found many useful items in the trash discarded by Helena whites. In October 1873, during that visit to Helena, a Salish man repaid two dollars he had borrowed two years earlier from Ben Stickney, Jr.[18]

In 1878 an article told of a Salish pony that had been sold to a Mr. Silverman in Helena. The pony went missing the next week. When the Salish seller returned home from the hunt, he found the missing horse had returned to its old pastures. On the next buffalo hunt the Salish man brought the horse to Helena and returned it to Mr. Silverman.[19] An 1880 Helena article mentioned that the Salish sold prime-quality buffalo robes for between four and six dollars each.[20] A Salish couple with two boys rode into Helena in 1882 on four horses. They sold three of the horses, and the four family members rode out of town on the single remaining horse.[21]

John Delaware told of one white trader at Helena during the late 1860s and early 1870s whom the Salish named "Hatchet." According to Delaware, Hatchet overcharged the Salish for guns and also made money by trading in Salish horses. Delaware remembered Hatchet paying fifty dollars for Salish horses and then auctioning them off and keeping the profit.[22]

Salish trade was also valuable to Bozeman merchants. A May 1880 article refers to the Salish in Bozeman "swapping furs and peltries for coin, grub and trinkets." In June 1881 Salish hunting parties arrived in Bozeman with "pony-loads of furs" to trade.[23]

Margaret M. Beal, a white woman living on a ranch near the site of Anaconda, remembered bartering butter and condiments for game or fish with Flathead Indians who had come to the Deer Lodge Valley to hunt. She moved there about 1877, so the trading must have taken place in the period around 1880.[24]

A visit in spring 1881 to a small trading post operated by the Barrows family in the Musselshell Valley offers another example of Salish commerce. According to John R. Barrows, the store had a lively trade for two days or so. Barrows knew some Chinook and sign language, and one Salish man was selected to be behind the counter as interpreter and house detective: "This individual was at once conscious of his elevated and important station, and helped himself to stick candy, dried apples and crackers, until I was sure he would die, but he lived through it and was really of great service to us. A few of our [Salish] Indian friends were again invited to sit at mother's table, where they behaved with more gentility than many of our Caucasian guests."[25]

At the twilight of the Salish buffalo hunts, a correspondent in Helena described the trade for a New York newspaper. Tanned buffalo hides sold for between four and ten dollars each, and there was a market for all the Salish could provide. The Salish man would first buy ammunition with the proceeds and then spend the rest on colorful blankets: "'They never boggle [*sic*] over prices,' said the proprietor of a Main Street store, 'but count their money, and if they find they have enough to buy the articles wanted, make the purchase there and then. If you treat the Indian fairly, and don't cheat him, you'll enjoy his whole tribe's custom whenever they come to town.'"[26]

### *Military Escorts*

The historical sources tell of other areas of cooperation between the Salish and white communities in the 1870s and 1880s. One of the most important was the military escort system for Salish buffalo hunting parties between 1876 and 1880.[27] During these turbulent years of Indian-white relations in Montana, the U.S. Army provided troops to escort Salish hunting parties between Missoula and the plains buffalo hunting grounds. From the viewpoint of the white settlers, the escorts reduced the possibility of drunken violence by the young Salish and also helped avoid any property thefts. For the Salish, the escorts would have had several benefits. First, they helped reduce the danger of conflict with whites fearing hostile Indian tribes. Second, they discouraged white men from selling alcohol to the young men. Third, they supported the efforts of the Salish leaders to keep the young men from raids that would disrupt the peace that Salish leaders were trying to maintain.

On February 16, 1876, Col. John Gibbon, of Fort Shaw on the Sun River near Great Falls, wrote the following instructions for Lt. C. A. Booth, who was preparing to escort a camp of Pend d'Oreille, Salish, and Spokane Indian buffalo hunters to Missoula:

> I am directed by the Commanding Officer to inform you that you will proceed with the camps of the Pend d'Oreille, Flathead and Spokane tribes of Indians now at this Post to the vicinity of Missoula M.T. having there seen all these parties depart toward their several reservations, you will return to this post. You will keep the Indians as much together as possible and make the trip as rapidly as is consistent with their modes of travelling. . . . Investigate all matters of complaints by whites against

> the Indians or the latter against the whites and apply such remedies as lie in your power. In communicating with the Indians, do so generally through their chiefs, and treat these with the greatest mildness and consideration, telling them plainly what you want in each case, and that you are acting in accordance with Instructions of Col. Gibbon. These Indians are especially jealous about their women and you will therefore see that your men are circumspect in their bearing towards them and that they are acting as protectors to the Camps. . . .[28]

On February 26, 1876, Booth's orders were modified. He was to return to Fort Shaw as soon as the Indians had been escorted across the Continental Divide. Booth was to assure the chiefs that Gibbon trusted the Indians to "get back to their homes without [Gibbon] hearing any complaints from them or against them."[29]

John Stanley served in the U.S. Army at Fort Logan, on the Smith River east of Helena, during the late 1870s. Years later he described a party of Salish Indians returning from a buffalo hunt with a young Salish man on a travois. The Salish man's ankle had been crushed when his horse fell on him. The post surgeon examined the patient and amputated his foot when he was under chloroform. Unfortunately, infection had set in, and the patient died and was buried on the hillside above the post.[30]

The last army escort for the Salish was in April 1880 between Fort Logan, on the Smith River east of Helena, to Missoula. Lt. Chas. B. Hinton, in charge of the soldiers, reported to a Helena newspaper that the roads were bad and volunteered that "he would be willing to trust the [Salish] Indians from this on without escort."[31]

### *Other Cooperative Incidents*

Some Salish-white military cooperation was more informal. As mentioned above, in January 1875 a camp of white woodcutters on the Missouri River fed Joseph Barnaby, Antoine Arlee, and Felix when the Salish were on their way to steal horses from the Sioux. They also gave Barnaby and the other Salish food on the return trip. Then the whites gave the Sioux pursuit party misleading information and did everything they could to delay them so the Salish could get away.[32]

The newspapers carried occasional articles mentioning Salish Indians attending church while in Helena. At 6 a.m. on June 27, 1875, a large number of Salish Indians camped near Helena and attended Mass in the city. The report noted that the Salish "assisted throughout the services with a devotion truly characteristic of well instructed people." They sang hymns and recited the rosary in Salish and listened to a sermon delivered in Salish by Father Philip Rappagliosi, S.J., who had previously served at St. Mary's Mission in the Bitterroot Valley.[33] In March 1877 a large party of Salish Indians stopped at Helena on their return from the buffalo hunt and attended Sunday Mass at the Church of the Sacred Heart. After the service they visited St. John's Hospital and found in the chapel the body of Miles Daily, a white man who had died in the hospital Saturday night. The Salish sang hymns and recited the prayers for the dead over the corpse.[34] In October 1877, after the Salish had protected the Bitterroot whites from harm during the Nez Perce War, the Salish visited Helena on their way to the buffalo hunt. On Sunday they attended the funeral of Professor Dietrich, a white man killed two months earlier by the Nez Perce. They came to the funeral "mounted and dressed in plumes and paint." The letter writer also described the baptism of a Salish child in Helena during which the adult sponsors and other Indians joined in singing the *Pater Noster* and *Credo* in Salish.[35]

Horses were frequently a source of friction between the Salish and white communities, but they also played a role in cooperation. In October 1878 a Salish hunting party found forty-three of their horses in the possession of a white rancher on Smith River. The horses had been stolen in spring 1878 while they were camped on the Marias River. The thieves may have been Blackfeet or white, but the horses passed through several hands before reaching the Smith River ranch. The Salish proved their ownership of the horses to the satisfaction of the local whites and were given possession of them.[36] On April 28, 1879, Maj. H. L. Chipman of Fort Missoula gave a letter of introduction to Pasha, a Salish Indian. Pasha was traveling to Fort Benton to retrieve Salish horses that had been recaptured from horse thieves. The letter asked that Pasha not be molested while on his journey.[37]

Sports competitions such as horse races and footraces also characterized Salish-white meetings on the buffalo hunts. In the Judith Basin area in 1879, the Salish raced one of their horses against a horse named Bally owned by a white man. Bally won, and the Salish declined further races against the horse.[38] Four Salish-white footraces made it into the newspapers. One was in Philipsburg, probably in 1881; the second was in White Sulphur Springs in March 1881; the third was in September 1881 in Deer Lodge; and the fourth was in June 1884 in Anaconda. The Salish runner won in all four cases.[39]

Charlie Young, a white man who grew up in the Ovando area in the 1880s, recalled Salish hunting camps with as many as fifty tepees pitched near his childhood home. Young told of playing with the Salish children: "Most of 'em couldn't talk English, but we picked up their signs quickly, and we'd get along in the sign language."[40]

Many of the friendly Salish-white interactions during the buffalo hunts could be loosely classified as "entertainment." Condescending whites often found Salish customs and conduct interesting and even amusing. The entertainment must have run in both directions as the Salish certainly observed the whites closely to see the strange actions of these newcomers. Cora Levengood Sparrow, a white woman who grew up on a ranch in Warm Springs, Montana, in the early 1870s, recounted large parties of Salish and Nez Perce Indians passing the Levengood ranch. She specifically remembered one incident when the Levengood children were alone in the house and her older sister attempted to start a fire in the fireplace. A young Indian boy of either the Salish or Nez Perce tribe came into the house and told Cora's sister that she did not know how to build a fire and then built it for her. The Levengood children were surprised and scared, but the Indian boy did not bother anything and left after he built the fire. The boy must have been hiding outside to see what the strange white people did and felt sorry for the fumbling white girl trying to start a fire.[41] Another example of Salish interest in strange white behavior was found in Missoula's first school in the early 1870s. Emma Slack Dickinson, the first teacher at the Missoula school, remembered the Salish coming to the window and leaning in to watch her teach.[42]

Most of the surviving examples of friendly Salish-white interaction, as each community observed the customs of the other, involved white observations of the Salish. On March 31, 1879, victorious Salish warriors triumphantly exhibited two scalps from a Sioux war party to the citizens of Helena. Helena whites welcomed the Salish victory, but seem to have been hesitant about the public celebration over the scalps.[43] Two weeks later, when the Salish camp returned to Missoula, fifteen or twenty mounted Salish warriors rode down Main Street and up Front Street firing blank cartridges and yelling for joy over one of the Sioux scalps. The Salish camp held a scalp dance near Missoula, and a number of the white residents went to observe the celebration. The *Weekly Missoulian* reported that the Salish were pleased to see the white spectators, but that the Salish were "the most sensitive people in the world to ridicule, and very properly resented anything that appeared like ridicule of their performance."[44]

A letter from Helena to a New York City newspaper in 1884 referred to the visit of a Salish couple to Helena during which the woman attacked the man and left the man's face bruised and swollen.[45] To nineteenth-century Helena whites, this was a remarkable case of female independence. White observations of Salish life and customs were probably seriously distorted as each community viewed the other through the smoky glass of cultural differences.

In a strange incident in 1882 in White Sulphur Springs, a Salish Indian traded a horse for a coffin and funeral service by the town's undertaker. The coffin was for a dying Pend d'Oreille. The funeral service was attended by one person only, the Salish boy who had nursed the dying man.[46] A Salish man died near Bozeman a little later in 1882, presumably as the result of a drinking binge. Local whites assisted the family by making a pine coffin for the body and digging the grave.[47]

An incident of Salish friendship for Montana whites that took place about 1880 involved John Delaware, a noted Salish warrior, who saved a white woman from drowning in the Madison River. There were other people standing on the shore doing nothing, but Delaware dove in and rescued her. She lived in Three Forks for many years after.[48]

## Salish-White Friction in the Late Nineteenth Century

### *Alcohol-Related Conflict*

Most of the surviving records of Salish-white hostility on the buffalo hunts attribute the violence to whiskey, stolen horses, or both. The written record is biased in favor of recording incidents of Salish hostility toward whites. White people could easily complain to the local newspaper about Salish hunters drunk with whiskey or blame passing Salish for missing horses, but few whites described selling whiskey to the Salish for exorbitant profits or stealing Salish horses. In May 1873 a Helena newspaper reported that "a few score" of Salish Indians were in town, and a few of them were on the streets drunk and "pugilistically inclined." Some of the Salish had been drunk daily while traveling from eastern Montana to Helena, and one Salish died during the trip.[49] In July 1874 a report reached Helena of a fight between a mixed-blood Salish and a white man named Sullivan on Sun River. The quarrel over $2.50 was well lubricated by bad whiskey, and the Salish man was shot through his lung, arms, and neck. He was taken to the Fort Shaw hospital and was expected to recover.[50]

A March 1878 conflict that involved both horses and alcohol took place at Camp Baker near White Sulphur Springs. A Salish man named Thomas Edwards claimed a mare held by Christopher Myer near Diamond City. Edwards, who was drunk, claimed he had lost the horse three years earlier on the Missouri. Myer countered that he had purchased the horse from a white man in Diamond City who had purchased it from another white man in Helena. When Lt. Col. C. C. Gilbert declined to intervene in the matter, Edwards became abusive and threatened to steal an army horse. Gilbert had Edwards locked in the guardhouse until the post's horses were rounded up that evening and Edwards sobered up. A white correspondent from White Sulphur Springs reported that Edwards had proven his claim to the horse to the satisfaction of the white men present, and the white men advised Myer to give up the animal. Myer refused, which infuriated Edwards.[51]

That fall, in October 1878, a Salish party passing through Smith River obtained alcohol. According to a report in the *Rocky Mountain Husbandman* some members of the party became drunk and insolent, throwing stones through the windows and against the door of a nearby ranch house. Fortunately causalities were avoided because the two white men in the ranch house refrained from firing their guns due to the size of the Salish party.[52]

According to a report in the *Helena Independent* in October 1879, a Salish man walked into a Helena liquor store and attempted to steal two bottles of Hostetter's Bitters. The theft was discovered, and the Salish man was beaten in the resulting altercation.[53]

Complaints about drunken Indians in Missoula were frequent, but the reports from the 1870s and 1880s rarely give the Indian's name or tribal affiliation. Some of the drunken Indians involved in violence in Missoula were probably Bitterroot Salish, but individuals from many other tribes also passed through or lived near the town. One case involving two Bitterroot Salish Indians in August 1880 probably involved alcohol. According to the report of Private Malstrom of Fort Missoula, he was peaceably walking near the Bitterroot bridge when he met two Salish, one of whom pointed a gun at Malstrom and demanded tobacco. Both Salish were arrested by the army and turned over to Thomas M. Pomeroy, a judge in Missoula, for prosecution. No record survives of the Indian side of the story.[54]

In February 1882, newspaper reports told of a war party of two Salish and four Shoshoni warriors visiting saloons at Judith Gap and Martinsdale. According to the reports, the Salish and Shoshoni pulled a gun to force the saloons to serve them. The story may not have been accurate, however, as the prospect of making a profit was usually enough to force most saloons to serve Indian customers. The alcohol-impeded war party was captured by an army contingent of white soldiers and Cheyenne scouts. Seventeen head of horses that the Shoshoni-Salish war party had stolen from a nearby camp of Red River Metis were returned.[55]

In October 1882 a party of fifty to a hundred Salish visited Helena on their way to the buffalo hunt in the Musselshell. Two or three of the Salish men got "beastly drunk" while in Helena. One drunken Salish pulled a gun on a white man who was attempting to return a hat that the Salish man had dropped. Another got so drunk that it took several white men to get him to the Helena jail. The two Salish men were later fined by the probate court in Helena and served out their fines in jail.[56] A few weeks later, some members of the same hunting party got drunk near White Sulphur Springs.[57]

In December 1884 a party of Salish camped near Ellison, west of Helena, was involved in a number of drunken brawls. One of the group was accused of assaulting a local white woman while he was drinking.[58] Other complaints of Salish destruction of white-owned property were probably linked to alcohol. In 1874 a small group of Salish was accused of ransacking and plundering the cabin of two white men near Philipsburg. The men were arrested and jailed at Philipsburg.[59] Alcohol could have been involved in the report in October 1881 that a Salish hunting party had stolen provisions, blankets, arms, and ammunition from several cabins on the Smith River.[60]

The white settlers' desire for profitable liquor sales intersected with the thirst of many young Salish for whiskey. Drunken altercations while on the buffalo hunts threatened the lives and health of many Salish community members. Alcohol-induced conflict with the white settlers also hindered the efforts of the Salish leaders to keep peace with the whites.

### *Stolen Horses*

Horse theft was another common threat to the peace between the Salish and white communities, but the charges against Salish for stealing horses owned by white people were often problematic. Some Salish probably took a few shortcuts in building up their herds, but few of the thieves left calling cards. Most of the charges seem to have involved accusing any Indian people who had been seen in the area before the theft. The presence of Salish hunting parties also attracted war parties of hostile Indians from other tribes who might not have been noticed by local whites but who could take white-owned horses when Salish horses were difficult to get.

Some of the records reveal that whites were involved in stealing Salish horses, so the traffic went in both directions. An example of charges of Salish theft of white-owned horses was in 1874, when several horses were stolen in the neighborhood of Camp Baker. The newspaper correspondent reported that the Salish were accused of the thefts because they had just passed through the area on their summer hunt.[61] In October 1879 two Salish chiefs, Adolph and Antoine, complained to the U.S. Army that six head of their horses had been stolen by white men while the Salish were camped twenty-two miles from Helena. The newspaper writer added a note to the story saying he hoped that the horses would be returned to the Salish and the thieves captured.[62]

In March 1881 a camp of Piegan Indians in the Sweetgrass area blamed the Salish for stealing horses belonging to local white settlers.[63] A white correspondent from the Yellowstone Valley wrote in May 1881 that sixteen Indian horse thieves stole all but two of the horses from the local stage station. The correspondent claimed the thieves were Salish but did not give any proof.[64] A few weeks later Chief Arlee was leaving the Jocko Reservation for central Montana to visit his son's grave. Arlee felt obligated to stop at the *Weekly Missoulian* office to warn white thieves to stay away from his horse herd.[65]

The Salish were accused of stealing horses from some white cowboys near Martinsdale on the upper Musselshell in December 1882.[66] Four Salish stole thirty or forty horses from a party of Metis in December 1882 in central Montana, but one of the owners of the horses came upon the Salish war party the next day and opened fire. He killed a Salish man and recovered the horses.[67]

In 1883 a Salish hunting party was thought to have stolen some horses from white settlers in the Musselshell along with horses from a nearby camp of Crow Indians.[68] On July 22, 1883, some Salish families arrived in the Bitterroot from the buffalo hunt after most of their horses had been stolen by white people.[69]

During April of 1884 two Bitterroot Salish, Frank Eneas and Peaille, were murdered by whites near Bozeman. The surviving evidence is confusing, but Peter Ronan reported that two other Bitterroot Salish had left stolen horses at a Salish hunting camp near Bozeman. Local white authorities arrested Frank Eneas and Peaille, suspecting they were the horse thieves.

They were released for lack of evidence but were later found murdered on the road home. The sheriff offered a reward of three hundred dollars for the arrest of the murderers, but no arrests were recorded.[70]

### Other Friction

During the early 1880s white cattlemen in the Musselshell Valley began complaining that Salish hunters were killing their cattle as well as wild game. Most of the charges were not specific. In February 1880 the *Rocky Mountain Husbandman* complained that the shrinking plains buffalo herds and pressure from the Sioux war parties were forcing the Salish hunters to kill cattle.[71] Granville Stuart, an early white cattleman in central Montana, fumed at the Salish and other western Indians who hunted buffalo in the area. In April 1881 he organized a petition calling for the secretary of the Interior to force an end to the buffalo hunts because he accused the western Indians, including the Salish, of killing cattle in place of wild game.[72]

The winter hunt of 1882–83 produced a number of complaints from whites about the Salish killing white-owned cattle. Game was unusually scarce in the Musselshell that winter, and the cattlemen complained loudly about filling in the food gap for the Salish and other Indians in the area.[73]

Other accounts of Salish-white friction while on the buffalo hunts record a variety of problems. During the fall of 1877 two white sheepherders near White Sulphur Springs complained that the dogs from a passing Salish camp had killed thirty-seven of their sheep. Charlo immediately took steps to prevent further attacks by the Salish dogs, but he refused to pay for the dead sheep because he felt the value of the dogs killed by the sheepherders equaled the value of the dead sheep. The sheepherders filed a claim with the commissioner of Indian Affairs for sheep killed and wounded between 1875 and 1877.[74] In 1879 in Helena, a four-year-old white boy was frightened by the dress and appearance of an elderly Salish lady. His groundless fear amused the surrounding whites.[75] During the summer of 1882 a camp of Salish, Nez Perce, and Spokane Indians were having too much fun at a camas area in the Big Blackfoot Valley. They had horse races and footraces every night, bathed naked in the creek every morning, and used a sweat lodge. The complaints of the whites also involved competition over grazing and access to meadows in the area.[76] That fall another incident in Helena involved a sixteen-year-old white boy trying to bully an eight-year-old Salish boy. The Salish boy stood up to the older white boy and forced him to retreat.[77]

These incidents of Salish-white friction during the buffalo hunts suggest continuing problems for the Salish during the 1870s and early 1880s. The surviving sources are certainly one-sided. Salish hunters could probably have told many tales of white perfidy and unprovoked hostility that were not recorded. Avoiding hostilities with the white settlers did not happen by accident. The Salish leaders needed to purposely restrain the inflamed emotions of the younger Salish and help the more responsible white settlers deal with outlaw whites.

## *White Hunting Regulations*

During the early 1880s the rights of the Salish to hunt buffalo were generally accepted by local whites, but white hunting regulations complicated matters. The earliest Montana law to conserve large game animals was passed in 1872 and included a closed season between February 1 and August 15 of each year. The 1872 law covered moose, elk, deer, mountain sheep, antelope, and mountain buffalo, but not the plains buffalo. In 1876 a revised law made it illegal to kill game and only use the hides. This provision was not enforced against the legion of white buffalo-hide hunters in eastern Montana in the late 1870s. These hunting regulations were imposed to protect large game from extinction, but other motives were also involved. The closed seasons were designed to accommodate the white sportsmen who hunted seasonally. The laws ignored the Indian and white subsistence hunters who needed smaller amounts of game on a regular basis throughout the year. The laws also left no room for commercial hunting. In 1889, five years after the extermination of the wild plains buffalo in eastern Montana, the state passed a ten-year closed season for the plains buffalo.[78]

In 1880 a rod and gun club was organized in Missoula to support enforcement of the Montana Territory game laws. Flathead Indian agent Peter Ronan was a charter member. The *Weekly Missoulian* noted that other than closed seasons during calving, the enforcement of the game laws was an open argument because "so many people depend much upon the wild game for their supply of meat."[79]

In a letter to the *New North-West* newspaper in Deer Lodge on March 20, 1880, Agent Ronan argued that by 1880 almost all the buffalo hunters were Bitterroot Salish and Spokanes. These groups were non-treaty Indians and not eligible for support from the Flathead Indian Agency. Ronan quoted an October 22, 1877, letter from the commissioner of Indian Affairs and a

June 4, 1879, decision from the U.S. Army adjutant general's office in Washington, D.C. The army decided that "The Flat Head Indians in the Bitter Root Valley are domesticated Indians, and should be allowed to come and go as free citizens Subject to the laws of Montana."[80] The *Rocky Mountain Husbandman* commented that if the Bitterroot Salish were subject only to state laws, they could be tried in white courts for horse theft or cattle killing and would be subject to Montana game laws. By this interpretation the Salish would also have a legal right to purchase alcohol. The writer felt that legal alcohol purchases could devastate the Salish tribe and its economy.[81]

During the early 1880s Salish-white friction over game laws occasionally spilled into the newspapers. In June 1880, O. P. Moore, a white man living near Virginia City, complained that a band of Salish in his area was slaughtering game.[82] During the summer of 1881 complaints were published about Indian hunting, presumably Salish, in the Deer Lodge, Big Hole, and Hell Gate valleys.[83] Other complaints were published about the Salish killing elk in the Deer Lodge area in April 1883 and hunting game during the summer of that year in the Gold Creek Mountains.[84] Grumbling also came from Bitterroot whites about Salish hunting during the closed season.[85]

The game laws attacked a critical component of the Salish economy at a time when game populations in western Montana were crashing due to overharvesting. New minefields were being laid as the Salish worked to keep the peace with the white settlers and adjust their economy to the decline in buffalo and other hunting and gathering resources. Examples of Salish efforts to keep the peace in the Bitterroot have survived and will be discussed further in other chapters, but it would be hard to argue that peace with the whites could have been maintained on the buffalo hunts without the concerted and determined efforts of a cadre of very capable Salish leaders. No statements of strategy have survived, and only a few incidents of deliberate efforts to keep the peace with the whites during the buffalo hunts were recorded in the historical sources, but the concrete incidents described above fit the pattern that would be expected if maintaining peace with Montana whites was a conscious diplomatic policy of the Bitterroot Salish.

CHAPTER 4

# Navigating a Minefield

## The Nez Perce War Crisis and Salish Relations with Missoula County Whites, 1870–1878

Salish efforts to keep the peace with their neighbors ran through a minefield of economic and political hazards erected by western Montana whites attempting to exploit the Salish and their allies to benefit the local white economy. The year 1877 marked the culmination of a six-year campaign by Missoula leaders and journalists to secure a U.S. Army post. They needed the post and its local spending to boost the sagging western Montana economy, and used the alleged danger of Salish-white hostilities to mask their economic goals. During the Fort Missoula campaign, white Missoula County leaders carried out political and tax policies that exacerbated racial tensions. By the time Missoula finally obtained its military post in 1877, western Montana whites needed military help and protection from the Bitterroot Salish during the Nez Perce War. Despite years of vexation and occasional harassment, the Salish decided their best interests lay in continuing peaceful relations with the local whites. The Salish provided warriors to help the U.S. Army at Fort Fizzle on Lolo Creek and to help local whites families reach safety, and they also insisted the Nez Perces not attack or plunder the white settlers. Keeping the peace despite provocation, incitement, and miscommunication was a daunting task. Convinced that the survival of the tribe hinged on avoiding conflict, despite the hysterical fears of many local white leaders, the Salish assured the St. Mary's missionaries, Fort Missoula army officers, and the new Flathead Indian agent of the tribe's peaceful intentions. They even sent Chief Adolph to Missoula to placate the town's residents.

An economic depression in the white community during the 1870s had fueled the campaign to obtain an army fort at Missoula. Exasperating tensions between the Salish and white communities was an important element of this campaign. Chauncey Barbour, the editor of the *Weekly Missoulian* between 1875 and 1879, regularly fanned any smoldering racial hostility. The Salish-white competition for grazing, farming, and hunting resources in the Bitterroot Valley was an open sore that Barbour frequently washed with vitriol. He must have reasoned that the threat of violence was not enough to justify a fort, but an outbreak of hostilities would surely bring a fort and its federal money to the Missoula Valley.

During the 1870s Missoula County was bankrupt from overspending and declining tax revenues, and desperately needed new funds. One new revenue source they explored involved taxing the Salish in the Bitterroot Valley. This would either (1) bring in new tax money; (2) ignite conflict between the communities, which would bolster the case for a local fort; or (3) force the Salish to remove to the Jocko Reservation, freeing up more resources in the Bitterroot Valley for white settlers. For some whites it was a win-win situation.

Two crises in the late 1870s fed into the campaign for a fort and further complicated the work of Salish leaders to keep the peace. After the defeat of Gen. George Armstrong Custer in 1876, local white hysteria intensified. Fears of a Salish alliance with the Sioux, traditional Salish enemies, were encouraged by the alcohol-enhanced paranoia of Flathead Indian agent Charles S. Medary. A fever pitch was reached in 1877 during the Nez Perce War. The *Weekly Missoulian* editor printed unsubstantiated rumors painting the Bitterroot Salish as hostile to the whites. Salish assurances of friendship were interpreted as duplicitous and further reason to fear them. After the Salish dramatically protected the Bitterroot whites when the Nez Perces passed through the valley, the federal government responded by prohibiting sales of guns and ammunition to Salish warriors and hunters. Peacekeeping in such an environment must have taken every diplomatic skill the Salish leaders could muster.

The Missoula newspaper played a central role in the campaign for an army post. Journalism in the American West during the 1870s was a small business, not a profession. The newspaperman generated income by pleasing local political patrons and businessmen. Political subsidies and advertising from local businesses resulted in an obligation to support the sponsoring political party and boost the local community.[1] Missoula was founded in

1860 as a trading post and grew rapidly by supplying mining camps in western Montana, especially Cedar Creek, near present-day Superior. Gold was discovered there in October 1869, and by spring 1870 an estimated fifteen hundred white people were living in Cedar Creek, representing about 60 percent of Missoula County's white population. Only three hundred whites were living in Missoula that year. The trade with Cedar Creek benefited Missoula greatly, but the prosperity was fleeting. In a few years the Cedar Creek population crashed, and by the mid-1870s Missoula was in an economic depression.[2]

White Bitterroot farmers were suffering from the lack of markets by early 1873. A correspondent to the *Weekly Missoulian* observed that "good farms can be bought for less than the actual value of the improvements," but he encouraged Bitterroot farmers to persevere and hang on until the Northern Pacific Railroad arrived to give the Bitterroot access to a broader market. The railroad was expected to be completed in a couple of years, but it actually took ten years.[3]

In July 1875 the *Weekly Missoulian* decried the local "depression in the valuation of property." Again in June 1876 the paper lamented that "an extreme dullness pervade[s] all branches of business" in Missoula County, which then covered all of western Montana.[4] The *Helena Daily Herald* observed in April 1875 that Missoula had an abundance of resources, but Missoula County farmers were located far from the mining camps, and even when the farmers transported their production to the camps, they were not assured of a quick sale. This "discouraged to a great extent" farming in Missoula County, and Missoula's white population was smaller in 1875 than it had been in 1870.[5]

The correspondence of the Missoula National Bank between 1873 and 1879 emphasizes the economic depression in the Missoula area.[6] In December 1873 Ferdinand Kennett, the bank's cashier, complained to Samuel Hauser, its major stockholder, that business was "getting duller all the time." By March 1874 the bank was considering moving to Deer Lodge because of the business decline in Missoula. Even in October 1879, C. P. Higgins, the bank's president, wrote that "It seems to me the people of this County are getting poorer every year. The large herds of Cattle are gone, grain can be raised in abundance but we are too far from market."[7]

Some Missoula leaders decided that securing a local army post with its federal spending was just what the town needed to rescue the local economy. After negotiating with Charlo and the Bitterroot Salish in 1872,

Congressman James A. Garfield complained to the secretary of the Interior that there was "imminent danger of trouble in the Bitter Root Valley, from the conduct of mercenary whites, who want a military post."[8] In 1875 the commander of the U.S. Army District of Montana, Col. John Gibbon, wrote that the Indians of the Bitterroot Valley were peaceful except when the whites sold them whiskey. Gibbon did observe that a military post at Missoula "would probably be very desirable to the inhabitants of that section" because Missoula County was "highly productive" and "supplies of all kinds" were raised there.[9]

## A Fort at Any Price: Missoula's Campaign for Military Dollars

If a military post could provide a market for Missoula County farmers and boost the local economy, who could object to drumming up white skepticism about Salish peacekeeping efforts? An outbreak of violence could be used to justify dispossessing the Salish of their Bitterroot Valley lands and eliminate Salish competition for grazing and hunting resources. Washington Jay McCormick began the campaign in 1871 and 1872 in conjunction with Garfield's efforts to remove the Salish to the Jocko Reservation, and Warren R. Turk continued the effort in 1874, but Chauncey Barbour, editor of the *Weekly Missoulian* between 1875 and 1879, was the most active in whipping up white hysteria. The Missoula newspapers did not speak for all white people in western Montana, as many white settlers had friendly and respectful relations with the Salish. The newspapers did, however, represent the views of part of the white community and complicated the efforts of the Salish leaders and those white people who sought to keep the peace between the communities.

Washington Jay McCormick was a lawyer from Indiana who served in the gentile administration that was installed in Utah Territory by the U.S. Army in 1857. McCormick became so unpopular with the Mormon hierarchy that he had to be smuggled out of Utah in a buggy in 1863. He moved on to Montana, where he practiced law and held various political offices, and he was acting Flathead Indian agent between August 1867 and January 1869. McCormick did little more than oversee the agency bureaucracy during his tenure, and he was dismissed in 1869 amid allegations of corruption. McCormick denied the charges and pointed out that the federal government had failed to send him the funds needed to carry out agency functions. In late 1871 McCormick became editor of the Missoula newspaper, then named the *Pioneer*.[10]

McCormick was ecstatic in December 1871 when William Clagett, the new Republican territorial delegate to Congress, secured a presidential order to remove the Salish from the Bitterroot Valley. He paused for a breath and then proceeded immediately to argue that Salish attachment to the Bitterroot Valley would cause them to resist removal "to the bitter end." McCormick argued that it would require "a strong military force to execute this order successfully, and with safety to the white settlers in the valley, and not only to remove them but to keep them in subjection, after they are placed upon the Jocko reservation." Consequently, he argued, Clagett should also secure a military post for Missoula.[11] McCormick acknowledged that the Salish "have hitherto been friendly and for many years harmless, but when aroused by the infliction of fancied wrongs, their native ferocity may at any day burst forth and commit irreparable wrongs and inhuman massacres on the settlers."[12]

In the summer of 1872, when Salish opposition to the removal was clear, McCormick's histrionics escalated. By August 3, 1872, McCormick was no longer thankful for Clagett's efforts to remove the Salish. What else could the president have done? Surely he would not surrender "'350,000 acres of the best lands of Montana' to a tribe of idle and thriftless Indians." Now, in McCormick's view, Clagett was derelict because he had not secured an appropriation for surveying the Bitterroot, had allowed James Garfield from Ohio to handle the removal rather than a Montanan, and had the nerve to expect the white trespassers in the Bitterroot Valley to pay $1.25 an acre for their land. Most galling, however, was Clagett's refusal to join the campaign for a fort for Missoula. Clagett did not believe the Salish would resort to violence against the whites.[13]

The August 10, 1872, issue of the *Pioneer* carried news of volunteer military companies being formed in the Bitterroot Valley and Missoula, and of petitions to the governor of Montana for arms and military assistance.[14] Congressman James A. Garfield traveled to the Bitterroot for his inconclusive negotiations with the Salish leaders. Charlo and most of the Salish refused to remove, but no violence broke out.[15] Garfield attributed much of the hysteria to "mercenary whites, who want a military post."

The nonviolent stalemate that followed Garfield's visit lowered the volume of the campaign for a fort for a couple of years. In 1874 and 1875 a new Missoula newspaper editor, Warren R. Turk, took up the cause. A consumptive Civil War veteran from Iowa, Turk had moved to Montana in 1871 for his health. Although trained as a printer, he tried farming in the

Bitterroot Valley, but in 1873 he returned to newspaper work as a partner with F. H. Woody in the *Weekly Missoulian.* In 1874 he became the sole proprietor, but his declining health forced him to sell the newspaper to Chauncey Barbour in May 1875. Turk died in Missoula a month later at the age of thirty-two.[16]

In 1874 and early 1875, as the economy of the white settlers in western Montana was declining, Turk had taken up the campaign for a military post at Missoula because "friendship for whites does not exist in the Indian mind except such as is induced by force." According to Turk, the 1862 attack by previously peaceful Santee Sioux Indians on white settlers in Minnesota proved that Indian friendship could not be trusted.[17] Turk argued that Indian people had no claim to the land they occupied because white settlers could use the land more efficiently. The government should assist the Indians to become "civilized" and self-supporting farmers, but "they should be taught that the bounty of the government comes to them upon . . . philanthropic grounds."[18]

In May 1875, with the purchase of the *Weekly Missoulian* by Chauncey Barbour, the campaign to justify a fort at Missoula took a portentous turn. Barbour exhibited few qualms about working to convince western Montana whites that the Salish were a threat. In his mind, securing a fort and its economic benefit for Missoula justified printing unsubstantiated rumors and working to stir up conflict between the Salish and their white neighbors.

Chauncey Barbour was born in Illinois in 1834 but had been in San Francisco in the mid-1850s before coming to the Montana gold mining camps in 1863. He probably did some mining in the Helena–Virginia City area, but also mentioned working as a lawyer. In 1870 he was listed in the census as a miner at Cedar Creek, near Superior. In 1872 he was justice of the peace at Cedar Creek, and in 1873 he was elected chairman of the Missoula County Republican Convention. He was editor of the *Weekly Missoulian* between May 1875 and August 1879. In his farewell editorial on August 29, 1879, Barbour saw the new fort at Missoula as the proudest accomplishment of his editorship. Barbour was still in Missoula, listed as a printer, in the 1880 census. In 1881 he worked for a Butte newspaper, and between 1883 and 1887 he was an editor in Walla Walla, Washington.[19]

Many Montana whites in the 1870s may have agreed with parts of Barbour's racist ideology, spelled out in the columns of the *Weekly Missoulian*, but they were able to temper their cultural prejudices with a desire to keep the peace and a willingness to treat their Salish neighbors courteously. Barbour preached that all Indians were dangerous barbarians because they lacked the restraints of white civilization and European-style government: "Unlicensed liberty and absence of restraint upon individual action means a want of civilization, such as is presented by the savages of this country. . . . If the whites were to adopt the habits of the Indians, living in idleness in large bodies, without restraint upon their actions, they would speedily develop into worse natures than the Indians now present."[20] Barbour made frequent references to the Santee Sioux in Minnesota and the Modocs of Oregon, who he felt had feigned friendship with the white settlers. According to Barbour, these tribes had abandoned friendship without warning to initiate treacherous and unjustified wars against their unsuspecting white neighbors.[21]

Parallel to Barbour's views about the inherent threat of conflict with the "barbarous" local tribes was his belief that only white economic exploitation could be the basis for ownership of land. In the April 26, 1876, issue of the *Weekly Missoulian*, Barbour printed a speech by Chief Charlo complaining about white perfidy and violence towards the Salish: "Can he [the white man] blush before his Maker, or is he forever dead. Is his prayer his promise—a trust of the wind? . . . No, no; his course is destruction; he spoils what the Spirit who gave us this country made beautiful and clean."[22] An editorial accompanying the speech expressed Barbour's reasoning that Charlo's complaints were largely unjustified. According to Barbour's view, government assistance to help the Salish develop a civilized or agricultural economy was charity, not payment for land the whites now claimed: "As a piece of solid argumentation the chief's effort will not take a high place. He proceeds on the assumption that the handful of Gods' [*sic*] creatures who originally inhabited this country had a right to its permanent occupancy to the exclusion of all other creatures. . . . The Indians themselves would not insist upon any such an absurd claim."[23]

Based on this theology that white civilization was needed to restrain man's natural barbarism, and that land could only be claimed by white exploitation of resources, Barbour endorsed forced economic and cultural change for the local Indian tribes. In December 1875 he wrote: "An Indian has no better conception of his own good than a child, and refined notions about restraining his liberty are misplaced. . . . The remedy for this state of things is most obvious: Give us a few troops to keep our Indians at home, and the necessities of their natures will soon drive them to some useful employment."[24] In July 1876, commenting on the Sioux War, Barbour claimed that "It is not necessary for us to become savages by pursuing a war of extermination; but the . . . Indians should be thoroughly and forever disarmed and put to agricultural pursuits."[25]

Barbour occasionally abandoned logic to report rumors or write diatribes that may have been intended to incite interracial violence to justify a military post in Missoula. A good example of this use of unsubstantiated rumor and hysterical reporting occurred after a September 1875 incident at the head of Flathead Lake in which white man named Jack Allen was reported to have been killed by a party of Kootenai Indians. Based on the initial rumors that reached Missoula, Barbour printed an extra edition headlined: "The First of a Series of Indian Outrages!" and "Three Men Killed and Others Missing!!" The report claimed three white men had been killed at the head of the lake, a pack train with five men was missing, and a white trader and other whites had to flee for their lives. A week later, Barbour followed up with one of his trademark editorials lamenting the "hopeless condition" of the western Montana whites who had to leave the murder of Jack Allen unavenged because of the large number of Indians in the area. Barbour concluded by saying, "let us hope the government will take notice of the fact that we really do need a military post." He grumbled that "the treachery of the Indians" would probably only be noticed if prominent white officials were killed.[26]

The *New North-West* in Deer Lodge printed a very different version of the incident: "Instead of three white men being killed only one was killed—Jack Allen—and there is no apprehension of further trouble growing out of the affair. It in fact seems as the circumstances are now related to us that the white men were the aggressors, or at least equally to blame, and the murder of Allen was in retaliation for the killing of a Kootenai hlaf-breed [*sic*]." Allen and two other white men had been driving a band of horses from Walla Walla, Washington, to "the Whoop-Up Country" on the Montana-Alberta border. While camped near Flathead Lake, they and a group of Kootenai Indians and mixed-bloods got drunk together. During the party, Allen killed a Kootenai mixed-blood named Findley [Finley?]. In revenge, a party of Kootenai Indians ambushed and killed Allen.[27] Barbour never corrected his earlier report or apologized to the Kootenais.

Another interesting example of Barbour's reasoning was presented on September 1, 1875. He argued that the Bitterroot Salish and other western Montana Indians were as warlike as the Crows and Blackfeet, and that they had probably killed some struggling white men over the years. His conclusion was that if any white man "goes to a remote part of this county with his life in his hand and a few kegs of whiskey he cannot expect to get back with a whole hide." To Barbour, the safety of outlaw white whiskey traders demanded military protection for the sellers rather than incarceration.[28]

Finally, in January 1876, Gen. Wesley Merritt visited Missoula and local whites pleaded successfully for a military post,[29] which Merritt recommended on February 8. He justified his recommendation because of the large number of Indians of different tribes who transited the valley on their way to buffalo, the refusal of the Salish to pay taxes, and the number of white whiskey traders. He could not point to any outbreak of violence: "I find that, though no actual violence to the extent of loss of life on the part of the settlers has been experienced, the Indians when in the valley in numbers rule matters by a sort of terrorism, having things pretty much their own way, to the extent of taking and appropriating to their own use such property as they want. . . . Although an outbreak is not imminent it is possible"[30] The U.S. Army and Treasury would protect western Montana whites from threatened violence and bankruptcy.

Barbour did not drop his venom after securing a fort. The conduct of the *Weekly Missoulian* during the 1876 Sioux War, the 1877 Nez Perce War, and the 1878 return of a band of Nez Perce refugees continued to undermine the peacekeeping efforts of Salish leaders.

## "The White Man Wants Us to Pay Him"

One consequence of the 1870s recession in the local white economy was a financial crisis for the Missoula County government. Not only did the decline in county tax revenues underline the need for a fort and the federal spending it would bring to Missoula, but taxes offered a new avenue to harass the Bitterroot Salish.

As early as February 1873 Missoula County had a debt of over $58,000. County expenses had exceeded income by $3,667 during the previous fifteen months.[31] In 1874 and again in 1875 the Missoula County commissioners ordered the county assessor to assess the property of the Bitterroot Salish for taxes.[32] Missoula County finances continued to worsen, and with the advent of Chauncey Barbour as editor, the *Weekly Missoulian* became much more vocal on the issue. In July 1875 Barbour deplored the continual county deficit spending. He recommended that election notices and returns be sent by mail rather than delivered in person, that the grand jury get bonds from witnesses to make sure they appeared in court when scheduled, and that county officers not be paid both per diem and mileage at the same time. Barbour figured the county could save hundreds of dollars a year with these policy changes.[33]

Barbour further recommended that the county collect taxes from property owners who were escaping taxation. He figured the county lost between $1,000 and $1,500 per year due to untaxed, white-owned property on the Flathead Indian Reservation. He realized the county could not collect on the reservation, but he argued taxation of the Bitterroot Salish could be enforced. The added tax revenue was needed because the county was poor, but even better, if "the order is enforced it will practically solve the Indian question relative to the Bitter Root valley; they will either pay taxes or will remove to the Reservation."[34]

On September 1, 1875, Barbour lamented that the Bitterroot Salish had refused to list their property for assessment or to pay taxes. To him it was only logical for the Salish to "bear their share of the public burden." Nothing prevented the Bitterroot Salish from voting in white elections, and besides, they "have the use of roads and bridges, pasture their herds on the commons, and have the full benefit of a stable and orderly society in the protection of their rights and property." From the Salish viewpoint, paying the white settlers for the use of traditional Indian travel routes and grazing areas made little sense. Barbour acknowledged that using force to collect the taxes was "liable to involve us in a collision with these people that will in the end prove disastrous" and "the attempt will cost more than the amount realized." Could not the federal government understand how much Missoula needed a fort? Faced with the opportunity to use taxes to precipitate violence between the white settlers and the Salish, Barbour hesitated and pleaded for a fort based on the *prospect* of violence.[35]

The Missoula County campaign to force the Salish to pay taxes paused during the winter of 1875–76. Montana governor B. F. Potts wrote to the secretary of the Interior in Washington, D.C., for a definitive determination of the legality of the taxes assessed on the Bitterroot Salish. Potts pointed out that the Salish had refused to accept the patents to their land and so were assessed only on their cattle, horses, and improvements.[36]

Telesphore Jacques DeMers was elected as a Missoula County commissioner in the 1875 election, and on December 6 he became chairman. DeMers was a successful merchant in Frenchtown, and his wife was a Pend d'Oreille mixed-blood. His brother-in-law was Michel Revais, who served for many years as Flathead Agency interpreter. DeMers did not record his personal feelings on the tax issue, but violence over the tax question was avoided while he was in office.[37]

The secretary of the Interior replied to Governor Potts on May 31, 1876. His decision was that the Bitterroot Salish were liable for taxes under the 1872 law that officially declared that the Bitterroot Valley was not an Indian reservation. The land patented to the Salish was inalienable, so it could not be sold for nonpayment of taxes. The secretary added his "hope that the proceedings for the collection of the taxes assessed on the personal estate of the Indians, will be conducted with a wise discretion, which shall avoid any collision with them." When Potts relayed the decision to Frank Woody, Missoula County clerk, on June 1, he emphasized that the "proceedings of the County authorities must be conducted 'with wise discretion,' and so far as possible avoid any collision or trouble with the Indians."[38] Barbour celebrated the decision of the white legal system that the Salish were liable for taxes but agreed "it is perhaps best not to go too far in this matter until we have force sufficient to teach the aborigine that no foolishness is intended"—that is, until Missoula got a fort.[39]

The idea that the Salish should pay taxes to support a white government that frequently failed to protect their lives and property, and could not even restrain white whiskey dealers, rankled Charlo and other Salish leaders. Working to maintain peace with the white settlers while some of the whites were trying to force the Salish to pay taxes must have pressed the Salish leaders to the limit.

Father Joseph Giorda, S.J., of St. Ignatius Mission, wrote the president on February 21, 1876, that he feared if the Bitterroot Salish were "driven to the wall," they might "go and join the hostile tribes on the plains." The Missoula County sheriff was trying to compel the Salish to pay taxes based on a treaty (the Garfield Agreement) that had not been signed by a "real chief, and has been protested against by the Mass of flatheads." The trouble and expense of hostilities could be avoided by a change in policy, because there was no other Indian tribe "so peaceable and friendly to the whites."[40]

Charlo complained bitterly in the speech published in the *Weekly Missoulian*: "Yes, my people, the white man wants us to pay him. He comes in his intent, and says we must pay him—pay him for our own—for the things we have from our God and our forefathers; for things he never owned and never gave us. What law or right is that? What shame or what charity?" Charlo could see no rational reason why the Salish should pay taxes to use the land and resources that God had provided the Salish: "I have more to say, my people; but this much I have said, and close to hear your minds about this payment. We never begot laws or rights to ask it. His laws never gave us a blade nor a tree, nor a duck, nor a grouse, nor a trout."[41] Charlo refused to pay his tax bill of fifteen dollars even after local whites offered to give him the money. The principle was too important.[42]

The campaign to extract taxes from the Bitterroot Salish sputtered on for another year. During the summer of 1876, after the Sioux victory at the Little Big Horn, Barbour was arguing that the taxes should be enforced by the troops when they arrived to establish Fort Missoula.[43] A Missoula correspondent wrote in the *Helena Independent* that Missoula officials did not think it prudent to pursue the issue before the troops arrived.[44] When the army troops did reach Missoula, Barbour was in the midst of whipping up hysteria against the Nez Perces and Salish. Charlo and the Bitterroot Salish somehow avoided conflict with the western Montana whites and protected the Bitterroot Valley whites from the hostile Nez Perces. The chagrined Bitterroot settlers circulated a petition asking the county commissioners to abolish the tax upon Salish property in the valley. They asked, "Is it worth while, for the sake of a few dollars in the county treasury, to risk the enmity of our old-time neighbors and allies?"[45] Even Barbour had to admit that taxing the Bitterroot Salish might not be expedient.[46] The effort to collect Salish taxes was quietly dropped.

Missoula County's financial crisis continued. During the summer of 1876 the situation was so bad that no one would buy county bonds at any price. In December 1876 county warrants were discounted fifty cents on the dollar, which effectively added a 100 percent surcharge on goods and services purchased by the county.[47] The situation forced the Montana legislature to pass a special act in 1877 to bail out Missoula County. The act provided for new property taxes to fund the existing debt; a provision to exchange bonds at sixty cents on the dollar for old, unpaid county warrants; and reductions in payments for court expenses.[48] On June 14, 1878, the *Weekly Missoulian* was asking creditors of the county government to reduce the principal of the county debt. Barbour rationalized that most of the creditors had purchased the notes at a discount so they would not be losing any money.[49] That December, Missoula County defaulted on its bonds.[50]

The Missoula County authorities pursued other new revenue sources in addition to taxing the Bitterroot Salish. In April 1876 the assessor was directed to assess "all persons" coming from the reservation, which mostly affected white people and mixed-bloods living on the reservation and trading in

Missoula.[51] In one case, the *Weekly Missoulian* complained that the owner of a band of horses being driven through Missoula County from Colville had been excused from paying Missoula County taxes because taxes had already been paid that year on the horses in Colville. Barbour thought the owner should be forced to pay taxes to every jurisdiction through which the horses traveled.[52] By 1880 traders from the Kootenai country had to leave their pack trains on the reservation and have their Missoula purchases shipped there. Missoula County taxed their pack trains if they entered county jurisdiction. The tax collection was so aggressive that it drove trade away from Missoula.[53]

## Custer on the Little Big Horn: Manufactured Hysteria in Western Montana

Rumbles from eastern Montana brought Missoula news of the June 25, 1876, defeat of General Custer on the Little Big Horn. The "Custer Massacre" aggravated white emotions and irrational racism just as the tensions building up over the Fort Missoula campaign and the tax confrontation reached their height. The Sioux were traditional enemies of the Salish and had killed many of their warriors over the years, but this did not prevent Barbour and Charles S. Medary, the new Flathead Indian agent, from stirring the waters with reports of imminent hostilities.

A former journalist, Medary was the son of Sam Medary, governor of Ohio. Charles Ewing, of the Bureau of Catholic Indian Missions in Washington, D.C., noted that Medary was a "member of one of the oldest [and] most influential families of Ohio, nearly if not quite all of whom are converts to the [Roman Catholic] Church." Ewing felt Medary would have more influence with the Indian Department than would anyone appointed from Montana.[54]

Unfortunately for Medary, soon after he arrived, the Missoula County commissioners asked for his help in forcing mixed-blood and white residents of the reservation to pay county taxes.[55] Medary wrote to the commissioner of Indian Affairs on January 28, 1876, for an official decision about the rights of mixed-bloods on the reservation, and whites married to tribal members.[56] At about the same time, DeMers had Alex Morigeau's team and wagon assessed and attached for taxes when Morigeau was in Missoula on business. DeMers claimed Morigeau was not a tribal member, but Medary felt DeMers was just being spiteful because Morigeau had ceased trading at DeMers's store. Medary also reported that DeMers had several hundred cattle illegally grazing on the reservation.[57] Since DeMers was the new chairman of the Missoula County Commission and a prominent merchant, Medary had acquired a fatal enemy. Arlee, the chief of the Bitterroot Salish who had moved to the reservation, and Duncan McDonald, a mixed-blood trader at Jocko, joined with DeMers to attack Medary. Medary accused Arlee and McDonald of being motivated by avarice, but their side of the argument did not survive in the historical record.

Medary had been active in drumming up support for a new military post at Missoula, and Barbour expressed appreciation.[58] The Custer defeat worried many Montana whites, but Barbour's first response was to recommend that the county charge ahead and use the tax issue to force the Salish out of the Bitterroot. The troops coming to Fort Missoula could coerce the issue.[59] The local Indians were becoming "insolent," but if the military would crush the Sioux, it would "inspire a wholesome fear" among the local Indians.[60]

Medary contributed to the local hysteria with a July 21, 1876, telegram to the commissioner of Indian Affairs pleading for two hundred troops to prevent an outbreak of the western tribes. Medary cried that the Blackfeet were already moving west of the Continental Divide to steal horses and make anti-white alliances with the western tribes.[61] Medary failed to point out that most of the horses stolen by the Blackfeet were owned by western Montana Indians. The alarm spread as Medary's telegram was published in a number of Montana newspapers.[62]

While Medary's fears were useful for Barbour, they may have been based on something other than rational analysis. According to the sales records of the Worden and Company store in Missoula, Medary was purchasing alcohol in large quantities: "June 23—1 dozen Champagne and ½ dozen Imported; July 3—1 case Kelly Island Wine and 3 bottles Champagne; July 4—4 bottles Champagne; July 7—1 gallon Sherry wine; July 10—1 dozen bottles Imported Wine; July 21—4 bottles Champagne Imported; and July 22—4 bottles Champagne." Some purchases were not itemized, so there may have been even more alcohol.[63] Medary could have used the alcohol to entertain guests, but it seems more likely that he consumed much of it himself and that his evaluation of local Indian sentiments was distorted by an alcoholic haze.

Barbour's propaganda war continued. On September 13, 1876, Missoula was full of western Indians on their way to hunt buffalo. The Indians were well armed with "needle Sharp and Spencer guns." Barbour admitted that the western Indians had shown "many proofs of their friendship in their dealings with the whites," but "every movement of these Indians is looked upon with distrust, and supposition of their being allies of the Sioux are rife."[64] Barbour did not point out that the western Indians and the Sioux were traditional enemies.

On August 5, 1876, the secretary of War rejected Medary's request for troops, saying that the army had only 526 men in the entire territory of Montana and could not station 200 of them at Flathead Agency.[65]

Medary's battles with T. J. DeMers, Chief Arlee, and Duncan McDonald continued. On December 7, 1876, Medary pleaded with Col. John Gibbon, head of the army district of Montana, for military protection.[66] Gibbon sent an officer and twenty men to Flathead.[67]

The U.S. attorney charged Medary with stealing government property, and Chiefs Arlee and Michelle testified at the grand jury with Duncan McDonald as interpreter.[68] Medary argued that he had legally traded government-owned shingles in Missoula for blacksmith work for the agency.[69] The grand jury dismissed the charges against Medary without leaving the jury box.[70] It was a hollow victory for Medary. It had cost him four hundred dollars for lawyer's fees, witnesses, and traveling expenses, and he felt disgraced by having his "name dragged before the people of Montana and possibly of the states, for the crime of 'Larceny of U.S. property.'"[71] On February 28, 1877, Medary lamented that his enemies had initiated a second suit against him for having stock on the reservation without permission of the chiefs.[72]

The charges and countercharges caused the commissioner of Indian Affairs to replace Medary because of "alleged dissatisfaction existing among the Indians." Medary was soon succeeded by Peter Ronan.[73] Medary's alcohol consumption and political problems may have proved his undoing as Flathead Indian agent. Sorting out the charges is difficult, given the evidence that has survived, but Medary did prove a valuable ally for Barbour and those Montana whites desperate for a fort at Missoula.

## The Supreme Test of Salish Diplomacy: White Hysteria and the Nez Perce War of 1877

The Nez Perce War and its aftermath through 1878 were certainly a supreme challenge for the Salish leadership. The drumbeat of rumor, hysteria, and propaganda for violence from the *Weekly Missoulian* during the 1870s built to a crescendo in 1877. During and after the Nez Perce War, Barbour's underlying anti-Indian prejudices led him to print rumors of Indian danger. Barbour even encouraged "preventative" violence against the Bitterroot Salish and other western Montana Indians. The Salish were faced with the herculean task of trying to calm the panicked white settlers of western Montana and, at the same time, restrain the anger of younger tribal members.

At the end of June 1877 two companies of infantry soldiers arrived in Missoula to begin construction of the new fort.[74] Their arrival coincided with the first news of Nez Perce–white conflict in Idaho. Barbour was quick to point out that the western Montana tribes were closely intermarried with the Nez Perces, and the local tribes had grievances over Bitterroot lands and taxes that "to the Indians' way of reasoning" could provide "the most ample cause for an uprising against the whites."[75] The Bitterroot Salish left the valley at the end of June on their normal seasonal cycle of digging camas, hunting, and fishing. Some local whites interpreted the move as preparations for hostilities.[76] Many Bitterroot whites abandoned their homes and cowered behind the protection of Fort Owen's bastions in Stevensville.[77]

Father Jerome D'Aste of St. Mary's Mission in Stevensville reported widespread fear among the Bitterroot whites, who exacerbated the situation by antagonizing and harassing the Salish. In an 1878 account D'Aste related that:

> The alarm grew to such an extent that they sent for arms, built three forts, and *some weeks* before the hostile party arrived, left their farms and shut up themselves and families in the forts. The newspapers of the county had frequent spicy articles full of calumnies against the Flat-Heads, and exciting in the settlers feelings of fear and distrust. Every movement of the Indians was watched; in their most innocent actions hostile intention were discovered by the alarmed people; no powder nor ammunition was allowed to be sold to them. It was of no use for me to tell the people that they had no reason to suspect the Flat-Heads; that by acting in so distrustful and cowardly a way without the least foundation for it, they were provoking the Indians and exciting them to revolt.[78]

Some voices of reason were raised in defense of the Bitterroot Salish. Capt. Walter DeLacy, the pioneer Montana civil engineer, surveyor, and cartographer, reminded the *Helena Daily Herald* of the seventy-year history of Salish-white friendship and alliance. He pointed out that Salish friendship had been steady despite "plenty of provocation," and while "other tribes seem to have been rewarded for their hostility, this one alone seems to have suffered for its fidelity."[79]

On July 8, 1877, Peter Ronan, the new Flathead Indian agent, met with Charlo at St. Mary's Mission, where he and his family were attending Mass. The chief assured Ronan that it was his father's—Chief Victor's—"boast that the blood of a white man never reddened the hand of a single Indian of the Flathead tribe. My father died with that boast on his lips. I am my father's son and will leave that same boast to my children. . . . I will do all in my power to defend the whites and their homes, but I cannot send my young men out to make war on the Nez Perces." Ronan concluded that there were "a number of wild stories afloat in regard to Indian massacres lately perpetrated, but . . . I feel perfectly confident, however, of the good faith of Charlos, the 'original' Flathead chief, and his band, as well as the Confederate tribe under my jurisdiction." Ronan was, nevertheless, going to take "every precaution to guard against danger or surprise."[80]

Charlo and the Salish leadership sent several delegates to Missoula to reassure the whites of Salish friendship and neutrality. Chief Adolph, the Salish war chief, was one of the envoys. He assured the Missoulians, saying, "I like all the whites, and if I had wanted to fight I would have commenced long ago. . . . I talk but one way, and that is friendship for the whites."[81] Fortified with whiskey, some local whites went to the Clark Fork River bridge overlooking Adolph's camp and began shooting towards the camp. Adolph promptly complained to the military authorities and leading citizens of Missoula. Barbour tried to argue that the incident was just a misunderstanding. Despite Barbour's continuing efforts to rile relations between the communities, he backed off from endorsing direct physical aggression and advised, "We must observe prudence, caution and forbearance in our intercourse with these people, to prevent the spark which now exists from being fanned to a flame."[82] The restraint that Adolph and his camp showed in not firing back at the drunken whites on the bridge testified to the seriousness of Salish efforts to avoid conflict with whites during the Nez Perce crisis.

Although Barbour counseled against attacking peaceful Salish camps and argued for the suppression of whiskey sales to Indians, he was also willing to print unsubstantiated, inflammatory rumors.[83] On July 20, 1877, he presented vague reports of suspicious Indian movements in arguing that the local Indians were not trustworthy. One rumor was that a white man,

James House, saw Indians with a mule loaded with "what appeared to be ammunition." House had only his suspicions to prove that the load contained ammunition.[84]

In this crisis atmosphere, and with the approach of the Nez Perce hostiles, Barbour continued his constant propaganda that the Bitterroot Salish and other local Indians could not be trusted. In the July 20, 1877, issue of the *Weekly Missoulian*, Barbour argued, "The interests of the two races are essentially hostile to each other. . . . It is claimed that the Indians of Missoula county will not go to war, because they say so. This is rather a bruised reed to lean upon."[85]

When Joseph and his Nez Perce refugees arrived in the Bitterroot Valley on July 25, 1877, the Salish proved that their own preservation was more important than their friendship with the Nez Perces. The Salish leaders had concluded that the interests of the Salish people required avoiding war with the white settlers. The historical record indicated that the Nez Perces had no desire to harm the white people in the Bitterroot Valley and were desperately seeking to escape the fighting in Idaho. As Chief Joseph later stated, "We understood that there was to be no more war [now that they had made it to Montana]. We intended to go peaceably to the buffalo country, and leave the question of returning to our country to be settled afterward."[86]

John P. Martens, a white resident of Victor in the Bitterroot Valley, wrote in his journal on July 26, 1877, that "Carlo the Flathaed Chef had sent word to the People that the Nes Perces wold be in the Vally the next Day at 10 o clok and he the Cheif advised all of us to go to Forht Owen for protextion." On July 21, while returning from town, Martens had passed a "cople Indians sin[g]ing Glory Haleluya." Presumably the singing was to reassure the passing whites that the Indians were peaceful.[87] Gen. Henry B. Carrington was later told by a white Bitterroot settler, possibly Amos Buck, that in 1877 Charlo "personally conducted the exposed white families to Fort Owen and other places of security and protected them until additional troops arrived in the valley."[88]

A number of Salish warriors joined the U.S. Army and white settlers behind the hastily erected fortifications at the mouth of Lolo Creek to prevent the Nez Perces from entering the Bitterroot Valley.[89] The attempt to block the entrance to the valley failed miserably when the Nez Perces merely skirted around the fort, which became known as "Fort Fizzle." The Salish at Fort Fizzle wore white cloths tied around their heads so the army and settlers would not shoot their allies in the confusion of battle.[90] The original muster roll compiled in 1877 included mostly mixed-bloods, including the Mattes, Clairmonts, Lumpreys, and Silverthornes.[91] The list of volunteers used in 1881 as the basis for paying the volunteers also included a number of full-blood Salish, including Martin Charlo (Chief Charlo's son), Antoine Moiese, Louis Pierre, and Antoine Ninepipe.[92] Father D'Aste recalled that "some half breeds had induced a few Indians, about 15, to join the whites, and they followed the whites, but they had neither arms nor ammunitions. It was probably this circumstance that saved the [white] settlement from a general massacre." Father D'Aste observed that the Nez Perces could easily have climbed the hills surrounding Fort Fizzle and used their rifles to pick off the whites behind the barricades. He figured the Nez Perces had avoided attacking the fort because some Salish were with the whites. An attack on Fort Fizzle would have put them at war with the Salish and their allies, the Pend d'Oreille, Kalispel, and Kootenai tribes.[93]

After the Nez Perce promised to pass through the Bitterroot Valley in peace and skirted the fortification at Lolo, Charlo met with Joseph. There is some confusion in the sources, but most indicate that Charlo insisted that the Nez Perces not attack or rob any of the Bitterroot whites. Charlo refused to shake hands with the Nez Perce chiefs because they had murdered white people in Idaho.[94]

During the time the Nez Perce hostiles were passing through the Bitterroot Valley, the Salish dramatically proved their commitment to peace. Carrie May Warren, a white woman in the Bitterroot Valley, remembered one particular incident:

> one man a black smith in stevensville refused to leave His home & move into the fort [Fort Owen]. the Nesperse camp being just across the river west of stevensville. some of the Wariors wer in town every day. this day some generious hearted white man had sold or given an [Nez Perce] Indian whiskey. When He was full of the fire watter He went on the war path took it into His evil head to kill this mans wife. in this act of murder. a flathead man steped in betwean the woman & drunken Indian saying no killem white woman killem me. the white People surly owed that oald flathead man a lot, had that woman ben killed war would have started right then we can easily guess what would have happened to the little hanfull of whit People in the valley at that time.[95]

In the 1970s, Salish elder Mary Ann Topsseh Coombs suggested that her father, Louis Pierre, was the Salish man who had protected the blacksmith's wife.[96]

The incident was also remembered by Henry Buck, a white merchant in Stevensville. On August 1, 1877, a large number of well-armed Nez Perce warriors rode into town, and the local Salish Indians gathered in Stevensville with their weapons to protect the whites. Buck related the story of Jacob Herman, the white blacksmith at Stevensville whose wife was defended by a Salish Indian. According to Buck, the Salish man grabbed the firearm from the drunken Nez Perce to defend Mrs. Herman. In later years Herman kept that Salish man "in provisions as a token of appreciation for his kindly act in saving the life of his [Herman's] beloved wife." Later the same day a Nez Perce man threatened to kill a white man in Buck's store, but "by a quick move of one of the Flatheads, his gun was wrenched from him before he could pull the trigger."[97] After this incident, Looking Glass, a Nez Perce chief, forced the Nez Perces to return to their camp outside of Stevensville.[98]

During a September 1883 interview with Senator George G. Vest and delegate Martin Maginnis at St. Mary's Mission, Charlo noted that "When the Nez Perces came here we protected the whites." To corroborate Charlo's statement, an unnamed "old gray-headed Indian" added: "I am old, and nearly blind; but when the Nez Perces were here I was told they were going to abuse a white woman, and I got my revolver, placed myself in front of her, and told them they would have to kill me before they injured the white woman. My white friends will tell you this is true."[99]

In 1947, Pierre Pichette, a Salish historian, related that in 1877 "the Selish fight [fought] their own Indian friends instead of seeing any of the whites harmed by the Nez Perce. Out there the Selish tribe stood by the whites and didn't want the Nez Perce to do any harm at all."[100]

Charlo and the approximately three hundred Bitterroot Salish not only declined to attack the Nez Perces, but they actively defended their one thousand white Bitterroot neighbors.[101] The Nez Perces moved south out of the Bitterroot Valley and worked to avoid conflict with the Salish and whites there. The only Nez Perce hostility in the Bitterroot took place when some young men rifled the cabin of Myron Lockwood, a white settler in the upper part of the valley, and stole some provisions. When Nez Perce chief Looking Glass learned what his warriors had done, he forced the robbers to leave three horses in Lockwood's field to pay for the stolen items.[102] Keeping the peace could hardly have been more difficult, but the Bitterroot

Salish avoided conflict with both the Nez Perce hostiles and the Bitterroot whites. Failure at this critical juncture could have cost the Salish considerable casualties and destroyed their economic base in the Bitterroot Valley.

Gen. Oliver Otis Howard, who most observers felt had been outgeneraled and made a fool of by Chief Joseph and the Nez Perces, later made vague charges that the Bitterroot Salish had sheltered a Nez Perce spy who informed the hostiles of Howard's movements. Howard did not explain the basis for his assertion. Rehabilitating his military reputation occupied much of Howard's later years, so he may not have had any proof for the charge of Salish collaboration with the hostile Nez Perces.[103]

At the same time in 1877 that Charlo and the Salish were trying to avoid conflict in the Bitterroot Valley, the Pend d'Oreilles were working to calm white apprehensions on the Jocko Reservation. When agent Peter Ronan considered sending his wife and children off the reservation, Pend d' Oreille chief Michelle promised that he and his warriors would protect the Ronan family from any harm.[104] One source did suggest that some Pend d'Oreille warriors had contacted the hostile Nez Perces in the Lolo Canyon before the Nez Perces entered the Bitterroot Valley in 1877. The account by Andrew Garcia's Nez Perce wife, In-who-lise, claimed a party of Pend d'Oreilles were interested in joining the Nez Perces in fighting the whites and wanted to guide them to the Jocko Reservation and farther north by the back trails.[105] The Pend d'Oreilles may have been offering to guide the Nez Perces around the white settlements to avoid conflict.

The Bitterroot Valley whites were relieved and thankful for the protection of their Salish neighbors. On August 8 they gave Charlo and the Salish a feast as a thank-you gesture. Charlo made a speech at the feast "recounting the past friendship of the Flatheads for the whites; urging his young men to always live in amity with them, and showing them how much better off they were than the Nez Perces who are now being pursued as outcasts in the earth."[106] A few weeks later Barbour visited the Bitterroot and found that all of the white residents spoke "in the highest terms of the honorable conduct of Charlos" during the period the Nez Perces were in the valley. The whites had concluded that the Nez Perces "were probably induced to a better course of conduct from a knowledge of Charlo's determination" to protect the Bitterroot whites.[107] As mentioned above, in early 1878 the white settlers in the Bitterroot circulated a petition asking the Missoula County commissioners to drop their efforts to tax the Bitterroot Salish because these "old Indian settlers have always lived on good terms with the whites, and in time of threatened Indian invasion, have proved an effective and preventive means of defense."[108]

As usual, newspaper reaction was mixed. The *New North-West* in Deer Lodge concluded that the Salish had "earned another credit mark and stood true through circumstances trying their fidelity to the utmost," and that the attitudes of the Salish during the Nez Perce transit "probably changed the whole course of events in Missoula county, and the faithfulness of a friend is more deserving of reward than the concessions of a foe. This thing should not be forgotten when peace is established."[109]

In the *Weekly Missoulian,* Barbour continued his diatribes with barely a pause. On August 24, Barbour repeated his calumnies that the western Montana tribes sympathized with and aided the Nez Perce hostiles. Barbour's charge was that the local Indians had altered their movements since the start of the Nez Perce hostilities, and these changes were "suspicious." Somehow he knew that Indian couriers were "seen to go and come," and this left him in no doubt that the local Indians "were in active communication with the hostiles." Even Barbour had to admit that the Bitterroot Salish and some of the Flathead Reservation Indians were not hostile. The effort of western Montana Indians to buy ammunition for the buffalo hunt—despite a government order forbidding sales of ammunition or guns to any Indians in Montana—was just further proof to Barbour of their disloyalty. He argued that military force should be used to stop the buffalo hunts and force the local Indians either to farm or starve.[110]

Barbour also included a note about a recent incident on Lolo Creek. According to Barbour's version, two white men had been threatened by a party of ten Indian men, probably Bitterroot Valley Nez Perces and Salish. When the white men responded by preparing to fight, the Indian party made signs of friendship and produced a letter from Father Jerome D'Aste that the Indian bearers were peaceful. Barbour claimed that the Indians would have killed the whites if they could have blamed it on the Nez Perce hostiles.[111]

Shortly after the thank-you feast from the Bitterroot whites, the federal government expressed its appreciation for Salish efforts to protect them. The government's response was to forbid sales of arms or ammunition to any Indian in Montana—friendly or hostile.[112] This order struck particularly hard on the Bitterroot Salish as they had neglected their crops during the Nez Perce excitement in order to protect the white settlers. A hailstorm destroyed most of their crops, and the Salish had to hunt buffalo to survive. Father D'Aste complained that the Bitterroot Salish had paid dearly for their guns and were now forbidden to purchase ammunition for the hunt.[113] D'Aste's description of the plight of the Bitterroot Salish failed to dent Barbour's racist ideology, but Barbour did endorse having the government feed the Salish and other local Indians until they could develop farms.[114] D'Aste wrote to Montana governor Benjamin F. Potts and Flathead Indian agent Peter Ronan pleading that the Bitterroot Salish be allowed to purchase arms and ammunition. Potts declined to endorse the change but forwarded D'Aste's letter to the secretary of the Interior. Ronan forwarded another letter from Father D'Aste to the commissioner of Indian Affairs and added a request that the government furnish provisions to support the western Montana tribes if ammunition sales were not allowed.[115]

Ronan wrote to Martin Maginnis, the Montana territorial delegate, complaining about "the great blunders which are being made at Washington—blunders which are more than likely to plunge this country into another Indian war." One of these blunders was the "incendiary orders" prohibiting sales of arms and ammunition to the friendly Indians of western Montana. The government "must make provisions to support the Indians who depend upon the hunt for a lively-hood, *or hunger will compell them to fight for food.*" After having defended the white people in Missoula and Bitterroot, "they naturally feel that in depriving them of their means of living that a great wrong is committed, and if things are pressed, without providing for their wants war will be sure to follow." Ronan pleaded that Maginnis help keep "the crimes of a handful of Nez Percz outlaws" from penalizing the tribes who remained friendly to the whites.[116]

Ronan also wrote to the U.S. Army at Fort Missoula to request a change in the sales ban. Col. John Gibbon, commander of the army district of Montana, recommended that each warrior of the Salish, Pend d'Oreille, and Kootenai tribes be allowed to purchase one rifle and up to sixty rounds of ammunition. Gen. William T. Sherman and the secretary of War overruled Gibbon and only allowed the western Montana tribes to purchase ammunition for muzzle loaders and not the much more useful breech-loading guns.[117]

Several Montana newspapers disagreed with the *Weekly Missoulian* and commented on the unfairness of the ban on ammunition sales. On October 20, 1877, the *Helena Daily Herald* editorialized that "The Flatheads are here and want ammunition to hunt buffalo. They are peaceable, their crops are deficient, and they have to get meat, steal or starve. Give them the ammunition."[118] On November 30, 1877, the *Helena Daily Herald* reprinted an October 23 letter written from Helena that had been published first in *McGee's Illustrated Weekly* in New York City. The writer reported that the order prohibiting the sale of ammunition to all Indians was "very perplexing" to the Salish, given their record of friendship toward the whites. The writer reported that the "Governor, United States Marshal, and leading citizens of Montana have telegraphed to authorize the sale [of ammunition] to them. . . . They can be trusted with more confidence than those white men now in the brush selling contraband goods to all Indians alike."[119] The *Rocky Mountain Husbandman,* at Diamond City east of Helena, complained on October 25 that the ban on ammunition sales to the Bitterroot Salish was "certainly unjust, and a poor return for the service rendered by this chief [Charlo] and his warriors to the settlers of the Bitter Root valley during the invasion of the Nez Perces."[120]

On October 29, 1877, the Bitterroot Salish passed through Little Prickly Pear Canyon north of Helena. A passing army soldier noted in his journal that the Salish "only now & then" had a rifle and "all carry their bow & arrows yet."[121]

The abusive conduct of the white settlers and the government was frustrating and confusing for the Salish. The ban on selling ammunition to friendly Indians hindered the fall buffalo hunt in 1877 and must have restricted the ability of the Salish hunters to protect themselves against enemy war parties. Little written evidence has survived, but apparently during the late 1870s an assortment of small unregulated white traders were operating in the buffalo country grounds in the Musselshell Valley. Andrew Garcia left a detailed description of one trading operation in the area during the winter of 1878–79.[122] These independent traders probably charged higher prices than the merchants in Missoula and Helena, but for a price they would be willing to sell ammunition to the Salish buffalo hunters during the fall 1877 hunt. The Salish may not have had much respect for the behavior and values of the whites, but the Salish leadership's decision to keep the peace was based on what they saw as the best long-term interests of the tribe.

Another aftermath of the Nez Perce War that had an impact on the Bitterroot Salish was the return of a band of Nez Perce refugees through Montana during the summer of 1878. As explained in the last chapter, this band left a trail of conflict across Montana and in July 1878 killed three white miners in Rock Creek. They were also involved in thefts and attacks on whites in the upper Bitterroot Valley. The Nez Perces were chased out of the Bitterroot by a party of soldiers and volunteers, including four leading Salish warriors: Francois Lamoose, Narcisse, Louis Vanderburg, and Martin Charlo.[123]

In the midst of the white panic over the movement of this hostile band of Nez Perce refugees through the territory in 1878, Barbour oiled up his hysteria machine with new attacks on the peaceful tribes of western Montana. On June 28, 1878, he charged that it was "an evidence of an impotent understanding to suppose that every Indian does not sympathize with every other Indian in his struggle with the whites."[124] By July 12, 1878, when the first exaggerated reports of robberies and murders by the returning Nez Perces in Deep Creek reached Missoula, Barbour argued that the peaceful local Indians should be presumed hostile and attacked if they did not make war on the Nez Perces:

> The chiefs and reservation Indians who are engaged in agriculture are certainly averse to war; it is only the vagabonds who lead a vagrant life and have nothing to lose that could be induced to go upon the warpath. It is a duty that the peaceably disposed Indians owe to their own welfare to make common cause with the whites against the vagrants . . . if they do not, peace with Indians may as well be considered at an end, and the business of shooting down Indians wherever found be commenced.[125]

Barbour was calling for the killing of innocent Indians who were trying to remain neutral and avoid taking part in the Nez Perce–white hostilities.

Given the continuing incitement by part of the local white community, Salish success in avoiding war seems remarkable. Some whites supported the Salish efforts to keep the peace, but the conduct of the predatory and mercenary portion of the white community severely challenged the diplomatic talents of the Salish leaders. The campaign to get a U.S. Army post in Missoula, the efforts of Missoula County to tax the Bitterroot Salish, and white reactions to the Battle of the Little Big Horn in 1876 and the Nez Perce War and its aftermath in 1877 and 1878 raised particular challenges for the Salish. Several specific efforts to assuage the fears of Montana whites in 1877 and 1878 were recorded. Explicit statements of Salish policy have not survived, but the *actions* of Salish leaders and people indicate the importance the tribe placed on avoiding conflict with western Montana whites.

The Bitterroot Salish delegation to Washington, D.C., 1884: *back row, left to right*, John Hill, Indian agent Peter Ronan, and Michel Revais; *middle row*, Antoine Moiese, Chief Charlo, and Louis Vanderburg; *front row*, Thomas Abel Adams. Photograph by John K. Hillers, National Anthropological Archives, Smithsonian Institution, Washington, D.C., negative no. 43,583.

Chief Arlee. From Peter Ronan, *Historical Sketch of the Flathead-Indians from the Year 1813 to 1890* (Helena, Mont.: Journal Publishing Co., 1890), p. 78.

Agent Peter Ronan, of the Flathead Indian Agency. From the photographic archives of the Montana Historical Society, Helena, negative no. MMM900-004.

Father Jerome D'Aste, S.J. From the Jesuit Oregon Province Archives, Gonzaga University, Spokane, Washington, negative 1037.2.

St. Mary's Mission, Stevensville, Montana. Photograph by Rollin McKay. From the Archives and Special Collections of the University of Montana-Missoula, negative no. 94-94.

Interior of St. Mary's Mission, Stevensville, Montana. From the Photographic Archives of the Montana Historical Society, Helena, negative no. 950-756.

Salish settlement near Stevensville, Montana, March 1891. Photograph by Chase Carrington. From the University of Pennsylvania Museum, Philadelphia, image no. 143356.

Before the removal of the Salish, October 15, 1891. Gen. Henry B. Carrington stands to the left of the tepee. The rest of the identifications are uncertain. Photograph by Chase Carrington. From the University of Pennsylvania Museum, Philadelphia, image no. 143362.

Before the removal, Stevensville, Montana, October 15, 1891. Chief Charlo is to the right of General Carrington. Photograph by Chase Carrington. From the University of Pennsylvania Museum, Philadelphia, image no. 143370.

Food distribution before the removal march, October 15, 1891. Photograph by Chase Carrington. From the University of Pennsylvania Museum, Philadelphia, image no. 142689.

CHAPTER 5

# Coping with the Great Father

## The Politics of Salish Survival, 1868–1886

Keeping the peace with the whites during the late nineteenth century was particularly problematic for the Bitterroot Salish because of the arrogance, dishonesty, and incompetence of the federal government in its efforts to entice or force the Salish out of the Bitterroot Valley. The 1855 Hellgate Treaty and the government's failure to carry out its designation of the Bitterroot Valley as a provisional Indian reservation left the Salish and Bitterroot whites in direct conflict over land and other resources.

On a late August day in 1872 the Bitterroot Salish chiefs received notice that an important "suyapi" wanted to meet with them near St. Mary's Mission at Stevensville. The visit was not unexpected as the Salish had heard of the president's fall 1871 order to force them out of the Bitterroot Valley. The Montana superintendent of Indian Affairs had traveled to the Bitterroot in July 1872 to warn the Salish leaders that Congress and "the Great Father" were sending a representative to make arrangements for their removal.

Salish leaders were mindful of a recent chain of troubling developments among western Montana whites. Their white neighbors in the Bitterroot Valley and Missoula had been agitated, aloof, and devious during the summer. Some Missoula whites had schemed for years to secure a U.S. Army post as a boost to the local economy. White militia companies had recently been organized in the Bitterroot and Missoula valleys, and petitions to the territorial capital had requested troops, guns, ammunition, and pay for the militias.

Seventeen years earlier governor Isaac Stevens had promised to keep white settlers out of the Bitterroot Valley and to furnish the tribe with tools, shops, schools, and economic aid. Most of those promises, made in 1855, were still unfulfilled in 1872. The Salish leaders were not interested in trading their Bitterroot Valley homes for more empty promises from another important government official, but they also recognized the need to maintain peace with the whites. They could not afford to lose their supply of guns, ammunition, and other trade goods in the midst of their struggle with the Plains tribes over the buffalo grounds. The Salish leaders who met Congressman James A. Garfield in 1872 faced a singular diplomatic challenge: how to stand up for their rights to their Bitterroot homes while avoiding conflict with the white government.

Except for the 1872 negotiations with Garfield, which were accompanied by a local white military buildup, government negotiations represented a secondary threat, rather than a direct one, to the community. Generally the most important challenges facing the tribe revolved around relations with local whites and surrounding tribes, and strengthening the tribe's social and economic fabric. The occasional irruptions of federal government representatives into the Bitterroot Valley were consequential, but they were only one portion of Salish concerns. Official treaties and agreements set the parameters for events in the Bitterroot Valley, but containing violence resulting from alcohol use, maintaining respectful relations with local white leaders, and helping Salish families expand their farms were just as important to the survival of the tribe.

A multitude of historical sources are available to document the government's actions and deliberations between 1868 and 1886, so only a sampling of the evidence can be discussed here.

## The Sully Negotiations, 1869

The Salish strategy of insisting on their right to remain in the Bitterroot Valley while avoiding conflict with the federal government was set in 1868 and 1869 when Victor was still chief. In August 1868 Victor's position on Salish rights in the Bitterroot was spelled out in a message to special Indian agent William J. Cullen: "He is opposed to leaving the Bitter root Valley & contends that in the treaty with Gov Stevens July /55 this Valley was to be Set aside for the Flathead tribes & that the White Men here have located & Made improvements in defiance of this treaty."[1]

Cullen and his party negotiated with Victor and the Salish leaders in an effort to induce them to move to Jocko. Unfortunately for Cullen, however, the Salish leaders remembered the promises the government had made in 1855: "The Indians complained, and we thought with good cause, that the provisions of the treaty made with them by Governor Stevens, July 16, 1855, had not been faithfully observed on the part of the United States."[2] Minutes of the speeches by Chiefs Ambrose and Adolph at the August 15, 1868, council with Cullen have survived. The chiefs outlined in detail the promised goods and benefits that had not been delivered, and they also protested the failure of the federal government to help keep the peace.

Ambrose complained that "Not one half of what was promised us [in 1855] has ever been received by us." Since many of the annuity goods seemed to get lost between Washington, D.C., and the Bitterroot Valley, Ambrose appealed for the Great Father to furnish the Salish with an inventory of what was sent so they could check the annuity goods that arrived. Ambrose requested that the annuities include farming tools, plows, axes, hoes, and other goods rather than just blankets.[3]

In his speech, Chief Adolph also complained about the failure of the government to deliver the goods and services promised in 1855. In the thirteen years since the treaty had been negotiated—and nine years since it had been ratified—the Salish had received annuities only five years. As for the shops and services: "[Stevens] promised us a hospital for our sick, a Doctor and a Blacksmith, and to build a school for our children. He also promised to build fences and houses for us all of which has never been done. The Grist mill and saw mill [at Jocko] are far away [and] we never see them." Adolph reinforced Ambrose's request for more useful annuities: "The Agents have told us we could select such goods [for annuities] as we wanted. We want farming tools. My hands! Look at them!! They are my tools. I scratch the ground with my nails. The Great Father wants us to make farms. He ought to send us tools." Adolph also protested that the failure of the government to recognize the Bitterroot Valley as a provisional reservation and keep white settlers out had complicated Salish efforts to keep the peace: "The young [Salish] men are sometimes bad and we are afraid to live among the whites lest we have trouble with them. We want to know if our Great Father allows the whites to settle upon our lands. Some of them threaten to shoot us."

Cullen was not able to reach an agreement with the Salish, but in October 1869, Gen. Alfred Sully, Montana superintendent of Indian Affairs, continued the negotiations. No transcripts of the Sully negotiations have survived, but Sully's report suggests that the arguments and positions of the Salish leaders in 1869 were similar to those recorded a year earlier. Sully reported to the commissioner of Indian Affairs that he had "offered these Indians every inducement to leave the Bitter Root valley and Settle in the Flathead Lake valley. I even offered them more than I was willing or I think the Government would have been willing to allow, to induce them to move, but all to no purpose." The Salish insisted that the 1855 treaty allowed them to remain in the Bitterroot in exchange for giving up their claim to the rest of western Montana. The unfulfilled commitments were mentioned: ". . . the Government had promised them many things [in 1855] which for ten years they had been looking for and now all they asked was to be allowed to live and die in their land they loved so well." Victor, Arlee, and Joseph signed an agreement with Sully that provided for a Salish reservation in the lower Bitterroot Valley between Corvallis and Lolo. Sully forwarded the proposed agreement to Washington, D.C., but did not approve of its terms: "I do not like the Treaty, the whites and Indians living together on the reservation will be a constant source of difficulties." Sully intimated in his report that Father Joseph Giorda, S.J., of St. Mary's Mission, had influenced the Salish. Sully could not understand why the Salish leaders would be wary of new government promises piled on top of the worthless pledges of 1855.[4]

The prospect of reserving even a portion of the Bitterroot Valley for the Salish unleashed a torrent of political vitriol among Montana whites. The *Helena Daily Herald* labeled the agreement an "odious treaty."[5] The political firestorm buried the Sully agreement before it could be seriously considered in Washington. On October 31, the Montana territorial delegate met with President Grant to protest against the agreement.[6] Not surprisingly, the unratified Sully treaty was quickly filed away in the Office of Indian Affairs and forgotten.

In 1870 Chief Victor died while hunting on the plains in Crow country, and his son Charlo was elected the new chief of the Bitterroot Salish.[7] Much to the disappointment of white government officials, Salish resistance to removal continued under Charlo.[8] On May 7, 1871, Charlo and six other Salish chiefs and leaders addressed an appeal to President Grant. Charlo objected to white settlers coming into the Bitterroot Valley before the valley had been surveyed and examined, as required by the 1855 treaty. The chiefs complained that "almost our entire valley is occupied and overrun by white settlers, who impose on us in many ways, subjecting us to annoyance, inconvenience and injustice, which seem to call aloud for redress at your hands." The letter concluded by requesting permission for a Salish delegation to travel to Washington to negotiate directly with the president.[9]

## Garfield's 1872 Negotiations with the Salish

The Bitterroot land questions quickly came to a boil again in the fall of 1871 after the election of William H. Clagett, a Deer Lodge lawyer, as the first Republican congressional delegate from Montana Territory. Clagett's election benefited from the vigorous efforts of the new territorial governor, Benjamin F. Potts, to revive and unify the Montana Republican Party.[10] Within days of Clagett's arrival in Washington, he approached President Grant, a Republican, about an executive order to remove the Salish from the Bitterroot Valley. Grant issued the order on November 14, 1871. The presidential order was clearly a political favor based on patronage rather than an effort to do justice to the Salish.[11]

The order falsely declared that the president's decision was based on a careful survey and examination of the Bitterroot Valley as provided for in the 1855 treaty. On the basis of this purported examination, Grant declared that the Bitterroot Valley was not "better adapted to the wants of the Flathead tribe than the general [Jocko] reservation."[12] As late as November 9, 1871, Clagett had written to the commissioner of Indian Affairs requesting an examination of the Bitterroot as provided for in the treaty.[13] Grant dispensed with the formalities of an investigation of the valley on the political advice of Montana Republican officeholders. For white Bitterroot settlers, the most important provision of Grant's order was the declaration that the valley would be legally open to white settlement after the Salish were removed. The order concluded with a section allowing Salish farmers in the Bitterroot to sever their tribal relations and obtain title to their farms.

By June 5, 1872, Clagett had pushed through Congress "An act to provide for the removal of the Flathead and other Indians from the Bitter-Root Valley, in the Territory of Montana." The first section of the act directed the president to remove the Bitterroot Salish to the Jocko Reservation "as soon as practicable." Section 2 specified how white settlers could obtain title to Bitterroot lands. Settlers could occupy and purchase up to 160 acres of land for $1.25 per acre in cash with payment due twenty-one months after the land was selected. The first $50,000 from the land sales was to be expended for the benefit of the Bitterroot Salish who had removed to Jocko. White settlers were not allowed to obtain free land in the Bitterroot Valley under the homestead or preemption laws.[14] The third section allowed Indians over twenty-one years old and the head of a family to preempt, without cost, Bitterroot land they were living on and cultivating on June 5, 1872. The Indian farmer who was "actually residing upon and cultivating any portion of said lands, shall be permitted to remain in said valley and pre-empt without cost the land so occupied and cultivated, not exceeding in amount one hundred and sixty acres for each of such Indians, for which he shall receive a patent without power of alienation." In exchange for the patent, the Indian farmer was required to abandon his tribal relations. Differing interpretations of section 3 were to foment considerable controversy during the implementation of the act. Section 4 allowed John Owen, the merchant proprietor of Fort Owen and an early Flathead Indian agent, to claim land under the 1850 Oregon Donation Act.

In 1872 the Salish diplomatic dilemma was perilous. Western Montana whites were being incited to fear and violence based on white bigotry and the prospect that war or rumors of war would bring federal dollars to the local economy. When Congressman Garfield arrived to negotiate with Charlo and the other Bitterroot Salish, he expressed apprehension of the "imminent danger of trouble in the Bitter Root Valley, from the conduct of mercenary whites."[15]

On August 5, sixty white residents of the Corvallis area responded to the incitement by forming a militia company and preparing to fight their Indian neighbors.[16] A white militia was also organized at Aetna in the Bitterroot.[17] Washington Jay McCormick, the editor of the Missoula newspaper and former Flathead Indian agent, played a leading role on August 6 in organizing an anti-Salish militia in Missoula. Frantic requests were dispatched to authorities in Virginia City for federal troops and guns, and ammunition for the militia.[18] Montana territorial governor B. F. Potts dispatched 260 breech-loading guns, ammunition, and other equipment to Missoula for the Bitterroot militias. Wanting only free government subsidies, the white Bitterrooters were unwilling to pay the shipping costs for the guns or give a bond to guarantee their return to Governor Potts at the end of hostilities.[19] The Salish chiefs watched these preparations for warfare with growing unease.

In late June 1872, Jasper Viall, the Montana superintendent of Indian Affairs, met with the Bitterroot Salish leaders. Viall informed the Salish of the government decision to force them to either remove to the Jocko Reservation or take up individual farms and sever their tribal relations.[20] The Salish response to this news has not survived.

On July 1, 1872, Charlo, Arlee, Adolph, the Pend d'Oreille chiefs, and the Kootenai chiefs signed a power of attorney designating James Fullerton of Washington, D.C., as the attorney for the Confederated Flathead Nation of Indians. Fullerton was to pursue any claims arising from the failure of the federal government to pay the annuities required by the 1855 treaty, and claims "relating to lands as connected with or growing out of such treaties." Flathead agent C. S. Jones swore that the agreement was "fairly and duly obtained" and had been fully explained to the chiefs.[21] No references to Fullerton's power of attorney appear in the records of the commissioner of Indian Affairs. Jones was locked in a fight with Jasper Viall, the Montana superintendent of Indian Affairs, for control of Flathead Agency funds, and he was removed as Flathead Agent soon after the power of attorney was signed. No evidence has been found explaining the background for this contract or describing any results from Fullerton's work.

To negotiate arrangements for the removal, the secretary of the Interior selected James A. Garfield, the congressman and Republican party leader who later became president. Garfield was a friend and patron of Montana governor Benjamin Potts. In return Potts arranged for Garfield to be hired as the attorney representing Montana Territory in a series of court cases during the 1870s.[22] The trip to Montana might have been just a pleasant adventure for Garfield, but some newspapers speculated he had arranged the trip because he was embarrassed to campaign for President Grant's reelection.[23]

Whatever Garfield's motivation for traveling to Montana, the Salish faced some delicate choices. If they refused Garfield's order to remove to Jocko, the government might classify them as outlaws and use military force against them. Agreeing to Garfield's demands would unjustly force the tribe out of the Bitterroot Valley and compromise the moral right of the tribe to its home. An answer of "no" combined with a little equivocation seemed the best hope for allowing the Salish to stay in the Bitterroot Valley and still avoid conflict with the whites.

The trip to Stevensville by Garfield's party had the aura of a summer recreational excursion. In accounts of the trip, bird hunting and fishing figure prominently. Garfield was disappointed that the Salish leaders did not appear promptly when called or agree readily to the removal. He arrived in Stevensville on Wednesday afternoon, August 21, 1872, and ended up spending two nights in the Bitterroot. Garfield summoned the Salish leaders to meet Wednesday afternoon but was forced to postpone the meeting until Thursday morning. On Thursday the negotiations ran for six hours, and

Garfield found them "somewhat tiresome." Friday morning the talks concluded, and the chiefs agreed to visit Jocko with Garfield.[24] Charlo, Arlee, and Adolph took the negotiations much more seriously than did Garfield.

Garfield made generous promises of money and economic assistance to the Salish but passed over the failure of the government to carry out provisions of the 1855 treaty. He only wanted to discuss arrangements for the removal. The surviving transcript of the negotiations, held near St. Mary's Mission, quotes Garfield as admitting: "The President and Congress are keeping all the treaties and paying all the money, that belong to them [the Salish and Kootenai tribes], and they know there are rascals [government employees?] that cheat them, but that is no fault of theirs [the president and Congress?]".[25]

Charlo responded that in 1855 Governor Stevens had agreed to the Salish remaining in the Bitterroot Valley. In addition, Charlo pointed out that the Great Father had neither visited western Montana nor had the Bitterroot Valley or the Jocko Reservation surveyed and examined to see which would be a better home for the Salish.

Arlee, the next speaker, stated that the government had failed to provide the Salish with a schoolmaster, a blacksmith, a carpenter, or a doctor as provided for in the 1855 treaty. (Garfield made a short response suggesting that these services were provided at Jocko.) Arlee then challenged the moral and legal authority of the white government to invade Salish territory and force them to adopt white culture, or to compel the tribe to leave their Bitterroot home: "Now if I was to ask you to be an Indian and do like Indians would you do it? If I was to find your people in another country as the white men found us here, and tell them to go away, that I wanted to put my people there would you like it?" Arlee concluded with a complaint that the Salish had not gotten the money promised them, and pointed out the long history of friendship and peace between the Salish and the whites. Garfield answered: "If the President can get men honest enough to give you this money you shall have it. We dont [*sic*] want you to become white men, We want you to be by yourselves."

The last Salish speaker was Adolph, who insisted that Stevens had agreed to the Salish remaining in the Bitterroot Valley. The 1855 treaty also required the Salish to keep the peace with the whites and other tribes, and Adolph asserted the Salish had worked hard to fulfill that commitment. Under the treaty the government was to provide the Salish with horses, cattle, and plows. These payments had never arrived, and Adolph had to plow with his own hands: "[T]hey are worn out."

Charlo refused to go to the Jocko Reservation: "We will not go, we will not accept the terms. I speak for my tribe."

Garfield then put his demands in the form of an ultimatum: "I want you to tell me before I go if you want me to say to the great father when I go back that his children the Flatheads will not leave the Bitter Root valley, and will not obey his order. You can give me your answer in the morning."

In light of the white militias and the war hysteria circulating among their white neighbors, the Salish leaders decided that night that equivocation might help defuse the crisis. The next morning Charlo informed Garfield: ". . . I don't want you to go back and tell the great father that his children the Flatheads will not obey his order. The Chiefs will go with you to the Jocko as you desire, and will then tell you what you may say to the great father for his children."

On Sunday, August 25, 1872, the council was reconvened at the Jocko Agency. Again Garfield made generous promises of aid and security if the Salish moved to the reservation. The chiefs insisted that they did not want conflict, but asked how they could believe Garfield's promises. Charlo's position was stated early in the negotiation: "We will not talk mean against the Great Chief. We do not like to come here [to the Jocko Reservation], nor do we like to become citizens and remain on the Bitter Root. How could I be a white man? My skin is red. This is my land as well as the Bitter Root. I do not see why he wants to put me here borrowing this land. I want you to tell me how it is going to be about this land [the Jocko]".[26]

Arlee expressed the fear that after a few years the government would want the land in Jocko for white farmers: "Some are afraid this land will go as the Bitter Root has. They told us we should always have that, but in a few years they take it away." Garfield countered that the white government would never be unfair to the Salish and they should trust the Great Father. Adolph cautioned, "Only one thing, Charlois and I do not believe all we hear." Chief Arlee took a more pragmatic approach and asked Garfield, "Will you give more?" Garfield offered Charlo a paper making him chief of the Flathead Reservation tribes, but Charlo's answer was succinct: "No."

Near the conclusion of the negotiations, Adolph returned again to his concern: "Will you move us from here if we come?" Garfield's glib response appears even more ironic in light of the forced opening of the reservation to white homesteaders in the early twentieth century: "We [the white people] should be everlastingly cursed if we do [take the Jocko Reservation land] without your consent."

A few lines later Adolph said that whites in the Bitterroot had told the Salish that after forcing the Indians out of the Bitterroot, the government would want the Jocko land for white farmers. Garfield again assured the chiefs: "There are some bad men who tell you these things."

At the conclusion of the meeting, only Arlee and Adolph signed the agreement. Charlo emphasized his desire for peace and hedged his refusal to sign to defuse the threat of violence from the whites: "I am not mad, but I must see what is done here [in the Jocko Valley] and see my people."

After the meeting concluded, the Salish chiefs returned to the Bitterroot Valley, and Garfield traveled east to report to the Office of Indian Affairs and later campaign for the Republican ticket in Ohio.[27] No violence broke out, and the white militias quietly disbanded. The immediate goal of the Salish chiefs—to remain in the Bitterroot Valley while avoiding conflict with the white government—had been achieved. The long-range goal of maintaining an independent Salish community in the Bitterroot was still in question.

Soon after Garfield's report was published, a bizarre controversy broke out about whether Charlo had signed the agreement. Garfield clearly stated in his official report that Arlee and Adolph had signed the contract, "but Charlot refused to sign." According to Garfield, Arlee and Adolph expected Charlo to agree to remove if he saw the government actually carrying out the terms of the agreement. Garfield instructed Jasper Viall, Montana superintendent of Indian Affairs, to proceed with house construction and other preparations at Jocko "in the same manner as though Charlot, the first chief, had signed the contract. I do this in the belief that when he sees the work actually going forward he will conclude to come here with the other chiefs and thus keep the tribe unbroken."[28] Thus, in two places in the published report Garfield clearly stated that Charlo did not sign the agreement, and the original agreement in the files of the commissioner of Indian Affairs has no mark after Charlo's name.[29] The published report, however, was printed with an "x" mark after Charlo's name.

Charlo, of course, was deeply offended when told that his mark had been added to the published document, and the "forged" document quickly became a staple of Salish history. If Garfield had wanted to forge Charlo's mark on the agreement, he would probably have added an X to the original copy and dropped the explicit statements in the report noting that Charlo had refused to sign. However, Garfield never tried to clear up the confusion over Charlo's X. Since Garfield represented Montana as legal counsel in several court cases and was a frequent correspondent of Governor Potts and other Montanans, he must have known about the controversy, but he made no effort to clarify the record. Shortly after his return east, Garfield wrote about his Montana trip for a New York City newspaper. In this article, Garfield mentions that two of the Salish chiefs signed the agreement, but he makes no reference to Charlo's refusal to sign.[30] In an April 27, 1878, House of Representatives debate over the funding for the Bitterroot Salish in Jocko, Garfield stated that Charlo was "a very intelligent and enterprising man," but "was unwilling to leave that place [the Bitterroot Valley], even for large pecuniary advantages."[31] The documentation on Garfield's trip does not clarify his role, if any, in adding Charlo's mark to the printed report or his intentions at the time. Even if he was not responsible for adding the X to the report, he did not seem anxious to clarify the record and highlight his failure to negotiate a removal agreement with all of the Salish chiefs.

When Garfield left Montana, he planned to impress Charlo by having the agreement "carried out scrupulously in all respects."[32] Unfortunately, he also had the Salish houses in the Jocko built on the cheap by using agency employees paid with funds from the 1855 treaty.[33] Horace Countryman was chosen as contractor for the houses based on his qualifications as a faithful Republican.[34] Bungling and incompetence characterized the work, but Arlee and his extended family removed to the Jocko Reservation during the fall of 1873.[35] Arlee was given the old agency building and farm because he was not satisfied with the house that the government had built for him. Indian inspector J. W. Daniels reported on November 13, 1873, that the new houses constructed by the government were made of green lumber that had "shrunk so bad that they are not fit for human beings to live in."[36] Congress failed to fund the Garfield agreement, and agent Daniel Shanahan had to use his personal credit to purchase a cooking stove that Garfield had promised Arlee.[37] In March 1875, agent Peter Whaley wrote to Washington for funds to provide Arlee with six hundred bushels of wheat specifically mentioned in the Garfield agreement.[38] Any possibility of impressing the Salish with the value and reliability of government commitments failed miserably. Charlo and Adolph watched the government's failure to carry out the Garfield agreement, and they, with most of the Bitterroot Salish, remained in the Bitterroot Valley.

At the same time the government was drawing up land patents for those who remained in the Bitterroot. The provision in the 1872 law granting Bitterroot Salish farmers patents to their improved lands was meant to allow individual farmers to leave the tribe and remain in the Bitterroot Valley.

The Salish exploited this provision in their attempt to secure a land base for an independent Bitterroot Salish community. The federal bureaucracy struggled with three issues surrounding the patents: (1) How many Bitterroot Salish were farmers and what defined a farm? (2) How much land should be patented to each Salish farmer? And (3) Had the Salish farmers abandoned their "tribal relations with said tribe," as required by the statute?

The first quandary for the Office of Indian Affairs was to determine how many Salish, twenty-one years of age or the head of a family, were on June 5, 1872, "actually residing upon and cultivating any portion of said lands." In 1871, Flathead agent C. S. Jones found thirty-five Salish farms in the Bitterroot Valley averaging twelve acres each.[39] On April 25, 1873, Flathead Indian agent Daniel Shanahan reported that fifty-two Salish families had planted crops in 1873.[40] On May 16, 1873, James Wright, Montana superintendent of Indian Affairs, referred to about fifty Salish families who were farming.[41] The *New North-West*, the Deer Lodge newspaper, claimed on October 25, 1873, that only fourteen Salish farmers were entitled to patents, and some of them were cultivating the same ground in common.[42] Fifty-one patents were finally issued in 1876. Many Salish farmers probably had a small cabin and garden and cooperatively worked a neighbor's field during planting and harvesting seasons. In the early 1870s most Salish farmers still relied on hunting and gathering for much of their sustenance.

The second question in implementing the patent provisions of the 1872 law was to determine how much land each Salish farmer would receive. Not surprisingly, Montana newspapers campaigned to have the law interpreted to give Salish farmers as little land as possible. They would limit the patents to only those forty acre subdivisions that were being cultivated by Salish farmers on June 5, 1872.[43] Given that most of the Salish farms were small and many were farmed cooperatively, few Salish farmers would get more than forty acres. Many would have gotten only part interest in a 40-acre parcel. Columbus Delano, then secretary of the Interior, decided to interpret the 1872 law liberally and give each Salish farmer remaining in the Bitterroot a patent for 160 acres. The commissioner of the General Land Office had proposed following the conservative interpretation advocated by Montana newspapers, but Delano ordered the office to take the more liberal approach. Delano argued that "great inequality" would result from giving Salish farmers patents to only those quarter sections on which the farmers had improvements. Farmers whose improvements were, by chance, in the middle of a quarter section would receive only 40 acres, while other farmers who straddled the quarter section boundaries would receive 80, 120, or 160 acres.[44]

The patent process for those Salish who decided to remain in the Bitterroot began with a list of farmers assembled by John R. Winslett for James Wright, the Montana superintendent of Indian Affairs, in spring 1873. Winslett was a native of Georgia who had come to the Bitterroot Valley in 1865. With his partner, John Houk, Winslett ran the first general merchandise store in Stevensville and knew most of the Salish.[45] Winslett's list had several categories. The first section of eighteen names was headed: "Names on this Column I Know to be Farming." This section included such prominent Salish as Charlo, Arlee, Adolph, Sappeal [Sapiel], Delaware Jim, Charles Lamoose, Antoine Ninepipe, Gabriel Lumprey, Joe Barnaby, Baptiste Matt[e], Joseph Matt[e], Francois Eneas [Lamoose], and Antoine Arlee. The second category included another thirty-three Salish: "Names on this Column Say they are Farmers." This portion of the list had Isaac Red Wolf, Shawnee Jack, Narcisse, Big Sam, Joseph Lamoose, John Kaiser [Kizer], Joseph Collooyah, and twenty-six others. Winslett's list closed with the names of five men who "Say they are not Farmers but will not leave," and eight women who told Winslett they were farmers.[46]

In June 1873, James Wright directed Washington Hall, the Missoula County surveyor, to survey the lands occupied by the Bitterroot Salish.[47] On July 25, 1873, Hall submitted maps and a list of fifty-four Salish "ranches." Eight or nine Salish who were away on a buffalo hunt and fifteen or twenty others who could not make it to Hall in time to sign the list were not included. Hall suggested that they could be located later on unoccupied land in the Bitterroot.[48] Since Arlee had not yet moved to Jocko, he was to receive a patent on land east of Stevensville. During spring 1874, Hall surveyed sixty-six additional farms for the Salish who were left off the first list.[49] Finally, in 1876, the General Land Office patented the land of fifty-one of the fifty-four Salish farmers on Hall's initial list. The claims of Widow Matte, Maltine, and Old Felix were suspended because portions conflicted with John Owen's Oregon Donation Act land claim.[50]

If Charlo and the Salish leaders accepted the patents, presumably that would indicate their willingness to abandon tribal relations and become U.S. citizens. It would also open the Salish to taxes and regulation by the laws of Montana whites. Since neither alternative offered by the federal government—to move to the Jocko Reservation or remain in the Bitterroot Valley as U.S. citizens—were acceptable, the Salish resorted to a strategy of calculated ambiguity. Charlo refused to agree to remove to Jocko but also stated that, even if the government used force to move him, he would not fight the whites.[51] This allowed the Salish to avoid conflict with the government and still remain in the Bitterroot Valley.

As the 1870s progressed, the Salish leaders needed a strategy to protect as much of their Bitterroot land base as possible while not giving up their tribal relations or legal status as Indians. Since the fifty-one land patents and three suspended applications had been recorded in the General Land Office, those lands at least were safe from claims by white settlers. The Salish refused, however, to accept delivery of the patents, and the documents remained at the Jocko Agency.[52] As part of the strategy, the Salish would not cooperate with the assessor or pay the taxes claimed by Missoula County.[53]

Despite the limitations of their situation, the tactics of the Salish in dealing with the Garfield negotiations and the removal efforts of the early 1870s had several positive results:

- The 1872 law allowed Bitterroot whites to receive title to their farms, so the Salish community was no longer a direct threat to the land claims of their white neighbors.
- The war hysteria among western Montana whites dissipated without violence, even though most Salish remained in the Bitterroot Valley.
- The land patents issued by the General Land Office protected at least part of the Salish land base from white claims.
- The Salish refused to abandon tribal relations or submit to Missoula County taxes while simultaneously emphasizing their desire to avoid conflict.

Given the explosive situation that Salish leaders were facing in early 1872, their strategy resulted in at least the temporary preservation and survival of a Salish community in the Bitterroot Valley.

One of the biggest crises for the Salish occurred during the summer of 1877 when the hostile Nez Perces passed through the Bitterroot Valley. The Salish warned the Nez Perces not to harm the Bitterroot whites, and they refused to attack the Nez Perces without provocation. Some Salish men, including Martin Charlo, joined the white soldiers and settlers at Fort Fizzle in an unsuccessful effort to prevent the Nez Perces from entering the valley. The federal government rewarded Salish friendship with a prohibition on sales of guns and ammunition to the tribe. Bitterroot whites, however, responded with a petition asking Missoula County to drop efforts to tax the Bitterroot Salish. The 1870s closed with the Salish at peace with the whites, and still on their farms and ranches in the Bitterroot Valley.

## Senator Vest Visits the Bitterroot

The next meeting between the Bitterroot Salish leaders and a high-level government delegation from Washington was in September 1883. This meeting occurred soon after August 25, 1883, when Charlo returned from the last plains buffalo hunt of the Bitterroot Salish. The hunt was a failure because the buffalo herds had been exterminated, and the hunters had lost most of their horses to thieves.[54] One of the foundations of the Salish economy had been destroyed, and the Salish leaders were confronting wrenching economic adjustments if they were to survive in the Bitterroot. On September 10, a little more than two weeks after Charlo's embarrassing return from the buffalo hunt, Senator George G. Vest of Missouri and Montana delegate Martin Maginnis arrived at Stevensville. Vest had been a senator since 1879 and had a special interest in Yellowstone National Park and the western territories.[55] On September 11, Vest and his party visited Father Anthony Ravalli, S.J., at St. Mary's Mission while waiting for Charlo to arrive. Charlo and four or five other Salish appeared two hours later and commenced a stormy meeting with Vest. Unfortunately, the transcript of the meeting has not survived, and only portions of the exchange are mentioned in the historical record. According to an unnamed Stevensville correspondent of the *Weekly Missoulian,* Vest made generous promises of improved ranches, wagons, homes, and horses if the Salish removed to Jocko. Vest also promised Charlo that the Salish could sell their improvements in the Bitterroot and keep the proceeds. Charlo was unimpressed with the new promises and "cooly [*sic*] refused" Vest's inducements.[56]

Vest then produced a printed copy of the 1872 Garfield report with the X next to Charlo's name and accused Charlo of signing the agreement and failing to keep his word. Since the Salish had refused to remove or accept the patents for their Bitterroot lands and become citizens, the senator argued that they no longer had any claim to lands in the Bitterroot. Vest threatened to call troops from Fort Missoula to arrest Charlo and forcibly carry him and his warriors to the fort "like so many bags of grain."[57]

Charlo replied indignantly,

> "You may carry me to Fort Missoula dead, but you will never carry me there alive. I heard before . . . that your great father had printed a book showing my name to the treaty, but I never signed nor told anybody else to sign it for me. As to carrying me to the fort like a bag of grain, you did not talk that way when your people were going to California and came through my country sick and hungry. I had many warriors then and could have killed them all, but we nursed and fed them and did all we could to make them happy. Nearly all my warriors are dead, and I have only women and children. You have your foot on my head now," he said, as he threw on the floor a fragment of an old woolen hat and put his foot upon it, "but then I had my foot on your head."

To accentuate the unfairness of any forced removal of the Salish from the Bitterroot, Charlo pointed to the Nez Perce War of 1877: "There is not a drop of white blood on the hands of my people, and when Joseph, the Nez Perce, my kinsman, marched through my country on his way to Canada I refused to take his hand because it had white blood on it, and told him that if he hurt a single one of the whites in Bitter Root Valley I would attack him with my warriors at once." Charlo then pointed to an old blind Indian in the room who in 1877 had put himself in danger to defend the white wife of the Stevensville blacksmith from being harmed by the Nez Perces. Charlo referred Vest to Father Ravalli as an eyewitness to the 1872 negotiations with Garfield who could verify that Charlo had never signed the contract.[58]

According to Vest's description of the meeting, he then made arrangements for the Salish leaders to be fed at the Stevensville tavern, and he himself slipped out to talk to Father Ravalli. Ravalli corroborated Charlo's statement that he had not signed the Garfield agreement. When the meeting resumed at St. Mary's Mission, a chastened Vest proposed that Charlo travel to Washington to negotiate directly with the Great Father, and Charlo agreed. On his return east, Vest went to the secretary of the Interior to check the original copy of the 1872 Garfield agreement and verified that it did not have Charlo's mark or signature on it. The secretary agreed with Vest that Charlo had suffered "a great outrage," and approved a visit to Washington by Charlo and a few members of his tribe.[59]

The response of the Montana white population and the local newspapers in 1883 was very different from their responses in 1872. By 1883 Bitterroot whites had title to their farms, Missoula had Fort Missoula and the Northern Pacific Railroad, and the Salish had demonstrated their desire for peace by defending Bitterroot whites against the Nez Perces. One article in the *Weekly Missoulian* on February 15, 1884, even referred to Charlo and the other Salish leaders as "prominent citizens of Missoula county."[60] The efforts of the Salish leaders during the 1870s to remain in the Bitterroot Valley but avoid military conflict with the whites had been successful. In 1883, however, the leadership faced a new trial in adapting their economy to the end of the buffalo hunts.

## The 1884 Salish Delegation to Washington

During the winter of 1883–84 the Office of Indian Affairs made arrangements for Salish leaders to visit Washington, D.C. On November 8, Flathead agent Peter Ronan recommended Michel Revais, the Flathead Agency's interpreter, to interpret for the Salish delegation. Ronan also advised that the delegation include several Bitterroot Salish headmen as well as Charlo.[61] On November 19, the commissioner of Indian Affairs authorized Ronan to visit Washington with Charlo, the agency interpreter, and two Bitterroot Salish headmen.[62] When Ronan and Charlo met to discuss the trip in early January 1884, Charlo requested that the Bitterroot delegation be enlarged to five so that all factions of the Salish community could be represented.[63] On January 10, the commissioner granted permission for Charlo, four Salish headmen, Ronan, and an interpreter to travel to Washington.[64]

On Thursday morning, January 17, Charlo, Antoine Moiese, Louis Vanderburg, Thomas Abel Adams, and John Hill departed Missoula accompanied by Flathead agent Peter Ronan and interpreter Michel Revais.[65] Once in Washington, Ronan and the Salish delegation plunged into a whirl of social engagements in addition to their negotiations with Henry M. Teller, the secretary of the Interior. Ronan and the delegates already knew several socially prominent Washingtonians, including Joseph K. McCammon, the assistant attorney general who had negotiated with the reservation Salish and Kootenais in 1882 for the Northern Pacific Railroad right-of-way; Capt. John Mullan, who had directed the building of the Mullan Road through western Montana thirty years before and was head of the Bureau of Catholic Indian Missions in 1884; and Senator George G. Vest of Missouri, who had visited the Bitterroot in 1883. The delegation was widely introduced to Washington society by Ronan's political mentor, Montana delegate Martin Maginnis. Soon after arriving in Washington, Ronan wrote to his wife in Montana that "Just now (I suppose for lack of other beasts) Agent Ronan and his Indians are the lions of Washington. I am actually over-run with invitations for myself and the other animals." A week later, Ronan observed that "Charlot is the hero of the day, and although there are four other Indian Delegations now in the city, he and his people receive most exclusive attention from the government officials and citizens."[66]

Charlo and the delegation had several meetings with President Chester A. Arthur while they were in Washington. On Monday, February 4, following the last negotiating session with Secretary Teller, the entire delegation was presented to the president by Maginnis. Maginnis made a speech outlining the history of Salish friendship with the whites, and President Arthur shook Charlo's hand and thanked him for the kindness the Salish had shown the white people.[67] The grand social event of the trip was the annual presidential reception on February 5 attended by more than three thousand people. By special request of the president, Ronan and the Salish delegation stood opposite the receiving line so they could hear the names announced and view the callers as they passed. The heat in the reception room was oppressive, so after an hour of viewing the introductions, Ronan, Charlo, and the other delegates exited to an ovation from the assembled crowd.[68]

Also providing a backdrop to the 1884 negotiations were operations seeking to restore Charlo's and Michel Revais's eyesight. Charlo was nearly blind from cataracts, and as a once-successful hunter, the loss of his eyesight had been particularly depressing. Revais, the agency interpreter, was totally blind and had to be led around by the arm. Senator Vest suggested that a doctor be engaged to operate on Charlo's and Revais's eyes as an aid to the negotiations. When Charlo and Revais consented, they were examined by Dr. William V. Marmion, a leading eye specialist. Vest cautioned Marmion to operate only if he was certain the operations would succeed. Charlo asked Ronan to be present during his operation, which was performed on Thursday, February 7. Charlo delivered a speech in Salish while anesthetized, which Revais interpreted for the benefit of Dr. Marmion. Charlo's operation was successful in restoring his eyesight, but Revais's was not.[69]

Although impressed with all the attention and excited about his restored eyesight, Charlo continued to insist on the right of the Salish to stay in the Bitterroot Valley. No transcript of Charlo's negotiations has survived, but the historical sources indicate that Teller used the familiar strategy of generous promises of material aid combined with the argument that moving to Jocko would benefit the Salish people. According to Vest, Teller offered

Charlo and each Salish head of family who moved to the Jocko Reservation houses, fenced and plowed farms, cattle, horses, seed, and agricultural equipment. In addition Charlo was to get an annual pension of five hundred dollars and government recognition as the chief of the Salish. Still skeptical of government promises, Charlo declined the inducements offered. He continued to insist on his right to remain in the Bitterroot because "The Bitter Root valley is my home, my land. I own it. The blood of my ancestors is mixed with its dust and I feel as though I were resting on my mother's bosom. I am like a tree whose roots are imbedded in the soil and nothing but a hurricane can tear me out."[70]

During the Washington visit, Charlo and the other Salish thought they had a government promise to provide the Salish with one hundred 160-acre farms in the Bitterroot, free from taxation.[71] According to Ronan the "one hundred" patent figure had been mentioned by "a private and unofficial gentleman" and was not a formal commitment. As it turned out, only the fifty-one patents issued under the Garfield agreement were available to the Bitterroot Salish.[72] Charlo and the delegation interpreted the reduction to fifty-one as further evidence of government chicanery.

Charlo and the other Salish delegates made specific complaints to the secretary of the Interior about Missoula County's repeated attempts to force the Bitterroot Salish to pay taxes. According to Ronan, "The Hon. Secretary stated emphatically to the Indians [in the 1884 delegation] that they would not be forced to pay taxes."[73] The bureaucrats in Washington later reinterpreted the secretary's promise to apply only to the land, not the stock or other property owned by the Salish. The commissioner of Indian Affairs wrote on May 8, 1885, that "it is believed that the Honorable Secretary had reference to the taxation of their *lands* which . . . are not subject to sale for non-payment of taxes assessed thereon."[74]

Secretary Teller did conclude in 1884 that since the Salish held title to the Bitterroot allotments, it would not be right to force them out of the Bitterroot Valley.[75] Teller agreed that the Salish could remain in the valley as long as they maintained peaceful relations with their white neighbors. Charlo agreed to not oppose the removal of those Bitterroot Salish families who chose to move to Jocko. No assistance was promised to those Salish who remained in the Bitterroot, but Ronan met with Teller later and outlined the economic poverty of the Bitterroot Salish. Teller gave Ronan verbal instructions to visit the band on his return to Montana and report to the Department of Interior about how the government could assist the tribe.[76]

After returning to Montana, Ronan met with Charlo and the other Bitterroot Salish in council for five days in March 1884. According to Ronan, at first Charlo agreed to not object or hinder those Salish families who wanted to remove to the Jocko Reservation. Later in the council, however, Charlo complained that the government had promised 103 or 104 patents but had delivered only 51, and that in Washington more financial support had been promised to those who removed than Ronan was offering. The final result of the council was that 21 of the 95 Bitterroot Salish families agreed to remove to Jocko. Each family was to receive

> 1st A choice of 160 acres of unoccupied land on this Reservation.
> 2d Assistance in the erection of a substantial house.
> 3d Assistance in fencing & breaking up of a field of at least ten acres.
> 4th The following gifts—
> Two Cows
> A wagon and harness
> A plow with other necessary Agricultural Implements
> Seed for the first year & provisions until the first crop was harvested.

Ronan's survey of Salish farmers in the Bitterroot found only five who had sufficient agricultural implements and other requisites "as to enable them to make a living by farming." The Salish farmers in the Bitterroot did "have some forty dwellings Surrounded by enclosed farms, and, in addition, about twenty small fenced fields. These they are not only willing but anxious to cultivate,—having a very fair knowledge of farming gained by hiring to their white neighbors during Seeding and harvesting times." Ronan enclosed an estimate for supplies, agricultural equipment, and clerical help to aid both those Salish who removed to Jocko and those who remained in the Bitterroot Valley.[77]

Secretary Teller endorsed Ronan's recommendations and sent Congress a request for $21,000 for the Bitterroot Salish.[78] The Indian Department Appropriations Act of 1884 included the $21,000 item to aid both the Bitterroot Salish who removed and those who chose to remain in the valley. The law specified that the money was to be immediately available on passage, but it was not signed by the president until July 4, 1884.[79] The funds were thus too late for the 1884 growing season, but Ronan did receive the appropriations needed to fulfill his promises to those Salish who had removed to Jocko and to give substantial economic aid to those who remained in the Bitterroot Valley. The 1885 Indian Department Appropriations Act included an additional $18,000 for Charlo's band.[80]

Problems remained, however, regarding the Bitterroot Salish land base. The fifty-one patents, plus three suspended entries, were filed under the names of individual Salish, not the tribe. Many of the patentees had removed to Jocko and were not using their Bitterroot claims, and others did not know where their land was located. Young heads of families and those who were left out of the 1873 list for patents were often willing to start farming or to expand their existing farms on unclaimed land, but they needed protection from white settlers later filing claims on their improved farms.

On February 7, 1885, Father Jerome D'Aste of St. Mary's Mission wrote a letter for Charlo with proposals to settle some of the land problems. Charlo agreed to accept the fifty-one patents issued under the 1872 law in lieu of the 100 patents he understood had been promised in Washington in 1884. Charlo requested that (1) the government "appoint some trusty man" to show the Salish farmers where the property lines ran; (2) assign those patents issued to Salish who were now on the Jocko Reservation to landless Bitterroot Valley Salish; and (3) issue patents to those Indians with improved farms on the public domain to protect them from claims by whites. Charlo also asked that the government fulfill its promise that the Salish holdings would be exempt from taxes. Ronan endorsed Charlo's proposals and forwarded the letter to Washington.[81]

The commissioner of Indian Affairs responded on May 8, 1885, that the patented lands could not be reassigned without an act of Congress, and in the meantime the patents belonged to the patentees or their heirs as determined by the Montana laws governing inheritance. Salish farmers with improvements on the public domain could get Indian homestead patents without paying fees or commissions by filing affidavits with the Missoula County clerk. Regarding taxes, the commissioner referred to an earlier decision that the 1872 Bitterroot Salish lands could not be sold for nonpayment of taxes. Under the Indian Homestead Act of 1875, any new Indian homestead patents were not taxable for twenty years after a patent was issued.[82] The commissioner's reply assumed that the stock and personal property of the Bitterroot Salish were taxable. No record has been found of any Indian Homestead Act claims being filed in the Bitterroot Valley during the late 1880s. The fifty-one patents issued under the 1872 law and the three suspended claims that partially conflicted with John Owen's claim seem to have been the extent of the Bitterroot Salish legal land base.

## Partial Success

By 1885 and 1886 Charlo and the other Bitterroot Salish leaders had weathered some harrowing storms. Their deft handling of Salish–U.S. government relations between 1868 and 1886 had helped the Bitterroot Salish community to survive. Their emphasis on maintaining peace with the white settlers, combined with an ambiguous refusal to acquiesce to government demands that they move to the Jocko Reservation, defused the immediate threat of war in 1872. Once Bitterroot whites received title to their lands and Missoula got its fort, the militias disbanded, and much of the white hysteria dissipated. Dealings with the U.S. government were an important facet of tribal survival, but managing relations with local whites and preserving the tribe's economic independence were more immediately critical to the Salish.

As successful as the peace strategy had been, it was only a prelude to a new crisis that threatened the Bitterroot Salish in the 1880s: how to cope with the loss of the plains buffalo and other game resources. The struggle to expand their farms to replace the shrinking hunting and gathering resources was a painful recourse for the Salish, but it was their only hope for maintaining economic independence and remaining in the Bitterroot Valley. In the mid-1880s Salish diplomacy had even resulted in significant economic aid to help expand Salish farms. Questions remained about whether the Salish controlled enough land in 1886 to support the community, but efforts to develop their farms and herds gave the Salish hope they could succeed and remain in the Bitterroot Valley.

CHAPTER 6

# Hesitant Friendship

## Salish-White Cooperation and Amity in the Bitterroot Valley, 1870–1891

Bitterroot Valley whites celebrated July 4, 1877, with a picnic near Sweathouse Creek, about a mile from Chief Charlo's ranch. The feast assembled by the white settlers was described by an admiring journalist, Will Sutherlin:

> There were light bread, boiled ham, chickens and turkey; there were currants, gooseberries, raspberries and strawberries, pies, great piles of them, doughnuts, cookies, jelly cakes, confectioneries, and great stacks of pound cakes, whitened and coated, carved and trimmed as neatly as if designed for a queen's table. Besides these, there was a great variety of nicknacks which were palatable. The desert [*sic*] was large dishes of delicious strawberries and cream.

After the white celebrants had eaten their fill, more than half of the food remained. Seventy or eighty Bitterroot Salish and Nez Perces were fashionably late, but in time for the second sitting with some recent white arrivals. Sutherlin mentions Flathead Brown, an Indian farmer; Delaware John [John Hill], an Indian Civil War veteran who had married into the Salish tribe; and Plenty of Bear [Many Bear], half Nez Perce and half Salish, dressed up in a stovepipe hat with a pretty feather in it. A half dozen young Salish and Nez Perces at the feast were "all painted and rigged up in fancy style." Among the other Indian guests, Sutherlin made special notice of Mary Lumprey, the eighteen-year-old mixed-blood daughter of the "wealthiest man in the Bitter Root valley." When the Indians were about through, Chief Charlo and his family arrived. Their white hosts made them welcome and treated them to cake and pies.

Sutherlin felt compelled to explain to his white readers in eastern Montana that the Salish and the white Bitterroot Valley settlers had a history of peaceful coexistence. Many of the Salish and Nez Perces living in the Bitterroot had "little farms of their own, and some of them have considerable property in horses and cattle." It was the custom of the white people of the Bitterroot to give their Salish neighbors "an occasional feast, and the Fourth of July is as well remembered by them as by most white people." After the feast, everyone enjoyed using a large swing erected between two trees, jumping rope, and racing each other on foot.[1]

Salish-white relations in the Bitterroot were not always as carefree and pleasant as on July 4, 1877. Some whites were attracted by the profits of selling whiskey to young Salish men. Cultural misunderstandings arose from the Salish tradition of sharing with friends and allies and expecting return generosity. White expectations of exclusive use of fenced grazing meadows and their refusal to respect Salish claims to traditional gathering and hunting sites added friction to the relationship.

Relations with the federal government were important for the Bitterroot Salish during the late nineteenth century, but during most of the period the Salish had an even more vital concern: managing contacts with the white residents of western Montana. Avoiding friction during day-to-day Salish-white dealings in the valley while protecting the property and interests of tribal members occupied more Salish leadership time than the occasional visits of government officials. The Salish also struggled to avoid the drunken brawl or revenge murder that might start a war with the white settlers and the U.S. government. During the summer of 1877 the Salish's Nez Perce allies to the west failed in their labors to avoid a conflict with the whites. The revenge murders of three white men in June 1877 ignited a war that the Nez Perce leaders had sought to avert. The subsequent Nez Perce War resulted in the death of many tribal members, the loss of herds and personal property, and years of exile.[2] The Nez Perce example accentuated the importance of the Salish struggle to maintain peace with the Bitterroot whites.

The relationship between the Salish and white communities in the Bitterroot Valley included both cooperation and conflict, but the Salish and the more responsible members of the white community were able to keep the peace. More incidents of cooperation and friendly exchange between the communities have been documented than those involving conflict, but compiling statistics on the interactions of each type would require a representative sample, which we do not have. The interpretation that the Salish actively worked to maintain the peace is bolstered by evidence of Salish leaders intervening to avoid conflict or mollify friction that did occur. As with most of the events described in this book, little direct evidence of motive has survived, but the actions of leaders in both communities suggest a shared effort to keep the peace. Most Bitterroot white settlers presumably accepted the nineteenth-century American ideology of white racial and cultural superiority. Somehow, despite their racial and cultural prejudices, they were able to treat their Salish neighbors with some respect and courtesy, and to work for peace.

The preponderance of evidence presented below gives white viewpoints of Salish-white interactions in the Bitterroot Valley. Despite this problem, the evidence does support several general conclusions. First, Salish-white relations in the Bitterroot Valley between 1870 and 1891 were generally peaceful and often friendly. Second, the Salish people made explicit efforts to keep the peace and avoid conflict between the communities. Third, there is no suggestion in the evidence that the Salish were intimidated. The evidence indicates the Salish chose coexistence in the Bitterroot because they rationally decided peaceful relations offered the best chance for the tribe's survival.

One Salish veteran of the Bitterroot removal, Victor Vanderburg, related that Charlo "had many White friends [in the Bitterroot] and used to go visit them, going from farm to farm and talking with the settlers. He even got so that he could get along without an interpreter."[3]

The success of the Salish policy was further supported by the memories of Mary Ann Topsseh Coombs, who in 1975 was the last Salish survivor of the 1891 removal from the Bitterroot Valley. She did not remember personal economic hardships in the Bitterroot before the removal and specifically noted that her white neighbors had been nice to her: "She especially remembers a blacksmith who was nice to their family. She said it was the government who made them move out, not the neighbors."[4] As mentioned previously, Mary's father was the man who had protected the blacksmith's wife from a drunken Nez Perce warrior in 1877.

## The Demographic Milieu

Salish-white cooperation and friction in the Bitterroot Valley during the late nineteenth century played out within a shifting population milieu. The two most important changes were (1) the dramatic expansion of the white community in the valley, and (2) frequent Salish intermarriage with whites and Indians of other tribes.

The explosive growth of the white population in the Bitterroot Valley complicated relations between the communities. In the late 1860s and early 1870s, the government estimated the Salish population at about 550. The 1870 federal census found 265 whites and 45 mixed-bloods in the valley. In 1870, the Salish band in the Bitterroot outnumbered the whites almost two to one. In twenty years the population figures showed a dramatic reversal. The 1890 federal census recorded approximately 3,500 white people living in the valley at a time when the Bitterroot Salish band had dwindled to just 176 members: the Bitterroot Salish were outnumbered twenty to one by the white Bitterroot residents (Figure 6.1). Consequently, the competition for declining hunting, gathering, and open grazing resources in the valley became increasingly intense.

The other demographic development that impacted the ability of the Salish to maintain peaceful relations with the white settlers was intermarriage. The St. Mary's Mission *Liber Matrimoniorum*, or *Book of Marriages*, recorded frequent Salish marriages to Indians of other tribes, white men, and mixed-bloods. Of the 154 Indian marriages recorded at St. Mary's

**Figure 6.1.** Indian and white populations in the Bitterroot Valley, 1869–1891

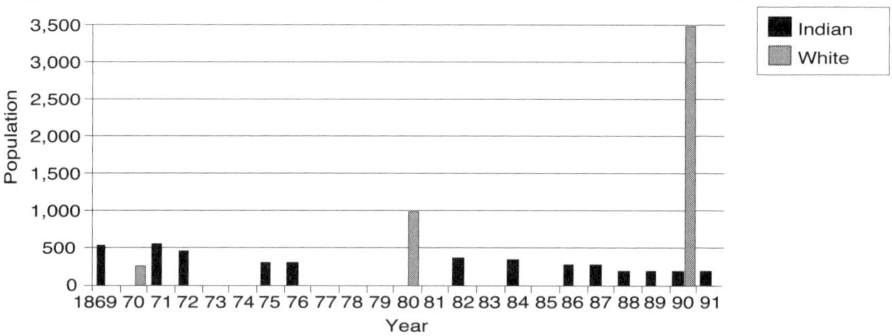


*Sources:* Annual Report of the U.S. Secretary of the Interior (ARSI), 1869, p. 740; Annual Report of the U.S. Commissioner of Indian Affairs (ARCIA), 1871, p. 610; ARCIA, 1872, p. 393; ARSI, 1875, p. 614; ARSI, 1876, p. 618; Jerome D'Aste, S.J., Diaries, entries for Jan. 2, 1882, and Aug. 5, 1884; Bitterroot Salish censuses, 1886–91, National Archives microfilm M595, r. 107; M593, r. 827 (MT, Missoula Co., Bitter Root Valley); National Archives microfilm T9, r. 742 (MT, Missoula Co., Bitter Root Valley); U.S. Census Office, *Compendium of the Eleventh Census* [1890], p. 259.

between 1866 and 1891, 91, or 59 percent, involved at least one partner who was non-Salish or part-non-Salish. Sixty, or 39 percent, of the marriages involved non-Salish Indians, and only 31, or 20 percent, had white or part-white partners. About 30 percent of the non-Salish Indian marriage partners mentioned in the *Liber Matrimoniorum* were white or mixed Salish-white. Seventy percent of the non-full-blood Salish Indian marriage partners mentioned in the *Liber Matrimoniorum* were Indians from other tribes or had parents who were Indians from other tribes. Twenty-eight of those marriage partners were Nez Perces or part Nez Perce; eleven were Kalispel; seven were Delaware; seven were Iroquois; seven were Blackfeet; six were Snake; and the rest were Shawnee, Crow, Kootenai, Assiniboine, Walla Walla, Coeur d'Alene, and Spokane.[5] Most of the out-marriage was with other Indians rather than white people. The 20 percent of the marriages involving white or part-white partners, however, does indicate significant interracial cooperation. The Salish and white communities in the Bitterroot Valley in the late nineteenth century were different, but the boundary between the groups was not fixed or sharp. Some people played roles in both communities.

## Labor and Trading: Salish-White Economic Cooperation in the Bitterroot Valley

Descriptions of Salish-white cooperation in the Bitterroot Valley between 1870 and 1891 include incidents of economic exchange and friendly social interaction. The economic exchanges often involved non-cash exchanges of goods and labor. This evidence suggests that the Bitterroot Salish played an active but limited role in the white Bitterroot economy. Whites had goods and employment opportunities that were desired by the Salish; the Salish had goods—such as meat, horses, and furs—and skills such as digging root crops and handling horses that were desired by the Bitterroot whites.

Economic exchange provided an important part of the positive cooperation between the Salish and white communities. Most of the Salish trade in Bitterroot and Missoula stores was probably based on cash or immediate exchange, which was not recorded in credit ledgers, so Indian commerce was probably more important than the surviving written records indicate. The dollar amounts in the evidence have not been adjusted for inflation. The reader needs to keep in mind that in the year 2008 it took about $22.21 to equal the spending power of $1.00 in 1880.[6]

### *St. Mary's Mission as an Economic Resource*

Extensive detail has survived about the economic relations of the Salish with one white organization in the Bitterroot: St. Mary's Mission. Father Jerome D'Aste's diaries from July 1878 to July 1887 provide a detailed record of financial aspects of the mission and its farm. D'Aste was responsible for mission finances and used his diary to keep a running record of who worked for the mission, who borrowed from the mission, and when wages and loans were settled. Because of the differences between the detail of D'Aste's diaries and the other sources, the evidence from the D'Aste diaries will be presented first. The analysis will be limited to only a sample year, 1879. This breakdown is incomplete but hopefully gives an indication of the mission's economic value to the Bitterroot Salish community.[7]

The priests at St. Mary's employed many local Indians and mixed-bloods, especially in operating the mission farm. Some were hired for wages, but most worked short-term for either money or trade goods during spring planting or fall harvesting. Activities such as getting rails, building fences, plowing, sowing, haying, and harvesting grain, potatoes, and other crops relied heavily on Indian labor. Other white-owned farms in the Bitterroot must have relied primarily on family labor, but many probably employed some Indians during the planting and harvesting seasons. Agent Peter Ronan reported to the commissioner of Indian Affairs on March 27, 1884, that the Bitterroot Salish had "a very fair knowledge of farming gained by hiring to their white neighbors during seeding and harvesting times."[8]

#### Employment

Father D'Aste hired Alexandre [Alexander Big Knife] on March 31, 1879, to work for the mission for $20 a month. Between April 1 and 5, with the help of Francois, Alexandre hauled rails and built a fence around a new garden area. On the afternoon of April 5 they helped kill a steer for the mission larder. From April 7 to 24 Alexandre plowed the mission fields. On April 23 he helped brand the yearlings in its herd. On April 29 Alexandre and his wife were part of the group of Salish Indians who sowed the garden. He left at noon on May 2. Alexandre received nine pounds of sugar, a shirt, a blanket worth $3.50, one hundred pounds of flour, and cash from Father D'Aste. On May 4 Alexandre borrowed eleven and a half bushels of wheat from D'Aste and agreed to return thirteen and a half bushels during the fall of 1879. Alexandre also borrowed five grain sacks to haul the seed wheat, which he returned the next day. Later that summer, on August 11, D'Aste hired Alexandre to help haul hay, and between August 11 and 23 Alexandre and the rest of the mission crew hauled at least fifty-five loads. Between August 25 and 30 Alexandre helped bind grain and haul wheat and oats. D'Aste paid him another $21.

Many other Salish worked for shorter periods. As mentioned above, between April 1 and 5 Francois (possibly Francis Lassoa) worked with Alexandre hauling rails, building a fence, and killing a steer. D'Aste paid Francois $3.50 in cash and gave him 42 pounds of beef. On July 26 Francois gave D'Aste 140 pounds of beef, and on September 23 D'Aste gave Francois 69 pounds of meat.

At the end of April D'Aste hired an Indian crew to sow the garden and plant potatoes. The diaries mention hiring "Felix and wife" (Felix Kezlshulkui and Cecilia), the "dummy and wife" (possibly Isaac Ntatkene and Ann), Alexandre and wife, Charlie's mother (possibly Mary, mother of Charles Koalsheni), and old Sosopie. D'Aste mentions paying four Indian women on April 30 for planting potatoes. During the harvest in late August, St. Mary's employed another Indian crew to bind and thrash grain consisting of John Delaware, Baptiste, Ignace Kaxpchin [Kizer], Stanislaus, Sapié, Martin Charlo, and Alexandre. D'Aste paid the harvesting crew in cash, with the workers getting between $1.00 and $9.00 each. On August 27 "the women" thrashed the peas. D'Aste mentions paying the women on the harvesting crew but did not record the amounts.

Other, more sporadic employment provided by St. Mary's Mission in 1879 included retrieving a horse, breaking a colt, castrating pigs, driving mission cattle across the Bitterroot River, washing clothes, and branding calves. In addition to cash, some of those workers received children's clothing, soda, sugar, blankets, and flour.

## Purchases by the Mission

Operation of St. Mary's Mission also involved purchases from the local Indian population. A few were major, but many involved small amounts of fish, buffalo tongues, or robes. The most costly purchase made by the mission was the neighboring farm owned by Felix. The purchase of Felix's claim and improvements was made before 1879, but payments continued into that year. On April 23 D'Aste paid Felix $60.00, leaving a balance of

$40.00. A few days later Felix received 200 pounds of flour, tea, tobacco, and sugar worth $2.00 for his son, and a mare valued at $25. The final $9.00 owed was paid with $6 to Eugenie on Felix's account on April 27, and $3 to Felix on April 29.

Salish parishioners regularly sold and traded cattle and horses with the mission. On April 6 D'Aste made a deal for a horse with Louis Seme [Vanderburg]. The price was $20 in cash plus twelve bushels of wheat (worth $9) and other goods worth $5. Louis borrowed a grain sack when he got the grain on April 20.

D'Aste traded "Charley's horse for another and paid 6. dollars to boot" on April 20. On May 20 D'Aste traded a red colt, $5 cash, and $5 in trade, and remitted Charley Koalsheni's debt to the mission in exchange for a roan horse. On June 12 D'Aste gave Joseph [Sinkutkuto] one hundred pounds of flour as final payment for a mare. Antoine Chamanà [Pellew] sold D'Aste a yearling steer on May 19 for $4 in cash, one hundred pounds of flour, and five pounds of coffee. Another steer was purchased from Pierre Snatzè on September 25 for $8 and four bushels of wheat to be delivered in spring 1880.

Between July 23 and August 13 the mission crew cut hay on Antoine Chamanà's place. D'Aste paid Antoine $5 on June 26 and $15 on July 29.

Purchases of fish appear regularly in the diaries. Apparently D'Aste was selling some of the fish he purchased in the Bitterroot to the nuns in Missoula and Deer Lodge, and several white men in Missoula.[9] On February 23 D'Aste paid $1.50 for fish, half in beads. On March 23 he gave 50 cents to Pliá for fish. D'Aste bought two lines of salmon on August 15. He made arrangements with "Michael the lame" for a hundred pounds of fish. D'Aste got eight pounds of fish from Joseph (probably Joseph Lamoose) on December 7, twenty-four pounds on December 14, and another eight pounds on December 15. On January 13 D'Aste paid Joseph $2, which could have been an advance payment or loan which was paid off in fish.

On April 5 D'Aste paid $3 for a buffalo robe. A little later, on April 20, D'Aste got nineteen buffalo tongues, for four of which he paid Pierre Snatzè.

## Loans or Purchases on Credit

The mission also made a number of loans or credit sales to Bitterroot Salish Indians. Most of the loans involved money, flour, seed grain, or grain sacks, but tools and miscellaneous items were also loaned. On March 19 Gabriel Lumprey borrowed a shovel and a pick; on April 9 D'Aste gave Antoine

Chamanà butter worth $1 on credit; on April 24 John Koalsheni got a blanket on credit; on June 24 Jemmy Delaware [Delaware Jim] borrowed a tea cup; on July 1 Ignace returned the wagon he had borrowed; and on November 9 Charles Koalsheni borrowed a saddle.

Flour was a commodity frequently loaned by the mission: D'Aste loaned fifty pounds to Pierre [Nkalkaltumsh], Cecile's husband; "the old Chen" [Stephen Kolentitie] got fifty pounds on credit; Charley Sinchelè borrowed fifty pounds; and D'Aste loaned Agnes, wife of Antoine [Felix], fifty pounds. Some returns were also noted. On September 15 Louis Seme returned the one hundred pounds of flour he had borrowed on January 3, and on September 19 Agnes returned fifty pounds of flour. Louise, the widow of Narcisse, gave fifty pounds of flour to D'Aste on September 26.

Cash loans were also made by the mission. D'Aste loaned $2 to Charles Koalsheni; $50 dollars to Joseph [Sinkutkuto], husband of Terese; $1 to the second boy of Joseph Barnabé; $4 to Jean Pierre; and $5 to Louis [Pierre], son of Pierre Ckkaepè.

St. Mary's Mission loaned wheat and grain sacks to farmers at planting season. Placide received ten and a half bushels of wheat on credit, and Samuel borrowed one grain sack. Antoine Chamanà [Pellew] borrowed four bushels and 51 pounds of wheat on April 21 for which he was to return six and a half bushels in the fall. Charles Koalshemi received 139 pounds of wheat from D'Aste on April 27. Gabriel Lumprey borrowed four grain sacks on May 4. On September 26 Mary, the widow of Shawnee Jake [Shawnee Jack], gave D'Aste three bushels of wheat. Presumably she was returning seed wheat loaned by the mission.

D'Aste gave [Joseph] Nustò a sack of seed potatoes on May 11. On September 1 Eugenie delivered to D'Aste one dollar's worth of meat in payment on her bill at the mission.

On July 10, when D'Aste had to haul 2,800 feet of lumber from the sawmill, he borrowed teams from a white man, a mixed-blood married to an Indian, and an Indian farmer: Joseph Lumprey, Joseph Deschamps, and Antoine Ninepipe.

## Gifts

In many cases D'Aste wrote that he "gave" something or "let" someone have something, but it is not always spelled out that these were gifts. St. Mary's Mission "gave the Indians a feast" on August 20. The mission furnished four hundred pounds of flour, twenty-five pounds of coffee, two pounds of yeast powder, twenty pounds of sugar, and thirty-five pounds of apples, and killed two steers for the event. On September 3 D'Aste gave Chen [Stephen] one dollar to buy lumber for a coffin for Agnes, his sixteen-year-old daughter.[10] Most of the gifts D'Aste recorded in 1879 were gifts of flour for Agnes; Jean Pierre; Pierre [Nkalkaltumsh] husband of Cecile; Gabriel Lumprey; Joseph, husband of Terese; and old Sosophie. In 1879 D'Aste recorded regular gifts of cash and other items given to Paul Koalsheni. Over the year D'Aste gave Paul two gifts of one dollar and three of fifty cents in addition to two shirts and a blanket. Father D'Aste also made cash payments to John Koalsheni [John Charley]; Antoine [Seme], a Snake Indian living in the Bitterroot Valley; and Antoine Delaware. Other gifts from D'Aste included four dresses given to four unidentified Indian girls and two dresses given to Spaiol (Anna) and Adelaide. Eugenie, daughter of Felix, got fifty cents' worth of coffee.

The gift giving went in both directions. On June 20 Antoine Chamanà gave the mission nineteen pounds of deer meat, and another nineteen pounds on June 22. D'Aste wrote that Antoine "did not ask any thing." On December 16 Joseph, son of Charles Lamoose, brought thirty-one pounds of deer meat and eleven pounds of fish.

The individual transactions were usually small, but St. Mary's Mission was a regular source of gifts, seasonal employment, and other economic assistance for the Bitterroot Salish Indians, and played an important economic, as well as religious and social, role for the Bitterroot Salish in 1879. The economic activity D'Aste recorded for St. Mary's Mission was probably more extensive than the dealings of the Salish with other white farms and businesses in the Bitterroot and Missoula.

## *Other Evidence of Salish-White Economic Interaction*

### Employment

One important part of the Salish-white economic relationship was employment, and St. Mary's Mission was not the only employer. Records of fifteen other cases of Salish working for white people, and two cases of white people working for Salish employers have survived in the historical literature. Hank Flanagin, a white man, was employed in 1870 by Narcisseau [Narcisse], a wealthy Bitterroot Salish stockman, to herd horses,[11] and at the time of the 1880 census George Redcrow, a prominent Nez Perce rancher who lived with the Salish, employed a white widow, Susan Davis, as a live-in housekeeper. Davis's sons, nineteen and fourteen years old, were also living in the Redcrow household and are listed as "laborers." A forty-five-year-old white man, V. R. Woodmancy, a farmer, also lived with Redcrow and probably worked for him.[12]

Most of the documented incidents of Salish working for whites involved herding and seasonal agricultural work, but some also worked as household domestics and one as an army interpreter. The seasonal agricultural work mentioned in the records included the 1870 employment of Albert Thomas Moore [Pi-Lu'-Ye-Kin], a ten-year-old Nez Perce boy living with the Bitterroot Salish, who helped a white man named Jackson care for a herd of cattle.[13] About the same time James Minesinger, a white man who had married into the Bitterroot Salish tribe, hired Indian workers to patrol his garden with brooms to keep grasshoppers out.[14] In 1871 Frank Marengo, a Salish mixed-blood, helped William E. Bass brand horses.[15] In 1877 John P. Martens of Victor employed two unnamed Indian women to help kill and dress twenty-three hogs, and later that year he paid Tyboo, an Indian boy, one dollar to deliver a mare to a neighboring farm. On December 20, 1877, Martens mentioned that Dutch Lumprey broke a bay cayuse mare for A. S. Blake, a white farmer.[16] Henry Minesinger, a Salish-Shoshoni-white mixed-blood, worked as a ranch hand for Neptune Lynch, a white settler near Plains, in the late 1870s.[17] A white man named McLain owed an unnamed Bitterroot Indian in 1885 for feeding McLain's steer over the winter.[18] According to Bass family records, they regularly employed Indian laborers on their Bitterroot farm to pick apples and other crops in the 1880s.[19]

Mary Minesinger and Ellen Silverthorne, Salish mixed-bloods, performed domestic work for prominent Missoula families in 1880.[20] During the 1880s John B. Catlin employed a mute Indian to saw wood, and Indian women to do laundry work for his Stevensville hotel.[21]

Other payments for work were incidental. Delaware Jim was paid five dollars for five days' work as interpreter for the U.S. Army during the Nez Perce War in 1877.[22] In 1878 a white packer named John Fahey paid an unidentified Salish ten dollars for retrieving a lost mule near the Montana-Idaho border.[23] In 1881 a Bitterroot sawmill hired a mixed-blood Indian worker for three or four days.[24] Lawton Sipple paid an unnamed Salish Indian in the early 1890s fifty cents for catching and returning a runaway horse and buggy.[25] In a February 8, 1878, editorial about the Missoula alcohol trade with local Indians, Chauncey Barbour provided a general outline of the role that Indians—including the Bitterroot Salish—played in the white Missoula economy. Barbour noted that Missoula whites employed Indian labor in "washing and scrubbing, sawing wood, carrying water in the winter, and pulling weeds from gardens in summer." According to Barbour, the Indian trade with Missoula businessmen from the proceeds of Indian labor and the sale of furs and skins was "considerable."[26]

## Trade

Another base of the Salish-white economic relationship in western Montana was trade, or economic exchange, of goods. Most of the documented exchanges refer to trades of Indian horses, furs, meat, fish, and berries for coffee, tea, money, and alcohol. Twenty-nine examples of economic trade between the communities were found in addition to the many examples in Father D'Aste's diaries.

Abram Mittower, a white man, moved to the Bitterroot Valley in 1880. According to family lore, he visited and smoked with his Salish neighbors on his arrival in the valley. During the 1880s the Salish kept the Mittower family supplied with fresh fish and wild game in return for watermelons and apples. Mittower was over six feet tall and was called "Heap Big Abe" by the Salish. Mittower and Charlo became friends as well as neighbors, and Charlo made his only return trip to the Bitterroot Valley after 1891 to testify in a water rights case as a witness for Mittower.[27]

On May 5, 1874, Father Philip Rappagliosi, S.J., a thirty-two-year-old novice missionary at St. Mary's, wrote his parents in Rome that coffee and tea were the common drinks accompanying meals in the Bitterroot Valley, and that the Salish often sold deer and buffalo skins in order to get coffee, tea, and sugar from the whites. Fresh fish were part of the missionary diet, and Rappagliosi mentioned giving a fishhook to a young Indian boy who in return brought a him a seven-pound fish that evening.[28]

Another case of trade involved James Upton Sanders, the son of Wilber Fisk Sanders, the prominent early Montana vigilante, attorney, and politician. James accompanied his father and congressman James A. Garfield to Stevensville on August 21, 1872. Shortly after the party left Missoula that morning, they split into two groups to hunt birds and to fish. The Wilber and James Sanders, Garfield, and W. H. Clagett, the Montana delegate to Congress, took guns to shoot birds on their way to Stevensville. Although unsuccessful, they did come across an unnamed Indian with a string of birds who was persuaded to sell his catch. The white hunters later tried to convince their fishing companions that the birds were their own kill.[29]

James Minesinger, a white man, moved to the Bitterroot Valley in the late 1850s and married Nellie Quick-To-See Smith Monteray, a lady of Spanish, Salish, and Shoshoni Indian descent. Their daughter, Emma Minesinger Magee, recorded that during the 1860s and 1870s, Nellie frequently traded garden produce with the Salish and Nez Perces for wild foods such as fruit, wild onions, wild carrots, camas, and bitterroot. Many Salish buffalo hunters obtained food from the Minesingers that they later paid for with buffalo robes, meat, and tongues. Emma remembered attending the Hell Gate School near Missoula in 1873 with her brother and sister. The Minesinger children took jerked buffalo meat for their lunches, and their white classmates eagerly traded cake, cookies, and pie for some of it.[30]

During the 1881–83 period several Salish tribal members had charge accounts at Chatfield & Bass, which provided blacksmith services and sold tobacco products in Stevensville. Delaware Jim paid one dollar in cash on December 1, 1881. On April 17, 1882, Antoine Ninepipe charged the fifty-cent fee for sharpening his plow. Alex and Baptiste Matte had charges in 1881. Several of the Lumprey children charged cigarettes, cigars, and horseshoeing. The Lumpreys' payments were mostly in cash, but on May 11, 1882, Henry Lumprey traded in a horse as partial payment on his bill for cigars.[31]

Most of the references to Salish-white trade in the Bitterroot Valley involved the Salish exchange of horses for cash or other goods. In 1877 Baptist Perrish, a Nez Perce rancher living with the Bitterroot Salish, sold a horse for one hundred dollars to a federal employee for use in the Nez Perce War. Two years later Perrish was still trying to collect for the horse.[32] In 1880 George Redcrow, another Nez Perce rancher living with the Salish, sold fifty mares to Montana territorial governor B. F. Potts.[33] Abe Williamson, a recent white arrival in the Bitterroot, described an active market for Indian ponies in Stevensville in 1881. Prices ranged from five to sixty dollars. According to Williamson, sellers who wanted whiskey sold their horses for the lower prices. Williamson had recently purchased a pair of Indian ponies for thirty-five dollars.[34] Two years later Francois Eneas [Lamoose], a Bitterroot Salish farmer, bought a horse, saddle, and gun from a white man named Al Clark for fifty dollars. Clark went with Francois to the Stevensville branch of the Eddy, Hammond & Company store where Francois banked his money. Clark got his fifty dollars, but he returned to Stevensville that December with two friends to rob the store. Francois was reported to have lost six hundred dollars in the robbery, but he got his money back.[35] When Delaware Jim, who was living with the Salish, was dying near Stevensville in 1887, he requested that one of his horses be sold to pay the five dollars he owed to three local white men.[36] Finally, in September 1889, a local Bitterroot newspaper mentioned that an Indian in Grantsdale tried to sell a horse for six dollars.[37]

In May 1875 Salish hunters who had recently returned from the plains were selling buffalo robes and pemmican in Stevensville.[38] In the late 1870s the Buck Brothers store in Stevensville purchased "silk buffalo hides" and chunks of native copper from Salish patrons.[39] A Bitterroot Valley correspondent to a Helena newspaper in August 6, 1881, complained that "Indians" (no tribe is specified) were slaughtering elk, moose, and deer in Hell Gate Canyon and selling the meat.[40] Two years later, on May 18, 1883, a Corvallis news item stated that "Indians supply some of our citizens with fresh elk meat."[41] In December 1883 the party of white men who had just robbed the Eddy, Hammond & Company store in Stevensville purchased a quarter of venison from Indian hunters in the Saphire Mountains.[42] Lula Wood Brooks remembered her mother in the Bitterroot in the middle 1880s trading sugar, flour, bread, beans, and smoked pork for the Indians' smoked buffalo tongues, tanned buckskin, moccasins, leather clothes, huckleberries, and fish.[43] Finally, Clara Blodgett Shults remembered her father trading butter to the Corvallis area Indians for meat in the late 1880s.[44]

As mentioned above, Father D'Aste regularly traded or purchased fish from the Salish, and Father Rappagliosi traded a fishhook for a large fresh fish in 1874. In another case in 1890, Jack Cox, a white man from Missoula, claimed to have caught a thirteen-pound fish in the Bitterroot, but others suggested "Jack caught it from a Bitter Root Indian for two dollars."[45]

In 1881, Sapiel, a Salish Indian man, traded a quarter of beef to Mrs. Hannah Ward for baby diapers.[46] Maclay family traditions relate that during the late 1880s David R. Maclay purchased cattle from Bitterroot Indian ranchers. The Indian neighbors also occasionally brought the Maclay family gifts of bear meat.[47]

Alice Chilson, a young white girl in the Stevensville area, remembered that during the mid-1870s the white women traded homemade bread with the Indian women for huckleberries.[48] Olive McCarty Wood remembered the Salish Indians in the mid-1880s bringing huckleberries to trade with the white settlers. One time Wood's mother had a batch of hard soap spread out to dry, and the Indian women came in and expressed their approval in Salish as they helped themselves to most of it.[49]

In 1881 John Chatfield, a white Bitterroot Valley resident, was charged with selling liquor to Henry Lumprey, a Salish mixed-blood, in Stevensville on January 1, 1879. Charles M. Gates, another white Bitterroot resident, was charged with selling liquor to Henry Lumprey on October 20, 1881.[50] In July 1891 the *Western News* in Stevensville described a clandestine economic deal between an unnamed white man and an unnamed Indian. The white man exchanged a bottle for something the Indian pulled out of his pocket.[51]

A final example of Salish-white trade involved Francois Eneas [Lamoose], a local Salish rancher who often came to John B. Catlin's hotel in Stevensville for his noonday meal. One day, sometime after 1879, Francois thought Catlin had undercharged him and insisted on paying Catlin the difference.[52]

Only a small sample of the incidents of Salish-white trade is documented in written sources. The number of cases that were found, however, suggests that trade was common between Salish and white residents of the Bitterroot Valley from 1870 to 1891.

## Begging and Loans

Five examples of begging were documented, besides the alms given by Father D'Aste. Alice Chilson's memories of the mid-1870s in the Stevensville area include giving food to local Indians who were begging, especially during the winter.[53] Carrie May Greenfield Warren, a young white girl living in Victor in the late 1870s, remembered the Salish in the late 1870s as "very good neighbours attending to their own business." In those days, she said, the white settlers never locked their chicken houses or smoke houses. She recalled that the Salish were very fond of "wattermellom" but "never would they go into the mellon patches untill after the fall frosts then Mr Indian would go help Himself a plenty & I doant mean maby."[54] On March 8, 1877, John P. Martens gave flour to two Indian ladies: "in the forenoon two Ladys of the Tribe of Lo paied me a visit told me that their Logdes were in mourning not for the lose of a brave but for the want of Flouer of course I gave them some Flouer and sendt them of[f] for who can widtstand the pleadings of the faier Sex." Martens also mentions that in December 1877 an Indian came to his home begging tobacco.[55] One case of begging seems to have involved a white man begging food from the Salish: on October 26, 1878, Father D'Aste noted in his diary that "A young man came here to night very poor begging food from the Indians."[56]

The historical record has preserved three examples of whites making loans to Indians. John P. Martens, a white settler near Victor, recorded loaning agricultural equipment to an Indian neighbor. On May 1, 1877, "an Indian named Kaiser came and wanted to barow a plow. I promised him one." Later that year, on December 12, 1877, an Indian lady returned a borrowed "Tin-Pan" to Martens.[57] A white resident of the upper Bitterroot remembered Salish hunting parties with fifty or sixty horses heading up the West Fork of the Bitterroot Valley, possibly about 1890. The writer noted that the Salish hunters "tended to their own business" and did not bother with the white residents. The Salish did stop at Billy Edwards's house and borrowed his Springfield needle gun for the hunt. Edwards "said they took better care of it than a white man and always returned it to him when they came back by the cabin."[58]

One example has survived of an Indian making a loan to a white man. In December 1883 a white posse was on the trail between Stevensville and Rock Creek chasing the three white men who had robbed the Eddy, Hammond & Company store at Stevensville. Near the summit the posse passed a band of about a dozen mounted Indians. The Indians declined to join the posse but did agree to take news of the pursuit to other local whites. One of the Indians loaned his gun and ammunition to an unarmed white man in the posse.[59]

## Other Economic Incidents

An assortment of miscellaneous examples of Salish-white economic exchange involved everything from mining and horse racing to robbery. Probably one of the most interesting of these incidents involved a joint Indian-white mining claim. In September 1882 Sternie Blake, a white prospector in the Bitterroot, filed three mining claims on a silver prospect near the divide between the Big Hole and Beaverhead valleys. Blake took two-thirds interest in the claims and assigned one-third to a Bitterroot Indian named Tybo. In 1881, Blake had given Tybo a rock sample containing silver and asked him to keep an eye out for similar rocks. In late summer of 1882, Tybo brought Blake a rock sample and escorted him to a thirty-foot-wide ledge of silver-bearing ore above the Big Hole Valley.[60]

Two other examples involved the popular pastime of betting on horse races. Francois Eneas [Lamoose], a Salish farmer and stock man, ran a roan pony named Little Blue in the cayuse race at the September 1879 Missoula County Fair. The race was a mile dash with fifty dollars in prize money, all to the first horse. Little Blue came in second.[61] Part of the July 4, 1883, celebration at Stevensville included a half-mile race for a fifty-dollar purse. An unnamed horse belonging to Francois [Lamoose] won the first prize of forty dollars.[62]

The December 1883 robbery of six hundred dollars of Francois Eneas Lamoose's money from the safe of the Eddy, Hammond & Company store in Stevensville by white robbers was also a form of economic interaction.[63]

One example of economic exchange also reflects on the white justice system in the Bitterroot Valley during the 1880s. In 1886 an unnamed Salish Indian shot a horse belonging to Newt Tillman, a white settler on Eight Mile Creek. The horse had broken the Indian's fence and destroyed his crop. Tillman had the Indian arrested, but a white jury in Stevensville acquitted the Indian, and Tillman later paid for the damage to the garden. Father D'Aste commented on the case in his diary on August 16, 1886: "a miracle! An Indian from 8 mile creek was tried on the charge of Killing a horse from a white man, because the horses were destroying his crop, and the Indian was acquitted! by a jury, in the Stevensville."[64]

Despite the limitations of surviving records relating to Salish-white economic interactions in the Bitterroot Valley between 1870 and 1891, the evidence indicates that much of the exchange was friendly. The economic exchanges between the communities were important and sustained, but there are no statistics to show how much the white community earned from Salish labor and goods, or how much Salish life was improved as a result of the new trade goods.

## Friendship through a Cloudy Glass: Salish-White Social Interaction in the Bitterroot Valley

In addition to referring to conflict and friction, historic sources frequently refer to friendly Salish-white social interactions. Any understanding of the relations between the Salish and white communities in the Bitterroot Valley between 1870 and 1891 must incorporate both the friction and the cooperation. The Salish probably did not understand or approve of all the actions of the Bitterroot whites any more than the whites understood or approved of all the actions of the Salish, but each side found amicable relations in its own best interests and generally worked to avoid conflict.

By far the most detailed description of Salish social customs as seen from a white perspective was recorded by Father Philip Rappagliosi, S.J., a novice priest at St. Mary's Mission in January 1874. His description of Salish social and hospitality customs in the 1870s illuminates areas of potential misunderstanding in Salish-white social interactions. Each community had a very different concept of proper hospitality and honorable social interaction. Rappagliosi was impressed with the friendly and open way he was received by the Salish, especially Agnes, Victor's widow. The Salish freely tutored him in their language and welcomed his visits to their homes. In May 1874 he was an honored guest at the memorial feast for the recently deceased Susanna. In June he wrote a long letter to his brother Luigi in Rome describing Salish visiting customs. Rappagliosi described an everyday visit of a Salish man to the priests' quarters at St. Mary's. The Salish visitor would enter without knocking or saying anything and might even ignore his white host after first entering. If the host immediately asked what was needed, the Salish guest would say "ta," which means "nothing." Finally, after half an hour or more of silence or small talk, the visitor would relate the purpose of his visit. If he asked for something and received it, the guest would just take it and leave. No "thank you" or response was given or required. According to Rappagliosi, the Salish tradition of hospitality allowed an Indian who was away from his home to enter the tepee of any other Indian and make himself at home for days, weeks, or months. Then, at the guest's pleasure, he would get up and move out without informing or thanking his hosts. Whenever an Indian entered a lodge, someone in the lodge automatically prepared a pipe, lit it, took three or four tokes, and then passed it around to everybody who was present. From this description one can see how easily friction and misunderstandings could arise in Salish-white social interactions in the Bitterroot Valley. The Salish visitor who arrived at a white home and behaved according to the Salish social customs described by Rappagliosi would have been acting unacceptably according to white social norms. In the same way, a white man who acted according to white social norms would be acting disgracefully according to Salish values.[65]

### *Celebrations and Public Events*

The sources indicate that the Bitterroot Salish and their white neighbors regularly joined together in friendly public celebrations. Salish Indians were guests of local whites at a Fourth of July celebration at Burnt Fork in 1872, and the report in the *Weekly Independent* of Deer Lodge suggests that the whites furnished the feast and ate first: "The citizens had furnished a sumptuous feast, more than the whites could make way with, but reinforcements from the Lo family soon made way with all that was left."[66] As mentioned above, a detailed description of the 1877 Fourth of July feast at Burnt Fork (discussed at the beginning of this chapter) was printed in the *Rocky Mountain Husbandman*. And in 1888, the Fourth of July celebration at Stevensville included an evening display of fireworks that was "greatly enjoyed by the people and by none more than the Indians, who had collected to see the display."[67]

New Year's festivities also involved both communities. Carrie May Warren's memories of her Salish neighbors in the late 1870s includes their custom of extending New Year's greetings to the whites, a custom that had been carried over from the Salish social jump dance:

> one of their friendly custums wer on the new year day to go into the homes of the White People & shake hands with them. that would mean wel [we'll] be friends all year. I well remember one perticular new year day we wer living in Stevensville, all day the Indians had ben coming in shaking hands with father & mother then going on Their way. in the evening an oald fellow came in He was quite a friend of fathers. this evening He had a fiew drinks of something stronger than watter. He came in went up to my fathe putting his arms around His neck & kept kissing Him & repeating my good friend my good friend, father dident seam to apresiate it yet He couldent resent it for fear of making the oald fellow angrey so He just sat & took all that loving without a murmer, we youngsters thot it a grate Joke on Dad to be kissed by a Buck Indian.[68]

Funerals could also involve both communities. Several entries in John P. Martens's diary in early 1878 expressed his sympathy on the death of two of the mixed-blood children of John Silverthorne. On May 20, 1878, Martens noted that the oldest son had drowned while crossing the river, and it was "rather hard on Mr. Silverthorn." One of Silverthorne's mixed-blood daughters, Mrs. Wm. Turnage, was buried on May 21, 1878, and Martens took a wagonload of white mourners to her funeral. He noted approvingly that "there was a good turnout" for the burial.[69]

White church services were sometimes visited by curious Salish. A report in the *Weekly Missoulian* on July 19, 1878, referred to Corvallis Indians coming around while Episcopal Sunday services were being held and evincing "their usual curious interest in such matters."[70] The *Weekly Missoulian* report on the July 23, 1881, Sunday services at Stevensville found that the "native element was . . . well represented." The day opened with preaching by bishop Leigh R. Brewer of the Episcopal Church of Montana. Other events included horse racing and "several bad cases of drunkenness, one of which was an Indian."[71]

Several incidents of Salish curiosity about the household activities of whites made it into the literature. John Waddell, a white freighter in the Bitterroot Valley in the mid-1880s, told of passing Indians hanging offerings on the Medicine Tree who greeted him with "Hello, John." Waddell's wife related stories of Indians peeking in the windows of their log cabin while she was alone with her daughter. She was fearful of them when she was alone, but was never harmed.[72] The reminiscences of a member of the Hollensteiner family on Lolo Creek in the mid-1880s also indicate a friendly curiosity on the part of the local Indians. Indian men visited the Hollensteiner home when only the women and children were there and looked through the family's possessions.[73]

The interest ran in both directions, and one white woman, Nora Simpson McLenegan, recorded her early fascination with Salish household life. As a young girl, in about 1890, McLenegan was living on Skalkaho Creek near Grantsdale. She and her young friends enjoyed watching the Salish Indians who camped near her home, and she particularly remembered the men sitting and visiting while the women set up the camp, started the fires, prepared the meals, and took care of the babies. The white children "liked to watch the babies, so we rustled wood for the women and brought water so they wouldn't mind our being around. . . . We were always glad to see the Indians riding by in their bright blankets, often with feathers in their hair."[74]

## Alcohol and Food

Some friendly interactions between the Salish and the local whites involved alcohol and food. About September 15, 1877, Baptiste Matte, a Salish mixed-blood, met a white neighbor in the Bitterroot (probably Cassius M. Nichols) and shared his bottle of liquor. An unnamed full-blood Indian passing by also shared in Matte's bottle.[75] The Bitterroot correspondent for the *Weekly Missoulian* on May 7, 1880, complained about gregarious Salish-white drinking. The writer grumbled that the Bitterroot Indians "ride about the country and ask their white acquaintances to drink with a carelessness of manner which shows that . . . their supply is inexhaustible."[76]

Alcohol was also involved in situations in which whites gave protection to Indian women being attacked by drunken Indian men. In May 1871 a band of Salish Indians were camped by the house of the Eliza Deery family near Missoula. At night a fight broke out between a drunken Indian man and a woman who ran to the Deery house for safety. The drunken man pursued her with a knife, but Mrs. Deery drove him off with a club. According to the newspaper, this had been the second time in a week that Indian women had fled to white households for protection against drunken Indian men.[77]

The sharing of food was involved in many Salish-white interactions. According to Oliver Gregg family traditions, a friendly Indian man arrived one particular morning and was invited to join the Greggs for breakfast. A plate full of homemade biscuits was politely passed to the guest first. In appreciation the Indian man complimented the "Goo-ood bread —Goo-ood bread" as he opened the front of his calico shirt and emptied the entire plate of biscuits into it. Mrs. Gregg got up and prepared another batch of biscuits for the rest of the hungry diners.[78] About 1880 John Summers had just fenced in a meadow in the Skalkaho area, and Loui Dominic, a mixed-blood Indian who had married into the Salish tribe, complained bitterly that Summers's fence obstructed access to his traditional hunting area. Summers finally agreed to let Dominic and his family pass through his fences. A short time later Dominic and his family returned for something to eat, and Summers's wife fixed lunch for them.[79] The children of George and Aquilla Dye, who lived in the Charlos Heights area south of Hamilton, were frightened and hid when they were alone and an Indian visited their home in the late 1880s. In later years their mother told her children "to feed the Indians, and be kind to them."[80]

## Miscellaneous

Other incidents of Salish-white cooperation preserved in the historical sources run from Chief Victor's deathbed gift to a white friend, to rescuing stranded white horse traders and holding a horse so an Indian mother could breast-feed her baby. Chief Victor's dying wish in 1870 was for his old war horse to be given to Angus McDonald as a sign of friendship. McDonald was the Hudson's Bay Company trader who married a Nez Perce woman and whose family became part of the Salish tribe on the Jocko Reservation.[81]

Some incidents of Salish-white interaction involved the giving of aid. In the fall of 1874 two Salish hunters, Martin Shallwain and his father, rescued two white horse traders, John Hammer and Charles Allard, Sr., who became snowed in on the Lolo Trail.[82] Less dramatic aid was involved in an 1881 incident during which Hannah Ward, a white resident, removed her bonnet and changed her hairstyle so she could hold the horse ridden by a young Indian woman who needed to nurse the baby she was carrying on her back.[83] In 1884 Rev. L. B. Stateler, a Methodist minister, wrote personal letters for Delaware Jim, a Delaware Indian who had married into the tribe.[84] According to Harlan family traditions, sometime during the 1880s Wilson B. Harlan sent for smallpox vaccine, vaccinated his children, and then vaccinated "a large number" of Indians living in the Como area.[85] One incident that might have involved providing aid or assistance occurred in July 1888, when Jeff Silverthorne, a Salish mixed-blood, was deputized for special duty by the justice of the peace court at Stevensville. The newspaper article does not describe his duties.[86] A series of exchanges were recorded by Frank L. Williamson, a white boy living near Florence during the late 1880s. Williamson remembered a distraught Indian woman appealing to his father and the other white employees at a local sawmill to help find her lost child. Her baby had been left in a cradle board tied to a horse while she was picking huckleberries. The horse came untied and wandered off, and the baby and cradle board were missing when the horse was located. Williamson also remembered a wagon trip with his brother to the family's winter home to plant a small plot of rye. On the last evening before the Williamson brothers were to return to the family's summer home near Florence, Sapiel, a Bitterroot Salish man, stopped at the Williamson ranch and spent the night. The next day he followed the Williamson boys' wagon on horseback as they returned to their summer home.[87] In 1941 Frank and his brother, Ernest Williamson, remembered being fed as children in Stevensville by Mary Lumprey, a Salish mixed-blood woman.[88]

Most of the remaining nine examples from the historical record of Salish-white social cooperation between 1870 and 1891 involved visiting or socializing. One of the more amusing cases involved the gathering of Indian and white Stevensville residents when the train arrived in town. A May 22, 1889, note in a Missoula newspaper observed that "an Indian tied his horse to the Bitter Root train Sunday, when the train stopped at Stevensville. When the train started up the horse managed to keep up with it until Conductor Wm. Houston stopped and untied the cayuse."[89]

One series of incidents involved both socializing and friction. When Peter Whaley was Flathead Indian agent for a couple of years in the mid-1870s, his daughter Julia learned to speak Salish. In the early 1880s the Whaleys lived near Stevensville, and many older Salish Indians came to the Whaley's house in order to visit with Julia in Salish.[90]

An account by John Tracy, Jr., tells of extensive social interactions between Tracy as a young boy and local Salish Indian children, including Victor Charlo, Chief Charlo's son. Tracy moved with his family to the Miller Creek area in 1884, when he was eight years old. He told stories of playing athletic games, attending church services at St. Mary's, taking a sweat bath, hunting, and fishing with his Salish friends. Since the account was recorded when Tracy was an old man, the story could have grown over the years, but some of the basic facts can be verified in contemporary nineteenth-century records.[91]

Other records of Salish-white visiting in the Bitterroot describe more limited contact. In August 1883 two white women and two white men floated down the Bitterroot River and were visited at one camping place by a "few Indians in gay blankets."[92] Olive McCarty Wood remembered seeing Salish Indian babies in beaded cradle boards in the 1880s. According to Wood, one Salish woman, Miley Sapiel (probably the wife of John Peter Koo loo) "was showing us her new baby and my mother asked if it was a girl or a boy, through a little hole that was left conveniently open, she flipped out a little thing and we knew it was a boy."[93] About the same time Alice Woody, the daughter of Judge Frank H. Woody of Missoula, accompanied her father to visit the Salish camp south of Missoula. Alice's long blond hair fascinated the Indian women, but their attention made Alice uncomfortable.[94] Allis B. Stuart reminisced that Sallie Blodgett, the mixed-blood daughter of Joseph and Ella McLeod Blodgett, was a popular young lady in the late 1880s who "was often on picnics and fishing excursions with the other young [white] people of the valley."[95] Also in the late 1880s, Edward Smith, a white pharmacist in the Bitterroot, learned to speak Salish in order to communicate with Charlo and the other Salish. Later, after he purchased the Medicine Hot Springs near Sula in the twentieth century, Smith socialized regularly with the Salish families who traveled to the upper Bitterroot to use the hot springs and harvest a nearby bitterroot field.[96] Finally, Maj. John B. Catlin called Charlo "as good a friend as I ever had," and told how before 1891 Charlo had visited the Catlins regularly on the chief's fortnightly trips to Stevensville.[97]

The incidents related above illustrate only one facet of a complex relationship, but they do support the conclusions that a significant part of the Salish-white interactions in the Bitterroot Valley between 1870 and 1891 were friendly, and the interactions were generally free and open.

## Other Salish-White Cooperation

Some incidents of Salish-white cooperation in the Bitterroot Valley between 1870 and 1891 that do not fit into the social or economic categories involved military cooperation. The Salish rendered the Bitterroot Valley whites military assistance during the Nez Perce War in 1877 and its aftermath in 1878. Despite provocations from some local whites and the fears flamed by Chauncey Barbour in the *Weekly Missoulian*, Charlo and the Salish leaders demanded that the hostile Nez Perces not harm the Bitterroot whites. A number of mixed-blood and full-blood Salish joined Capt. C. C. Rawn's soldiers and white volunteers at Fort Fizzle to confront the Nez Perces coming east over the Lolo Trail. The Salish also assisted the army and white volunteers in 1878 in pursuit of a party of Nez Perce refugees involved in several murders and robberies of whites in western Montana. The Salish and white volunteers returned to the Bitterroot after the trail of the Nez Perces reached Idaho.

Salish-white cooperation in the Bitterroot occurred throughout the 1870–1891 period, but interracial friction and tension also occurred during that time. The incidents of cooperation described in this chapter need to be considered in conjunction with the hostile interactions described in chapter 7. The conflicts between the Salish and white communities laid out there emphasize how much work was required of the Salish to keep the peace. It would take only one hostile interaction involving violence to spiral out of control and drag Montana territorial officials and U.S. Army troops into conflict with the small community of Indians living in the Bitterroot Valley.

CHAPTER 7

# Keeping the Lid On

## Salish-White Friction in the Bitterroot Valley, 1870–1891

One well-documented crisis in Stevensville in 1881 dramatizes the tightrope that Salish leaders walked as they struggled to both protect the rights of the Salish people and keep peace with Bitterroot whites. On Sunday evening, October 16, 1881, a Bitterroot Salish by the name of Cayuse Pierre tried to reclaim a horse ridden by the young son of James Morris, a white employee of Chatfield & Bass, a local blacksmith shop. The Morris boy called for help from some nearby white men, including Howard Preece, one of James Morris's coworkers. In the ensuing melee, Pierre struck Preece with a rock but was forced to leave without the horse. According to news reports, Pierre had recently traded the horse to Morris for two bottles of whiskey.

While at work the next day, Preece nursed his rock wound and lubricated his anger with alcohol. When he saw Pierre enter the Stevensville store of Eddy, Hammond & Company, Preece recruited James Morris's help to attack or "put a head" on Pierre. Morris and Preece entered the store, where Preece started pounding on Pierre. Most of the bystanders, Indian and white, ran for safety, but John Delaware started walking toward Pierre. Morris then pummeled Delaware with his fists, grabbed an ax, and hit him on the head. Pierre assisted the seriously injured Delaware as they retreated from town to the nearby Indian camp. Morris and Preece, meanwhile, withdrew to a saloon to celebrate their victory.[1]

John Delaware ended up surviving the attack, but both Indians and whites assumed his injuries had been fatal. Pierre and Sapiel, another Salish man, armed themselves and returned to town to even the score. When they opened fire on the saloon where the white men had sought refuge, Morris and Preece returned fire, and Pierre was mortally wounded. The court records suggest that Morris fired the fatal shot.

The murder of Cayuse Pierre marked the end of the altercation on the Stevensville streets, but the beginning of a complicated dance between Chief Charlo, Missoula County law enforcement officials, and local Stevensville whites to quiet the immediate situation, seek a modicum of justice, and keep the peace between the Salish and white communities in the Bitterroot Valley. After Charlo demanded that Morris and Preece be turned over to him for punishment, the army troops at Fort Missoula prepared to march to Stevensville as a show of force.

Flathead Indian agent Peter Ronan then arrived at Fort Missoula and recommended against sending troops. Ronan argued that from his "knowledge of . . . Chief Charlo's good judgment, and friendly disposition, that such a display of force would be more hurtful than beneficial."[2] At Ronan's urging, the Missoula County sheriff went to Stevensville alone, arrested Morris and Preece, and placed them in county jail.[3] Leaders of the Salish and white communities in Stevensville met in the St. Mary's Mission residence on October 18, the day after the shooting, and the whites promised the Salish that justice would be done for Cayuse Pierre's murder.[4]

The white Missoula County legal system slipped into action. On October 22 a coroner's jury disinterred and examined Pierre's body. In addition to some of the leading Bitterroot whites, the coroner's jury included Father D'Aste and two Indians, Francois [Lamoose] and Delaware Jim.[5]

Morris and Preece's trial was set for the November 1881 term of the Missoula District Court. The defense attorney began his case with a request for a change of venue, charging that Missoula County whites were willing to sacrifice his clients in order to keep the peace with the Bitterroot Salish. The change of venue motion was denied. When the trial was held, testimony was heard from Indian, mixed-blood, and white witnesses. Notes on the testimony of Nicholas, a Salish full-blood, and the mixed-bloods John Vincent, Jr., and Mary Lumprey have survived in the record.[6] The published list of county expenses indicates Sapiel, Big Mouth Charley, Dominic, and Francois Lamoose were also paid witness fees.[7] The all-white jury, however, was unable to agree after twenty-two hours of deliberation and was discharged. Morris and Preece were returned to the county jail, and because neither was able to make bail, that is where they remained.[8]

Howard Preece died on December 5, 1881, at the age of twenty-seven, while still in custody.[9] Morris remained in jail at least through January 6, 1882.[10] The case file for *Territory vs. James Morris* includes a bond dated July 14, 1882.[11] Morris had been incarcerated for at least two months, and possibly eight months, awaiting trial.

Because the November 1881 jury had deadlocked on the charge of killing Pierre, Morris was tried again on the murder charge in July 1882. He was found not guilty. He was then tried for the assault on John Delaware. On July 11, 1882, another jury found Morris guilty of assault and imposed a fine of fifty dollars. The case was continued several times until July 1883, when the prosecution was dropped, canceling the guilty verdict and fine.[12]

If the verdict had been imposed, Morris's fine for assaulting Delaware would have been similar to the punishment Missoula courts imposed on white defendants for assaulting other white men: on November 28, 1882, Dennis Gaffney was fined fifty dollars for simple assault on Richard D. Frislow; on June 9, 1884, Marion Gleason was sentenced to three months in the county jail for assault with a deadly weapon on John Danby; and on June 25, 1886, Isaac Kingrey was fined fifty dollars for simple assault on Guy McCune. The one Missoula County case between 1875 and 1886 that did not result in a comparable punishment for assault was an 1885 incident involving three Indians who were charged with assaulting a white man, which resulted in much harsher penalties. Michael, Benway, and Bazille, all from the Jocko Reservation, pleaded guilty to assault to do bodily harm to Thomas Shaughnessy, a white man. On November 14, 1885, Michael was sentenced to one and a half years at hard labor in the territorial prison, Benway got two years at hard labor, and Bazille got one year in prison.[13] They were, however, pardoned by acting Montana governor William Webb in March 1886, about four months into their terms, after three Flathead Reservation chiefs traveled to Helena to plead for clemency.[14]

The historical record fails to answer many questions about the murder of Cayuse Pierre and the prosecution of Howard Preece and James Morris. The white Missoula County justice system was not color-blind, but the handling of the cases that grew out of the October 1881 events in Stevensville illustrate the intricate maneuvers performed by Salish and white leaders in the Bitterroot Valley as they attempted to keep the peace between the communities.

According to federal law in 1881, off-reservation Indians were under the jurisdiction of the local white court system. An 1872 law had declared that the Bitterroot Valley was not legally a reservation, and that the Salish who remained in the valley had officially severed tribal relations. The Bitterroot Salish were in a state of legal limbo because they had refused to accept the patents for the allotments issued under the 1872 law. It was a struggle for the Salish to receive justice from a system that did not recognize them as a tribal community.[15]

An important part of Salish peacekeeping often involved efforts to prevent or control tribal members' use of alcohol. On September 1, 1878, Antoine Moiese was drunk at a horse race near Stevensville and fought with another Salish spectator. Narcisse, a prominent Salish farmer in the Bitterroot, intervened and received a fatal knife wound in the arm. After sobering up, Moiese went to Charlo to express contrition and receive his punishment. Charlo whipped Moiese so severely that for several days he was thought to be dying. A newspaper report claimed Moiese received four hundred lashes.[16]

The *Weekly Missoulian* Stevensville correspondent reported on July 27, 1883, that a group of drunken Indians attempted to break into Louis Solomon's store but were frightened off when he fired a pistol at them.[17] Two months later, on October 31, 1883, the Stevensville correspondent for the *Missoula County Times* complained that the Indian drinking parties there were so bad they had made it "unpleasant and unsafe for the church-going portion of our community to find their way to the place of worship on Sabbath evenings."[18]

Father Jerome D'Aste's diary mentions specific efforts by Charlo and the Salish leadership to curtail Indian drinking. On August 12, 1883, D'Aste described a meeting with the Salish headmen during Charlo's absence during which D'Aste requested an end to drinking in the camp. The headmen were reluctant to act until Charlo returned, so the only result of the meeting was a promise by one of them, Louis Vanderburg, to keep drunken Indians away from the church and camp. During the Christmas celebration at St. Mary's Mission in 1885, D'Aste sent a delegation of tribal elders to Charlo to pressure him into stopping drunkenness in their camp. D'Aste reported an immediate cessation of drunkenness, and after Christmas he gave Charlo and the Salish police and headmen a "great dinner . . . to encourage them to go on so well." On January 4, 1886, Father D'Aste noted in his diary that "two Indians, the two Martin[s] were whipped by Charlo (one his son) for drunkness!! [*sic*] a thing which had not been done since Narcise was cold." On January 3, 1887, D'Aste wrote, "To day George [Red] Crow (at his demand and Poè [Pierre Lamoose] were publicly whipped by the Chief for drunkness!!"[19] D'Aste often complained that Charlo did not exert even tighter control, but D'Aste's own diaries indicate that Charlo intervened repeatedly to punish Salish drinking.

In November 1889 Charlo rushed out of a meeting with Gen. Henry Carrington in response to "a message that some of his people were drunk."[20] Records of only a few of Charlo's efforts to curb Salish drinking have survived, but Charlo did make a sustained effort to punish drunkenness.

In March 1873 an unnamed Salish shot and butchered a cow owned by Billy Sanders, a white man. When Charlo learned of the theft, he quickly apprehended the offender and administered a severe whipping of 150 or 180 lashes.[21] The *Helena Daily Herald* reported on May 13, 1873, that "Occasional thefts and depredations have been committed by odd members of the [Salish] tribe, but the offenders have, almost without exception, been apprehended, tried, convicted and severely punished by their own system of police courts."[22] The peacekeeping efforts of Charlo and the other Salish leaders were manifest in their vigorous punishment of Salish malefactors.

## Other Salish-White Conflict in the Bitterroot Valley

The existence of friction between the communities suggests that peace was not an accident. "Keeping the lid on" must have required the determined efforts of both Salish and white leaders in the Bitterroot Valley. The interests of both communities in avoiding conflict showed up in several different areas.

### *Free-Range Livestock*

The historical sources describe two incidents in which white-owned horses and cattle destroyed Indian crops, and two cases of Indian-owned horses damaging the crops of whites. In August 1878 a cow owned by Peter Whaley, a white man and former Flathead Indian agent, trampled the corn of a Salish farmer named Paul. Enraged, Paul shot at the window of the Whaley house, barely missing Peter's sixteen-year-old daughter, Julia. Knowing Salish, she confronted Paul, who told her about the damage to his crop. After Julia promised that her father would pay for the damage, Paul apologized for shooting at the house. According to Whaley family traditions, Paul later became "good friends" with the Whaleys.[23]

In December 1878 a court case was tried that was the inverse of the Whaley incident. Three white farmers in the Willow Creek area sued Perrish, a Nez Perce rancher living with the Salish, after his horses damaged their grain crops. The justice court awarded the white farmers compensation for the damage, but the district court dismissed the case over questions of the jurisdiction of territorial courts over non-reservation Indians.[24]

Roswell Parkhurst, a white farmer in the Skalkaho area, complained in June 1880 to Martin Maginnis, the Montana territorial delegate, that Indian-owned horses were not being tended by their owners and during the dry period in August had broken into his grain field. He had two fences—one five boards high and one nine rails high—and he had hired a man to care for the crop, but the horses had still damaged it.[25]

One case illustrates both competition and cooperation. In August 1886 a Salish farmer killed a horse owned by Newt Tillman because it had broken a fence and destroyed his crop. The Salish was charged with killing the horse and kept in jail, but when the case came to trial, a white jury acquitted him of the charge. According to family traditions, Tillman later paid for the damages and lived on friendly terms with his Salish neighbor.[26] The problem of free-range stock centered on the question of whether farmers were responsible for fencing their fields to keep animals out or the stock owners were obligated to herd their stock to keep them away from farmers' crops. During the 1870s, white Montana law made it the farmers' responsibility to fence their fields to keep horses and cattle out.[27]

### *The Case of Peter Matte*

At first glance the March 9, 1878, lynching of Peter Matte for stealing horses appears to be a case of Salish-white conflict. Peter Matte was of Piegan and white descent, but his family had been adopted into the Salish tribe and was considered part of the Salish community. Matte was in the custody of the Missoula County sheriff and on the way to the county jail when he was lodged for the night in a room over Plummer's saloon in Stevensville. During the night Matte was taken from the room by "unknown" parties and lynched outside of town. Matte had been accused of a series of horse thefts over the previous five years, and complicity in the 1873 murder and robbery in Idaho of a white man named Goodwin. The *Weekly Missoulian* claimed that "the Indians and halfbreeds in the [Bitterroot] valley" were "highly incensed" over the lynching. Matte's father, Louis Matte, a white

Stevensville blacksmith, mourned that "My son is a villain but his instigators [lynchers] are greater villains and are afraid of him."[28]

On closer inspection, however, Peter Matte's place in Salish-white relations in the Bitterroot Valley becomes much more complicated. According to his confession, the murder and robbery of Goodwin was committed by James Gash, a white Bitterroot Valley resident. The sixteen-year-old Matte had been traveling with Gash and assisted in the robbery and attack on Goodwin, but the older Gash appeared to have been the ringleader in the affair.[29] The 1878 Missoula court case against Matte for horse theft suggested that, in at least some of the thefts, Matte was working under the direction of William G. Brown, a white man.[30] To further confuse the situation, some of the horses that Matte was accused of stealing belonged to members of the Bitterroot Salish tribe. Many of the stolen horses belonged to Francois [Lamoose], a wealthy Salish farmer and rancher.[31] Evidence in the 1878 court case suggests that horses were also stolen from tribal members Medicine Pierre, Lame Dominic, and Sapiel.[32] In 1878 an unnamed Pend d'Oreille reported seeing a band of stolen horses near the Blackfeet Agency in the possession of Johnny Jackson, a Piegan mixed-blood. The horses had been stolen from the Bitterroot Valley by Peter Matte and Bill Brown, and included animals owned by Medicine Pierre and Bitterroot whites.[33]

Even more interesting was an 1875 incident in the Blackfoot River valley. A camp of Salish on their way to hunt buffalo met Peter Matte and a Piegan Indian accomplice driving a band of twenty horses north to the Whoop Up Country. The Salish recognized the horses as belonging to an unidentified "Flathead Chief in Bitter Root." The Salish and some local white men pursued Matte and captured him and the stolen horses. The Salish took back the horses, stripped Matte, and sent him off on foot.[34] It would be hard to portray Matte's criminal activities as directed only at Bitterroot whites, but his criminal career and extralegal execution did add to the grievances felt by Indians and whites in the Bitterroot Valley.

### *Salish Hunting Rights*

Conflict over the declining wild game resources impacted the Salish while they were in the Bitterroot as well as when they were hunting buffalo on the plains. The 1855 Hellgate Treaty had guaranteed traditional Salish rights to hunt, fish, and gather roots and berries "in common with citizens of the Territory. . . . upon open and unclaimed land."[35] In the nineteenth century, however, "in common with citizens" was interpreted to mean that the Salish and Kootenai were subject to white hunting laws when they were off the reservation. In 1872 the Montana legislature adopted a closed season between February 1 and August 15 for moose, elk, deer, mountain sheep, and some other large game animals. In 1865 the legislature had declared that trout fishing must be done only with a rod, line, and hook. That act outlawed the use of dams, seines, or nets and also traditional Salish fish traps. These laws were passed in the name of wildlife conservation, but they were also designed to serve the interests of the seasonal sportsmen over those of subsistence hunters.[36]

A correspondent in the Bitterroot complained in 1881 that Indians (tribe not given) were "slaughtering the elk, moose and deer in the Hell Gate canyon" above Missoula and selling the venison.[37] In 1884 and 1885 a writer from Como complained about seeing Indian hunting parties during the official closed season.[38] In March 1886 Flathead agent Peter Ronan wrote to Charlo asking him to call back the Salish who were then hunting in the Lolo Valley and insisting that the Salish hunters had to observe the white hunting seasons.[39]

The friction over hunting rights came to a head in the spring of 1887. In early March Ronan received a complaint from a Missoula member of the conservationist Rod and Gun Club that Indians were hunting in the Lolo during the closed season. Ronan replied that the Bitterroot Salish were not under his jurisdiction since they were off-reservation. Ronan concluded that Indians were subject to territorial law while off the reservation, but he was "not prepared to say if it is a crime for an Indian to kill game for food at any season of the year."[40] On March 26, 1887, Father D'Aste wrote that "An Indian has been arrested and brought to Missoula for Killing a deer!"[41] The register of prisoners for the Missoula County Jail included "Levy an Indian," incarcerated on March 27, 1887, for "Killing Deer." He was released on April 14, 1887.[42] No other arrests of Bitterroot Salish hunters were recorded in the Missoula County records before their 1891 removal to the Jocko Reservation.

In 1889, however, Ronan reported that the Office of Indian Affairs in Washington, D.C., had concluded that the hunting rights of the off-reservation Bitterroot Salish were limited by white game laws. In this case an Indian hunting party in Rock Creek was reported to have been hunting with dogs and killing more than two hundred deer. The Office of Indian Affairs reasoned that the 1855 treaty gave the Bitterroot Salish the right to hunt off the reservation "in common with citizens of the territory." They concluded that "these [hunting] rights are now defined and limited by law, and apply to the Indians just the same as to citizens."[43] The legal argument over the hunting rights of western Montana Indians continued until the mid-twentieth century, when Salish tribal rights to hunt on public lands in western Montana without observing Montana game laws were finally recognized.

Only one incident in the historical record illustrates the impact on Salish hunting of the white fondness for fences and exclusive use of "private" property. Chaffin family tradition holds that a conflict occurred between John Summers, a Chaffin in-law, and Loui Dominic shortly before 1891. Summers claimed a large ranch in the Skalkaho area and fenced off the trail that Dominic had traditionally used when hunting in the surrounding mountains. When Dominic demanded access through the fence, Summers insisted that he detour around "his" property. After a heated exchange, Summers relented and allowed Dominic and his party to use the direct route.[44] Many similar confrontations must have occurred that were not recorded.

The Montana law limiting trout fishing to the rod, line, and hook used by white sportsmen and proscribing fish traps interfered with some traditional Salish fishing practices.[45] In September 1878, Carrie Strahorn, an early white tourist in the Bitterroot, observed a Salish fish trap in Lolo Creek.[46] No conflict with white fish and game authorities over Salish fish traps seems to have occurred while the Salish were still in the Bitterroot Valley.

### *Land Conflicts*

The evidence of Salish-white conflict over the use of land and resources in the Bitterroot Valley before 1891 is surprisingly limited. Early problems probably involved reduced common range caused by whites enclosing valley bottoms, and fencing and claiming ownership of traditional Salish plant-gathering sites. Col. George Gibson, the newly arrived commander of Fort Missoula, was informed in 1879 that "when the season for planting sets in, . . . many troubles arise in the Bitter root valley caused by the encroachments of the whites upon Charlot's band."[47] By the late 1880s whites began filing claims on land that was occupied and had been improved by Salish farmers and ranchers but had not been registered in their names with the local land office. These conflicts arose over Indian-used lands that were not included in the 1872 patents.

Charlo complained in 1885 that a white man, Peter Lafountain, was attempting to force an unnamed Salish off land on Eight Mile Creek that he had farmed for several years and on which he had constructed a house. Charlo asked Indian agent Peter Ronan to have the matter investigated and grant the Salish a patent if he had first right to the land.[48]

In 1886, Thomas H. Gibbons, a white man, filed a claim on land in the Willow Creek area near Corvallis that had been occupied and improved by Baptiste Perrish, a Nez Perce rancher who was part of the Salish tribe. Perrish had lived on the land for five or six years and had erected a house that cost more than $1,200. Father Jerome D'Aste of St. Mary's Mission forwarded a complaint to Ronan, who asked the Office of Indian Affairs in Washington for instructions. The office referred Ronan to a General Land Office circular from 1884 specifying that "Registers and Receivers" were to refuse white entries on land "in the possession of Indians who have made improvements of any value whatever thereon." Ronan was instructed to make sure Perrish appeared at the local land office and contested Gibbons's filing. The General Land Office in Washington told the local office to request affidavits from Ronan if Perrish failed to appear.[49]

In 1887, Newton J. Tillman, a white man, claimed land in the Eight Mile Creek area near Florence on which two Salish, Joseph and Paul, had a house and a cultivated field. Ronan reported that the two Salish men appeared with legal counsel to contest the case. The land officers decided that the Indian improvements were not extensive enough to justify rejecting Tillman's claim. Tillman thus won the case, although he did offer to pay the Salish for the improvements. Charlo, however, advised them not to compromise. The chief's many efforts to keep the peace between the Salish and white communities in the Bitterroot did not extend to giving up part of the tribe's land base.[50]

Two incidents of conflict over land between Charlo and his white neighbors were briefly mentioned in the sources but not described in detail. In January 1877, Charles Medary, the Flathead Indian agent, reported to the Bureau of Catholic Indians Missions in Washington that the official surveys to locate the boundaries for Charlo's patent cut off "his best land."[51] Ten years later, in September 1887, the Missoula County commissioners ordered Charlo, Indian Alex, and Fisher John to remove their obstructions from a public road near Stevensville.[52] Charlo and the two other Salish may have been objecting because the county had built a public road through their farms.

The remaining case of Salish-white conflict over land in the Bitterroot during this period hinged on white legal technicalities rather than conflict between the communities. The Bitterroot patents issued under the 1872 law were inalienable, but Chief Adolph traded his land to John Hill, a Nez Perce living with the Salish, and Hill later traded the land to Stephen James, another Salish farmer. James wanted the timber removed from the land, and in October 1887 sold it to Thomas M. Slocum, a white man, for five hundred dollars. After two hundred dollars' worth had been cut, Agent Ronan learned of the transaction. Since Chief Adolph had no legal right to sell or trade the land, the Slocum logging was officially a timber depredation on Chief Adolph's land. Ronan ordered a halt to the timber cutting, and the Office of Indian Affairs in Washington agreed to drop the matter because "Slocum was guiltless of any criminal intent."[53]

### *Assaults*

Ten cases of assault have been identified between members of the Salish and white communities, in addition to the series of events in Stevensville in October 1881 that were detailed at the beginning of this chapter. Five cases involved whites assaulting Indians, four involved Indians assaulting whites, one involved a Chinese assailant and an Indian victim, and another case did not identify the initiators of the violence. In Chief Charlo's famous speech in April 1876 he mentioned several cases of Salish-white friction and conflict. During a bitterly cold night the previous winter, Keneth, a one-eyed Indian in his seventies, had been refused shelter in four different white homes. Another aged Indian lived with his wife and daughter in a poor lodge. During a cold winter night, two lost and freezing white men were welcomed into their home. The white men were warmed, fed, given new moccasins, and offered shelter for the night, but they insisted on going on. The white men returned later that night to murder and rob their Salish benefactors. The next day they met a young Salish man on the road and killed him and stole his horse.[54]

Other white assaults on Bitterroot Salish included the February 1878 incident in which a drunken white man drove a carriage or wagon over George Redcrow, an "inoffensive" Nez Perce living with the Salish.[55] In the early 1880s Elijah Chaffin was accosted by a young, inebriated Salish man. When the young man offered Chaffin a drink of whiskey, Chaffin threw him into Burnt Fork Creek.[56] In May 1889, Joseph Uesse, a young Salish man, was killed while drinking whiskey with white men in Deer Lodge County. The white whiskey seller and murderer were arrested, but the murderer was "discharged on the plea of self-defense."[57]

A novel white assault with a broom occurred in the Bitterroot during the early 1880s when Mrs. Hannah Ward had a run-in with some of the local young Indian men. Mr. Ward had been gone for three months, and Mrs. Ward was afraid of her Indian neighbors. When a young Indian man tried to force her ten-year-old son to draw water for his horse, Mrs. Ward confronted him with a broom, gave him the bucket, indicated he should draw his own water, and took her son back into the house. She heard the Indians outside whooping and yelling and looked out. The other Indians in the party were "bent over with laughter at the one she had threatened with the broom."[58]

Alice Chilson, a white child in the Bitterroot in the late 1870s, recorded memories of Salish threats, but not assault. She was afraid of her Salish neighbors, but her parents were friendly and gave them food in the winter. Alice, however, remembered Salish men "hollering and shooting off their rifles" in celebration on Christmas Eve. On another occasion she hid in fear in a grain field when an Indian man rode up to her on a road. The man called out to her but she refused to come out of hiding until after he left. In yet another incident she felt an Indian man was following her as she rode into town to the store. She stayed in town until the Indian went away. She also related that Big Mouth Charley, a Salish man, once rode up to the Chilson family wagon on the road and threatened to kill her father. When her father insisted that that was not a good idea, Big Mouth Charley rode off.[59]

The Charley family was also involved in an altercation on the road between Stevensville and Missoula on an August night in 1891. According to James Phelps, Sr., a white man, Paul Charley assaulted him as Phelps and his son were driving two wagonloads of poultry to Missoula. Phelps was hit in the side with a large stone before Charley was driven off. When Charley was arrested by the deputy sheriff a week later, his father, Big Mouth Charley, attempted to attack the sheriff with a butcher knife but was restrained by another one of his sons. The justice court in Stevensville bound Paul Charley over to the grand jury with three hundred dollars' bail.[60]

The other two cases of Salish assaulting whites took place in 1874 and 1880. In June 1874 George A. Baker was riding his horse past an Indian encampment near Missoula when a pack of dogs began barking at him. Baker pulled his gun and started shooting at the dogs, and an Indian fired a shot at Baker. The Indian was arrested but was released a few days later.[61] In August 1880, Priv. Franse Malstrom was assaulted just off the Fort Missoula grounds by two Bitterroot Salish. The men were captured by the army and turned over to the local white authorities for prosecution.[62]

It is unclear who started the conflict in one incident. A Missoula newspaper report in April 1871 described a recent "row" in Stevensville between local whites and Indians. The whites were led by Johnny Parker, and the Indian combatants included a mixed-blood named Louis. The newspaper report claimed that the whites won the brawl.[63]

A case of Chinese-Indian violence on November 28, 1888, was reported by a Missoula newspaper. According to the story, a Chinese man in Missoula "attempted to outrage the daughter of one of the Flathead chiefs" and was wanted by the local white authorities. The woman involved could have been from either the Jocko Reservation or the Bitterroot Valley.[64]

One case of Indian-on-Indian violence was punished by the white judicial system. In the same November 1881 term of the Missoula District Court when the white judicial system was making its befuddled attempt to prosecute Cayuse Pierre's killers, another Bitterroot Indian named Pierre was being tried for second degree murder. The twenty-nine-year-old Pierre was convicted of the murder of Joseph Garvis, an Indian, and sentenced to twelve years in prison. He died in January 1885 while still confined at Deer Lodge. The fragmented historical record of this case does not indicate whether Charlo objected to Pierre's arrest or the course of the case.[65]

### *Theft*

Six incidents of theft involving Indians and whites are found in the historical record for 1870–91. In May 1878 Perrish, a Nez Perce who lived with the Bitterroot Salish, complained at Fort Missoula that an unnamed white man had stolen a bay horse from him, and the stolen horse had ended up in the possession of Slug-eh, another Salish. Perrish requested that the army help him get it back. The commanding officer declined to intervene but wrote a letter to Charlo asking him to settle the matter.[66]

Shortly after Charlo and the Bitterroot Salish moved to the Jocko Reservation in October 1891, Carrington complained that the Salish's recently vacated cabins had already been broken into and vandalized. A Stevensville newspaper commented that "Such work is not conducive to the health of the parties committing the same. The Indians have never been known to have molested a white man's house in the whole history of the valley and now some cowardly whelp is guilty of work as described above."[67]

Two cases of Indian theft of white property involved childhood pranks and a probable cross-cultural misunderstanding. As an old man, Baptiste Lumprey told of stealing apples as a child in the late 1880s from a white man in the Bitterroot named Bass. When he hollered at Lumprey and the other Salish children, one of the children said Bass must want them to shake the tree, so they did. Bass hollered again, and the children ran off with the apples.[68] The other case probably involved a misunderstanding over taking meat from a dead animal. In June 1887 three Bitterroot Indians were fined ten dollars each in Justice Court for skinning a dead cow belonging to a white man. They were identified as Malteen, Can Pee, and "old Dummy."[69]

Joseph Wagner, a white Bitterroot resident, told of an undated attempted horse theft, possibly in the 1880s. An Indian whose name and tribe were not recorded took a horse out of Wagner's barn. When Wagner "showed the Indian his crucifix, the Indian looked at it, took the horse back to the barn and left."[70] In another case, probably in the mid-1880s, several drunken young Indian men approached Mary Harlan, a white woman in the Como area, and demanded food and other goods. Mrs. Harlan lured them into the family root cellar and locked them in until her husband, Wilson B. Harlan, returned. Mr. Harlan gave them a "tongue-lashing" and sent them away.[71]

## *White Fears of Indians*

Three reminiscences reveal that some white children of the period were afraid of Indians. Most of Olive McCarty Wood's childhood memories of her Salish neighbors in the Bitterroot in the early 1880s were positive, but she remembered that some young Salish men were "mean and liked to scare the [white] children when ever they got a chance, would run at us whooping and holloring [*sic*] and how they would laugh because we were scared of them."[72] Lula Wood Brooks, a white child in the Bitterroot in the mid-1880s, remembered her mother and the children being very afraid of the local Indians. When trading with them, her mother would be so afraid that she would give them whatever they wanted. Brooks observed later that the Indians "were very kind hearted and could not understand our being afraid of them."[73] Edna Hollensteiner Tucker, a white child in the Lolo Creek valley during the late 1880s, remembered curious Indian men visiting their cabin when the men of the family were gone. According to

Tucker, the Indian visitors "would fondle the [white] children and examine everything. They frightened mother terribly, but little could she do. When the [white] men showed up, they'd leave. What a relief!"[74]

### *Other Conflict*

On the evening of November 24, 1881, a mixed-blood Salish woman, Ellen Silverthorne, was "badly frightened" while returning home alone by a white object mysteriously rising from a woodpile near the road. She "was so severely frightened that she was thrown into a fit and it is feared the shock may result in serious illness." The newspaper correspondent warned "our smart young men" that "playing such tricks is dangerous not only to their victims" since "people have been known to shoot at ghostly apparitions."[75] On April 10, 1877, John P. Martens, a white settler in the Victor area, went to Anderson Buker, the local justice of the peace, to get John Silverthorne, Jr., arrested. The diary does not explain what complaint Martens had against Silverthorne, a mixed-blood Salish, or whether Silverthorne was ever prosecuted. Later that year, on November 14, 1877, Martens found cattle in his pasture after "the Indians" had left the fence down.[76]

In late 1878, Baptiste Matte, a Piegan mixed-blood who was a member of the Salish tribe, feuded with his white neighbor. This neighbor testified that in September 1877 Matte shared a friendly drink of alcohol with the neighbor and a passing Salish mixed-blood. Matte was found guilty of giving liquor to an Indian, but the jury insisted that the punishment not exceed one day in prison.[77] In March 1884 John Vincent, Jr., a Salish mixed-blood, was discovered in a burning Chinese laundry and residence. Vincent was acting as if he were trying to put out the fire, but the local justice court decided that Vincent had broken into the locked building and had set it himself. Shortly after Vincent was jailed in Missoula on the arson charge, all the prisoners but one escaped: Vincent, who could have fled, stayed in jail.[78]

The final incident of Salish-white friction during this period involved the refusal of Delaware Jim to assist Scott Sherrill in getting his wagon unstuck from the Bitterroot River during the mid-1880s. Sherrill had to let the horses go and leave the wagon in the river to get other help. According to Sherrill, Delaware Jim lounged on the bank and watched Sherrill's predicament but was unwilling to assist.[79]

There must have been other cases of Salish-white friction that did not get recorded in the historical documents. For example, two leaders of the

Bitterroot Salish, Arlee and Ninepipe, traveled to the Jocko Agency on January 17, 1871, to meet with Flathead agent C. S. Jones to complain of the "harassments to which they were subjected in their present homes [in the Bitterroot Valley], and the demoralization which has ensued consequent upon the incoming of so many whites amongst them." Unfortunately the "harassments" were not described in Jones's letter to the commissioner of Indian Affairs.[80]

Only limited documentation describing the peacekeeping efforts of the Salish in the Bitterroot Valley between 1870 and 1891 has survived. The infrequency of friction between the Salish and white communities in the Bitterroot, and documented Salish efforts to contain those incidents that did occur, support an interpretation that the peace between the peoples was not an accident. Indians and whites in the Bitterroot had so many conflicting political, social, and resource interests that the need to maintain the peace was one of the few areas of agreement between the two communities. The Salish always ran the risk that drunken violence or conflicts over property could start a chain of events that would result in military conflict between the Salish and the U.S. government. Avoiding such a conflagration could help avert the physical destruction of the Bitterroot Salish people.

CHAPTER 8

# "I Have Ploughed with My Hands, They Are Worn Out"

## Salish Agricultural Development in the Bitterroot Valley, 1870–1889

During the summer of 1877 Will Sutherlin of the *Rocky Mountain Husbandman* was traveling through the Bitterroot Valley looking for newspaper subscribers when he observed a settlement southwest of Stevensville of six or seven Salish families living in log homes with small fields of grain. Sutherlin recorded some of the most detailed descriptions of the results of the growth in the Salish farming economy in the Bitterroot Valley since the 1840s. Despite limited equipment and agricultural supplies, the Salish had managed over the last thirty years to diversify their economic resources to include herds of cattle and small grain and vegetable farms. Sutherlin paid particular attention to Chief Charlo's farm: "Charlos, the Flathead chief, has a home in their midst. His dwelling is a two-story log house with four rooms, and his farm which covers over a pretty little park before his house, encloses seven or eight acres, upon which there is a good growing crop of wheat."[1]

Sutherlin's next trip through the Bitterroot was in 1887. The decade since his last visit had been traumatic for the economy of the Bitterroot Salish. The destruction of the plains buffalo herds in the early 1880s deprived the tribe of a critical resource. As a result, during the mid-1880s the federal government provided seed, tools, and other equipment to help the Salish expand their farms to replace the buffalo. Victor Vanderburg recounted in later years that Charlo actively encouraged the Salish to develop their farms in the Bitterroot.[2] The impact of Charlo's efforts and the government aid was seen by Sutherlin in his 1887 visit: "I observed in passing by that his fences have been reset and his fields widened somewhat since my last visit. Several stacks of hay and grain were noticed. The hay was mostly timothy, of which he has a good stand. He lives in the same two-story log house which he had ten years ago, and though things thereabouts seemed to have a progressive appearance, I cannot note any advancement in the line of fruit-growing."[3]

Despite the signs of progress in 1887, in the fall of 1889 Charlo's farm showed the painful impact of a devastating drought. On Wednesday morning, October 30, 1889, retired general Henry B. Carrington drove southwest from Stevensville to Charlo's farm for a social call. When Carrington and his party arrived, Charlo had his horses harnessed and was fixing a plow to dig potatoes. Carrington observed "a corn stack" in front of Charlo's cabin, a "few acres of wheat stubble . . . , half an acre, perhaps, of corn stumps, and a smaller spot of meadow with old harrows, wagons, broken wheels, a few farm and garden tools, a very small smoke house, and one half-covered tepee, . . . a rude rack which supported some old harness, three lean horses, a few hogs, some chickens, more dogs, and a cow crumping dry corn fodder." Carrington noted many evidences of Charlo's efforts at farming, but he could also see his economic poverty.[4]

Other, more scattered evidence has survived, giving a few more details of the extent and seriousness of Charlo's farming efforts. In 1872 Charles Shafft (or Schafft), a longtime Flathead Agency employee, noted that at that time Charlo "was the proprietor of a nicely-fitted ranch."[5] On March 14, 1872, Louis Matte, a white blacksmith at Stevensville who with his Blackfeet wife had been adopted into the Salish tribe, fixed a plow for Charlo for one dollar and repaired his whipple trees for two dollars. On April 20, 1872, he sharpened Charlo's plow again for one dollar.[6] According to a January 1874 article in the *Weekly Missoulian*, sometime between 1872 and 1874 Charlo purchased a new location and moved his farm.[7] Flathead agent Charles Medary reported in January 1877 that the official surveys to locate the boundaries for Charlo's patent cut off "nearly every acre of his best land and includes it in the survey of land belonging to a white man, and runs the balance of his farm over on to another survey of land as poor as the portion left him."[8] During the white hysteria before the hostile Nez Perces came through the Bitterroot in the summer of 1877, a correspondent to the *Helena Daily Herald* pointed out that Charlo was peacefully working his farm and was busy putting up hay.[9] On May 1, 1884, Father D'Aste wrote to Flathead agent Peter Ronan that Charlo "had prepared two fields to put in crops" but was having trouble getting enough seed wheat.[10] In 1889

Henry B. Carrington noted that the first half of Charlo's allotment was "well located" and appraised at ten dollars per acre. This half of the allotment was occupied by Charlo and had "$300 in value of improvements. There is timber for fuel, and a few saw-mill trees. A few acres, not more than 20, have borne good crops." The second part of the allotment, which was not contiguous due to a surveying correction, had "considerable good timber" and was appraised at eleven dollars per acre.[11]

After the end of the buffalo hunts in 1883, the Salish community worked to expand their farms and herds in order to maintain their economic independence and remain in the Bitterroot Valley. Although they certainly would have preferred to continue their hunting-based economy, the extermination of the plains buffalo left them with a stark choice: either become dependent on the federal government or expand their farms and herds. Salish farming emphasized sharing resources and work among tribal farmers, and between farmers and their nonfarming relatives.

The mixed economy of farming and hunting and gathering was referred to by Charlo in July 1877 when he assured newly appointed Agent Ronan that the Salish were keeping to their normal seasonal round and not preparing to join the Nez Perce hostilities. Charlo explained, "It is usual every year after my people put in their crops for them to go to the different camas prairies for the purpose of digging those roots for winter use and while the . . . [women] and children perform that duty the young men fish and hunt. When the crops begin to ripen they return to their homes. They are on their way home now."[12] In 1871, Jasper A. Viall, the superintendent of Indian Affairs for Montana, noted in his annual report that the Bitterroot Salish "do not remain on their farms the year round, but every spring and fall go on a buffalo hunt."[13] Even after the extermination of the plains buffalo, seasonal hunting continued to be important for the Salish. Paul Antoine, a Salish elder, remembered going on fall and winter trips in the 1880s to hunt and trap around Bozeman and in the Big Hole Valley.[14] After the disastrous farming season of 1889, many Salish families relied on expanded fall hunts to help them survive. In November 1889, Carrington waited in Stevensville for the return of Antoine Ninepipe, the Ciselles, and Cisilene from a hunting trip in Rock Creek.[15]

Several Salish elders have left descriptions of the cooperative work patterns that distinguished their farms from those of their white neighbors. In 1939 Martin Charlo related that in the Bitterroot, the Salish "helped each other with the farm work. One Indian farmer had two or three plows going at the same time. Everyone helped everyone else in the harvest."[16] In the mid-1930s, Paul Antoine recalled how those "who had crops of grain were assisted in harvesting by those who didn't and the latter were paid in grain. . . . During the summer when one had a crop and one went hunting for a few days, one of his neighbors would look after it for him. . . . Groups of four or five men would join together and help to harvest each others grain."[17] Flathead agent C. S. Jones's 1871 report found thirty-five farms among the Bitterroot Salish averaging twelve acres each. Since the total Salish population was 558, that would mean there was one farm for every 16 people. In 1870 almost every Salish person must have been either related to a farmer or close friends of one.[18]

The principal factor limiting Salish farm production seems to have been the lack of sufficient farming equipment. Martin Charlo remembered that the Salish "didn't have any threshing machines. We put the grain on buffalo hides that the women had sewed together. Then we led horses over the grain to separate it. Several of the men would lift the robes and shake them to let the wind blow the chaff out."[19] An 1872 correspondent of the *New North-West* newspaper described a scene of Indian women threshing in the Bitterroot: "They lay the sheaves on a large cloth, and then with a pole a dozen feet in length, pelt out the grain. Each one of these noble women, of whom there were a number in the field, had taken a shock apiece and were laying on with a vim that was a caution to Woman's Rights." According to the correspondent, the men and boys were fishing in the nearby river while the women threshed the grain by hand. The writer did meet one unnamed Indian farmer who was prosperous enough to have his threshing done by machine.[20] In March 1884, agent Peter Ronan reported to the commissioner of Indian Affairs on the agricultural equipment problems handicapping the Bitterroot Salish farmers:

> Of the whole number of families, (ninety-five in all) I found there were only five, So provided with agricultural implements and other requisites, as to enable them to make a living by farming. . . . Among them are only three wagons and five plows, with a like dearth of all other aids to tillers of the Soil. Still they have some forty dwellings Surrounded by enclosed farms, and, in addition, about twenty Small fenced fields. These they are not only willing but anxious to cultivate,—having a very fair knowledge of farming gained by hiring to their white neighbors during Seeding and harvesting times . . .[21]

As a result of Ronan's report and the visit of the Bitterroot Salish delegation to Washington, D.C., in 1884, the tribe received government help to expand their farms during the middle 1880s.

The event that propelled Salish ranching and farming from being a secondary resource to a primary one was the loss of the plains buffalo herds in the early 1880s. The last Salish plains buffalo hunt occurred between September 1882 and August 1883. An outbreak of smallpox within the tribe in September 1882 was combated with vaccination and the dispersal of the uninfected Salish into hunting parties. On September 25, 1882, Charlo started for buffalo with a "few Indians." The buffalo hunters lost most of their horses to thieves and had trouble returning to the Bitterroot Valley. On July 31, 1883, Father D'Aste recorded in his diary that "Two Indians started with horses to go and meet Charlot who is a foot." Charlo finally made it home on August 25, but he had "not a horse left."[22] This humiliating finale to the Salish plains buffalo hunts highlighted the economic crisis confronting the Bitterroot Salish. The extermination of the buffalo obliged Salish leaders to develop a strategy to expand their farms in the Bitterroot to replace the buffalo.

## *Other Evidence of Salish Farming*

References to Salish farming in the Bitterroot Valley before 1889 are episodic, not comprehensive. The available sources indicate that the Salish farming effort was substantial and probably involved most of the adults at least part-time. No surveys or production figures have survived to describe the crops raised, amount of farmland used, or the value of farming to the Salish economy.

The Montana superintendent of Indian Affairs, Alfred Sully, wrote in 1869: "Many of these [Bitterroot] Indians were living in houses and had flourishing farms. In fact, some of them had proved themselves as good farmers as the white settlers." When Sully reported Chief Victor's death to the commissioner of Indian Affairs, he commented that years before Victor had "turned his attention to farming and thus set the example to the rest of his nation, many of whom now, are very successful farmers."[23] In September 1870, William F. Wheeler, the U.S. marshal for Montana Territory, reported from the Bitterroot that "Some three hundred and fifty of these Indians make the Bitter Root Valley their home, and some twenty or more families live in log houses, cultivate from an acre to twenty acres of land with success, and raise large numbers of horses. The majority of the young men live by hunting and fishing, and upon the food raised by the industry of their relatives."[24] Flathead agent C. S. Jones wrote that in 1870 the Bitterroot Salish grew 2,000 bushels of wheat, about 5,000 bushels of oats, about 650 bushels of potatoes, and about 60 bushels of corn, and they owned about 600 head of horned cattle, about 100 hogs, and 1,100 horses. On January 29, 1871, he noted: "Of the ninety heads of families composing the [Bitterroot Salish] Tribe, forty-four are well to do farmers—some of them making five or six hundred bushels of wheat annually."[25]

Some of the references to Salish farming during the early 1870s need to be viewed with special caution because the estimates were being used to justify removing the Salish from the Bitterroot Valley. For example, Jasper Viall, the superintendent of Indian Affairs for Montana in the fall of 1871, claimed there were only "three really good Indian farms in the [Bitterroot] valley."[26] In contrast, a white Bitterroot correspondent of the *Weekly Missoulian* claimed that a summer 1872 census of the Bitterroot Valley Salish found thirty-one families cultivating the soil.[27]

Fragmented business records of two Bitterroot blacksmiths show that Bitterroot Salish farmers were frequent customers for work on plows and agricultural equipment. The government paid Louis Matte for blacksmith work for Salish Indians during March and April 1872. That spring Matte fixed, sharpened, or added parts to plows for sixteen Salish farmers: Lebrun [Peter Brown?], Charlos (twice), Narcissa [Narcisse], Big Sam, Big Sam's mother, Antoine Pedro [Antoine Pellew?], Chas. Lamoose, Alexander, Baptiste, Antoine, Ignace, Sophie, Marie, Barnaby, Pierre, and Francis. Matte also repaired whipple trees for three Salish: Ignace, Lebrun, and Charlos.[28]

Chief Adolph mentioned his farming efforts when he complained to congressman James A. Garfield on August 22, 1872, at St. Mary's that the government had failed to keep the promises of economic aid it had made in the 1855 Hellgate Treaty: "Gov. Stevens promised us two horses and two cows each where are they, he promised us plows, where are they? I have plowed with my hands, they are worn out."[29] At a later meeting with Garfield at the Jocko Reservation, Chief Arlee described his farm in the Bitterroot Valley: "I have a place in the Bitter Root. Three houses and fields, good crops like white man, I get money for it."[30]

The most comprehensive list of Bitterroot Salish farmers was compiled in the course of carrying out the Garfield agreement of 1872. During the spring of 1873, John R. Winslett, a white Stevensville storekeeper, prepared a list of Salish farmers in the Bitterroot requesting land patents. The list included eighteen Salish whom Winslett personally knew to be farming, and thirty-three men and eight women who "say they are farmers."[31]

An 1873 *Weekly Missoulian* correspondent reported "large herds of horses and cattle" owned by Burnt Fork Salish farmers.[32] At least one of Arlee's sons farmed in the Bitterroot: on September 13, 1873, Father D'Aste complained that Arlee's son had joined a horse-stealing expedition and left without harvesting his crops.[33] In 1874 a *Weekly Missoulian* correspondent claimed that there were only fifteen cultivated Salish farms, and a government inspector reported only about twenty.[34]

Francois Eneas Lamoose was probably the most successful Salish farmer in the Bitterroot. In July 1877 Will Sutherlin described his farm for the *Rocky Mountain Husbandman*: "He lives in a two story log house, has a good barn and stables, and about 15 acres of land under fence, but not in cultivation. He is represented to be very wealthy, his wealth being in cattle and Indian horses. He speaks English and is said to be a good financier."[35] Francois moved to the Jocko Reservation before 1889, but Carrington valued the improvements on his Bitterroot allotment (under the name "Eneas Fransway") at $660. According to Carrington, most of the allotment had been used for pasture, but part was tilled, and there were three cabins, a corral, and fences on the property.[36]

In 1877 Father D'Aste mentioned that Salish farmers lost their crops to a hailstorm while standing guard to protect white settlers during the Nez Perce War.[37]

The 1880 federal agricultural census described the Bitterroot farm of George Redcrow, a Nez Perce who lived with the Salish. Noncitizen Indian farmers in the Bitterroot were not included in the census, but Redcrow was Nez Perce and had legal title to the land he farmed. According to the census, Redcrow owned 160 acres valued at $1,200, machinery valued at $250, and livestock valued at $21,000. In 1879 his production was $450, including 800 bushels (5 acres) of oats and 240 bushels (7 acres) of wheat. On June 1, 1880, Redcrow had 700 head of horses and one milk cow.[38]

In September and October 1880, W. F. Wheeler again traveled through the Bitterroot and described the Salish farms: "I passed through many small farms up the Bitter Root which were cultivated by Indians. They had as good crops as their neighbors, though their farms were not as large. Beside, they own many horses."[39]

The value of livestock in the Salish economy is suggested by an incident described by Abe Williamson, a white Bitterroot immigrant, in 1881. According to Williamson, a Stevensville sawmill hired a mixed-blood Indian laborer for fifty dollars a month, but the worker quit because "if he wanted money he would sell a pony said thats easier than working by the month." Williamson concluded by noting that "you can buy poneys here of the Indians from 5 dollars to 60."[40]

The ledger for Chatfield & Bass in the Bitterroot recorded a $1.50 charge to Lame Eneas (Indian) for sharpening and pointing a plow on April 5, 1882. On May 10 Eneas was charged another fifty cents for plow sharpening. On April 17, 1882, Antoine Ninepipe was charged fifty cents for sharpening a plow.[41]

In his diary, Father D'Aste twice refers to the Salish leaving St. Mary's Mission in August 1883 to work their fields.[42] On March 25, 1886, a Salish farmer named Anthony Chimmilchi [Antoine Chonemelche] got $2.50 from Father D'Aste to pay for filing his water rights, which suggests that Chimmilchi had an irrigation ditch on his land.[43] Chimmilchi was possibly the man referred to as "Antoine Numchee" in Carrington's 1889 appraisal list, which describes the allotment as "entirely fenced. A small cabin and fence are worth $280." Carrington appraised the land at six dollars per acre.[44]

In 1889 Carrington described the Salish Indian improvements on individual Bitterroot allotments. He presumably ignored any that he did not consider valuable enough to add to the appraisals. Twenty of the fifty-seven appraisals included Salish agricultural development.

> Peter Brown had a cabin, root-house, stable and 2 miles of fencing (the later out of order) worth $440. Aquois-poo-ka-nee [Isaac] was using irrigation to cultivate part of his allotment. Antonine-koo-koo-wee [Antoine Kokouil (Cocowee)] has had portions under culture for ten yrs. his cabin and more than a mile of fence are valued at $220; he has raised wheat, potatoes, corn, and grass. Narcisse Trochee, Joseph Pehotchee [Joseph Npigozin?], Sappelle Chinlough [John Peter Chimlo], Delaware Jim (deceased), Widow Nine Pipes, and Frank Murengo [Marengo] (deceased) had fences and cabins on their land. Joseph LaMoose, Charles Qualchinee, Charles La Moose (deceased), John Kiser [Kizer], Antoine Nine Pipes, and Louis Vandenburg had unspecified improvements and some fencing.

Carrington made vague references to cultivation on the allotments of Widow Therese Brooks (deceased) and Francois Kiser [Kizer]. The Carrington appraisal evidence is spotty, but in 1889 a number of the Bitterroot allotments showed the results of Salish farming.[45]

Finally, according to a story told by Bitterroot Valley whites, Salish Indian women in the nineteenth century would tie the hind legs of their milk cows during milking. After many years of doing this, the cows only needed to feel the touch of the rope on their hind legs while being milked. If the cows' legs were not tied or did not feel a rope, the cows refused to be milked.[46]

## Assets and Impediments to Bitterroot Salish Agricultural Development, 1883–1889

### *Government Agricultural Assistance*

In early 1884, Charlo, Antoine Moiese, Louis Vanderburg, Thomas Abel Adams, and John Hill traveled to Washington, D.C., with Flathead agent Peter Ronan and interpreter Michel Revais. The delegation met with Henry M. Teller, secretary of the Interior, and Senator George G. Vest, who tried to induce Charlo and the other delegates to move from the Bitterroot Valley to the Jocko Reservation. Charlo and the Salish delegation, however, saw the trip as an opportunity to insist on their right to remain in the Bitterroot. After the meeting, the secretary decided to aid the Salish farmers who remained in the Bitterroot as well as those who moved to the Jocko Reservation. In a meeting in the Bitterroot Valley in March 1884, Agent Ronan explained the benefits being offered to those families who moved to Jocko. In his report to the commissioner of Indian Affairs on March 27, 1884, Ronan included an estimate for subsistence supplies and agricultural equipment to help the Salish who chose to remain in the Bitterroot and the twenty-one families who had agreed to remove.[47]

On April 9, 1884, the commissioner of Indian Affairs, Hiram Price, formally requested a congressional appropriation to assist both groups of Salish. On August 29, the commissioner gave Ronan permission to spend three thousand dollars in western Montana for flour, oats, potatoes, and wheat. The harness, harrow teeth, plows, sugar, tea, wagons, bacon, and baking powder for the Salish were to be ordered by the commissioner's office under existing contracts and forwarded to Montana as soon as possible.[48]

No cumulative list has survived showing what equipment each Bitterroot Valley Salish farmer received, but many records confirm that the federal government provided substantial amounts of agricultural equipment and supplies as well as subsistence provisions in 1885 and 1886. On January 23, 1885, the *Weekly Missoulian* reported that Agent Ronan was in the Bitterroot distributing, among other things, sixty plows, fifty sets of harnesses, and ten wagons to Salish farmers.[49] On March 22, 1885, Father D'Aste noted in his diary that all the Salish were in from the winter hunt, and a "good many [were] camping by the Mission waiting for the seed."[50] On April 3, 1885, the Stevensville correspondent to the *Weekly Missoulian* noted that the "Indian farmers in the valley are all appearing with new wagons, new harness, and new plows." In addition, Ronan had brought 600 bushels of seed wheat, 1,200 bushels of oats, and 300 bushels of potatoes on his last visit.[51] The next spring, on March 19, 1886, the newspaper related that Charlo "returns from the Agency with a long line of wagons. . . . Every team attached to a wagon driven by a Flathead Indian, and the wagons are laden with agricultural implements of every description, as also bacon, coffee, tea, sugar, oatmeal, soap, etc."[52]

Between January 1885 and October 1886, Father D'Aste coordinated many distributions of agricultural equipment and seed and subsistence supplies provided by the government to help the Salish expand their farms. His diary entries refer to the following agricultural equipment provided by the government: 30 wagons, 60 sets harness, 60 plows, seven boxes casting for plows, three boxes iron, 12 plow-handles, 36 axes, 59 axe handles, 36 cradles, 36 scythes, 24 hay forks and rakes, 24 hoes and garden rakes, 12 shovels, 12 manure forks, 97 harrows teeth, two grinding stones, six cross-cut saws, and one sewing machine. In addition, D'Aste mentions 300 bushels of potatoes, 600 bushels of wheat, and 1,200 bushels of oats for seed. D'Aste also received two shipments of garden seed, a "good lot" and a barrel of garden seed.[53] Just as the Bitterroot Salish farmers were working to expand their farms to replace the lost buffalo herds, they received agricultural equipment, seed, and provisions. Unfortunately, no production estimates are available for the Bitterroot Salish for the mid-1880s to show the impact of this assistance.

Father D'Aste's diaries for the 1883–87 period give indirect evidence suggesting that, especially in 1885, the Bitterroot Salish farmers successfully expanded their production. The quotations reproduced below are references that either record Salish farmers borrowing harvesting equipment or grain sacks or having grain or flour to sell or pay back debts. The diaries include two such references in 1883, five in 1884, fifteen in 1885, three in 1886, and two in 1887.[54] The following references, all from 1885, are quoted below to help the reader see the nature of this indirect evidence:

> March 17: Charles La Mousse sent 75 lbs of corn (poor corn) for what he owes.
> July 27: I let Alexandre [Alexander Big Knife?] have the cradle.
> August 21: Alexandre has 11 sacks belonging to the Mission, and Martin one.
> August 22: Anthony the snake [Antoine Seme] gave back the two sacks of oats.
> August 28: I let Martin Kaltemgu have a hay fork.
> August 30: I let Joseph La Mousse have a hay fork, long handle.
> September 12: Alexandre gave 100 lb oat to pay for the Dollar he owed, . . . James De la Wair gave back the 50 lbs flour he took two years ago.
> September 13: Martin Charlo got 4 grain sacks, Alexandre brought back 6 sacks.
> September 17: Martin Kaltemi gave back the 50 lb flour; Alexandre gave back another sack.
> October 7: Ignace [Kizer] Kaoshin paid in wheat 3.25 he owed on the hay bought last winter, he gave 2 bushels over.
> October 8: Martine gave back the sack of flour her Father had borrowed 2 years ago.
> October 9: I got back the sacks from Martin Charlos.
> October 30: Ignace NKatò [Ignace Nkuto Finley] gave 2 sacks of wheat 2.00 present.[55]

Unfortunately, the evidence from D'Aste's diaries is only suggestive, but it does imply that Salish farmers had some success in using the U.S. government's assistance to expand their agricultural production.

### *Winter Grazing Lost to White Enclosures*

Another factor in the shrinking resource base of the Bitterroot Salish in the 1880s was the dwindling winter range for their herds of cattle and horses. The enclosure of much of the grassland on the valley bottom by white settlers, combined with severe winters of 1885–86 and 1886–87, forced Salish farmers to switch from wintering their herds on open range to stockpiling and feeding hay. In 1870 the estimated 550 Salish shared the valley with 265 white people.[56] Twenty years later the stock of the 176 remaining Salish residents had to compete with the herds of an estimated 3,500 white people.[57]

Even as early as 1880, competition for range was becoming a problem in the Bitterroot. In October of that year W. F. Wheeler reported in the *New North-West* that overgrazing was forcing a reduction in Bitterroot livestock herds. The white farmers complained that Salish herds of horses and cattle were forcing them to reduce their own herds.[58] In March 1881, the *Weekly Missoulian* reported that George Redcrow, a Nez Perce rancher who lived with the Bitterroot Salish, had lost three hundred head of horses over the winter.[59]

The real crunch for Salish livestock herds was during the hard winters of the mid-1880s, especially 1886 and 1887. On December 26, 1886, Father D'Aste wrote in his diary that the "Indians are running away to their houses for their horses."[60] On February 22, 1887, Father D'Aste wrote to Agent Ronan that the Bitterroot "Indians continued to lose their horses, and if the snow keeps on much longer, only a few will have teams able to put in any crop with, next spring."[61] Nathaniel E. (Than) Wilkerson, a white settler who arrived in the Bitterroot Valley in July 1886, vividly remembered the 1886–87 winter. The weather was so bad that "All the stock, horses as well as cattle that were not fed, perished," and none of the Salish, and few of the whites, had enough hay to see their stock through until spring.[62] The Stevensville correspondent for the *Weekly Missoulian*, however, reported that stock loss was "very light" for those who put in sufficient hay, and he glossed over the losses of those without enough hay.[63]

In the mid-1930s, Martin Charlo recalled an especially bad year for stock in the Bitterroot Valley, probably 1886–87. During that winter, his father, Chief Charlo, lost his entire herd of sixty horses. According to Martin, before the 1880s the Bitterroot Valley bottomlands "were covered with thick bunch grass and there was abundant slough grass in bottoms and horses had plenty of feed. Intrusion of white farming destroyed these natural pastures."[64] The fall 1887 description of Chief Charlo's Bitterroot Valley farm by Will Sutherlin in the *Rocky Mountain Husbandman*, quoted above, noted a "good stand" of timothy hay.[65]

Paul Antoine, a Salish elder during the 1930s, remembered a very similar situation in the Bitterroot Valley in the 1880s as Salish farmers were forced to abandon the free range for wintering horse and cattle herds:

> About six families in the Bitterroot had large herds of cattle when Paul was a boy, but many families had one or two cattle. Six families had large herds of horses and some of these were also the families who owned many cattle. The families with one or two cows would milk their cows, and use the milk themselves; they seldom made butter. Those with long [*sic*] herds of cattle did make some butter for their own use. There was plenty of grazing at that time. . . . In the old days (P. boyhood) those who went hunting allowed their cattle to run loose as little of the land was fenced in at that time.[66]

The loss of winter free range in the Bitterroot Valley for Salish cattle and horse herds reached a climax during the winter of 1886–87.

White farm enclosures also cut off Salish access to traditional root and berry gathering sites in the Bitterroot. Unfortunately, and rather surprisingly, very few records of Salish-white conflict over these sites have survived. On May 1, 1884, Father D'Aste wrote to Agent Ronan that the "roots, this year, are scarce, most of the places where they were used to dig them having been fenced in, or being rooted out by hogs who are running abroad every where here in the [Bitterroot] valley."[67] U.S. government land laws did not provide any mechanism for tribal groups to patent seasonal gathering sites for communal use.

The only record found of conflict over enclosures was the confrontation between John Summers, a white Bitterroot farmer, and Loui Dominic, a Salish Indian, shortly before 1891. As described above, Summers's fence obstructed Dominic's access to hunting areas in the surrounding mountains. In this case, the white farmer finally relented and allowed Dominic and his party to travel through his land.[68] Some white farmers may have continued to allow Salish access to traditional gathering sites within their fences. The efforts of Salish leaders to keep the peace with the whites might also have caused Salish gathering parties to acquiesce when access was denied. In any event, white farm enclosures and plowing impacted the availability of traditional root and berry crops in the Bitterroot Valley.

### *Wild Game Population Crash*

Yet another element in the shrinking assets of the Bitterroot Salish was the big game population crash in western Montana during the late nineteenth century. Newspaper comments on local hunting success probably had more to do with mountain storms than the total game population. For example, in November 1888 one of the Stevensville newspapers reported that large game was being found by hunters in "great abundance," the result of "late mountain storms having driven them to the low range."[69]

The dramatic decline in the region's big game populations was caused by the increased hunting pressure resulting from the explosive growth of white mining and agricultural settlements. Two authors have documented the abundance of big game in western Montana before the white mining boom of the 1860s. Both of them combed the journals of the early white travelers for references to how abundant game was before 1860.[70] Elers Koch, a long-time U.S. Forest Service employee in western Montana, concluded from his historical research and personal experience that the big game populations in western Montana reached their lowest level in the 1890s and early twentieth century.[71] In 1900, Joseph Barlow Lippincott reported on a summer 1897 U.S. Geological Survey reconnaissance of the Bitter Root Forest Reserve, which included the Bitterroot Mountains and the adjacent area of east-central Idaho. Lippincott traveled 876 miles through the reserve and saw only one elk and two deer.[72] In October 1900 an unnamed Stevensville correspondent wrote: "The elk is fast becoming extinct in this region, or being driven from Montana into Wyoming and Idaho."[73] The available evidence suggests that in the 1880s a rapidly declining big game population in western Montana combined with game laws that favored recreational sportsmen over subsistence hunters to cripple yet another underpinning of the traditional Bitterroot Salish economy.

### *The Drought of 1889*

Faced with the extermination of the plains buffalo herds, shrinking winter grazing for their livestock, restricted access to berry and root gathering sites, and rapidly ebbing big game populations, Charlo and the Bitterroot Salish farmers used equipment and supplies furnished by the U.S. government to expand their agricultural production. No production figures are available, but as noted above, there is some indication in Father D'Aste's diaries that Bitterroot Salish agricultural production was expanding during the mid-1880s. Unfortunately, however, the record drought of 1889 devastated the farms of the Salish and many of their white neighbors.

Data are available to compare the Missoula rainfall during the 1889 crop cycle (October 1888 through September 1889) to the historic average. Average annual precipitation in Missoula is 14.01 inches. Between

October 1888 and September 1889 Missoula received only 6.55 inches, or 47 percent of average. Even more dramatic was the comparison between average and 1889 precipitation during the May–September growing season. The average for those five months is 6.96 inches. In 1889 Missoula received 2.81 inches, or only 40 percent of normal.[74]

Agent Peter Ronan described the situation on the Jocko Reservation, immediately north of Missoula, in his August 20, 1889, report to the commissioner of Indian Affairs. Ronan lamented,

> The outlook for the Indians this year is gloomy in the extreme. The drought of the summer has been unknown to the oldest Indians. The country is parched and the usually luxuriant bunch grass is burned to the roots on prairie and upland. Nothing green remains save along the banks of the rivers and the line of the irrigation ditch. The hay crop is almost a total failure; the grain and vegetable crops have suffered in the same way, and not one-quarter of the usual amount can be harvested this season.[75]

In his January 1890 report to the commissioner of Indian Affairs, General Carrington observed: "During the last year of unprecedented drought in the valley, very few of the older Indians secured even a fair crop for themselves or their stock. . . . Even Charlos was compelled to seek aid."[76]

Local newspapers were caught between their desire to print the news and their role as boosters of western Montana. The *Weekly Missoulian* exhibited such boosterism in a local news column in September 1886 asking readers to "Send us word about the big yields of grain and vegetables, the fine fruits, and everything that helps to show up the country."[77] Reports of drought did not "show up the country." In June 1889, however, the situation was so bad that the *Missoula Gazette* reported that in the Bitterroot Valley, "Everything, crops, hay and produce of all kinds is withering for want of moisture."[78] The *Weekly Missoulian* related about the same time that "It must be admitted that the outlook for crops in Missoula county is discouraging. The reports from Flathead Lake are not as bad as from the Bitter Root valley." The *Weekly Missoulian* went on to emphasize that the drought had much less effect on irrigated crops.[79] On July 17, 1889, the *Weekly Missoulian* carried multiple reports that emphasized the success of irrigated crops and the willingness of the railroad to haul hay to Missoula for ten dollars a ton, and feed grain for sixty cents per hundred pounds.[80]

No production figures are available for the Bitterroot Salish farms in 1889, but the results must have been a devastating drain on their farms, herds, and determination to build an economically independent Salish community in the Bitterroot Valley. Despite their farming success during the mid-1880s, the 1889 drought combined with their shrinking grazing, gathering, and hunting resources would have been a crushing blow.

It was not only the Salish farmers who were squeezed by the drought. The number of white farmers in the Bitterroot Valley with delinquent taxes doubled and tripled afterward. Twenty-five owners of Bitterroot acreage were delinquent on their 1887 taxes, and 31 were in 1888. In 1889, 56 were delinquent, and in 1892, 74.[81] The 1889 drought ruined many Bitterroot farmers, white as well as Salish.

Even if the drought of 1889 had not put an end to the development of the Bitterroot Salish farms, the Salish might have eventually run out of land to develop. Since some of the land patented to the Salish was actually controlled by white encroachers, it is hard to determine exactly how much farmland Salish farmers had available. In addition, the land was patented to individuals, not the community, meaning Salish leaders could not give unused patented land to landless Salish who were willing to farm. The available evidence does suggest that in 1889 the Salish farmers still had access to land to expand their farms. In December 1888, M. J. Haley, a special agent for the General Land Office, reported that "scores of tracts of land, allotted to Indians, during the past 15 years in the Bitter Root Valley, Montana . . . have been abandoned. In nearly all cases the land was patented. In the vicinity of Stevensville there are a dozen or more of such cases where the land was abandoned more than seven years ago. The greater part of this is excellent farming land."[82] General Carrington's appraisals of the Salish Bitterroot Valley lands also suggest that in 1889 some of the patented land was still available to expand Salish farms. Of the fifty-seven tracts that Carrington appraised, fifteen had white-owned improvements and had been encroached upon by whites. Twenty had Salish-owned improvements and had been developed by Salish farmers. Nine were identified as having no improvements, and thirteen more had no improvements mentioned. Presumably at least some of these unimproved tracts were still available to expand Salish farms. In addition, the Salish-developed tracts still had options for expanding production. For example, in 1889 Charlo had only developed about twenty of his 160 acres for grain.[83] The historical evidence indicates that the Salish bumped into the drought of 1889 before they ran out of land resources to expand their farms.

## Economic Survival Strategies of the Bitterroot Salish, 1870–1889

The Bitterroot Salish community faced a crisis of survival in the 1880s. The plains buffalo herds were extinct, and other parts of the traditional Salish economy were imploding. But the Salish were determined to stay in the Bitterroot, and expanding their farms offered the prospect of maintaining an independent Salish community there. Government aid during the mid-1880s provided agricultural equipment and tools and supplies to help the Salish increase their farm production. We do not have the minutes of the meeting of Salish leaders where this strategy was chosen, but we have considerable evidence of substantial and sustained Salish efforts to operate and expand their farms. If we assume intelligence on the part of the Salish, their decision to pursue agricultural development most likely resulted from a strategy to preserve the tribe's economic independence and give the Bitterroot Salish community a chance to survive.

As described in earlier chapters, the economic crisis of the loss of the buffalo was the second major challenge confronted by the Salish leaders and people between 1870 and 1891. The diplomacy of the Salish leaders had been successful in protecting their military supply lines and safeguarding their flank as they fought the Plains tribes for access to the buffalo herds. While the loss of the buffalo brought intertribal peace, it also spawned an economic exigency that the Salish met by struggling to expand their farming and grazing assets. In the 1870s and early 1880s livestock herds and part-time farming operations were already an important part of the Salish economy, but they supplemented the buffalo hunt and seasonal harvest of wild berries and roots. After 1883, the farms and herds were needed to support the bulk of the Salish economy.

Ultimately, however, the farms of the Salish and many of their white neighbors were destroyed by drought in 1889, before the Salish had been able to accumulate the capital in equipment, improved fields, and irrigation works that might have enabled them to survive such misfortune. Defeated in their effort to maintain an independent Salish community in the Bitterroot, the Salish reluctantly agreed to remove to the Jocko Valley during the fall of 1889. Charlo and the other Salish leaders had developed an economic survival strategy to cope with the loss of the buffalo, but their concerted efforts had been wrecked by a dramatic climatic event beyond their control.

CHAPTER 9

# "Charlot Loves His People!"

## The Defeat of Salish Aspirations for an Independent Bitterroot Valley Community, 1889–1891

Sunday, November 3, 1889, was a historic and traumatic day in Stevensville, Montana. After attending Mass, Chief Charlo called on retired general Henry B. Carrington to sign an agreement allowing the sale of his Bitterroot Valley allotment.[1] Charlo lamented that "the young [Salish] men would hunt and sell their game for fire-water, and he could not stop it[;] . . . they followed the words of bad white men and stole what they wanted to eat, without working for it." Just the day before, Charlo had rushed to break up a drunken row between two young Salish men. He had knocked the fighters down and whipped them. Before signing the agreement, Charlo asked for assurances that the Salish graves in the cemetery near St. Mary's Mission would be secure. Carrington pledged that the cemetery "would be protected, just as well as the other burial places near the white man's churches." Charlo also sought confirmation that the Salish would receive good cabins on the Jocko Reservation, located on unoccupied sites of their choosing. With Carrington's guarantees, Charlo stepped forward to sign, saying "The Great Spirit said to me last night, 'Trust the white Chief.' Charlot loves his people! Charlot will change and do right! Charlot will sign the paper, and then, the white Chief can write down what Charlot wants."

Before that meeting, according to Carrington's English-language record of the negotiations, Charlo had emphatically refused to move to Jocko: "I would kill myself first."[2] Carrington claimed that he had avoided pressuring or threatening Charlo because he believed that would be counterproductive.

Many previous white negotiators had used threats combined with generous promises, but Charlo no longer believed the promises and for almost twenty years had consistently refused to bow to any threats. Carrington was convinced that Charlo had been won over by his brilliant argument that only God never changed, and Charlo should move for the good of his people. It is just as likely, however, that when faced with the destruction of the Salish farms by drought, Charlo and the Salish community reached the painful decision to move based on what would be in their best interest. On November 2, Charlo had closed a meeting with Carrington with these words: "Goodbye! Charlot will think, all night, and do what is right, if he can."[3]

The agreement between Charlo and Carrington included a specific government commitment to support the drought-stricken Salish farmers until their removal to Jocko in spring 1890.[4] Many problems and conflicts arose over the government's halting efforts to fulfill the commitments Carrington made that day. Most devastating was a two-year delay, until the fall of 1891, in funding the removal. Surviving without crops for two years further impoverished the Salish farmers, who were already reeling from the grinding drought of 1889.

### *The Origins of the Carrington Visit*

The genesis of Carrington's visit in 1889 was a January 1888 petition from Bitterroot whites to Joseph K. Toole, the Montana Territory delegate to Congress. The historical evidence does not identify the author of the petition or the white Bitterroot residents who circulated it. The petition asked for legislation to permit the sale of land owned by those Salish patentees who had already moved to the Jocko Reservation or who lived in the Bitterroot Valley but were willing to sell their allotments and remove to Jocko. The 1872 law governing the Bitterroot Salish patents had made them permanently inalienable. According to the unidentified author of the petition, many of the Bitterroot Salish would be willing to remove to Jocko if they could sell their land and improvements in the Bitterroot Valley.[5]

On February 27, 1888, Toole introduced a bill in the House of Representatives "to provide for the sale of lands patented to certain members of the Flathead band of Indians in Montana Territory, and for other purposes."[6] The bill was reported out of the House Committee on Indian Affairs with minor amendments on May 22, 1888,[7] but did not come up for debate until 1889. The House debated the bill and made minor changes on February 6,

1889, and the Senate followed on February 26.[8] The act directed the secretary of the Interior to sell the Bitterroot lands owned by assenting Salish Indian patentees or heirs. Proceeds from the land sales—less the pro-rata expenses for obtaining consents and making appraisals—were to be paid to the Salish owners in cash or expended by the government for the benefit of the owners. Five hundred dollars was appropriated to carry out the provisions of the act. Section 6 provided for the removal to the Jocko Reservation of those Bitterroot Salish who agreed to sell their lands, but only after the lands had been sold.[9]

By the time the appropriation became available and draft instructions were prepared by the Office of Indian Affairs, it was September 1889. Retired army general Henry B. Carrington was offered the appointment to negotiate with the Salish and appraise the lands. Carrington accepted the assignment on September 21 with the encouragement of Senator Henry L. Dawes, who assured him that more money would be available if the five hundred dollars that had been appropriated was "found insufficient to meet the expenses of the labor."[10] By the fall of 1889 the record drought of that year had devastated crops and impoverished the Salish.

Carrington had been a brigadier general of volunteers during the U.S. Civil War, in charge of raising, organizing, and training troops. He never served in combat, which limited his opportunities in the regular army after 1865. Carrington's military career effectively ended on December 21, 1866, near Fort Phil Kearny, Wyoming, when he ordered Lt. Col. William J. Fetterman to assist a wood train from the fort that was under attack by Sioux, Cheyenne, and Arapaho Indians. Fetterman and the eighty other men with him fell into an ambush and were annihilated that day. The Fetterman action was part of the futile army effort to force the Sioux, led by Chief Red Cloud, to accept the Bozeman Trail and white encroachment on Sioux hunting grounds. As Fetterman's commander, Carrington was disgraced, and he spent the rest of his life explaining and defending his actions. After being removed as commander of Fort Phil Kearny, Carrington accidentally shot himself in the thigh. He retired from the army in 1870 and developed another career as a professor of military science and an author of books and articles on military history. Carrington also became involved with the Friends of the Indian, a white Protestant movement that worked to save Indians by protecting them from white military aggression, but that also wanted to coerce them into white American cultural patterns and values.[11] The Friends of the Indian opposed other late nineteenth-century whites who wanted American military forces to crush Indian tribes and confiscate their resources for white use.

The missionary, imperialist cast of Carrington's views of Indians was expressed in an 1875 speech he gave before the British Association for the Advancement of Science. Carrington sermonized that "the Anglo-Saxon, in his westward march, still meets the red man. It is the old story of an issue of races, in the expansion of the stronger. The inferior must perish. . . . [W]e must work . . . to Christianize, and thereby civilize, the world."[12] On November 1, 1889, during his negotiations with the Salish, Carrington wrote the commissioner of Indian Affairs: "Dear General Morgan, I tell you, that you have a trust in your charge, that is worthy of the mission of Christ to earth, to save America from the reproach of being unequal to its obligations to this fading race."[13]

Despite these views, Carrington was apparently able to treat Charlo with respect and avoid pressuring him and threatening military force during most of their dealings. One of Carrington's first actions after arriving at Jocko on October 19, 1889, was to meet with Michel Revais and Francois Saxa [Lamoose], two prominent Salish, to seek their advice about "the best methods of reaching Charlot and securing his co-operation in the removal."[14] In his manuscript about the removal, Carrington claimed Revais and Saxa were his "tireless and trustworthy advisors and companions" during 1889 and 1891.[15] Revais and Saxa were probably more interested in the survival of the Salish tribe than in helping Carrington, but it is likely that on October 19, 1889, they advised Carrington to avoid using threats when negotiating with Charlo. Carrington did threaten to cut off Salish subsistence supplies in October 1891, but his account asserts that during the 1889 negotiations he carefully avoided intimidation.[16]

The only detailed descriptions of the Charlo-Carrington negotiations were written by Carrington. Charlo's version of the discussions was not recorded. Carrington's account does portray Charlo as independent and capable, concerned about the interests of the Bitterroot Salish, but also his own best interests. Three problem areas appear in Carrington's accounts:

1. Carrington had a tendency to magnify his personal role. For example, he emphasized the importance of his skilled arguments in convincing Charlo to change his mind and move to Jocko. Charlo could also have honestly and painfully evaluated the changing circumstances facing the Bitterroot Salish and decided that at that point removal was their only remaining option.

2. Like most white officials, Carrington did not understand the Salish tradition of collective leadership. Charlo was the spokesman for the tribe, but the decisions he communicated must have been based on many long, and probably stormy, meetings of Salish leaders and tribal members. The details of the debate within the Bitterroot Salish community have not survived in the written record.

3. As a result of viewing the Bitterroot Salish community as an autocracy, Carrington often assumed Charlo's decisions were based on pride and personal ego. For example, he and other white observers frequently interpreted Charlo's refusal to remove during the 1880s as a result of personal animosity between Charlo and Arlee. According to this view, Chief Arlee's death in August 1889 and a government promise to recognize Charlo as head chief would motivate Charlo to move to Jocko.[17] But Charlo had already been offered—and had declined—government recognition as head chief.[18] Charlo's actions can be better understood as a rational struggle to remain in his Bitterroot homeland and pursue what he saw to be the best interests and collective goals of the Bitterroot Salish tribe.

## The Negotiations Unfold: Carrington and Charlo in 1889

When Carrington arrived at the Jocko Agency in October 1889, he invited the Salish to meet at Indian agent Peter Ronan's house the next day following Mass. At this meeting "the new contract [to sell Bitterroot allotments] would be submitted and their signatures requested," but "None were to be asked to sign, until responsible and influential men should declare their willingness to execute the contract, regardless of Chief Charlot's dissent, or his threats. It was also decided that Charlot should be advised of the proposed interview, and be invited to be present if he so desired."[19] When Charlo replied that he did not want to discuss the land question until after he returned to the Bitterroot, Carrington replied that "the Commissioner would call upon him at his cabin in Bitter Root Valley, and talk no business until they became acquainted, and Charlot's views could be considered; but, that if he was willing to join in a smoke, in Major Ronan's parlor, with Francois, Michell, Big Sam, and others, he was welcome to do so and would not be asked to sign, or to talk business at all."[20]

During that Sunday afternoon meeting, Carrington placed the land sale agreement on the table, "accessible to all," and Father Jerome D'Aste was available as interpreter,[21] but Carrington emphasizes in his account that no pressure was put on anyone to sign. Charlo arrived, was seated on a large rocking chair, and given cigars. Carrington then visited with Charlo about his family, the neighboring Nez Perce tribe, railroads, and the Sioux-white war of 1868. According to Carrington, the time was spent in "miscellaneous talk" and answering questions, and he made "no request of any [patent holders] to sign."[22]

Carrington promised to visit Charlo at his home in the Bitterroot Valley so that they could become acquainted and Carrington could "consider" Charlo's views on the removal question.[23] The next day, as Charlo left the agency for the Bitterroot, Charlo reminded Carrington of his promise to visit: "'Tell white Chief, that he promised to come and see Charlot in his cabin.' 'That is what they always say; and then they send for Charlot to come and see them.' 'Nobody ever came to see Charlot in the woods, to find out whether or not he lied when he said he was poor.' 'White Chief talks kind, like all the rest, He would go home and see if this last one lied like all the rest.'"[24] A week later, on October 30, Carrington and Michel Revais, with an unnamed Indian guide, undertook a three-hour buggy ride southwest from Stevensville to Charlo's farm on McCalla Creek.[25] On arriving, Carrington invited Charlo to "a conference" in Stevensville regarding removal to Jocko. Carrington's visit was taken up with discussions about Charlo's farm, his crops, and family, and Carrington gave Charlo a present of cigars. Charlo was invited to send to Stevensville for food supplies and tobacco as a gift from Carrington. As they left, Charlo said that Carrington was "'the first white man from Washington that ever visited Charlot's cabin,' that 'he promised, when at Jocko, and he did not lie!'" Charlo paid a formal return visit to Carrington the next day at Stevensville.[26]

As part of Carrington's strategy not to pressure Charlo, Carrington claimed that he avoided calling on military help from Fort Missoula, but that the soldiers "added a moral support to the negotiations."[27] Presumably indicating how difficult a decision removal was for Charlo, Carrington noted that there were times during the process when Charlo seemed "most obstinate, violent, and threatening." At Stevensville, Carrington again laid the agreement out on a table, and "no pressure was brought to bear upon any, save the simple announcement of the general purpose of the visit." Carrington did, however, point out that the patentees would receive "considerable sums of money" from the sale of their lands and improvements.[28]

When Carrington and Charlo finally began their negotiations, Charlo complained about the failure of the government to fulfill the terms of the

1855 treaty. Charlo asked for the "literal execution of the Stephens treaty," but Carrington did not respond. Charlo continued, saying that despite the broken government promises, he and the Bitterroot Salish had continued to be friends to the white settlers and had protected the whites in 1877 during the Nez Perce War:

> "this is what I said to [Chief] Joseph, 'Charlot, never lies! Charlot never betrays his friends. You are in the land of the Flatheads, where you never had a home. You want to go through the land of my fathers to kill my friends. If you will go through the valley in peace, Charlot will say,—yes—but will not take your hand, for it is the hand of the white man's enemy. You may go through: but if you steal a calf, or a little chicken from Charlot's friends, Charlot and his soldiers will strike you as his fathers knifed the Blackfeet, on all sides, and spare nobody! Go Joseph! Charlot has no more words for Joseph.'"

Carrington recorded that Charlo personally escorted some of the outlying white families to the safety of Fort Owen in 1877.[29]

Carrington's strategy was to isolate Charlo from the rest of the Bitterroot Salish and then appeal to his ego. His arguments and promises—or the devastation of the Salish farms—slowly convinced many Salish to sign the consents, despite Charlo's objections. In one dramatic episode, Carrington produced the original Garfield agreement from 1872 to corroborate Charlo's claim that he had never signed it.[30] Carrington's promise to give Charlo the late Chief Arlee's ranch in Jocko and a "two-seated, covered, spring wagon" were part of his strategy to appeal to Charlo's vanity.[31] Carrington seems to have been unaware of the long and torturous meetings of the Salish community that were probably occurring behind the scenes to grapple with the crisis facing the tribe.

Carrington's account describes Charlo as repeatedly and emphatically refusing to remove because he feared he would look weak if he changed his mind. According to Carrington, Charlo "declared that 'he never would sign, but kill himself first . . . [because] the women will call Charlot a coward and a liar, if he change his promise and sign.'"[32] Carrington claimed he countered Charlo's refusal to consent to the removal with the argument that only God never changes, and that all people start as children and adapt as they grow, sometimes even changing their plans to account for bad weather.[33] Carrington argued that Charlo needed to remove to Jocko to help keep the young Salish men away from gambling, alcohol, brawls, and stealing. According to Carrington, Charlo responded to these arguments with a promise to "think, all night, and do what is right, if he [I] can."[34]

Later that afternoon, on Saturday, November 2, 1889, Charlo was called on to break up a drunken brawl among some young Salish men. Charlo whipped the recalcitrants until the Salish women begged for mercy for the offenders. Carrington offered to have the white men who had furnished the liquor arrested if they could be identified.[35]

Following Mass on Sunday, November 3, Charlo arrived at Carrington's headquarters in Stevensville and made a dramatic speech lamenting the economic decline and breakdown of tribal discipline resulting from the wrenching economic and political crises of the past decade:

> In simple words, with no reference to the incidents of the previous day, he made a full statement of the poverty and wretchedness of the Flatheads of the valley, especially naming several very aged men and women who could not help themselves and whom the young men would not help. He said that "the young men would hunt and sell their game for fire-water, and he could not stop it," that "they followed the words of bad white men and stole what they wanted to eat, without working for it." He dwelt tenderly upon the burial place near the church, asking "if it would be dug up by white men when his people went to Jocko?" Upon being told that "it would be protected, just as well as the other burial places near the white man's churches," he made very explicit inquiry as to what would be their privileges and holdings at the Jocko." He was informed that "he would have his own choice of land so far as possible, but that good cabins would be built for all and that whatever he thought best for his people would be put upon paper when he was ready to explain their greatest needs."
>
> He then stepped forward, with extended hand, and replied, "The Great Spirit said to me last night, 'Trust the white Chief.' Charlot loves his people! Charlot will change and do right! Charlot will sign the paper, and then, the white chief can write down what Charlot wants."[36]

After the speech, Charlo affixed his X to the agreement and then bargained for some additional benefits. The agreement provided for Charlo to be given Chief Arlee's ranch in Jocko; promised food assistance until the removal, which was to take place in spring 1890; and guaranteed that the burial ground at St. Mary's Mission would be protected. A note attached to the agreement provided assurances that the proceeds from the sale of Charlo's land would be paid directly to him. The note promised Charlo "a new wagon and harness," and also a "two-seated, covered, spring wagon." There was a provision, however, that the two-seated spring wagon was to be charged to Charlo "if the Government can not furnish." Carrington claimed that Charlo understood that he would be charged personally for the cost of the spring wagon if Washington did not approve the purchase. According to Carrington's official report, when the Salish arrived at Jocko, each Salish family "having young children, but no cow, should be supplied with a cow." Carrington's unpublished manuscript, "The Exodus of the Flatheads," however, refers to furnishing *every* Salish family "having young children . . . [with] a fresh cow." The note attached to the agreement also reemphasized the government's commitment to give Chief Arlee's old farm to Charlo, saying the Arlee property had been promised to him when he was in Washington, D.C., in 1884. Carrington added: "I confirmed the promise by embodying it in the contract. Widow Arlee and her heirs are satisfied." In his manuscript describing his work among the Salish, Carrington claimed that Charlo had been promised the Arlee ranch only "if just arrangements could be made with Arlee's widow."[37] This restriction was not mentioned in the agreement itself or in Carrington's report to the secretary of the Interior on January 29, 1890. Presumably, when writing the manuscript, Carrington knew about the problems that flowed from this provision and was not above inventing a self-justifying caveat to the promise. Trying to fulfill these vague and sometimes contradictory promises was to complicate Charlo's and Agent Ronan's lives for years after Carrington returned east in 1891.

After Charlo reluctantly and painfully consented to the sale of his land, Carrington continued to collect consents and examine and appraise the lands and improvements. On November 1, 1889, several hundred Bitterroot whites assembled at the Stevensville High School for speeches, supper, and a ball to celebrate the upcoming removal and the opening of Salish lands to white settlement. According to Carrington's account, Charlo "had a special seat of honor" at the gala, and Louis Vanderburg, Michel Revais, Francois Saxa [Lamoose], and "other prominent Indians were favored guests." The evening, which was nonalcoholic, included poetry, toasts, and speeches by various Bitterroot whites. Speeches were delivered about the Salish, the early white settlers, and farming, lumbering, and mining in the valley. Some of the white orators pompously exhibited their arrogance by calling the

Salish "savages" in Charlo's presence. Charlo always used an interpreter in his dealings with Carrington, but he knew enough English to visit regularly with white friends and neighbors in the Bitterroot.[38] The next day Charlo complained to Carrington that "The men who talked, talked rough about the Flatheads. It made me feel bad." Carrington tried to reassure Charlo that none of the white speakers meant to be unfriendly.[39] Another Stevensville assembly on November 15 approved resolutions praising Montana delegate Joseph Toole, General Carrington, and Agent Ronan for opening the Salish lands "to settlement and occupation by [white] people who will aid us in the development of our Infant state."[40]

Carrington claimed that after Charlo signed the agreement to sell his land, he had "the cordial co-operation of the Flathead Chief" in tracking the heirs of the original allottees and finishing the surveys and appraisals of the lands.[41] Carrington continued until late December 1889 gathering consents, making appraisals, and filing court petitions to have adults declared the legal guardians of minors and one insane Indian.[42] The commissioner of Indian Affairs directed that questions regarding heirs and guardians be resolved by the local courts based on the Montana laws governing inheritance.[43] Carrington acted as counsel in order to avoid attorney fees.[44]

Finally, in late December, Carrington returned to Boston to complete his report. The commissioner of Indian Affairs had advised him on December 5 that it was "very desirable that none of the work should be left unfinished, and that you should close it all up while on the ground," but "the entire cost of your work must be brought within the appropriation of five hundred dollars."[45] On January 29, 1890, Carrington submitted his report to the secretary of the Interior along with a bill for $1,057.50 in addition to the $500 already spent, representing a 212 percent cost overrun.[46] Presumably based on the assurances of Senator Henry L. Dawes in September 1889 that Congress would reimburse any extra costs, Carrington had obtained a bank loan to cover his extra expenses for the Montana trip.[47] On February 28, 1891, Carrington wrote to the commissioner of Indian Affairs that "Another *dun* from the bank where I borrowed the money has come. I need it, greatly. Dont let it fail. It is ruin!"[48] The 1891 Indian Appropriation Bill finally included money to pay Carrington $1,057 and settle the 1889 expenses.[49]

The Office of Indian Affairs seems to have been unimpressed with Carrington's budgeting, and his official instructions for the 1891 removal included the proviso that "you [Carrington] will, *under no circumstances*, exceed the limit of $1,000. The amount for your compensation and expenses, fixed by the Honorable Secretary of the Interior in your commission."[50] In October 1891, when the secretary of the Interior suggested that Carrington be put in charge of the removal of the Bonners Ferry Kootenai from northern Idaho to the Flathead Reservation, the Office of Indian Affairs rushed to assure him that Agent Ronan was "fully acquainted with the situation" and "can attend to the matter [the Kootenai removal] satisfactorily and without aid from the outside."[51] During 1890 and early 1891 Carrington did receive an assignment from the Department of the Interior's Census Bureau to take a census of the Iroquois Six Nations' reservations in upstate New York.[52]

Carrington had promised the Salish that he would return the following spring to arrange for the sale of the Bitterroot allotments and removal to the Jocko Reservation. However, Congress initially balked at spending more money on the removal and did not make new funds available until July 1, 1891.[53] The agreement with Carrington provided that the Bitterroot Salish, "who, on account of the dry season last past [in 1889], have had scant crops, and who in view of their removal in the spring [of 1890] will need aid, shall have sent to Stevensville for distribution, according to their actual necessities, sufficient flour, sugar, coffee, tea, rice, and bacon, to prevent suffering, until the time of their removal."[54] In December 1889 the Office of Indian Affairs authorized Ronan to spend five hundred dollars for subsistence supplies for the Bitterroot Salish.[55] R. V. Belt, the acting commissioner of Indian Affairs, claimed in his February 12, 1890, cover letter for Carrington's report that "The fulfillment of the promise to furnish provisions has been complied with."[56] As 1890 dragged on, however, the Office of Indian Affairs was delinquent in authorizing further distributions, and apparently in March 1890, Ronan had to use some of the supplies intended for needy Indians on the Flathead Reservation to assist the Bitterroot Salish.[57] In June 1890 the Bitterroot Salish faced the choice of hunting in violation of state game laws, living off offal from nearby slaughterhouses, or starving.[58]

Agent Ronan gave two slightly different explanations of why the Bitterroot Salish failed to plant crops during the 1890 growing season. On June 2, 1890, Ronan wrote to the commissioner that in spring 1890 the Bitterroot Salish had "asked for seed to plant if removal to this reserve was not at once contemplated by the Government."[59] The drought of 1889 had left the Salish without seeds to plant in 1890. One short item in a Missoula newspaper on March 18, 1890, suggested that Ronan had arranged to purchase "seed wheat, potatoes and like articles" for the Salish farmers,[60] but the official correspondence in the National Archives indicates that Ronan was only authorized to purchase subsistence supplies for the Salish. In his annual report written on August 14, 1890, however, Ronan claimed that the Bitterroot Salish "could not be induced to plow or sow their land in the Bitter Root Valley," because they had relied on Carrington's promise that the removal would occur during spring 1890.[61]

Regardless of which of Ronan's explanations was correct, the failure to plant crops in 1890 had a devastating effect on Bitterroot Salish resources. Ronan reported on December 6, 1890, that "the wagons, harness, plows, and other agricultural implements, and even their stoves which I issued to those Indians [the Bitterroot Salish] in previous years are being bartered away to white settlers for provisions to feed their families and themselves."[62] Charlo related in December 1890 that the Bitterroot Salish would have starved during the winter of 1889–90 if their "horses and cattle had not died in great numbers," providing meat for the band.[63]

At the end of July 1891, when Carrington returned to the Bitterroot to facilitate the land sales and arrange for the removal to Jocko, he described the impact on the Salish of the eighteen-month hiatus: "Many are very destitute. Wagons and plows were sold, for provisions, or expecting to leave, and Charlots statement made this morning, as to some, is confirmed by the [white] citizens."[64] Carrington later affirmed the economic destitution wrought by the 1889 drought, and compounded by the government's failure to act before the 1890 and 1891 growing seasons were over: "No crops had been planted by the Indians. They [the Salish] lived quite largely upon roots and game, except as partially aided from the Flathead Agency at Jocko, sinking daily in misery, wretchedness, and want until fifteen hundred dollars had been expended by the Indian Bureau to save them from actual starvation."[65] The removal of 1891 began based on Salish economic desperation rather than any confidence or trust in Carrington's competence or integrity. When Carrington returned to Stevensville and met Charlo on July 29, 1891, Charlo was "solemn and apparently more grieved than angry" and insisted "Charlot will talk no business, until his people are fed."[66]

## Exodus from the Promised Land: The 1891 Removal to Jocko

Two interconnected problems confronted Carrington and the Bitterroot Salish leaders in 1891 as they wrestled over the land sales and removal: (1) Could, or should, the Salish remove to the Jocko Reservation before the

Bitterroot lands were sold? and (2) Did Carrington's appraisals represent the real value of the Bitterroot Valley allotments?

The 1889 law providing for the removal included a provision that "in the event of the sale of the [Bitterroot] lands" the secretary of the Interior was "to remove the Indians whose lands shall have been sold."[67] Carrington interpreted this to mean that the removal was contingent on the sale of the allotments, and presumably he conveyed this timetable to Charlo during their negotiations. As a result of Carrington's reading of the law, he was alarmed by the slow pace of the General Land Office's preparations for the sales. Carrington feared that if Charlo did not see the land being advertised and sold, he would "think the *removal* a *trick* to get them over into Jocko."[68] The commissioner of Indian Affairs, however, decided that under the 1889 law the Salish could be removed "pending the sale of their lands."[69] From Charlo's viewpoint, the changing timetable could not help but arouse suspicions.

One practical problem with removing before the lands were sold was that those Salish who had the more valuable farms "did not dare leave them for fear that their fields would be stripped of fences and their cabins plundered during their absence."[70] The danger of looting by predatory Bitterroot whites proved well founded, and only a few weeks after the Salish did leave the valley, some of the Salish farms had been plundered and vandalized: "General Carrington informs us that some of the Indian huts have been broken into during their absence and timothy seed and other things which they could not take have been stolen; some of their fences thrown down and hauled away, and windows broken."[71]

An interrelated problem facing Charlo and Carrington was whether Carrington's appraisals represented the actual value of the Salish allotments in 1891. These appraisals served as the minimum prices that the General Land Office would accept when the allotments were offered for sale. The 1889 act providing for the sales stated that the land was to be valued as if it were unimproved, and improvements were to be appraised separately.[72] In his 1890 report, Carrington claimed that his appraisals, of at least those lands that had been improved by white farmers, were not set at "their highest possible value, but at a price so fair that the settlers could afford to buy them in without straining sacrifice, and yet invite competition."[73]

On October 30, 1890, Mary Sedgwick, an elderly white woman living in Stevensville, wrote the commissioner of Indian Affairs asking for a price break on one of the Salish allotments near Stevensville. Carrington had set the value of the eighty-acre parcel at seven dollars an acre, despite pointing out that one-third of the parcel consisted of a dry gulch running through the center. Sedgwick asked to buy the land and pay seven dollars per acre only for the two-thirds of the tract that had any value. She complained that "its more than could be produced off the land to pay $7.00 acre for the ⅔ that can be cultivated."[74]

Even if Carrington's appraisals did fairly reflect the 1889 value of the land, the economic situation had changed by 1891. A national economic panic and recession had spread to western Montana by the time the lands were being sold, and local land values were depressed. On July 31, 1891, Carrington defended his 1889 appraisals as reasonable and claimed that only an expeditious sale of the allotments would provide for "a speedy end of Indian occupation" of the Bitterroot lands.[75] On September 29, 1891, Carrington acknowledged that "Times are hard. Money is scarce. Real estate is down." He also feared that having the sale in Missoula on a Monday rather than in Stevensville on a weekend would "tell upon the result."[76]

Carrington had originally led Charlo and the other Salish leaders to believe that the lands would be sold rapidly, and in short order the Salish would remove to Jocko and be able to spend their money as they settled into new farms. Delays in the land sales, tardy authorization for Ronan to prepare the new homes, and the impact of declining land prices threatened to abort the entire removal program. To complicate the sale further, the General Land Office had originally planned to charge white occupants of Salish allotments for improvements they had made on the land. The improvement costs were to be refunded to the white trespassers at a later date. Only at the last minute did the secretary of the Interior decide that white owners of improvements could purchase the land without paying for the improvements they had made.[77] The Missoula Land Office finally offered the lands for sale on October 5, 1891, and just four pieces were sold. One newspaper report claimed "The appraisement is too high to suit purchasers"; but another noted that "An opinion is held in some quarters that a combination has been formed to prevent bidding in hopes of a new appraisement at lower figures."[78]

Carrington's correspondence with the commissioner of Indian Affairs during the fall of 1891 suggests he was under increasing stress. Neither the Missoula Land Office nor the Flathead Agency was receiving timely instructions or moving fast enough for him. Carrington saw himself as the messiah of the Salish, and he became convinced that only he had Charlo's trust and could complete the removal successfully. Carrington's letters to Washington during July and August of 1891 increasingly emphasized his belief in his own indispensability and Charlo's faith and trust in him personally:

> July 29, 1891: "They [the Bitterroot Salish] had begun to distrust every-body; but patience and care will wear that off."[79]
>
> July 29, 1891: The Congressional delay of the removal until 1891 "has deservedly made the Indians mistrustful; and, only a kind, patient, and firm management will get them moved and settled."[80]
>
> August 17, 1891: "The Indians have confidence in what I say; and, are thus kept in patient preparation. . . . Charlot seems to have lost confidence in the Agent. . . ."
>
> "If, as per Instructions, he [Agent Ronan] is to locate the Indians, and provide for their winter comfort, it should be, UPON CONFERENCE WITH ME. I am positive as to the wisdom of this deliberate opinion; —for solid reasons."[81]
>
> August 25, 1891: "I also mail to Agent Ronan, this day, careful maximum estimate, by a competent mechanic, under my supervision, of cost and material and labor to erect" houses for the Salish to be removed to Jocko.[82]

On August 26, 1891, the commissioner of Indian Affairs specifically rebuked Carrington's efforts to control the settlement of the Salish at Jocko in addition to the removal itself. He assured Carrington that Ronan would be responsible for the Salish after they arrived at Jocko.[83]

Looking through the lens of his ego, Carrington assumed that Charlo and the Salish had confidence in his promises and trust in his benevolence. Charlo and the other Salish leaders, however, must have recognized Carrington as self-important and prone to make promises he could not keep. In 1889 Carrington had promised the Salish subsistence until the removal scheduled for spring 1890, but the Office of Indian Affairs had failed to back up this promise. Carrington tried unsuccessfully during September 1891 to convince Charlo and the other Salish to move to Jocko before the lands were sold.[84] After only four allotments were sold on October 5, Carrington tried to entice the Salish by promising them wages to help erect the new houses in Jocko, and also tried to pressure them by threatening to end government subsistence if they did not move.[85]

On October 11, 1891, the Salish held a community-wide council to wrestle with the bleak options facing them.[86] This was one of the few cases where Carrington was cognizant of the collective consensus building behind Charlo's statements. The drought of 1889, combined with the lack of crops in 1890 and 1891, had so impoverished the Salish as to force them to trust the government to carry out its promises of resettlement aid. According to Carrington, Charlo spoke to him on the afternoon of October 11, saying:

> "I could not sleep, at first, last night. I remembered my father Victor and that his people expected me to do what he would approve, for their good. I told everybody to come together in the morning as soon as the sun was up to say prayers to the Great Spirit. That made me feel better, and I could go to sleep. Then, the Great Spirit gave me these thoughts. 'Charlos, go with your people. They will starve, or freeze here. Nobody will buy your land if you stay. Go and pick out good land and build houses before winter. Shut your ears to lies which bad people tell you.' So I come, to say, we will all go, and go together. We dont want any soldiers with us, or any other whitemen except, White Chief [Carrington] and Joe McLaren. . . ."[87]

Consent to the removal could not lessen the pain of defeat after the twenty-year struggle of Charlo and the other Salish leaders to keep the peace with the Bitterroot whites and protect their economic independence after the extermination of the buffalo herds.

Carrington's account of the removal emphasized Charlo's insistence on directing the march and avoiding any white military escort. Because of Charlo's determination, Carrington scuttled plans to use an army ambulance and soldier escort for Carrington's "personal convenience." Charlo feared that "if white soldiers went with the Indians, it would appear to his people and to other Indians and to white people, that he went under force and not because he wanted to keep the treaty."[88] Charlo organized the march as a military operation and enforced the same strict discipline that the Salish used in moving camp on the plains, where the chief's "emblem of authority was a whip, with a short and strong oak handle, and such was the regularity observed in their marches that if any of the tribe left the order of march and fell out, without consent of the war chief, the disobedient warrior instantly received a severe flagellation at his hand. . . . Chief Charlot himself as late as 1891, exercised this function with undisputed discretion in punishment of disorderly young men on his final march to the Jocko Valley."[89] Carrington related that when arrangements were being made for the party's transit through Missoula, the young Salish warriors supervised the cross-streets, and white soldiers were kept out of town.[90] The Fort Missoula correspondence, post orders, and post returns indicate that the Fort Missoula soldiers were not involved with the Salish march to Jocko.[91] Other contemporary records and eyewitness accounts of the removal do not indicate the presence of U.S. Army troops, but most represent white rather than Salish viewpoints, and they did not specifically state that troops were not involved.[92]

In an 1892 interview with a Catholic newspaper in Boston, Carrington reiterated the absence of white troops during the removal, but explained the move as based on what he fancied as Salish love and respect for him personally. Carrington's suggestion that the removal was a pleasurable experience for the Salish conflicts with other eyewitness accounts. It is hard to tell if Carrington could not sense the emotions of the Salish or if he felt a need to dress up what actually happened.[93]

The Confederated Salish and Kootenai Tribes' Salish–Pend d'Oreille Culture Committee in St. Ignatius, Montana, is currently editing a collection of Salish oral accounts that indicate Carrington did use U.S. Army troops during the removal. Unfortunately, their tribal history book is not yet complete or available to researchers.[94] A 1998 Salish–Pend d'Oreille Culture Committee publication does indicate painful Salish consent: "Chief Charlot gathered the people together. They prayed, and announced that they would go." The trauma of the move was testified to by elders who described the trip as a "funeral march," and who remembered the strict discipline enforced during the trip.[95]

We do not have corroborating evidence of Charlo's insistence that the army not be involved in the removal to Jocko, but this stand is consistent with his attitude in earlier negotiations. As noted above, Charlo had a history of resolutely refusing to capitulate to intimidation. The threat of military force was clear in 1872 and 1883, but Charlo refused to bow. Avoiding U.S. Army involvement in the removal was consistent with Charlo's position before 1891. But nothing could blunt the fact that even if removal to Jocko was the only means to preserve the Salish tribe in 1891, it was a crushing defeat and an agonizing end to Charlo's twenty-year struggle to preserve an independent Salish Indian community in the Bitterroot Valley.

Carrington described Charlo on Thursday morning, October 15, 1891—as he organized the Salish for the actual march to the Jocko Reservation—as defeated but not broken. According to Carrington, the Salish were divided into three groups. One of the Lamooses was in charge of the Salish on the west side of the Bitterroot River, Charlo was in charge of the lead Salish party starting at Stevensville on the east side of the river, and Louis Vanderburg directed the second Salish party starting from Stevensville.[96] A Stevensville newspaper reported that Charlo "looked sad, as he was taking his farewell view of Stevensville and the long familiar scenes of the valley and neighboring mountains. . . . When all was ready he gave the signal to march by lifting a large white wing—the emblem of his chieftainship—and the procession, of perhaps three hundred, moved forward."[97] Washington J. McCormick, Jr., a white eyewitness to the move, remembered that Charlo was in "over-all command" and rode in the rear of his party: "He was the last to leave, but his heart he left behind."[98] Charles Amos Buck, another Bitterroot white, noted the older Salish men "sat on their ponies straight as arrows and looking straight ahead very sober and not a word was spoken." The older Salish women, however, "were bent over crying."[99] The heartbreak and emotion of the trip were emphasized years later by Mary Ann Coombs, a Salish survivor: "She remembers all the people crying about having to leave. . . . Charlo held prayer in the evenings at camp. This helped relieve the agonizing gloom that hung over the camp."[100]

Thursday night the Salish camped just southwest of Missoula on land owned by a white farmer named David Maclay.[101] On Friday, October 16, the Salish passed through Missoula, but the surviving sources do not agree on the route followed. Some of the sources could be inaccurate, but it is also possible that not all of the Salish followed the same route through Missoula. Carrington wrote later that Louis Vanderburg commanded a party of young warriors who blocked the Higgins Avenue bridge in Missoula until the Salish column could be organized for "a compact march through the city." The young men then "guarded at every cross-street" as the Salish passed through the city under the curious gaze of the white Missoula residents. According to Carrington, after the party had set up camp northwest of Missoula on Friday night, three young men, including Martin Charlo, slipped back to town for some "liquid refreshment."[102]

Ellen Big Sam, however, remembered crossing the Clark Fork River at a traditional ford just below the present-day Orange Street bridge to avoid downtown Missoula.[103] In 1891 there were already some buildings along Orange Street—then known as Harris Street—and intersecting city streets that might have required warrior guards.[104] The *Weekly Missoulian* of October 21 referred to the Salish passing "through the city" but did not specify the route.[105]

The second day's march ended at a camp near DeSmet, a railroad station just northwest of Missoula. The third day they crossed the Coriacan Defile, or Evaro Hill, and continued to the Jocko Agency, where the Salish were welcomed with Mass in the church and a feast provided by agent Peter Ronan.[106] Mary Ronan, an eyewitness to the Salish arrival at Jocko, wrote to her sons at Gonzaga College in Spokane describing the arrival. She indicated that Charlo was in charge and did not mention the presence of any U.S. Army troops.[107] Carrington reported that Vanderburg and his party declined to join Charlo and the other Salish at the benediction service held in the agency church immediately after the Salish arrived.[108] This could have been a symptom of the divisions and pain within the tribe over the removal.

Charlo's twenty-year battle to preserve a Salish Indian community in the Bitterroot Valley had been lost. The campaign for the physical survival of the Salish people and control over the changes affecting the tribes, however, continued. Carrington soon returned east, but Charlo and Agent Ronan were left with the challenge of getting the Office of Indian Affairs to fulfill Carrington's promises.

## The Aftermath of Removal

On his return to Hyde Park, Massachusetts, Carrington submitted recommendations for an enlarged irrigation system in the Jocko Valley and a new government boarding school at the agency.[109] He also filed a claim for $360.85 in personal compensation in addition to the $1,000 that had been budgeted for his pay and expenses. Carrington blamed the 36 percent cost overrun on the bureaucratic delays in the Office of Indian Affairs and General Land Office, and Agent Ronan's tardy preparations to house the Salish at Jocko.[110] Carrington had hoarded $176.14 remaining from the $500 he had been allocated for removal expenses, and this was paid to him as additional personal compensation.[111] The balance of $184.71 that Carrington claimed was covered by Congress in the deficiency appropriation bill of July 28, 1892.[112] Carrington's influence with Congress made it possible for him to collect all the money he claimed for his work in Montana, but no evidence has surfaced of any effort on his part to ensure funding to cover his promises to Charlo and the Bitterroot Salish.

In Montana it fell to Charlo and Ronan to sort through Carrington's unfunded promises. Carrington had agreed to give Charlo Chief Arlee's farm in the Jocko, but Arlee had willed the farm to his granddaughter and her husband. Ronan objected that throwing Arlee's heirs off the farm would be unfair, and he attempted to negotiate a compromise to solve the problem that Carrington's promise had created. Charlo was willing to accept the Jocko Valley farm owned by Mrs. Joseph Couture, the part-Kootenai widow of a French Canadian who had worked for the Flathead Agency in the 1870s, but Ronan estimated that it would cost the government $5,000 to purchase Mrs. Couture's improvements. Ronan reported that Charlo was also willing to accept the Flathead Agency farm, and he requested permission to turn it over to Charlo. Ronan included a criticism of Carrington in his December 14, 1891, report on the subject: "Unguarded promises should never be made by any person dealing with Indians. It is generally left to the Agent to fulfill them or to cope with the embittered feelings of the Indians who profess to believe it is his fault if not carried out. I have no complaint to make against Chief Charlot—he is a just and agreeable man, but is a believer in the fulfillment of promises."[113] In early March 1891, Ronan turned the Flathead Agency farm over to Charlo in lieu of the Arlee farm promised by Carrington.[114]

Carrington had also promised Charlo "a big two story house" at Jocko, but he had left it to Ronan to convince the Office of Indian Affairs to cover the cost. In lieu of a two-story house, Charlo agreed to a sixteen-foot extension and a brick fireplace and chimney added to the basic cabin provided the other families. On December 15, 1891, inspector Benjamin H. Miller of the Department of the Interior filed a report supporting Ronan's request for $150 to cover the labor and materials for the extension.[115]

The 1889 agreement between Charlo and Carrington had also promised Charlo a new wagon and harness and a "two-seated, covered, spring wagon, to use in visiting his people, and getting them settled at work."[116] On January 23, 1892, Ronan wrote to the commissioner of Indian Affairs that he had a farm wagon and harness on hand to issue to Charlo, but the commissioner needed to make provision for the two-seated covered spring wagon.[117]

Carrington seems to have promised the Salish assistance with fencing and plowing their new farms in Jocko, but this was not mentioned specifically in their November 3, 1889, agreement. On January 23, 1892, Ronan requested funds to fence and plow at least ten acres of land for each of the

Salish families removed to Jocko, and funds to construct an irrigation system to water the new fields.[118] On April 2, 1892, Ronan wrote that "Every head of a family of Charlots band removed here last fall from the Bitter Root Valley will be the cultivator of a field of wheat, oats and vegetables this year." The Salish farmers had accomplished this feat by jointly farming the old agency farm now belonging to Chief Charlo and obtaining permission from previously established Jocko Valley farmers to plant land these farmers had fenced but were not cultivating.[119] Ronan mentioned the failure to provide fencing and plowing in a January 11, 1893, letter, and a correspondent for the *Anaconda Standard* reported the same situation on October 30, 1893. According to Ronan, in January 1893 the Salish farmers were still waiting "upon promises given [by Carrington] that fields would be fenced and plowed, etc., for their use."[120]

As mentioned above, Carrington had promised a cow and calf for either all Salish families with young children or all Salish families with young children who did not already have a cow and calf. Ronan requested funds to purchase the cows on January 23, 1892.[121] As late as December 2, 1897, then-agent Joseph Carter repeated the request for funds to fulfill this promise.[122] In 1939 Martin Charlo reported that this promise had never been kept.[123]

Carrington also had promised the Salish rations after they arrived in Jocko. The exact terms of the promise were vague, as Ronan assumed the rations would end with the 1892 harvest season, but at least some Salish expected rations until they received money from the sale of their Bitterroot lands.[124] In March 1892 Ronan ran out of beef for the rations, and in July of that year he reported that the food rations were totally exhausted and his new annual food requisition had not yet arrived.[125] In February 1892 the *Stevensville News* reported that "The Flathead Indians complain bitterly of short rations. Big Mouth Charley says that every Sunday morning each Indian gets one cup of coffee, one cup of sugar, one cup of salt, one cup of beans and about five pounds of bacon, all of which they eat on Monday and then wait until the following Sunday for more."[126] Similar Salish reports of insufficient rations were recorded in the Stevensville newspaper on September 13, 1892, and June 27, 1893.[127] According to Ronan, Carrington specifically promised that two beeves a week would be slaughtered to feed the Salish removed to Jocko, but Ronan was never provided with funds to fulfill this promise.[128] In the 1939 interview referred to above, Martin Charlo mentioned this unfulfilled promise but indicated that seven steers had been promised per week.[129]

To compound the bureaucratic bungling and bad faith in dealing with the Salish who had removed to Jocko, the government failed to promptly pay the Salish for those allotments that were sold. More than a year after the removal, on November 30, 1892, after seventeen tracts had been sold, Agent Ronan wrote to Washington asking for the money to be paid soon as a token of good faith. Ronan argued that the money was needed to enable the Salish to fence and improve their farms in Jocko.[130] On January 14, 1893, the commissioner of Indian Affairs petitioned the secretary of the Interior to have the Bitterroot monies paid out to the Salish as soon as it was received.[131] The Stevensville newspaper reported on June 27, 1893, that the Salish had "received no money yet from the sale of their lands."[132] Ronan repeated his plea for prompt payment in his annual report on August 5, 1893.[133]

It was not until March 1894—twenty-nine months after the removal—that the Salish received their first payment of $16,000 for Bitterroot allotments that had been sold.[134] The next month a second payment of $18,000 was disbursed at the First National Bank in Missoula. The Missoula bureau of the *Anaconda Standard* reported a bonanza of sales in Missoula stores for consumer luxuries, clothes, saddles, and craft supplies, while heads of households also purchased plows, spring wagons, harrows, and harnesses.[135] The sixteen-year-old son of Big Sam, a Salish leader, insisted on paying the Missoula Mercantile $20 to settle an overdue bill owed by his father.[136] The Salish appreciated the belated payments for the Bitterroot allotments, but they were unhappy when the government deducted a pro rata share of Carrington's pay and expenses from the land payments. The Salish landowners were forced to pay for Carrington's work in Montana in 1889 and 1891.[137]

A January 1896 payment of $8,800 also resulted in newspaper stories celebrating the honesty of the Salish who settled up old debts from their years in the Bitterroot Valley.[138] One story described Chief Charlo intervening to convince Widow Ninepipe to uphold the honor of the tribe and pay $500 she owed on a ranch she had purchased for her son while they were still in the Bitterroot.[139] Much of the money from the laggard payments went to improve the Salish farms in the Jocko, but the failure of the government to pay the money promptly added to the feeling of betrayal that the Salish felt over government handling of the removal and its aftermath.

The government's ineptitude in handling the land sales was further emphasized by a January 1893 decision by the General Land Office to sell the allotments in eighty-acre units without redoing the appraisals.[140] The Salish complained that this allowed a purchaser to select the choicest eighty acres from an allotment and buy it at a bargain rate. The worst eighty acres then could not be sold since the appraisal had been set at the average value of the entire 160-acre allotment.[141]

Sales of the Bitterroot allotments continued to be hampered by questions about Carrington's appraisals. Agent Ronan reported on January 11, 1893, that Carrington "placed so high a valuation upon it [the Salish land], that purchasers cannot be found who would pay the prices set upon most of the farms."[142] On June 20, 1894, the Missoula correspondent for the *Anaconda Standard* reported that "When they [the Bitterroot Salish lands] were appraised, this section of the country was on the crest of a boom wave and the prices placed upon the Indian lands were considered somewhat high at that time.[143] On October 10, 1896, Indian Affairs inspector C. C. Duncan reported that only a third of the Bitterroot allotments had been sold, and the remaining lands could not be sold at the appraised price "owing to the depreciation in the values of land in the Bitter Root Valley." Duncan recommended that the land either be reappraised or offered for sale at two-thirds of Carrington's appraisals.[144] The commissioner of Indian Affairs, however, concluded that the lands could not be reappraised without new congressional action.[145] Congress did authorize the reappraisal in July 1898, and in July 1899 the Interior Department finally sent inspector Cyrus Beede to obtain consents and reappraise the remaining forty-one tracts.[146] It was September 12, 1900, before Beede completed the reappraisals.[147]

In the end, thirty allotments were reappraised. Thirteen of these were 80-acre units that remained after the best 80 acres of the allotment had been sold at the appraised price per acre set for the entire 160 acres. The reductions in the appraisals for these thirteen units averaged 39 percent. The largest reduction was 71 percent, on Chief Adolph's allotment, but this also reflected that timber had been clear-cut from the allotment after 1889. Seventeen of the reappraisals were on the same 160-acre or 80-acre units appraised by Carrington. Beede's appraisals of these seventeen allotments averaged 33 percent less than Carrington's.[148]

A public sale at Missoula on February 2, 1901, sold all but twelve of the reappraised parcels. The General Land Office then offered the remaining units for private sale.[149] The newspaper story of the sale reported that some bidders colluded to avoid bidding up the prices.[150]

Carrington also seems to have made a mistake in the lands he recorded for Antoine Koo-koo-wee [Kokouil] and Isaac Black Moon [Aquois Poo-ka-nee]. According to a report by Flathead agent Joseph Carter on March 27,

1896, Carrington had accidentally switched the legal descriptions of the farms cultivated by these two Salish men. Consequently, neither man could prove that he occupied the land he had been allotted, and the allotments were canceled and homesteads granted to two white men in the 1890s.[151]

Given this record of unkept promises and bureaucratic bungling, it is hardly surprising to learn that Charlo was bitter and hurt over his treatment by Carrington. In 1896 a reporter for the *Anaconda Standard* described Charlo's attitude: "Charlot feels that he and his people were deeply injured by these officials [government negotiators] and has never forgiven the white race for this injury. It is doubtless true that some of the promises made by General Carrington at the time the transfer was made have never been fulfilled, and the grouty [*sic*] old chief has some reason for his hostility."[152]

## Lost Battle and Continuing Struggle

Between 1870 and 1891 the Salish confronted major diplomatic/military and economic crises. They developed a strategy that allowed them to safely thread their way between military powers that could have physically exterminated the tribe. Then they worked to counter the economic dislocation resulting from the extermination of the buffalo herds and were apparently having some success before the drought of 1889. In that year Charlo and the other Salish were finally forced to accept a painful strategic retreat and remove to the Jocko Reservation. The Salish were thus defeated in their struggle to maintain a community in the Bitterroot Valley, but the larger conflict, to preserve the Salish Indian people and protect as much of Salish Indian culture as possible, continued after the move to Jocko. The 1891 removal concluded the story of Salish survival strategies in the Bitterroot Valley, but it was only a pause in the struggle to influence the terms of Salish adaptation to the white invasion of western Montana.

# Epilogue
## The Struggle Continues

After the removal to Jocko, Charlo and the Bitterroot Salish joined the battle of the Pend d'Oreilles and Kootenais to control the pace and scope of cultural and economic change on the reservation. Charlo accepted having a school at Jocko but refused to permit the students' hair to be cut in the white man's style. He wanted the Salish students to learn English and white economic skills, but not to lose valuable aspects of Salish culture. He supported the Catholic Church and opposed praying in the sweat lodge and recounting traditional Salish legends, but he adamantly fought any sale of reservation land. In 1898 and 1901 Charlo played a leading role in successfully opposing land sales proposed by the federal government. After 1904, when Joseph Dixon forced a Flathead Reservation allotment bill through Congress without the consent or approval of the Salish and Kootenai tribes, Charlo was one of the leaders in fighting to reverse the decision, or delay and mitigate its impact. Charlo died in 1910 as the U.S. government was preparing to sell "surplus" Flathead Reservation land to white homesteaders at well below market prices.

U.S. Indian policy during the late nineteenth century centered on the exploitation of natural resources, the theft of Indian assets, and the use of coercion to force cultural change. The program was founded on the belief held by most white Americans that Indians were inferior and did not make adequate use of their land and other resources. The attitudes of individual Americans ranged from the few who advocated using military force to exterminate Indian people, the many who would have been satisfied if Indian people adopted European culture and disappeared as distinct communities, and the few who could coexist with native communities. The natural resource values promoted by the ideology behind government policy extolled man's manipulation and control of the physical environment for private gain. This policy required continual reduction of the Indian reservation land base, destruction of tribal community organization, education that promoted the values of white society, and removal of Indian communities from "public" lands. Military pressure was used against some of the tribes or bands that objected to living on reservations.

While the Salish were busy navigating a rapidly changing diplomatic and economic landscape during the nineteenth century, the advancing white population was expanding its economic activity in western Montana. The fur trade, gold rush, mining industry, railroads, and creation of commercial agriculture all represented new ways to exploit the landscape. White expansion required displacing the Salish from much of their lands and curtailing many traditional Salish economic activities. The boom in the white economy continued through the twentieth century, leaving a legacy of untreated mining wastes, soil erosion, fire-prone forests, and poorly planned subdivisions. But that is another story.

Bitterroot Salish leaders in the late nineteenth century did not need to deal directly with white ideology: the Salish needed to cope with the facts on the ground. The white settlers might have believed in their superiority, but the immediate challenge for the Salish was to avoid conflict with the expanding white population and protect enough resources to preserve their economic independence. Federal Indian policies posed the threat of white military intervention, but as long as the Salish could manage their relations with their white neighbors and avoid conflict, the U.S. Army was unlikely to attack. Bitterroot Salish life during the late nineteenth century was molded by the local situation they faced and their efforts to cope with the changes around them.

Between 1870 and 1891 the Bitterroot Salish confronted crises on both the military and economic fronts. There is little direct historical evidence of the debates and reasoning of Salish leaders as they developed strategies to cope with these crises. Fortunately, however, a large number of historical sources document the implementation of these strategies. The white invasion of western Montana did not rely on military battles but on competition from an expanding population of whites, who like locusts consumed resources traditionally used by the Salish. Many local white settlers were willing to treat their Salish neighbors honorably and with respect, but even the white people who had positive relations with the Salish increased pressure on the local resource base and undermined their economy. Since the Salish were locked in a long-running battle with the Plains tribes in the nineteenth century for access to the buffalo herds, the Salish actively worked to maintain peaceful relations with the growing white population. This strategy protected their supply lines of guns and ammunition, gave the Salish more allies against the much larger Plains tribes, and protected them from a multifront war that could have decimated the tribe. The arrogant and possessive western Montana whites were not easy to get along with, but with hard work, this strategy allowed the Salish to survive a military competition against much more powerful forces.

Salish efforts to get along with western Montana settlers were demonstrated most dramatically in 1877 when they refused to join their Nez Perce allies' fight against the whites. The Salish pursued what they saw as their own best interests. In 1872 the Salish came perilously close to conflict as local whites formed militias before Congressman James A. Garfield came to the valley to negotiate with the Salish leaders. The Salish adroitly navigated the crisis and avoided war. One outcome of the 1872 negotiations was that local whites gained title to their farms, which defused their conflict with Salish land claims. A virulent campaign by local business interests and the Missoula newspaper for a U.S. Army fort in the 1870s threatened to antagonize race relations in an effort to support the local white economy. While Missoula leaders were searching for federal military dollars, they attempted to harass Salish farmers and ranchers in the Bitterroot with taxes. Many specific incidents described in previous chapters offer proof of Salish efforts to maintain amicable relations with Bitterroot Valley whites while protecting the rights and property of tribal members.

The loss of the buffalo herds in the early 1880s ended intertribal warfare, but the Salish faced catastrophic economic dislocation. In response they worked to expand their farms and herds in the Bitterroot Valley. Declining western Montana wild game populations, winter stock deaths, and loss of traditional gathering sites amplified the economic crisis and the importance of growing their farms and herds. There is some evidence that Salish farms were making progress in the mid-1880s, but climatic crises—including hard winters and a severe drought—wiped out the Salish farmers before they could develop the financial reserves that might have enabled them to survive as an economically independent community in the Bitterroot Valley.

One question remains unanswered by the sources: did the Salish control enough resources in the Bitterroot Valley in the 1880s to support their community, even with expanded farming? Did the Salish Bitterroot lands and seasonal wage labor offer enough economic potential to replace the buffalo and other reduced hunting and gathering resources? We do not know if the 1889 drought just hastened the inevitable collapse of the Salish economy in the Bitterroot Valley or whether the drought prevented the Salish from reaching their goal of economic self-sufficiency. The surviving historical evidence is too sketchy to give us a detailed measure of the resources that the Bitterroot Salish had access to in the 1880s. We do not know what could have happened if the 1889 drought had not intervened.

During the nineteenth century the Bitterroot Salish developed survival strategies to protect the tribe and allow the community to survive. This pattern of peaceful resistance, selective cultural borrowing, and active efforts to protect tribal interests is a thread that continued through the twentieth century and into the twenty-first.

Between 1898 and 1910 the Salish and Kootenai tribes of the Flathead Reservation fought against efforts of predatory Montana whites to allot and open the reservation to white settlers. Government policy at the time was based on transferring Indian land to white ownership at far below market value. Tribal leaders successfully resisted the earliest attempts to sell reservation land but were unable to counter the assault launched by Congressman Joseph M. Dixon in 1904. Right up to the opening of the reservation in 1910, the tribes opposed the sale of their land and worked to stop or mitigate the policy.

During the 1910s the tribes fought government policies to use tribal funds to subsidize construction on the reservation of an irrigation system that primarily benefited white homesteaders. Tribal representatives testified in Congress opposing irrigation appropriations charged against the tribes. They had some success, but the battle over funding the Flathead Irrigation Project dragged on for most of the twentieth century.

The federal policy of forced land patents on Indian allotments during the 1910s threatened remaining tribal lands, but the tribes fought the policy politically and in the courts. Land was lost through bargain sales, but the tribes probably slowed the damage until the national policy was reversed in the 1930s.

In the 1920s the first proposals to develop the Kerr Dam hydroelectric power site included use of the income to subsidize white irrigators on the reservation. With the aid of a national crusade led by John Collier, the tribes forced the government to recognize their ownership interest in this valuable property. The tribes were also actively involved in the battle over who would get the federal license to build the dam. The white irrigators did finally receive a subsidy from the dam site rentals, and the tribes' choice did not get the license, but the tribes benefited from substantial revenues from the site.

National Indian policy during the 1950s terminated federal recognition of some tribes, which devastated their land bases and other assets. The Confederated Salish and Kootenai Tribes (CSKT) were an early target for this policy. They avoided termination by cultivating support from Montana politicians who were sympathetic to the tribes and concerned about the cost of termination to local white taxpayers.

During the 1960s and later, efforts to protect the tribes centered on educational and economic development to grow their skills and assets. Tribal members completed academic degrees in a variety of fields, and many were employed by the tribes, who began to assume more responsibility for self-government. The CSKT also expanded their political influence in Washington, D.C., Helena, and Polson. The tribes fought these assaults and even won some of the battles, but they never gave up their efforts to preserve the tribes and protect their interests. The same resourcefulness and adaptability that distinguished Bitterroot Salish history between 1870 and 1891 characterized the history of the Flathead Indian Reservation tribes during the twentieth century.

The Salish in 2010 are still struggling for physical survival and trying to protect important parts of their culture. These contemporary battles parallel the nineteenth-century struggles of Chief Charlo and the Bitterroot Salish. In the twenty-first century the CSKT supports a large natural resources department charged with protecting the Flathead Indian Reservation's land, water, and game resources. In 2009 they were working to have a say in managing the U.S. National Bison Range and mitigating the ecological and social impact of rebuilding U.S. Highway 93 through the reservation. The tribal health department is focused on preventing alcohol abuse and promoting the physical health of the Salish and Kootenai people. The CSKT Cultural Preservation Department, the Kootenai Culture Committee, and the Salish–Pend d'Oreille Culture Committee are documenting and preserving traditional cultural knowledge and practices for future generations. Tribal history is littered with battles won and lost, but as long as a distinctively Salish Indian community remains, the fight for survival continues.

Many earlier histories of the Salish and other tribes were based on the assumption that the Indian people were helpless, pathetic victims, incapable of understanding or responding to their changing situation. I believe that more detailed case studies of the concrete, day-to-day events that impacted the various tribes might reveal that, like the Salish, other tribes were actively involved in developing strategies to protect their communities and interests during the cataclysms of Indian-white contact in nineteenth-century America. Histories that examine Native Americans during the late nineteenth century need to reconstruct the efforts of tribal communities to cope with the dire situations they faced. The ideology and philosophy of the white government and church bureaucracies were only part of the drama. Historians must rise above the biases and bigotry in the records and reconstruct tribal actions, not just describe the activities and viewpoints of white people dealing with Indians. Native American history is primarily the story of what the tribal people did in response to the situations they confronted.

# Notes

## Abbreviations

| | |
|---|---|
| AAAG | Acting Assistant Adjutant General |
| AAG | Assistant Adjutant General |
| ARCIA | Annual Report of the U.S. Commissioner of Indian Affairs (U.S. Government Printing Office, Washington, D.C.) |
| ARSI | Annual Report of the U.S. Secretary of the Interior (U.S. Government Printing Office, Washington, D.C.) |
| AS | Anaconda (Mont.) Standard |
| BCIM | Bureau of Catholic Indian Missions, Marquette University, Milwaukee, Wis. |
| *BR Trails* | *Bitterroot Trails* (Bitterroot Valley Historical Society, Darby and Stevensville, Mont., 1982–2007), 4 vols. |
| BRVPS | Bitterroot Valley Pioneer Society Papers, SC 1053, Montana Historical Society, Helena |
| Carrington MS | Henry B. Carrington, "The Exodus of the Flatheads," unpublished manuscript, Carrington Family Papers, Sterling Library, Yale University, New Haven, Conn. |
| CommIA | U.S. Commissioner of Indian Affairs |
| DAI | Dissertation Abstracts International |
| D'Aste, Diaries | Jerome D'Aste, S.J., Diaries, PNTMC, rr. 29–30 |
| *DM* | *Daily Missoulian* (Missoula, Mont.) |
| FH agent | Flathead Indian agent, Flathead Reservation, Mont. |
| GLO | U.S. General Land Office |
| LR | Letters Received |

| | |
|---|---|
| LS | Letters Sent |
| LB | Letter Book |
| MHS | Montana Historical Society, Helena |
| MslaCtRec | Missoula County Court Records, Missoula County Courthouse, Missoula, Mont. |
| NA | National Archives |
| NAmf | National Archives microfilm publication |
| *NNW* | *New North-West* (Deer Lodge, Mont.) |
| PNTMC | Pacific Northwest Tribes Missions Collection of the Oregon Province Archives of the Society of Jesus, edited by Robert C. Carriker and Eleanor R. Carriker, microfilm edition (Scholarly Resources, Wilmington, Del., 1987) |
| *RMH* | *Rocky Mountain Husbandman* (Diamond City, Mont., and other locations) |
| Schaeffer Papers | Claude Schaeffer Papers, Glenbow-Alberta Foundation, Calgary, Alberta |
| SecInt | U.S. Secretary of the Interior |
| SuptIndAff | U.S. Superintendent of Indian Affairs |
| Toole Archives | Ross Toole Archives, Mansfield Library, University of Montana, Missoula |
| UM | University of Montana, Missoula |
| *WM* | *Weekly Missoulian* (Missoula, Mont.) |

## Chapter 1

1. See, for example, Cressman, *Prehistory of the Far West*; Binnema, *Common and Contested Ground*, 55–85.

2. Teit, "Salishan Tribes of the Western Plateaus," 359.

3. Thompson, *David Thompson's Narrative*, 240. See also Jackson, ed., *Letters of the Lewis and Clark Expedition*, 2:528.

4. Binnema, *Common and Contested Ground*, 86–106. See also Secoy, *Changing Military Patterns*, 45–64.

5. Turney-High, "Diffusion of the Horse to the Flatheads," 183–85.

6. Teit, "Salishan Tribes of the Western Plateaus," 318–19, 346.

7. Moulton, ed., *Journals of the Lewis & Clark Expedition*, 5:188.

8. Stevens, "Report of Explorations," 1:148.

9. Bradley, "Lieut. James H. Bradley Manuscript," 288. See also Ewers, "Were the Blackfoot Rich in Horses?"

10. Thompson, *David Thompson's Narrative*, 240–43.

11. Henry, *Journal of Alexander Henry*, 2:378.

12. Ibid., 480–81, 527.

13. Thompson, *David Thompson's Narrative*, 389–93.

14. Mengarini, *Recollections of the Flathead Mission*, 193–94.
15. Smith to Greene, Feb. 6, 1840, in Baird and Baird, *In Nez Perce Country*, 89.
16. "Louise Lumprey" notebook, Schaeffer Papers, file 118, 22–24.
17. Boyd, "Introduction of Infectious Diseases," 95.
18. Teit, "Salishan Tribes of the Western Plateaus," 315–16.
19. Reuben Lewis to Meriwether Lewis, Apr. 21 [1810], Meriwether Lewis Collection, Missouri Historical Society.
20. Menard to Chouteau, Apr. 21, 1810, in Chittenden, *American Fur Trade*, 2:897–98.
21. "A Great Squaw Man," *AS*, Feb. 19, 1893, 9.
22. Bigart and Woodcock, eds., *In the Name of the Salish*, 33.
23. Stuart, *Forty Years on the Frontier*, 1:174–76.
24. Vaughn, *Then and Now*, 211–12.
25. Meredith, "Bannack and Gallatin City," 249.
26. "The Indian War," *Montana Post*, July 8, 1865, 2.
27. "Helena Letter," *Montana Post*, Mar. 17, 1866, 3.
28. "A Buffalo Hunt in the Muscleshell [*sic*] Country, [No. 2]," *Helena Weekly Herald*, Feb. 27, 1868, 1.
29. "Red Skins," *Helena Weekly Herald*, July 19 [16], 1868, 8.
30. Ewers, "Nicholas Point Drawings," 30.
31. Ewers, "Identification and History of the Small Robes Band," 400.
32. De Smet, *Life, Letters, and Travels*, 1:338, 363.
33. Larpenteur, *Forty Years a Fur Trader*, 2:259–60.
34. Mullins, "Report of First Lieutenant John Mullins," 164.
35. De Smet, *Life, Letters, and Travels*, 2:524.
36. Stevens, "Report of Explorations," 1:150.
37. Honig, *James Bridger*, 114–16; Alter, *Jim Bridger*, 144, 218.
38. Turney-High, *Flathead Indians of Montana*, 41–43.
39. Palladino, *Indian and White*, 8–29.
40. Wyeth, "Correspondence and Journals," 193–94.
41. Spier, *Prophet Dance*.
42. Point, *Wilderness Kingdom*, 39–42.
43. De Smet, *Life, Letters, and Travels*, 1:317, 328–30, 336–37.
44. "Reductions of Paraguay," *New Catholic Encyclopedia* (1967) 12:165–66.
45. De Smet, *Life, Letters, and Travels*, 1:224, 227.
46. Ibid., 332–33.
47. Ibid., 321–22.
48. Ibid., 363–66; Buckley, *Nicolas Point, S.J*, 249–59.
49. De Smet, *Life, Letters, and Travels*, 1:319–23.
50. Point, *Wilderness Kingdom*, 189–92.
51. De Smet, *Oregon Missions*, 394–96; Mengarini, "Rocky Mountains," 30–31, 144–49.

52. De Smet, *Life, Letters, and Travels,* 1:338.

53. Ibid., 2:589.

54. Ibid., 3:949–56; Point, *Wilderness Kingdom,* 199.

55. Schaeffer, "First Jesuit Mission," 227–50.

56. Palladino, *Indian and White,* 67.

57. "Father Mengarini," 93–97.

58. Stevens, "Narrative and Final Report," vol. 12, bk. 1, p. 124.

59. Suckley to Stevens, Dec. 19, 1853, in Stevens, "Report of Explorations," 1:292–93.

60. [Menetrey], "Extract from a Letter," 300–302.

61. See Bigart, ed., *Life and Death at St. Mary's Mission;* Rappagliosi, *Letters from the Rocky Mountain Indian Missions,* 24–45.

62. Elwood Evans, journal of 1853 expedition, Beinecke Library, Yale University.

63. Mullan to Stevens, Dec. 14, 1853, NAmf M234, r. 907, fr. 171.

64. Bigart and Woodcock, eds., *In the Name of the Salish,* 22.

65. Ibid., 33–34.

66. Richards, *Isaac I. Stevens,* 226–34.

67. Bigart and Woodcock, eds., *In the Name of the Salish,* 51.

68. Ibid., 55.

69. Ibid., 56–62.

70. Ibid., 15.

71. Stevens, "Narrative and Final Report," vol. 12, bk. 1, p. 221.

72. Burns, "Jesuit at the Hell Gate Treaty," 108–109. See page 104 for the original French. Alexander called the governor "un homme à doubles bouches," or "a man with two mouths."

73. Bigart and Woodcock, eds., *In the Name of the Salish,* 9.

74. Kappler, ed., *Indian Affairs,* 2:736.

75. Owen to Doty, Apr. 25, 1857, NAmf M5, r. 22, fr. 121.

76. Lansdale to SuptIndAff, Sept. 22, 1857, ARSI (1857): 666–67.

77. Stevens to Lansdale, Sept. 7, 1855, NAmf M5, r. 1, fr. 350.

78. Lansdale to Stevens, Oct. 2, 1855, NAmf M5, r. 22, fr. 35.

79. Bigart and Woodcock, eds., *In the Name of the Salish,* 44.

80. Stevens to CommIA, Sept. 16, 1854, ARSI (1854): 409–11.

81. Mullan to Stevens, Nov. 18, 1853, in Stevens, "Report of Explorations," 1:437.

82. Doty, "Visit to the Blackfoot Camp."

83. Owen, *Journals and Letters,* 2:168–69, 199.

84. Bigart and Woodcock, eds., *In the Name of the Salish,* 12.

85. Ibid., 153.

86. Ibid., 158–59.

87. Owen, *Journals and Letters,* 2:223.

88. Hutchins to SuptIndAff, June 30, 1863, ARSI (1863): 573.

89. SuptIndAff to Owen, Sept. 6, 1860, NAmf M234, r. 612, fr. 491; SuptIndAff to CommIA, Oct. 19, 1862, ARSI (1862): 538.

90. Chapman to CommIA, Oct. 28, 1866, NAmf M234, r. 488, fr. 327.

91. Cullen to CommIA, Aug. 22, 1868, ARSI (1868): 678.

92. "Minutes of Remarks," Aug. 1868, NAmf M234, r. 489, fr. 306.

93. Bigart and Woodcock, eds., *In the Name of the Salish*, 12–13.

94. Cullen to CommIA, Aug. 22, 1868, ARSI (1868): 677; but see also McCormick to CommIA, Mar. 1, 1869, NAmf M234, r. 489, fr. 376.

95. Galbreath to SuptIndAff, Sept. 6, 1869, ARCIA (1869): 296. See also Sully to CommIA, Oct. 11, 1869, NAmf M234, r. 489, fr. 635.

96. Chapman to SuptIndAff, Apr. 2, 1866, NAmf234, r. 488, fr. 210.

97. McCormick to CommIA, Mar. 1, 1869, NAmf M234, r. 489, fr. 376.

98. Affidavit of William H. Norton, Dec. 28, 1871, NAmf M234, r. 492, fr. 92; Viall to CommIA, Aug. 5, 1872, NAmf M234, r. 493, fr. 177.

99. Wells to CommIA, Apr. 15, 1867, NAmf M234, r. 488, fr. 509.

100. Viall to Jones, Sept. 21, 1872, NAmf M234, r. 492, fr. 449.

101. Garfield to CommIA, Nov. 15, 1872, NAmf M234, r. 492, fr. 199.

102. Medary to CommIA, Sept. 24, 1875, NAmf M234, r. 502, fr. 661; "Death of a Pioneer," *Missoula (Mont.) Gazette* (daily), Mar. 19, 1891, 1; Schafft, "Sketch of a Life," 26–37.

103. Viall to CommIA, Sept. 25, 1872, ARSI (1872): 660.

104. Viall to CommIA, Dec. 8, 1870, NAmf M234, r. 490, fr. 849; Cavanaugh to CommIA, Apr. 7, 1871, NAmf M234, r. 491, fr. 104; Jones to CommIA, May 17, 1872, NAmf M234, r. 492, fr. 335; Jones to CommIA, July 1, 1872, NAmf M833, r. 2, fr. 153.

105. Hutchins to CommIA, Jan. 17, 1865, NAmf M234, r. 488, fr. 62.

106. U.S. Department of the Interior, *Register of Officers and Agents*, 1869, 172; 1871, 178–79; 1873, 323; 1875, 365–66; and 1877, 287.

107. "Minutes of Remarks," Aug. 1868, NAmf M234, r. 489, fr. 306.

108. McCormick to CommIA, Mar. 1, 1869, NAmf M234, r. 489, fr. 376.

109. Galbreath to SuptIndAff, Sept. 6, 1869, ARCIA (1869): 298.

110. "Minutes of Remarks," Aug. 1868, NAmf M234, r. 489, fr. 306.

111. De Smet, *Life, Letters, and Travels*, 1:342–58.

112. Palladino, *Indian and White*, 47. Some of Father Palladino's details may have become hazy over time as the Salish traditionally used wild onions as condiments and were accustomed to their strong taste. See Hart, *Montana—Native Plants and Early Peoples*, 10.

113. Woody, "Sketch of the Early History of Western Montana," 92–93.

114. Weisel, ed., *Men and Trade*, 7.

115. Wheeler, "Judge Caleb E. Irvine," 476.

116. Ewers, "Iroquois Indians in the Far West," 2–10.

117. Weisel, ed., *Men and Trade*, 5, 30.

118. Owen, *Journals and Letters*, 1:50, 242.

119. Ibid., 87.

120. Weisel, ed., *Men and Trade*, 31.

121. Ibid., 28.

122. Ibid., 30.

123. George Suckley, Journal, MS in the Natural History Library, Smithsonian Institution, entry for Oct. 7, 1853.

124. F. H. Burr, Diary, 1858, Beinecke Library, Yale University, entry for Feb. 22, 1858.

125. Weisel, ed., *Men and Trade*, 60–61.

126. Harris, Journals, MHS, entry for May 13, 1860.

127. Owen, *Journals and Letters*, 1:127.

128. Ibid., 128, entry for May 21, 1856.

129. Harris, Journals, MHS, entries for Sept. 22, 1864; Oct. 11, 1867; Sept. 29, 1868.

130. Owen, *Journals and Letters*, 2:35, entry for Oct. 27, 1866.

131. Ibid., 185.

132. Owen to SuptIndAff, May 31, 1859, ARCIA (1859): 424.

133. Owen, *Journals and Letters*, 2:193. See also Owen to SuptIndAff, Aug. 10, 1859, NAmf M5, r. 22, fr. 156, where date is Aug. 10, 1859.

134. Owen, *Journals and Letters*, 2:223.

135. Ibid., 265.

136. Harris, Journals, MHS.

137. Ibid.

138. Owen, *Journals and Letters*, 1:262.

139. Ibid., 322.

140. "The National Rail Road," *Oregon Spectator*, Dec. 24, 1853, 3.

141. Saxton to Stevens, Feb. 1854, in Stevens, "Report of Explorations," 1:260–61.

142. Suckley to Stevens, Dec. 19, 1853, in Stevens, "Report of Explorations," 1:292–93.

143. Suckley, Journal, Natural History Library, Smithsonian Institution.

144. Tinkham to Stevens, July 19, 1854, in Stevens, "Report of Explorations," 1:279.

145. Gibbs to McClellan, Mar. 4, 1854, in Stevens, "Report of Explorations," 1:415.

146. Weisel, ed., *Men and Trade*, 76.

147. John Owen, Diaries, 1851–63, John Owen Papers, Diary 4a (1854), MHS. There are assorted unpublished memos and accounts in the diaries.

148. Owen, *Journals and Letters*, 1:116.

149. Frederick H. Burr, Diary, Jan. 1, 1857–Jan. 4, 1858, Beinecke Library, Yale University, entry for Feb. 19, 1857.

150. Owen, *Journals and Letters*, 1:171.

151. Ibid., 194.

152. Ibid., 2:195. See also Owen to SuptIndAff, Oct. 10, 1859, NAmf M5, r. 22, fr. 161.

153. Owen, *Journals and Letters*, 1:214.

154. Ibid., 226.

155. Ibid., 230–31.

156. Harris, Journals, MHS, entry for Feb. 18, 1862.
157. Owen, *Journals and Letters,* 1:244.
158. Harris, Journals, MHS.
159. Owen, *Journals and Letters,* 1:250.
160. Ibid., 255, entry for July 5, 1862.
161. Harris, Journals, MHS.
162. Owen, *Journals and Letters,* 1:252.
163. Harris, Journals, MHS, entry for May 17, 1862.
164. Owen, *Journals and Letters,* 1:265.
165. Harris, Journals, MHS, entry for May 8, 1863.
166. Ibid., entry for Jan. 21, 1864.
167. Ibid., entry for Feb. 20, 1864.
168. Owen, *Journals and Letters,* 2:72.
169. Ibid., 105, 110, entries for Apr. 7 and May 29, 1868.
170. Owen, *Journals and Letters,* 1:194.
171. Owen to SuptIndAff, Oct. 26, 1859, NAmf 5, r. 22, fr. 169.
172. Harris, Journals, MHS.
173. Ibid., entry for May 19, 1861.
174. Ibid., folder 3.
175. Harris, Journals, MHS.
176. Hutchins to SuptIndAff, Dec. 2, 1862, encl. of SuptIndAff to CommIA, Jan. 6, 1863, NAmf M234, r. 908, fr. 95.
177. Harris, Journals, MHS, entry for May 11, 1863.
178. Hutchins to SuptIndAff, June 30, 1863, ARSI (1863): 575.
179. Hutchins to Edgerton, Jan. 27, 1865, Charles Hutchins Letters, MHS.
180. Owen, *Journals and Letters,* 1:330.
181. Hutchins to SuptIndAff, June 30, 1865, ARCIA (1865): 247.
182. Owen, *Journals and Letters,* 2:4–5.
183. Chapman to CommIA, Aug. 31, 1866, ARCIA (1866): 315.
184. Owen, *Journals and Letters,* 2:27–29, 58.
185. Cummings to CommIA, June 27, 1867, NAmf M234, r. 488, fr. 559.
186. SuptIndAff to CommIA, July 20, 1867, NAmf M234, r. 488, fr. 579; Owen, *Journals and Letters,* 2:58.
187. Owen, *Journals and Letters,* 2:115.
188. Ibid., 125–27.
189. Ibid., 125.
190. Ibid., 126.
191. Cullen to CommIA, Aug. 22, 1868, ARSI (1868): 680.
192. Owen, *Journals and Letters,* 2:138.
193. "Visitor Recalls Early Days," *DM,* Sept. 4, 1916, 8.
194. R. W. Nicol, "Early Pioneers," *Western News,* Mar. 7, 1894, 8, and Mar. 14, 1894, 1.

195. GLO to CommIA, June 2, 1868, NAmf M234, r. 488, fr. 1197.

196. "A Scheme to Surrender Bitter Root Valley," *Helena Weekly Herald*, Sept. 3, 1868, 4.

197. Sully to CommIA, Oct. 20, 1869, NAmf M234, r. 489, fr. 653.

198. J. A. Simms to Vincent Colyer, Nov. 24, 1871, LR, Records of the Board of Indian Commissioners, RG 75, NA.

199. Galbreath to SuptIndAff, Sept. 6, 1869, ARSI (1869): 739.

200. McCormick to SuptIndAff, Aug. 31, 1868, ARSI (1868): 672.

201. Galbreath to SuptIndAff, Sept. 6, 1869, ARSI (1869): 739.

202. Cullen to CommIA, Aug. 22, 1868, ARSI (1868): 679; SecInt to CommIA, Jan. 7, 1869, NAmf M234, r. 489, fr. 303.

## Chapter 2

1. "The Chief of the Flatheads Dead," *Rocky Mountain Weekly Gazette*, Aug. 22, 1870, 3; Sully to CommIA, July 30, 1870, NAmf M234, r. 490, fr. 563.

2. McGinnis, *Counting Coup*, 109, 136.

3. Stevens, "Report of Explorations," 1:151.

4. Calculated from Bigart, ed., *Life and Death*, 117–77.

5. See Bigart, ed., *Life and Death*, especially 207–18.

6. Walter S. Campbell Collection, box 105, notebook 24, p. 37, Western History Collections, University Libraries, University of Oklahoma.

7. Vestal, *Sitting Bull*, 118–24; Walter S. Campbell Collection, box 105, notebooks 4, 13, and 24, Western History Collections, University Libraries, University of Oklahoma; White Bull, *Warrior Who Killed Custer*, 41–47; Utley, *Lance and the Shield*, 99–100.

8. "Indian Fight," *Weekly Independent*, July 21, 1871, 3; "From the Buffalo Hunt," *Missoula Pioneer*, July 27, 1871, 3; Jones to SuptIndAff, Sept. 1, 1871, ARSI (1871): 842; "The Indian Feast of Mourning," *Missoula Pioneer*, Aug. 10, 1871, 3.

9. "A Nice Operation," *NNW*, Apr. 25, 1874, 3.

10. Bigart, ed., *Life and Death*, p. 138, no. 219.

11. "Indians on the Move," *NNW*, Mar. 16, 1872, 3.

12. Shanahan to CommIA, Mar. 1, 1873, NAmf M833, r. 2, fr. 240.

13. Switzer to AAG, Dept. of Dakota, Mar. 7, 1875, Fort Ellis, Mont., LS, RG 393, NA. A similar report in a Helena newspaper declared that these tribes were fighting the Sioux in the Judith Basin; "Judith Basin," *Helena Daily Herald*, July 12, 1875, 3.

14. Moore, *Pi-Lu'-Ye-Kin*, 20–21, 37.

15. "Kootenai Notes" notebook, Flathead and Kootenay Field Notebooks, folder 161, no page numbers, Schaeffer Papers.

16. Gibbon to Booth, Feb. 26, 1876, Fort Shaw, Mont., LS, RG 393, NA; Gibbon to Terry, Apr. 21, 1876, LS, District of Mont., RG 393, NA.

17. Ronan to Maginnis, Aug. 21, 1877, Martin Maginnis Papers, MHS; Potts to SecInt, Oct. 1, 1877, NAmf M234, r. 517, fr. 21

18. *Helena Independent* (daily), Mar. 29, 1878, 3.

19. "The Scalpers," *Helena Independent* (daily), Apr. 1, 1879, 3; *WM*, Apr. 18, 1879, 3 (two articles).

20. *Helena Daily Herald*, July 17, 1879, 3; *Helena Independent* (daily), Nov. 16, 1879, 3. The July 1879 report may have pertained to Chief Arlee's reservation band of Salish, who visited Helena on the way to Missoula in late July; "The Flatheads," *Helena Independent* (daily), July 29, 1879, 3.

21. "Returning Flatheads," *Helena Daily Herald*, Apr. 6, 1880, 3.

22. Telegram from Gibson to AAG, St. Paul, Minn., Apr. 12, 1880, Fort Missoula Correspondence, LS, 1879–1881, copy at Mansfield Library, UM.

23. "Sweet Grass," *Helena Independent* (daily), Apr. 20, 1880, 3.

24. Culbertson, *Joseph Culbertson's Indian Scout Memoirs*, 34–35.

25. Sully to Camp, Jan. 9, 1870, NAmf M833, r. 3, fr. 138.

26. Charles M. Lee, Journals, UM, entry for Feb. 22, 1870.

27. Moore, *Pi-Lu'-Ye-Kin*, 2–3, 10.

28. "Sophie Moiese" notebook, Flathead Field Notes, folder 118, p. 9, Schaeffer Papers.

29. Dusenberry, "Samples of Pend d'Oreille Oral Literature," 114.

30. Two Leggings, *Two Leggings*, 89–93. The fallen Salish man whom Two Leggings almost scalped survived. Years later they met as friends, and the Salish man said he was paralyzed but could feel Two Leggings lift his head by the hair and waited for the scalping knife. The Salish man partially recovered but was never again able to use his left hand.

31. "Martine Vanderburg" notebook, Flathead Field Notes, folder 118, pp. 4–5, Schaeffer Papers.

32. Stone, *Following Old Trails*, 151–52. A photograph of Big Sam wearing the painted robe is in Keyser, *Five Crows Ledger*, 87.

33. "Identification of Stolen Horses," *Rocky Mountain Weekly Gazette*, Aug. 21, 1871, 3.

34. Browning to AAG, Dept. of Dakota, St. Paul, Minn., Nov. 13, 1871, LR 874/1871, Div. of the Missouri, RG 393, NA; "The Interior," *Helena Daily Herald*, Feb. 28, 1872, 1.

35. "Kootenai Notes" notebook, Flathead and Kootenay Field Notebooks, folder 161, Schaeffer Papers.

36. Shanahan to CommIA, Jan. 21, 1874, NAmf M234, r. 500, fr. 262; Bigart, ed., *Life and Death*, p. 134, nos. 174 and 175.

37. Leforge, *Memoirs of a White Crow Indian*, 48–50. See also Topping, *Chronicles of the Yellowstone*, 93–94.

38. Shanahan to CommIA, Jan. 21, 1874, NAmf M234, r. 500, fr. 262. An incident reported in a Bozeman newspaper in March 1873 may have been another account of the same fight; "Flathead Indian Killed," *Bozeman Avant Courier*, Mar. 28, 1873, 3.

39. Bigart, ed., *Life and Death*, p. 136, no. 194.

40. Switzer to Davis, May 23, 1873, Fort Ellis, Mont., LS, RG 393, NA.

41. Brunot, "Report of the Commission to Negotiate with the Crow Tribe," 119–20.

42. Switzer to AAG, Dept. of Dakota, Oct. 6, 1873, Fort Ellis, Mont., LS, RG 393, NA; D'Aste to Shanahan, Sept. 13, 1873, BCIM Papers.

43. Marquis, *Wooden Leg,* 29.

44. Shanahan to CommIA, Jan. 21, 1874, NAmf M234, r. 500, fr. 262.

45. Switzer to AAG, Dept. of Dakota, Jan. 5, 1874, Fort Ellis, Mont., LS, RG 393, NA.

46. Bigart, ed., *Life and Death,* p. 138, nos. 213 and 214.

47. "From Judith Basin," *Bozeman Avant Courier,* Feb. 20. 1874, 3.

48. "Eastern Montana Items: From the Courier, Aug. 21," *NNW,* Aug. 29, 1874, 3.

49. Whaley to CommIA, Sept. 12, 1874, ARCIA (1874): 263.

50. *WM,* Oct. 14, 1874, 3.

51. *RMH,* Apr. 10, 1879, 3.

52. Barrows, *Ubet,* 85–86, 110–12; "Missoula County," *NNW,* Apr. 8, 1881, 3; "Missoula County," *NNW,* June 10, 1881, 2.

53. D'Aste, Diaries, entry for Aug. 7, 1881.

54. Bigart, ed., *Life and Death,* p. 152, no. 343.

55. *RMH,* Mar. 16, 1882, 3; Mar. 30, 1882, 6.

56. Maerdian, "Pioneer Ranching in Central Montana," 415.

57. "An Indian Fight," *Daily Enterprise,* Nov. 12, 1883, 1; *Bozeman Weekly Chronicle,* Nov. 14, 1883, 3; "A Skirmish Between Indians," *Weekly Avant Courier,* Nov. 15, 1883, 3.

58. "Murder of Two Indians," *Bozeman Weekly Chronicle,* Apr. 16, 1884, 3; "Foully Murdered," *Weekly Avant Courier,* Apr. 17, 1884, 3; "Those Two Indians," *Bozeman Weekly Chronicle,* Apr. 23, 1884, 3.

59. Ewers, "Identification and History of the Small Robes Band," 397–401.

60. Ewers, *Blackfeet,* 252–53.

61. "Letter from the Blackfoot Agency," *Helena Daily Herald,* Dec. 29, 1870, 1; "The Blackfeet Indians," *Helena Daily Herald,* Oct. 21, 1871, 3.

62. Wissler, "Social Life of the Blackfoot Indians," p. 50, no. 31.

63. "Blackfoot Agency," *Helena Daily Herald,* Mar. 13, 1872, 1; "The Lo Family," *Pioneer,* Mar. 23, 1872, 3.

64. "Sophie Moiese" notebook, Flathead Field Notes, folder 118, pp. 36–40, Schaeffer Papers.

65. NAmf M1350, r. 1, fr. 2 and 29, nos. 74 and 1038.

66. Bigart, ed., *Life and Death,* p. 138, no. 215.

67. Malouf, *Economy and Land Use,* 29.

68. Turney-High, *Flathead Indians of Montana,* 64.

69. Moore, *Pi-Lu'-Ye-Kin,* 20–21, 37.

70. Lancaster, *Piegan,* 280–83.

71. Stone, *Following Old Trails,* 151–52. See also Keyser, *Five Crows Ledger,* 87.

72. Schultz, *Why Gone Those Times?,* 100.

73. Telegram from Gibson to AAG, St. Paul, Minn., Apr. 12, 1880, Fort Missoula Correspondence, LS, 1879–1881, copy at Mansfield Library, UM.

74. *RMH*, Apr. 29, 1880, 3.

75. "Indian Depredation on the Yellowstone," *Bozeman Avant Courier*, Mar. 24, 1881, 2.

76. Uhlenbeck-Melchior and Uhlenbeck, *Montana 1911*, 306.

77. "Capture of a Piegan Indian," *RMH*, Jan. 25, 1883, 6.

78. Eagle Calf and Heavy Breast, interpretations, *Picture Writing*, 20.

79. Untitled MS on cards, GLAC 9813, Glacier National Park Archives.

80. Uhlenbeck-Melchior and Uhlenbeck, *Montana 1911*, 310.

81. Untitled MS on cards, GLAC 9813, Glacier National Park Archives.

82. Dempsey, *Blackfoot War Art*, 374, 382.

83. Wissler, "Social Life of the Blackfoot Indians," 37.

84. Eagle Calf and Heavy Breast, interpretations, *Picture Writing*, 22.

85. Untitled MS on cards, GLAC 9813, Glacier National Park Archives.

86. Dempsey, *Blackfoot War Art*, 383.

87. "Charlos the Flathead," *Helena Independent* (daily), Sept. 16, 1883, 4; D'Aste, Diaries, entries for July 31 and Aug. 25, 1883; *RMH*, Aug. 16, 1883, 3.

## Chapter 3

1. "The Indians on Deep Creek," *Helena Daily Herald*, July 29, 1875, 3; "The Savages on Deep Creek," *Weekly Independent*, Aug. 5, 1875, 4; "That 'Raid' Into Missouri Valley," *Weekly Independent*, Aug. 5, 1875, 4; "A Big Scare!" *Helena Daily Herald*, July 30, 1875, 3; Nelson to Post Adjutant, Camp Baker, Mont., Aug. 1, 1875, LR 4675/1875, Military Div. of the Missouri, RG 393, NA.

2. Switzer to AAG, Dept. of Dakota, June 2 and Sept. 9, 1873, Fort Ellis, Mont., LS, RG 393, NA; Wright to CommIA, Apr. 22, 1874, NAmf M234, r. 500, fr. 781.

3. *RMH*, July 26, 1877, 3.

4. *RMH*, Aug. 1, 1878, 3.

5. "Wayside Notes," *Helena Independent* (daily), June 5, 1878, 3; Gilbert to AAAG, Dist. of Mont., May 20, 1878, NAmf M666, r. 415, fr. 694–702; "The Last Raid," *Helena Weekly Herald*, May 30, 1878, 2.

6. "Full Particulars of the Indian Raid," *RMH*, May 30, 1878, 2.

7. "The Murder of Joy, Elliott and Hayes," *NNW*, July 19, 1878, 2; "A Race for Life," *NNW*, July 19, 1878, 2.

8. "The Hostiles," *Helena Independent* (daily), July 21, 1878, 3; "Editorial Correspondence," *WM*, July 26, 1878, 2.

9. *WM*, July 19, 1878, 3.

10. "Pursuit of the Murder Party," *NNW*, Aug. 2, 1878, 2; "Editorial Correspondence," *WM*, Aug. 2, 1878, 2; "Avenged," *WM*, Aug. 2, 1878, 2; C. S. Nichols, "Stevensville Pioneer Tells Interesting Story," *DM*, May 28, 1916, pt. II, 1.

11. Duncan McDonald, "An Appeal to Reason," *NNW*, Aug. 16, 1878, 3; *NNW*, Aug. 16, 1878, 2; "'Friendlies' or 'Hostiles,'" *NNW*, Aug. 30, 1878, 3.

12. "From Philipsburg," *NNW*, Aug. 30, 1878, 3.

13. "Smith River Items," *Helena Independent* (daily), June 5, 1878, 3; *WM*, June 7, 1878, 2; *RMH*, June 13, 1878, 3; Gilbert to AAG, Dept. of Dakota, June 14, 1878, LR, Dept. of Dakota, RG 393, NA.

14. "Capture of a Piegan Indian," *RMH*, Jan. 25, 1883, 6.

15. *Helena Daily Herald*, July 18, 1871, 3; Oct. 18, 1871, 3.

16. "Indians," *Rocky Mountain Gazette* (weekly), Oct. 21, 1872, 3.

17. NNW, Mar. 1, 1873, 3; "Indians," *Weekly Rocky Mountain Gazette*, May 7, 1873, 4.

18. " 'Lo,' the Poor Indian," *Helena Daily Herald*, Oct. 24, 1873, 3; *Weekly Rocky Mountain Gazette*, Oct. 29, 1873, 4.

19. "An Honest Indian," *Helena Daily Herald*, Oct. 14, 1878, 3.

20. *Helena Daily Herald*, Apr. 6, 1880, 3.

21. *Helena Independent* (daily), Oct. 13, 1882, 3.

22. Malouf, *Economy and Land Use*, 41.

23. *Bozeman Avant Courier*, May 13, 1880, 3; June 16, 1881, 3.

24. "Mrs. Beal Tells Story of Early Days in Valley," *RMH*, Mar. 22, 1928, 3.

25. Barrows, *Ubet*, 85–86, 110–12.

26. "The Flatheads in Town," *Northwest* (New York) 2, no. 4 (Apr. 1884): 12.

27. For a history of the escorts and a survey of the debate about the policy within the U.S. military and newspapers, see Farr, "Going to Buffalo."

28. Gibbon to Booth, Feb. 16, 1876, Fort Shaw, Mont., LS, RG 393, NA.

29. Gibbon to Booth, Feb. 26, 1876, Fort Shaw, Mont., LS, RG 393, NA.

30. W. H. Banfill, "Keeping the Peace on the Musselshell River," *RMH*, Oct. 16, 1930, 1.

31. *Helena Daily Herald*, Apr. 5, 1880, 3.

32. "Kootenai Notes" notebook, Flathead and Kootenay Field Notebooks, folder 161, no page numbers, Schaeffer Papers.

33. "The Indians Attend Church," *Helena Daily Herald*, June 28, 1875, 3.

34. "Flathead Indians," *Helena Independent* (daily), Mar. 6, 1877, 3.

35. "Rocky Mountain Correspondence."

36. *RMH*, Oct. 24, 1878, 3.

37. Chipman to "To all whom it may concern," Apr. 28, 1879, Fort Missoula Correspondence, LS, 1879–81, copy at Mansfield Library, UM.

38. "The Judith and Its Mines," *Helena Independent* (daily), Nov. 9, 1879, 3.

39. "Meagher County Items," *Helena Independent* (daily), Mar. 29, 1881, 3; *NNW*, Sept. 23, 1881, 3; "Territorial News," *WM*, June 13, 1884, 4.

40. H. McDonald Clark, "Charlie Young Still Going Strong at 85," *Great Falls Tribune*, Feb. 13, 1955, Montana Parade, 10–12.

41. Cora Levengood Sparrow, "Reminiscences of the Levengood Family," Montana Pioneers Collection, folder 17, MHS.

42. "Missoula's First School Open in '69," *DM*, Apr. 30, 1933, Anniversary section, 4.

43. "The Scalpers," *Helena Independent* (daily), Apr. 1, 1879, 3.

44. *WM*, Apr. 18, 1879, 3 (two articles).

45. "The Flatheads in Town," *Northwest* (New York) 2, no. 4 (Apr. 1884): 12.

46. *RMH*, Feb. 23, 1882, 3.

47. "Burying an Indian," *Helena Independent* (daily), Mar. 29, 1882, 3.

48. Malouf, "Place Names According to John Delaware," box 17, folder 1, Carling I. Malouf Papers, UM.

49. "Reprehensible," *Helena Weekly Herald*, May 8, 1873, 8.

50. "Shooting Scrape," *Daily Independent*, July 8, 1874, 3.

51. Gilbert to AAAG, Dist. of Mont., Mar. 24, 1878, NAmf M666, r. 405, fr. 254–60; "Indian Troubles," *Helena Daily Herald*, May 24, 1878, 2.

52. *RMH*, Oct. 31, 1878, 3.

53. *Helena Independent* (daily), Oct. 23, 1879, 3.

54. Williams to Pomery, Aug. 8, 1880, Fort Missoula Correspondence, LS, 1879–1881, copy at Mansfield Library, UM.

55. "Drunken Indians at Martinsdale," *Helena Daily Herald*, Feb. 11, 1882, 2; "Impudent Indians," *Benton Weekly Record*, Feb. 9, 1882, 5; "Judith Matters," *RMH*, Feb. 16, 1882, 6.

56. "Drunken Indians," *Helena Independent* (daily), Oct. 14, 1882, 3; Oct. 17, 1882, 3.

57. *RMH*, Oct. 26, 1882, 3.

58. "Bad Indians," *NNW*, Dec. 5, 1884, 3.

59. " 'Lo,' " *NNW*, Aug. 8, 1874, 3.

60. *RMH*, Oct. 13, 1881, 3.

61. "Meanderings of the 'Judge,'" *Helena Daily Herald*, June 19, 1874, 1.

62. "Indian Ponies Stolen," *Helena Independent* (daily), Oct. 25, 1879, 3; *Bozeman Avant Courier*, Nov. 13, 1879, 2.

63. "Indian Depredations in the Yellowstone," *Bozeman Avant Courier*, Mar. 24, 1881, 2.

64. "Indian Depredations on the Yellowstone," *Bozeman Avant Courier*, May 26, 1881, 3.

65. "Missoula County," *NNW*, June 10, 1881, 2.

66. "Flatheads Depredating," *Helena Daily Herald*, Dec. 9, 1882, 3; *RMH*, Dec. 14, 1882, 3.

67. "Unsuccessful," *Helena Daily Herald*, Dec. 29, 1882, 3.

68. Maerdian, "Pioneer Ranching in Central Montana," 415.

69. D'Aste, Diaries, entry for July 22, 1883.

70. "Those Two Indians," *Bozeman Weekly Chronicle*, Apr. 23, 1884, 3; "Neighborhood News," *NNW*, May 9, 1884, 2; *Bozeman Weekly Chronicle*, Apr. 16, 1884, 2; "Murder of Two Indians," *Bozeman Weekly Chronicle*, Apr. 16, 1884, 3.

71. *RMH*, Feb. 26, 1880, 2.

72. Overholser, "Livestock Growers Threatened by Indians"; Montana Historical Society, *Not in Precious Metals Alone*, 98–99.

73. *RMH*, Nov. 23, 1882, 3; "Flatheads Depredating," *Helena Daily Herald*, Dec. 9, 1882, 3; *RMH*, Dec. 14, 1882, 6; *RMH*, Jan. 11, 1882 [1883], 6.

74. Sec. of War to SecInt, Dec. 7, 1877, NAmf M234, r. 508, fr. 1011; Ronan to CommIA, Jan. 10, 1878, *NAmf* M234, r. 511, fr. 505; Indian Depredation Claim no. 1783 (RG 75), no. 8422 (RG 205), and no. 8422 (RG 123), NA.

75. "Genuine Fright," *Helena Weekly Herald*, Oct. 23, 1879, 7.

76. "From the Northwest," *NNW*, July 7, 1882, 3.

77. *Helena Independent* (daily), Oct. 14, 1882, 3.

78. Brownell, "Genesis of Wildlife Conservation in Montana," 13–43.

79. *WM*, Feb. 20, 1880, 3; "Rod and Gun Club," *WM*, Feb. 27, 1880, 3.

80. "Roving Indians," *NNW*, Mar. 26, 1880, 3. Quote taken from Fort Missoula letter book as the newspaper version was garbled. Gibson to Hartman, Mar. 17, 1880, Fort Missoula Correspondence, LS, 1879–1881, copy at Mansfield Library, UM.

81. *RMH*, Apr. 1, 1880, 2.

82. *Helena Daily Herald*, June 14, 1880, 3.

83. *NNW*, July 1, 1881, 3; "Bitter Root Items," *Helena Independent* (daily), Aug. 6, 1881, 3.

84. *NNW*, Apr. 20, 1883, 3; Jan. 11, 1884, 3.

85. "Como," *WM*, Mar. 14, 1884, 3.

## Chapter 4

1. See Dary, *Red Blood and Black Ink*.

2. Coon, "Economic Development of Missoula, Montana," 60–63, 84–86.

3. "Our Bitter Root Letter," *WM*, Feb. 28, 1873, 2; "Bitter Root Correspondence," *WM*, Mar. 28, 1873, 2.

4. "Our County Affairs," *WM*, July 15, 1875, 2; "A Glance Backward and Forward," *WM*, June 7, 1876, 2.

5. "Debt of Missoula County," *Helena Daily Herald*, Apr. 3, 1875, 3.

6. The Panic of 1873 and the resulting national economic slowdown apparently had little effect in western Montana. Economist Shirley Coon blamed the local depression mainly on the decline of the gold mining camps. Coon, "Economic Development of Missoula, Montana," 80, 84.

7. Kennett to Hauser, Dec. 27, 1873, and Mar. 9, 1874; and Higgins to Hauser, Oct. 14, 1879, Samuel Hauser Papers, MHS.

8. Garfield to SecInt, Sept. 7, 1872, "Removal of Flathead Indians, 1871–72," vol. 9, series 11, r. 131, James A. Garfield Papers, Library of Congress.

9. Gibbon to Terry, Apr. 4, 1875, "Post at Hell Gate, Montana Territory, Mar. 1875–May 1877," Special Files of Headquarters, Div. of the Missouri, NAmf M1495, r. 2.

10. Addison Howard, "When Missoula Was Very Young," *DM*, Jan. 22, 1928, pt. II, 1; Weisel, ed., *Men and Trade*, 233–34; Seifried, "Early Administration of the Flathead Indian Reservation," 56–62; "Old Pioneer Received Present Name in '73," *DM*, May 4, 1919, pt. II, 1.

11. "Bitter Root Question Settled," *Pioneer*, Dec. 9, 1871, 2.

12. "An Appeal for a Military Post," *Pioneer*, Dec. 16, 1871, 2.

13. Various articles, *Pioneer*, Aug. 3, 1872, 2.

14. "Bitter Root Items," *Pioneer*, Aug. 10, 1872, 3; "Petition," *Pioneer*, Aug. 10, 1872, 2; "Citizen's Meeting," *Pioneer*, Aug. 10, 1872, 2.

15. Garfield, "Report," ARCIA (1872): 109–18.

16. "Died," *WM*, June 23, 1875, 3.

17. "A Military Post a Necessity," *WM*, May 28, 1874, 2. During the nineteenth century many anti-Indian whites used the Santee Sioux outbreak of 1862 to attempt to justify their views. See Meyer, *History of the Santee Sioux*, 109–32, for a detailed account of the 1862 events.

18. "Our Indian System," *WM*, Jan. 20, 1875, 2.

19. Barbour, "Two Vigilance Committees," 285–91; NAmf M593, r. 827, Mont., Missoula Co., Cedar Cr. Mines, 11, line 27; Will Cave, "Cedar Creek," *DM*, July 3, 1921, pt. II, 1; "County Republican Convention," *WM*, June 27, 1873, 2; "Old Pioneer Received Present Name in '73," *DM*, May 4, 1919, pt. II, 1; "Farewell," *WM*, Aug. 29, 1879, 2; NAmf T9, r. 742, Mont., Missoula Co., Missoula, ED 25, p. 450, line 25; *Bozeman Avant Courier*, Aug. 11, 1881, 3; *Weekly Avant Courier*, Sept. 27, 1883, 3; *WM*, Jan. 6, 1888, 3.

20. "The Need of Military Protection," *WM*, July 7, 1875, 2.

21. "Need of Military Protection," *WM*, Jan. 26, 1876, 2.

22. "Indian Taxation," *WM*, Apr. 26, 1876, 3. Barbour gave no indication of how much he altered the English translation of the speech before publishing it. The irony is that the speech Barbour published to show how ridiculous the Salish viewpoint was became a celebrated piece of "Indian" literature in the twentieth century. See, for example, Armstrong, "*I Have Spoken*," 99.

23. "The Local Indian Question," *WM*, Apr. 26, 1876, 2.

24. "Treatment of Indians," *WM*, Dec. 8, 1875, 2.

25. "The Sioux War," *WM*, July 26, 1876, 2.

26. *WM*, Sept. 22, 1875, 3; "The Indians," *WM*, Sept. 29, 1875, 2.

27. *NNW*, Oct. 1, 1875, 2.

28. "Indians Generally," *WM*, Sept. 1, 1875, 2.

29. "Our Distinguished Visitor," *WM*, Jan. 26, 1876, 3.

30. "The Post Established," *WM*, Mar. 29, 1876, 2.

31. "County Finances," *WM*, Mar. 28, 1873, 2.

32. "To Be Assessed," *WM*, Mar. 19, 1874, 3; "Board of County Commissioner's [*sic*] Meeting," *WM*, June 16, 1875, 3.

33. "Our County Affairs," *WM*, July 15, 1875, 2.

34. "Property Not Taxed," *WM*, July 22, 1875, 2.

35. "Taxing Indians," *WM*, Sept. 1, 1875, 3.

36. Potts to SecInt, Jan. 20, 1876, 1:173–74, Montana Governors' Papers, MHS.

37. O'Neil, *Two Men of Demersville*, 6–32.

38. "Taxation of Indians," *WM*, June 21, 1876, 2.

39. *WM*, June 21, 1876, 2.

40. Giorda to Grant, Feb. 21, 1876, BCIM Papers.

41. "Indian Taxation," *WM*, Apr. 26, 1876, 3.

42. "Bitter Root Items," *NNW*, May 5, 1876, 3.

43. *WM*, July 19, 1876, 3.

44. "Missoula Items," *Helena Independent* (daily), Aug. 5, 1876, 3.

45. *WM*, May 3, 1878, 3.

46. *WM*, June 7, 1878, 2.

47. "Missoula County Bankrupt," *Helena Weekly Herald*, Oct. 19, 1876, 2; "County Finances," *WM*, Dec. 6, 1876, 2.

48. "Missoula County Act," *WM*, Feb. 28, 1877, 2.

49. "Must We Compound?" *WM*, June 14, 1878, 2.

50. "Missoula County Bonds," *Helena Weekly Herald*, Dec. 12, 1878, 2.

51. "Proceedings of the County Board," *WM*, Apr. 19, 1876, 2.

52. *WM*, Aug. 2, 1876, 3.

53. *WM*, May 14, 1880, 3; *WM*, July 30, 1880, 3.

54. *NNW*, July 9, 1875, 3; Ewing to Van Gorp, ca. Apr. 19, 1875, BCIM Papers.

55. *WM*, Dec. 15, 1875, 3.

56. Medary to CommIA, Jan. 28, 1876, NAmf M234, r. 505, fr. 194.

57. Medary to CommIA, Feb. 11, 1876, NAmf M234, r. 505, fr. 204.

58. *WM*, Jan. 26, 1876, 3.

59. *WM*, July 19, 1876, 3.

60. *WM*, July 26, 1876, 3.

61. "Precautionary Measures," *WM*, July 26, 1876, 3.

62. "Trouble with Northern Indians Apprehended," *NNW*, July 28, 1876, 3; "The Indian Situation in Western Montana," *Helena Daily Herald*, July 29, 1876, 3.

63. Day books vols. 27 and 39, Francis L. Worden Papers, UM.

64. *WM*, Sept. 13, 1876, 3.

65. Sec. of War to SecInt, Aug. 5, 1876, NAmf M234, r. 505, fr. 1115.

66. Medary to Gibbon, Dec. 7, 1876, NAmf M234, r. 505, fr. 706.

67. Gibbon to Medary, Dec. 21, 1876, encl. in Medary to "My Dear General," Jan. 11, 1877, BCIM Papers.

68. Atty. Gen. to SecInt, Jan. 8, 1877, NAmf M234, r. 508, fr. 382.

69. "Indictment of Agent Medary," *NNW*, Dec. 22, 1876, 3.

70. "Acquitted," *Helena Daily Herald*, Jan. 2, 1877, 3; *WM*, Jan. 9, 1877, 3.

71. Medary to "My Dear General," Jan. 3, 1877, and Jan. 18, 1877, BCIM Papers.

72. Medary to CommIA, Feb. 28, 1877, NAmf M234, r. 508, fr. 261.

73. Ewing to Medary, Mar. 28, 1877; Medary to "My Dear General," Apr. 28, 1877, and May 6, 1877, BCIM Papers.

74. "At Last," *WM*, June 22, 1877, 3.

75. "Indian Excitement," *WM*, June 29, 1877, 2.

76. Ronan to Potts, July 10, 1877, NAmf M234, r. 507, fr. 271; "Letter to Gov. Potts," *Helena Independent* (daily), June 29, 1877, 3.

77. "Alarm in Missoula," *Helena Independent* (daily), July 2, 1877, 3.

78. D'Aste to "Rev. and Dear Father," 181. Emphasis in original. See also [D'Aste], "The Nez Perce War of 1877," PNTMC, r. 30, fr. 342–49.

79. "Justice to the Flatheads," *Helena Daily Herald*, June 30, 1877, 1.

80. "Charlos," *Helena Independent* (daily), July 15, 1877, 2; Ronan to CommIA, July 11, 1877, NAmf M234, r. 507, fr. 268.

81. "Making Medicine," *WM*, July 13, 1877, 2.

82. *WM*, July 13, 1877, 3; "Missoula County Notes," *NNW*, July 20, 1877, 3; "Old Letters Tell of Troubles," *DM*, May 21, 1910, 18; "Indian Temper and Our Duty," *WM*, July 13, 1877, 2.

83. *WM*, July 13, 1877, 3; *WM*, July 20, 1877, 3.

84. *WM*, July 20, 1877, 3; "Indian Troubles," *RMH*, July 26, 1877, 2.

85. "Is There Danger?" *WM*, July 20, 1877, 2.

86. [Chief Joseph], "An Indian's Views of Indian Affairs," 426.

87. John P. Martens, Journal, MHS, entries for July 21 and July 26, 1877.

88. Carrington, "Exodus of the Flatheads," unpublished manuscript (hereafter Carrington MS), chap. 7.

89. "Startling News from Western Montana," *Helena Daily Herald*, July 30, 1877, 2.

90. W. B. Harlan, "The Fiasco at Fort Fizzle," *DM*, Mar. 18, 1917, pt. II, 1.

91. Niles et al., "Muster Roll 'Co.' Montana Militia, Stevensville," Montana Secretary [Territorial and State] Records, MHS.

92. [Leeson, ed.], *History of Montana*, 145–49. See also Eneas Granjo testimony in Tunison, "Before the Indian Claims Commission," 2:40–42.

93. [D'Aste], "The Nez Perce War of 1877," PNTMC, r. 30, fr. 342–49.

94. D'Aste, "Rev. and Dear Father," 179–84; "Always Friendly," *DM*, Sept. 11, 1911, 10; Ronan to CommIA, Aug. 13, 1877, ARSI (1877): 530–31.

95. Carrie May Warren, Reminiscences, UM.

96. Matt, "Mary Ann Topsseh Coombs."

97. Henry Buck, Reminiscence, 29, 32, MHS.

98. "Trip to Stevensville," *WM*, Aug. 31, 1877, 3.

99. "Chief Charlos," *Helena Independent* (daily), Sept. 13, 1883, 5.

100. Pierre Pichette, interpreter, "Stories Related by Members of the Selish Tribe," Hansen and Wright, leaders, "Full Blood Flathead Indian Montana Study Group, Arlee, Montana," appendix, 2.

101. Salish population, ARSI (1877): 692; white population calculated from NAmf T9, r. 742; Gibbon, *Adventures on the Western Frontier*, 181, 206.

102. McWhorter, *Hear Me, My Chiefs!*, 361.

103. Howard, *Nez Perce Joseph*, 193–94.

104. Clark, *Indian Sign Language*, 301.

105. Garcia, *Tough Trip Through Paradise*, 273–78.

106. *WM*, Aug. 10, 1877, 3.

107. "Trip to Stevensville," *WM*, Aug. 31, 1877, 3.

108. *WM*, May 3, 1878, 3.

109. *NNW*, Aug. 10, 1877, 2.

110. "The Future," *WM*, Aug. 24, 1877, 2.

111. *WM*, Aug. 24, 1877, 3.

112. *WM*, Aug. 17, 1877, 2.

113. Potts to SecInt, Oct. 1, 1877, NAmf M234, r. 517, fr. 21.

114. *WM*, Aug. 24, 1877, 2.

115. Potts to SecInt, Oct. 1, 1877, NAmf M234, r. 517, fr. 21; Ronan to CommIA, Aug. 20, 1877, NAmf M234, r. 507, fr. 378; Ronan to CommIA, Oct. 1, 1877, NAmf M234, r. 507, fr. 465.

116. Ronan to Maginnis, Aug. 21, 1877, Martin Maginnis Papers, MHS. Emphasis in original.

117. Ronan to CommIA, Jan. 16, 1878, NAmf M234, r. 511, fr. 523.

118. *Helena Daily Herald*, Oct. 20, 1877, 2.

119. "Rocky Mountain Correspondence," *Helena Daily Herald*, Nov. 30, 1877, 2. The letter was originally published in *McGee's Illustrated Weekly* 3, no. 1 (Nov. 24, 1877): 3.

120. *RMH*, Oct. 25, 1877, 2.

121. Zimmer, *Frontier Soldier*, 142.

122. Garcia, *Tough Trip Through Paradise*, 3–333.

123. Nichols, "Stevensville Pioneer Tells Interesting Story," *DM*, May 28, 1916, pt. II, 1.

124. "The Indians," *WM*, June 28, 1878, 2.

125. "Are Our Indians Peaceable?" *WM*, July 12, 1878, 2.

## Chapter 5

1. Owen, *Journals and Letters*, 2:121.

2. Cullen to CommIA, Aug. 22, 1868, ARSI (1868): 679.

3. SecInt to CommIA, Jan. 7, 1869, NAmf M234, r. 489, fr. 306. Quotes from Chief Adolph's speech at the 1868 negotiations in the following paragraphs are also from this source. See also Cullen to CommIA, Aug. 22, 1868, ARSI (1868): 679.

4. Sully to CommIA, Oct. 20, 1869, NAmf M234, r. 489, fr. 653; "Treaty Between the United States and the Flathead Indians," Oct. 7, 1869, NAmf M833, r. 3, fr. 153.

5. "Odious Treaty with the Flatheads," *Helena Daily Herald*, Oct. 27, 1869, 4.

6. "Washington and Montana," *NNW*, Nov. 19, 1869, 1.

7. "The Chief of the Flatheads Dead," *Rocky Mountain Weekly Gazette*, Aug. 22, 1870, 3.

8. Viall to CommIA, Dec. 16, 1870, NAmf M234, r. 490, fr. 881.

9. President to SecInt, May 29, 1871, NAmf M234, r. 491, fr. 349.

10. Spence, *Territorial Politics and Government in Montana*, 79–81.

11. "Settled at Last," *NNW*, Dec. 9, 1871, 2; "The Bitter Root Valley," *NNW*, Dec. 9, 1871, 2.

12. "The Bitter Root Valley," NNW, Dec. 9, 1871, 2.

13. Clagett to CommIA, Nov. 9, 1871, NAmf M234, r. 491, fr. 127.

14. *U.S. Statutes at Large,* June 5, 1872, 17:226–27.

15. Garfield to SecInt, Sept. 7, 1872, "Removal of the Flathead Indians, 1871–72," series 11, 9:38, r. 131, James A. Garfield Papers, Library of Congress.

16. "Bitter Root Items," *Pioneer,* Aug. 10, 1872, 3.

17. Garfield to SecInt, Aug. 17, 1872, NAmf M234, r. 492, fr. 184.

18. "Citizen's Meeting," *Pioneer,* Aug. 10, 1872, 2.

19. Garfield to SecInt, Aug. 17, 1872, NAmf M234, r. 492, fr. 184; Potts to Bass, Nov. 5, 1872, Benjamin F. Potts Papers, MHS.

20. NNW, July 6, 1872, 2.

21. Charlo et al., [power of attorney with James Fullerton], July 1, 1872, "Treaty with United States," box 124, MONAC Collection, Eastern Washington State Historical Society.

22. Spence, *Territorial Politics and Government in Montana,* 83, 84, 92, 134, 200, 236.

23. *Pioneer,* July 20, 1872, 2; "Hiram," *Garrettsville Journal,* Sept. 19, 1872, 3.

24. J. V. Sanders, "When Garfield Visited Montana," AS, May 24, 1908, 7; Garfield, *Diary,* 2:78–83.

25. "Indian Council," *Pioneer,* Aug. 31, 1872, 2. All quotes from the 1872 St. Mary's negotiations in the following paragraphs are from this source. The notes taken at the council are preserved in "Flathead Council, Aug. 22, 1872," "Removal of the Flathead Indians, 1871–72," series 11, vol. 9, 20–29, r. 131, James A. Garfield Papers, Library of Congress. The notes are abbreviated but seem to agree with the quotes used above.

26. Garfield, "Conference," 171–74. All quotes from the 1872 Jocko negotiations in the following paragraphs are from this source. The original notes recording this council are in "Aug. 24, 1872, F. Agency," "Removal of the Flathead Indians, 1871–72," series 11, vol. 9, 30–35, r. 131, James A. Garfield Papers, Library of Congress.

27. Garfield, *Diary,* 2:83–109; *Garrettsville Journal,* Sept. 19, 1872, 3.

28. Garfield, "Report," ARCIA (1872): 111, 115.

29. Garfield to CommIA, Nov. 15, 1872, NAmf M234, r. 492, fr. 199. See also fr. 232.

30. James A. Garfield, "The Indian Question," *Independent,* Oct. 31, 1872, 1.

31. *Congressional Record,* 45th Cong., 2nd Sess., vol. 7, pt. 3 (Apr. 27, 1878): 2894–95.

32. Garfield, "Report," ARCIA (1872): 115.

33. SuptIndAff to CommIA, Mar. 28, 1873, NAmf M234, r. 496, fr. 444.

34. "The Flathead Treaty," *Weekly Independent,* Feb. 1, 1873, 3; "Buildings at Jocko," NNW, Feb. 8, 1873, 3; Jones to CommIA, Sept. 26, 1872, NAmf M234, r. 492, fr. 443.

35. Shanahan to CommIA, Oct. 11, 1873, NAmf M234, r. 496, fr. 117.

36. Inspector J. W. Daniels to CommIA, Nov. 13, 1873, Inspection Reports File, RG 75, NA.

37. Shanahan to CommIA, Jan. 29, 1874, NAmf M234, r. 500, fr. 281; Shanahan to CommIA, Sept. 16, 1873, NAmf M234, r. 496, fr. 51.

38. Whaley to CommIA, Mar. 17, 1875, NAmf M234, r. 503, fr. 278.

39. Jones to SuptIndAff, Sept. 1, 1871, ARSI (1871): 841.

40. "Removal of the Flatheads," *WM*, Apr. 25, 1873, 3.

41. Wright to GLO, May 16, 1873, encl. in SecInt to CommIA, June 2, 1873, NAmf M234, r. 495, fr. 179.

42. "The Bitter Root Valley," *NNW*, Oct. 25, 1873, 2.

43. Ibid.; "The Bitter Root Question," *Weekly Independent*, Nov. 1, 1873, 2.

44. SecInt to CommIA, May 14, 1873, NAmf M234, r. 495, fr. 160.

45. Stevensville Historical Society, *Montana Genesis*, 95.

46. SuptIndAff to CommIA, Mar. 11, 1873, NAmf M234, r. 496, fr. 331; SuptIndAff to CommIA, Mar. 15, 1873, NAmf M234, r. 496, fr. 359. Winslett's list included eight women "who say they are Farmers": Matt[e], Daughter of Esuck [illegible word]; Margaretta; Susanah; Maltine (Husband Crazy); Victor's Widow; Pallaceno; Sustein; and Mary Mushell.

47. SuptIndAff to CommIA, June 30, 1873, NAmf M234, r. 497, fr. 263.

48. SuptIndAff to CommIA, Aug. 12, 1873, NAmf M234, r. 497, fr. 345.

49. Whaley to CommIA, Dec. 5, 1874, NAmf M234, r. 500, fr. 1334.

50. GLO to CommIA, Mar. 29, 1876, NAmf M234, r. 505, fr. 129.

51. SuptIndAff to CommIA, Apr. 26, 1873, NAmf M234, r. 496, fr. 608.

52. Ronan to CommIA, Aug. 6, 1877, NAmf M234, r. 507, fr. 347.

53. "From Missoula," *NNW*, Oct. 1, 1875, 2; "Bitter Root Items," *NNW*, May 5, 1876, 3.

54. D'Aste, Diaries, entry for Aug. 25, 1883.

55. Dawes, "Senatorial Career of George Graham Vest."

56. "Stevensville," *WM*, Sept. 14, 1883, 3.

57. G. G. Vest, "Charlot: Chief of the Flathead Indians," *Washington Post*, July 26, 1903, 11. Information and quotes from the 1883 meeting with Vest in the following paragraph are from this source.

58. For slightly different accounts of the exchange between Charlo and Vest, see "Council with Chrlos [*sic*]," *Helena Daily Herald*, Sept. 12, 1883, 3; and "Some Recollections of Senator Vest," *AS*, Aug. 10, 1904, 2.

59. Vest, "Charlot," *Washington Post*, July 26, 1903, 11.

60. *WM*, Feb. 15, 1884, 2.

61. Ronan to CommIA, Nov. 8, 1883, NA CommIA LR 20926/1883.

62. CommIA to Ronan, Nov. 19, 1883, finance, letter press, vol. 93, pt. 1, p. 182, NA CommIA LS.

63. Telegram from Ronan to CommIA, Jan. 9, 1884, 444/1884 NA CommIA LR; *WM*, Jan. 11, 1884, 3.

64. CommIA to Ronan, telegram, Jan. 10, 1884, finance, letter press, vol. 94, pt. 2, p. 469, NA CommIA LS.

65. D'Aste, Diaries, entry for Jan. 18, 1884.

66. Margaret Ronan, "Memoirs of a Frontiers Woman," 357, 360.

67. "Returned from Washington," *WM*, Mar. 14, 1884, 2; Ronan, "Memoirs," 358–59.

68. "The President's Public Levee," *New York Times*, Feb. 6, 1884, 1; Ronan, "Memoirs," 360.

69. Vest, "Charlot," *Washington Post*, July 26, 1903, 11; Ronan, "Memoirs," 356, 360–62; "Returned from Washington," *WM*, Mar. 14, 1884, 2; "Charlo's Eyesight Restored," *Washington Post*, Feb. 9, 1884, 4.

70. "Returned from Washington," *WM*, Mar. 14, 1884, 2; Peter Ronan, *Historical Sketch of the Flathead Indian Nation*, 71–72.

71. "Stevensville," *Missoula County Times*, Mar. 12, 1884, 2.

72. Ronan to CommIA, Mar. 27, 1884, 6629/1884 NA CommIA LR.

73. Ronan to CommIA, Feb. 12, 1885, 3554/1885 NA CommIA LR.

74. CommIA to Ronan, May 8, 1885, land, LB 135, p. 371, NA CommIA LS.

75. "The Flathead Indians," *Evening Star*, Jan. 31, 1884, 1.

76. Ronan, *Historical Sketch*, 72–73.

77. Ronan to CommIA, Mar. 27, 1884, 6629/1884 NA CommIA LR.

78. CommIA to SecInt, Apr. 9, 1884, finance, letter press, vol. 99, pt. 1, p. 125, NA CommIA LS.

79. *U.S. Statutes at Large*, July 4, 1884, 23:90.

80. *U.S. Statutes at Large*, Mar. 3, 1885, 23:377.

81. Ronan to CommIA, Feb. 12, 1885, 3554/1885 NA CommIA LR.

82. CommIA to Ronan, May 8, 1885, land, LB 135, p. 371, NA CommIA LS.

## Chapter 6

1. "Fourth of July on the Bitter Root," *RMH*, Aug. 23, 1877, 7.

2. Josephy, *Nez Perce Indians*, 510–18.

3. Dusenberry, "Samples of Pend d'Oreille Oral Literature," 116.

4. Matt, "Mary Ann Topsseh Coombs," 8–9. See chapter 4 for more about Mary Coombs's father, Louis Pierre, protecting the wife of the blacksmith from a drunken Nez Perce warrior.

5. Calculated from data in Bigart, ed., *Life and Death*, 77–115. These calculations assume that those Indian marriages for which no tribe is mentioned were between two Salish, so it is probably a minimum estimate of the degree of out-marriage.

6. Calculated from U.S. Bureau of the Census, *Historical Statistics*, 1:210–11; and *Statistical Abstract of the United States* 1987, 463; 2008, 469; and 2010, 466.

7. This entire St. Mary's Mission section is based on Jerome D'Aste's diary for 1879; PNTMC, r. 29, fr. 245–92.

8. Ronan to CommIA, Mar. 27, 1884, NA CommIA LR 6629/1884.

9. D'Aste, Diaries. See entries for Mar. 15 and 20, and Nov. 27, 1879.

10. Bigart, ed., *Life and Death*, p. 148, no. 309.

11. Hank Flanagin, "Other Days in the Old West," *DM*, May 4, 1930, 6.

12. NAmf T9, r. 742, Montana, Missoula County, Bitter Root Valley, ED 24, p. 2, lines 20–26.

13. Moore, *Pi-Lu'-Ye-Kin*, 47.

14. Patterson, *Montana Memories*, 15–16.

15. [William E. Bass], Diary, 1871–72, Bass Family Papers, UM, entry for May 12, 1871.

16. Martens, Journal, MHS, entries for Nov. 15–16, Sept. 12, and Dec. 20, 1877.

17. Bud Ainsworth, "Neptune Lynch Family Were First Settlers," *RMH*, Aug. 4, 1932, 1.

18. D'Aste, Diaries, entry for Mar. 3, 1885.

19. Jo Rainbolt, "Bass Brothers Ran First Experimental Station," *Missoulian*, Sept. 3, 1979, 12; Bass, *Our Tapestry*, 14.

20. NAmf T9, r. 742, Montana, Missoula County, Missoula (town), ED 25, p. 7, ll. 1–10, and Stevensville, ED 24, p. 15, ll. 43–47.

21. Belle C. Hershey, "John B. Catlin," Montana Pioneers Collection, box 1, folder 3, MHS.

22. Chipman to D'Aste, Feb. 22, 1879, Fort Missoula, Montana, Fort Missoula Correspondence, LS 1879–1881, copy at Mansfield Library, UM; MacDonald, "The Nez Perces," *Idaho Yesterdays* 21, no. 4 (Winter 1978): 5.

23. *WM*, Aug. 23, 1878, 3.

24. Stevensville Historical Society, *Montana Genesis*, 109.

25. *North West Tribune*, Oct. 16, 1891, 3.

26. *WM*, Feb. 8, 1878, 3.

27. Jeff Langton, "Mittower, Pioneer Bitter Root Man," *Daily Ravalli Republican*, July 26, 1967, 6.

28. Rappagliosi, *Letters*, 34–35.

29. Sanders, "When Garfield Visited Montana," *AS*, May 24, 1908, 7.

30. Patterson, *Montana Memories*, 16–17, 35, 46.

31. Chatfield & Bass, ledger, 1881–83, Bass Family Papers, r. 5, frame 536+, UM.

32. Woodbridge to D Aste, Oct. 16, 1877, and Woodbridge to D Aste, Nov. 2, 1877, Fort Missoula, Montana, LS July 1, 1877–June 30, 1878, SC 45, r. 1, UM; Chipman to AAG, District of Montana, May 3, 1879, Gibson to Commanding Officer, Fort Lapwai, Idaho Territory, Aug. 20, 1879, and Williams to Buck, Dec. 15, 1879, Fort Missoula, Montana, Fort Missoula Correspondence, LS 1879–1881, copy at Mansfield Library, UM.

33. *WM*, Oct. 1, 1880, 2.

34. Stevensville Historical Society, *Montana Genesis*, 109.

35. *WM*, Dec. 21, 1883, 3; "Stevensville," *Missoula County Times*, Dec. 19, 1883, 2.

36. Stanley, *Life of Rev. L. B. Stateler*, 288–90; "Martine Vanderburg" notebook, folder 118, p. 21, Schaeffer Papers.

37. *Bitter Root Bugle*, Sept. 6, 1889, 1.

38. "Up the Bitter Root and Back," *WM*, May 12, 1875, 3.

39. "75-Year History of Buck Mercantile," *DM*, Mar. 25, 1951, 6.

40. "Bitter Root Items," *Helena Independent* (daily), Aug. 6, 1881, 3.

41. "Corvallis," *WM*, May 18, 1883, 3.

42. *WM*, Dec. 21, 1883, 3; "Stevensville," *Missoula County Times*, Dec. 19, 1883, 2.

43. Lula Wood Brooks, Reminiscences, MHS.

44. "Clara Blodgett Shults," BRVPS, folder 3, MHS.

45. *Missoula Gazette* (daily), Aug. 15, 1890, 8.

46. "George Washington Ward," *BR Trails I–II*, 346.

47. *Some Bitterroot Memories*, 51.

48. "Interview with Alice Chilson (Hickey)," BRVPS, folder 1, MHS.

49. "Memoirs of Olive (Mc Carty) Wood," BRVPS, folder 4, MHS.

50. Territory vs. John Chatfield, Nov. 12, 1881, case 489, criminal (mf. r. 7, fr. 1909–48), MslaCtRec; Territory vs. Chas. M. Gates, Nov. 12, 1881, case 491, criminal (mf. r. 7, fr. 1950–63), MslaCtRec.

51. *Western News*, July 28, 1891, 2.

52. Belle C. Hershey, "John B. Catlin," Montana Pioneers Collection, box 1, folder 3, MHS.

53. "Interview with Alice Chilson (Hickey)," BRVPS, folder 1, MHS.

54. Warren, Reminiscences, UM.

55. Martens, Journal, MHS, entries for Mar. 8 and Dec. 14, 1877.

56. D'Aste, Diaries, entry for Oct. 26, 1878.

57. Martens, Journal, MHS.

58. Mrs. Ira Hendrikson, "Recollections," *BR Trails I–II*, 286–87.

59. *WM*, Dec. 21, 1883, 3; "Stevensville," *Missoula County Times*, Dec. 19, 1883, 2.

60. *WM*, Sept. 15, 1882, 3.

61. "County Fair," *WM*, Sept. 12, 1879, 3.

62. "Stevensville," *WM*, July 13, 1883, 2.

63. *WM*, Dec. 21, 1883, 3; "Stevensville," *Missoula County Times*, Dec. 19, 1883, 2.

64. *Some Bitterroot Memories*, 17; D'Aste, Diaries, entry for Aug. 16, 1886.

65. Rappagliosi, *Letters*, 42–44.

66. "The Fourth at Stevensville," *Weekly Independent*, July 13, 1872, 3.

67. "The 4th at Stevensville," *Missoula Gazette* (weekly), July 7, 1888, 2.

68. Warren, Reminiscences, UM.

69. Martens, Journal, MHS.

70. *WM*, July 19, 1878, 3.

71. "Bitter Root Items," *WM*, July 29, 1881, 3.

72. L. M. Powell, "John Waddell Family," *BR Trails I–II*, 257–59.

73. Edna Hollensteiner Tucker, "Tucker," in Lolo History Committee, *Lolo Creek Reflections*, 102.

74. Nora Simpson McLenegan, "Memories of the Bitterroot Valley," *BR Trails I–II*, 425.

75. Ronan to CommIA, Dec. 28, 1878, NAmf M234, r. 515, fr. 12; Ronan to CIA, Feb. 5, 1879, NAmf M234, r. 515, fr. 69; Territory vs. Baptiste Matte, July 2, 1878, case 375, criminal (mf. r. 6, fr. 719–55), MslaCtRec.

76. "Bitter Root Items," *WM*, May 7, 1880, 3.

77. "Drunken Indians," *Missoula Pioneer*, June 1, 1871, 3.

78. S.O.S. Writers' Club, *Montana's Little Legends*, 66–67.

79. Chaffin, *Last Horizon*, 28–29.

80. Hazel Blodgett and Violet Rennaker, "The Dye and Odell Families," *BR Trails III*, 214–16.

81. "The Dying Chief's Souvenir," *Missoula and Cedar-Creek Pioneer*, Nov. 3, 1870, 3.

82. "Charles Allard, Sr.," vertical file, MHS; "A Close Call," *WM*, Nov. 25, 1874, 3.

83. "George Washington Ward," *BR Trails I–II*, 346.

84. Stanley, *Life of Rev. L. B. Stateler*, 288–90.

85. "Wilson B. Harlan," *BR Trails I–II*, 322.

86. *North West Tribune*, July 27, 1888, 1.

87. Frank L. Williamson, "Frank L. Williamson (Doc)," BRVPS, folder 4, MHS.

88. Glenn Chaffin, "Mission 'Belles-Lettres,'" *DM*, Aug. 28, 1941, 3.

89. *Missoula Gazette* (weekly), May 22, 1889, 3.

90. Albert C. Tillman, "The Whaley Family," BRVPS, folder 4, MHS; *Some Bitterroot Memories*, 17.

91. Tracy, *Uncle Jack's Fiddlin Around*, 17, 21–71.

92. "Leaves From a Diary," *WM*, Sept. 7, 1883, 1.

93. "Memoirs of Olive (Mc Carty) Wood," BRVPS, folder 4, MHS.

94. Davis, "Miss Woody," 21–22.

95. Allis B. Stuart, "More About Joseph Blodgett," in Whealdon et al., *"I Will Be Meat for My Salish,"* 204–206.

96. Jonathan Kirpatrick et al., "Barton Smith," *BR Trails III*, 393–94.

97. "Chief Charlot Journeys to Happy Hunting Ground," *DM*, Jan. 11, 1910, 1.

## Chapter 7

1. The historical sources about the events of October 16–17, 1881, in Stevensville differ on many details. This reconstruction is based on information from "Murder at Stevensville," *WM*, Oct. 21, 1881, 3; *Ty. vs. Morris & Preece*, Oct. 20, 1881, case 488, criminal (mf. r. 7, fr. 1831–1908), and *Ty. vs. James Morris*, June 21, 1883, case 567, criminal (mf. r. 8, fr. 2066–2158), MslaCtRec.

2. Ronan to CommIA, Nov. 1, 1881, 20142/1881 NA CommIA LR.

3. Telegrams from Jordan to Breck, Oct. 18, 1881; Jordan to Ronan, Oct. 18, 1881; and Jordan to AG, Oct. 20, 1881, Fort Missoula Correspondence, LS 1879–81, copy at Mansfield Library, UM; *NNW*, Nov. 4, 1881, 3.

4. D'Aste, Diaries, entries for Oct. 17 through Nov. 14, 1881.

5. Ibid., entry for Oct. 22, 1881.

6. *Ty. vs. Morris & Preece*, Oct. 20, 1881, case 488, criminal (mf. r. 7, fr. 1831–1908), MslaCtRec.

7. "An Exhibit," *WM*, Mar. 31, 1882, 4.

8. "Court Proceedings," *WM*, Nov. 25, 1881, 3.

9. *WM*, Dec. 9, 1881, 3.

10. *WM*, Jan. 6, 1882, 3.

11. *Ty. vs. James Morris*, June 21, 1883, case 567, criminal (mf. r. 8, fr. 2066–2158) MslaCtRec.

12. Ibid.; *WM*, July 7, 1882, 3; "Court Proceedings," *WM*, Nov. 17, 1882, 2; *WM*, July 6, 1883, 3.

13. Judgment Record Book A (1867–87): 323, 387, 498–500, and 544, MslaCtRec.

14. "Indians Pardoned," *Helena Daily Herald*, Mar. 19, 1886, 3.

15. For a history of federal law regarding the status of noncitizen Indians, see Strickland, ed., *Felix S. Cohen's Handbook*, 640–45.

16. *WM*, Sept. 6, 1878, 3; *WM*, Sept. 27, 1878, 3; "Mrs. Louis Coombs," noteboook, Flathead Field Notes, folder 118, p. 22, Schaeffer Papers; D'Aste, Diaries, entry for Sept. 2, 1878.

17. "Stevensville," *WM*, July 27, 1883, 3.

18. "Stevensville," *Missoula County Times*, Oct. 31, 1883, 2.

19. D'Aste, Diaries, entries for Aug. 12, 1883; Dec. 19–27, 1885; Jan. 4, 1886; and Jan. 3, 1887.

20. Carrington to CommIA, Nov. 4, 1889, NA CommIA LR 32102/1889.

21. "Our Bitter Root Letter," *WM*, Mar. 7, 1873, 2; *WM*, Mar. 7, 1873, 3; "The Flathead Indians," *Helena Daily Herald*, May 13, 1873, 3; Shanahan to CommIA, Sept. 8, 1873, ARSI (1873): 619.

22. "The Flathead Indians," *Helena Daily Herald*, May 13, 1873, 3.

23. *Some Bitterroot Memories*, 17; Albert C. Tillman, "The Whaley Family," BRVPS, folder 4, MHS; D'Aste, Diaries, entry for Aug. 22, 1878.

24. "Summons," *WM*, Nov. 1, 1878, 2 (3 summons); *WM*, Dec. 13, 1878, 2; "Court Proceedings," *WM*, Nov. 14, 1879, 3; D'Aste, Diaries, entry for Dec. 3, 1878.

25. Maginnis to CommIA, June 30, 1880, NAmf 234, r. 517, fr. 81.

26. *Some Bitterroot Memories*, 17; D'Aste, Diaries, entry for Aug. 16, 1886.

27. *WM*, Dec. 13, 1878, 2.

28. "Judge Lynch," *WM*, Mar. 15, 1878, 3; *WM*, Mar. 15, 1878, 3; McDonald to Knowles, Mar. 24, 1878, Hiram Knowles Papers, box 1, folder 2, MHS.

29. "A Man Murdered and Robbed in Idaho!" *WM*, Nov. 14, 1873, 3.

30. *Ty. vs. Brown, Matte, and Matte*, Feb. 21, 1878, case 362, criminal (mf. r. 6, fr. 170–207), MslaCtRec.

31. "Horse Stealing," *WM*, Sept. 5, 1873, 3; *WM*, Feb. 15, 1878, 3.

32. *Ty. vs. Brown, Matte, and Matte*, Feb. 21, 1878, case 362, criminal (mf. r. 6, fr. 171–73, 179–85), MslaCtRec.

33. *WM*, Nov. 1, 1878, 3.

34. "Matte Again," *NNW*, Oct. 1, 1875, 3; "Peter Matte's Expedition," *NNW*, Oct. 15, 1875, 3.

35. Bigart and Woodcock, eds., *In the Name of the Salish*, 12.

36. Brownell, "Genesis of Wildlife Conservation," 13–43.

37. "Bitter Root Items," *Helena Independent* (daily), Aug. 6, 1881, 3.

38. "Como," *WM*, Mar. 14, 1884, 3; "Como," *WM*, Mar. 13, 1885, 1; "Como," *WM*, May 29, 1885, 2.

39. D'Aste, Diaries, entry for Mar. 5, 1886.

40. "Deer Killing by Indians," *WM*, May 13, 1887, 1.

41. D'Aste, Diaries, entry for Mar. 26, 1887.

42. "Register of Prisoners Confined in County Jail, 1882–1893," Missoula County Records, UM, 110:4.

43. "An Interesting Letter," *WM*, Nov. 27, 1889, 1.

44. Chaffin, *Last Horizon*, 28–29.

45. Turney-High, *Flathead Indians*, 123–24.

46. Strahorn, *Fifteen Thousand Miles*, 1:128–29.

47. Gibson to Sackett, Oct. 8, 1879, Fort Missoula Correspondence, LS 1879–81, copy at Mansfield Library, UM.

48. Charlos to Ronan, Feb. 6, 1885, encl. in Ronan to CommIA, Feb. 12, 1885, 3554/1885 NA CommIA LR.

49. CommIA to GLO, May 21, 1886, land, LB 148, p. 292, NA CommIA LS; CommIA to Ronan, May 22, 1886, land, LB 148, p. 318, NA CommIA LS; *WM*, June 4, 1886, 3; GLO to CommIA, June 8, 1886, 15507/1886 NA CommIA LR; CommIA to Ronan, June 15, 1886, land, LB 149, p. 190, NA CommIA LS; GLO to CommIA, July 16, 1886, 19222/1886 NA CommIA LR.

50. CommIA to Ronan, May 2, 1887, land, LB 159, p. 261, NA CommIA LS; Ronan to CommIA, May 18, 1887, 13478/1887 NA CommIA LR; CommIA to Ronan, Jan. 22, 1889, land, LB 180, p. 409, NA CommIA LS.

51. Medary to "My Dear General," Jan. 11, 1877, BCIM Papers.

52. "The County Board," *WM*, Sept. 9, 1887, 2.

53. Ronan to CommIA, Aug. 17, 1888, 21158/1888 NA CommIA LR; GLO to CommIA, Jan. 2, 1889, 192/1889 NA CommIA LR; CommIA to Ronan, Nov. 24, 1888, land, LB 179, p. 46, NA CommIA LS; Harrison, "Message from the President," 9.

54. "Indian Taxation," *WM*, Apr. 26, 1876, 3; "The Local Indian Question," *WM*, Apr. 26, 1876, 2.

55. "Bitter Root Items," *WM*, Mar. 8, 1878, 3. Presumably the same incident, with some confusion about the victim, is referred to in Martens, Journal, MHS, entry for Feb. 28, 1878.

56. Chaffin, *Last Horizon*, 99–100.

57. Ronan to CommIA, Aug. 20, 1889, ARCIA (1889): 231; Bigart, ed., *Life and Death*, p. 176, no. 534.

58. "George Washington Ward," *BR Trails I–II*, 346.

59. "Interview with Alice Chilson (Hickey)," BRVPS, folder 1, MHS.

60. "An Indian on the Warpath," *Western News*, Sept. 8, 1891, 3; *Western News*, Sept. 8, 1891, 3.

61. "Indian Difficulty," *WM*, June 4, 1874, 3; *WM*, June 4, 1874, 3; *Helena Daily Herald*, June 4, 1874, 3.

62. Williams to Pomery, Aug. 8, 1880, Fort Missoula Correspondence, LS 1879–81, copy at Mansfield Library, UM.

63. "Fight in the Bitter Root Valley," *Missoula Pioneer*, Apr. 20, 1871, 3.

64. *Missoula Gazette* (weekly), Dec. 1, 1888, 3.

65. Montana State Prison Records, r. 4, p. 73, MHS; *Ty. vs. Pierre (Indian)*, Nov. 14, 1881, case 471, criminal (mf. r. 7, fr. 1175–96), MslaCtRec.

66. Chipman to "Shiloh," May 16, 1878, and Chipman to D'Aste, May 16, 1878, Fort Missoula, Montana, LS July 1, 1877–June 30, 1878, UM.

67. *North West Tribune*, Oct. 30, 1891, 3.

68. Clarence Charlo, "The Flathead Indians," unpublished student term paper, Arlee High School, Arlee, Mont., 1965. Copy in possession of author.

69. *North West Tribune*, July 1, 1887, 1.

70. *Some Bitterroot Memories*, 17.

71. "Wilson B. Harlan," *BR Trails I–II*, 322.

72. "Memoirs of Olive (Mc Carty) Wood," BRVPS, folder 4, MHS.

73. Brooks, Reminiscences, MHS.

74. Lolo History Committee, *Lolo Creek Reflections*, 102.

75. "Stevensville Ghosts," *Helena Independent* (daily), Nov. 29, 1881, 3.

76. Martens, Journal, MHS, entries for Apr. 10, Apr. 26, and Nov. 14, 1877.

77. Ronan to CommIA, Dec. 28, 1878, NAmf M234, r. 515, fr. 12; Ronan to CommIA, Feb. 5, 1879, NAmf M234, r. 515, fr. 69; *Ty. vs. Baptiste Matte*, July 2, 1878, case 375, criminal (mf. r. 6, fr. 719–55), MslaCtRec.

78. "Stevensville," *WM*, Mar. 14, 1884, 3; "Stevensville," *Missoula County Times*, Mar. 26, 1884, 2; *WM*, Mar. 28, 1884, 3.

79. Mrs. Theodore (Lena) Sherrill, "Sherrill Family," *BR Trails I–II*, 81–83.

80. Jones to CommIA, Jan. 29, 1871, NA mf M234, r. 339, fr. 715.

## Chapter 8

1. "West Side of the Bitter Root—Sweat House Farmers," *RMH*, Aug. 16, 1877, 2.

2. Dusenberry, "Samples of Pend d'Oreille Oral Literature," 116.

3. "Jottings of Our Traveling Man," *RMH*, Dec. 8, 1887, 2.

4. Carrington to CommIA, Nov. 1, 1889, 31955/1889 NA CommIA LR; Carrington MS, chap. 7.

5. Shafft, "General Garfield and the Flatheads," 20.

6. SuptIndAff to CommIA, Mar. 28, 1873, NAmf M234, r. 496, fr. 427. Whipple trees are crossbars that were used to attach the harnesses of draft animals pulling plows or wagons.

7. "The Bitter Root Imbroglio," *WM*, Jan. 8, 1874, 2.

8. Medary to "My Dear General," Jan. 11, 1877, BCIM Papers. See also Ronan to CommIA, Aug. 20, 1878, NAmf M234, r. 511, fr. 731.

9. "Honor to the Flatheads," *Helena Daily Herald*, July 17, 1877, 2.

10. D'Aste to Ronan, May 1, 1884, encl. in Ronan to CommIA, May 5, 1884, 8856/1884 NA CommIA LR.

11. Harrison, "Message from the President," p. 16, no. 41.

12. "Charlos," *Helena Independent* (daily), July 15, 1877, 2.

13. SuptIndAff to CommIA, Sept. 15, 1871, *ARSI* (1871): 829.

14. "Sophie Moiese" notebook, Flathead Field Notes, folder 118, pp. 20–21, Schaeffer Papers.

15. Carrington to CommIA, Nov. 25, 1889, 34449/1889 NA CommIA LR; Carrington to CommIA, Nov. 27, 1889, 34579/1889 NA CommIA LR.

16. Dusenberry, "Samples of Pend d'Oreille Oral Literature," 118.

17. "Sophie Moiese" notebook, Flathead Field Notes, folder 118, pp. 19, 21, 23, Schaeffer Papers.

18. Jones to SuptIndAff, Sept. 1, 1871, ARSI (1871): 841.

19. Dusenberry, "Samples of Pend d'Oreille Oral Literature," 118.

20. "Up the Bitter Root," *NNW*, Nov. 23, 1872, 3.

21. Ronan to CommIA, Mar. 27, 1884, 6629/1884 NA CommIA LR.

22. D'Aste, Diaries, entries for Sept. 19–26, 1882; and July 22, 31, and Aug. 25, 1883.

23. Sully to CommIA, July 30, 1870, NAmf M234, r. 490, fr. 563; Sully to CommIA, Sept. 20. 1870, ARSI (1870): 656

24. "A Trip to the Westside," *Helena Daily Herald*, Sept. 23, 1870, 1.

25. Jones to SuptIndAff, Sept. 1, 1871, ARSI (1871): 841; Jones to CommIA, Jan. 29, 1871, NAmf M234, r. 339, fr. 715.

26. SuptIndAff to CommIA, Sept. 15, 1871, ARSI (1871): 829–30; SuptIndAff to CommIA, Oct. 16, 1871, NAmf M234, r. 491, fr. 954.

27. "Survey of Indian Ranches," *WM*, Aug. 26, 1874, 2.

28. SuptIndAff to CommIA, Mar. 28, 1873, NAmf M234, r. 496, fr. 427.

29. "Indian Council," *Pioneer*, Aug. 31, 1872, 2.

30. "The Chiefs in Council," *Pioneer*, Sept. 7, 1872, 3. Sometime between 1874 and 1883, after he had moved to the Jocko Valley, Arlee withdrew one of his sons from the St. Ignatius Mission school because he had been put to work on the harvest. In 1883 Arlee complained: "he had sent the boy there to learn how to read and write, not to work like a squaw." The historical record does not make clear if this represents a change in Arlee's attitude toward farming or if he was just angry at the mission. Vest and Maginnis, "Report," xiv. See also Rappagliosi, *Letters*, 55–58.

31. SuptIndAff to CommIA, Mar. 15, 1873, NAmf M234, r. 496, fr. 359.

32. "A Trip Up Bitter Root Valley," *WM*, July 11, 1873, 2.

33. D'Aste to Shanahan, Sept. 13, 1873, BCIM Papers.

34. "The Bitter Root Imbroglio," *WM*, Jan. 8, 1874, 2; Inspector J. D. Bevier to CommIA, July 18, 1874, no. 37, CommIA Inspection Report file, RG 75, NA.

35. “Up the Bitter Root Valley,” *RMH*, July 26, 1877, 2.

36. Harrison, “Message from the President,” p. 16, no. 31.

37. D’Aste to Ronan, Aug. 18, 1877, encl. in Ronan to CommIA, Aug. 20, 1877, NAmf M234, r. 507, fr. 378; Potts to SecInt, Oct. 1, 1877, NAmf M234, r. 517, fr. 21; Ronan to CommIA, Oct. 1, 1877, NAmf M234, r. 507, fr. 465.

38. NAmf M1794, Montana Territory, Missoula County, Bitter Root Valley, ED24, p. 1, no. 3.

39. W. F. Wheeler, “Missoula County,” *NNW*, Oct. 8, 1880, 2.

40. Stevensville Historical Society, *Montana Genesis*, 109.

41. Chatfield & Bass, ledger, 1881–83, Bass Family Papers, r. 5, pp. 185, 307, UM.

42. D’Aste, Diaries, entries for Aug. 20 and 29, 1883.

43. Ibid., entry for Mar. 25, 1886.

44. Harrison, “Message from the President,” p. 15, no. 15.

45. Ibid., abstracted from 8, 11–17. Carrington’s report did not say who occupied the allotments of Salish who were deceased in 1889.

46. “How Indian Milk Maids Fooled the Kicking Cow,” *Ronan Pioneer*, Nov. 17, 1916, 3.

47. *Missoula County Times*, Feb. 6, 1884, 2; Feb. 20, 1884, 2; “Returned from Washington,” *WM*, Mar. 14, 1884, 2; Ronan to CommIA, Mar. 27, 1884, 6629/1884 NA CommIA LR.

48. CommIA to SecInt, Apr. 9, 1884, finance, letter press, vol. 99, pt. 1, p. 125, NA CommIA LS; CommIA to Ronan, Aug. 29, 1884, finance, vol. 105, pt. 1, p. 471, NA CommIA LS.

49. *WM*, Jan. 23, 1885, 3.

50. D’Aste, Diaries, entry for Mar. 22, 1885.

51. “Stevensville,” *WM*, Apr. 3, 1885, 3.

52. “The Indians,” *WM*, Mar. 19, 1886, 2.

53. D’Aste, Diaries, entries for 1885 and 1886.

54. Ibid., entries for Apr. 22, 1883; Sept. 3, 1883; Mar. 7, 1884; Sept. 8, 20, 22, and 30, 1884; Sept. 5 and 16, 1886; Dec. 4, 1886; Jan. 5, 1887; and May 3, 1887.

55. Ibid., entries for 1885.

56. Galbreath to SuptIndAff, Sept. 6, 1869, ARSI (1869): 740; NAmf M593, r. 827, Montana, Missoula Co., Bitter Root Valley.

57. NAmf M595, r. 107, fr. 376–84; U.S. Census Office, *Compendium of the Eleventh Census*, 259.

58. Wheeler, “Missoula County,” *NNW*, Oct. 8, 1880, 2.

59. “Missoula County Items,” *Helena Independent* (daily), Mar. 20, 1881, 3.

60. D’Aste, Diaries, entry for Dec. 26, 1886. See also Feb. 25, 1887.

61. D’Aste to Ronan, Feb. 22, 1887, encl. in Ronan to CommIA, May 18, 1887, 13478/1887 NA CommIA LR.

62. “Nathaniel E. (Than) Wilkerson,” *BR Trails I–II*, 164–65.

63. “Stevensville,” *WM*, Mar. 4, 1887, 2; “Stevensville,” *WM*, Mar. 25, 1887, 2.

64. "Martin Charlo" notebook, Flathead Field Notes, folder 118, p. 3, Schaeffer Papers.

65. "Jottings of Our Traveling Man," *RMH*, Dec. 8, 1887, 2.

66. "Sophie Moiese" notebook, Flathead Field Notes, folder 118, box 13, pp. 24–25, Schaeffer Papers.

67. D'Aste to Ronan, May 1, 1884, encl. in Ronan to CommIA, May 5, 1884, 8856/1884 NA CommIA LR.

68. Chaffin, *Last Horizon*, 28–29.

69. *WM*, Nov. 21, 1888, 3.

70. Walcheck, "Montana Wildlife"; Koch, "Big Game in Montana."

71. Koch, "Big Game in Montana," 368.

72. Lippincott, "Grandeur in an American Forest," 25–28.

73. "Game Law a Dead Letter," *AS*, Oct. 28, 1900, 14.

74. U.S. Department of Agriculture, Weather Bureau, *Summaries of Climatological Data by Sections*, section 28—Western Montana, 6; U.S. Department of Agriculture, *Climate and Man*, 957.

75. Ronan to CommIA, Aug. 20, 1889, ARCIA (1889) 229.

76. Harrison, "Message from the President," 19.

77. *WM*, Sept. 10, 1886, 3.

78. "The Outlook," *Bitter Root Bugle*, June 14, 1889, 1.

79. "The Crop Outlook," *WM*, June 19, 1889, 3.

80. *WM*, July 17, 1889, 2, 3.

81. "Tax Sale Book, 1871–1889," Missoula County Records, Missoula County Courthouse, Missoula, Mont., 10, 14, and enclosure; "Delinquent Tax List," *WM*, Jan. 30, 1889, 4; "Delinquent Tax List of Missoula County," *WM*, Dec. 28, 1892, 2–3. No delinquency lists for 1890 or 1891 were located.

82. GLO to CommIA, Jan. 22, 1889, 1849/1889 NA CommIA LR.

83. Harrison, "Message from the President," 11–17.

## Chapter 9

1. The description of Carrington's and Charlo's final negotiations on the weekend of Nov. 2–3, 1889, are from Carrington MS, chap. 8; Carrington to CommIA, Nov. 4, 1889, 32102/1889 NA CommIA LR.

2. Carrington MS, chap. 7.

3. Ibid.

4. Harrison, "Message from the President," 13.

5. "To Remove the Flatheads," *NNW*, Jan. 20, 1888, 3.

6. *Congressional Record*, 50th Cong. 1st Sess., vol. 19, pt. 2 (Feb. 27, 1888): 1516.

7. U.S. Congress, House, "Sale of Lands of Flathead Indians."

8. *Congressional Record*, 50th Cong., 2d Sess., vol. 20, pt. 2 (Feb. 6, 1889): 1588–89; pt. 3 (Feb. 26, 1889): 2329.

9. *U.S. Statutes at Large*, Mar. 2, 1889, 25:871–72.

10. SecInt to CommIA, Sept. 24, 1889, 27337/1889 NA CommIA LR.

11. McKeen, "Henry Beebee Carrington."

12. Carrington, *Indian Question*, 5, 14.

13. Carrington to CommIA, Nov. 1, 1889, 31955/1889 NA CommIA LR.

14. Carrington MS, chap. 6.

15. Ibid., chap. 12.

16. Carrington to CommIA, Oct. 11, 1891, 37294/1891 NA CommIA LR.

17. Carrington MS, chaps. 4, 6.

18. Garfield, "Conference," 173; Vest, "Charlot: Chief of the Flathead Indians," *Washington Post*, July 26, 1903, 11.

19. Carrington MS, chap. 6.

20. Ibid.

21. Father D'Aste states in his diary that he was at the Jocko Agency on Oct. 20, 1889, but he does not mention interpreting for Carrington. D'Aste, Diaries, entry for Oct. 20, 1889.

22. Carrington MS, chap. 6.

23. Ibid.

24. Ibid. Punctuation in original.

25. Carrington's chronology of his first few days in Stevensville in October 1889 is confusing, and the date of the visit to Charlo's farm could be off by a day.

26. Carrington MS, chap. 7; Carrington to CommIA, Nov. 1, 1889, 31955/1889 NA CommIA LR.

27. Carrington MS, chap. 7.

28. Ibid.

29. Ibid.

30. Ibid.

31. Harrison, "Message from the President," 12–13.

32. Carrington MS, chap. 7.

33. Unfortunately, the page detailing a large part of Carrington's argument (MS, chap. 7) is missing from the manuscript preserved at Yale University. Carrington to CommIA, Nov. 4, 1889, 32102/1889 NA CommIA LR.

34. Carrington MS, chap. 7.

35. Ibid., chap. 8; Carrington to CommIA, Nov. 4, 1889, 32102/1889 NA CommIA LR.

36. Carrington MS, chap. 8; Carrington to CommIA, Nov. 4, 1889, 32102/1889 NA CommIA LR.

37. Harrison, "Message from the President," 12–13; Carrington MS, chap. 8.

38. Dusenberry, "Samples of Pend d'Oreille Oral Literature," 116.

39. Carrington MS, chap. 8; "A Great Banquet," *Helena Journal*, Nov. 6, 1889, 2.

40. "Resolutions," *WM*, Nov. 20, 1889, 1.

41. Carrington MS, chap. 9.

42. Harrison, "Message from the President."

43. CommIA to Carrington, Nov. 14, 1889, land, LB 191, p. 289, NA CommIA LS.

44. Carrington MS, chap. 9.

45. CommIA to Carrington, Dec. 5, 1889, land, LB 192, p. 167, NA CommIA LS.

46. Harrison, "Message from the President," 6–23.

47. SecInt to CommIA, Sept. 24, 1889, 27337/1889 NA CommIA LR; Carrington to Noble, Apr. 7, 1890, 11613/1890 NA CommIA LR.

48. Carrington to CommIA, Feb. 28, 1891, 8339/1891 NA CommIA LR.

49. *U.S. Statutes at Large*, Mar. 3, 1891, 26:1009.

50. CommIA to Carrington, June 30, 1891, land, LB 219, p. 234, NA CommIA LS. Emphasis in original.

51. CommIA to SecInt, Oct. 21, 1891, land, LB 224, p. 260, NA CommIA LS.

52. McKeen, "Henry Beebee Carrington," 319–22.

53. "Valley Indians," *Missoula Gazette* (daily), Oct. 9, 1890, 1.

54. Harrison, "Message from the President," 13.

55. Ronan to CommIA, Jan. 2, 1890, 709/1890 NA CommIA LR.

56. Harrison, "Message from the President," 5.

57. Ronan to CommIA, telegram, Mar. 17, 1890, 8311/1890 NA CommIA LR; Ronan to CommIA, Apr. 9, 1890, 11409/1890 NA CommIA LR.

58. Ronan to CommIA, June 2, 1890, 17468/1890 NA CommIA LR.

59. Ronan to CommIA, June 2, 1890, 17468/1890 NA CommIA LR.

60. *Missoula Daily Gazette*, Mar. 18, 1890, 4.

61. Ronan to CommIA, Aug. 14, 1890, ARCIA (1890): 124.

62. Ronan to CommIA, Dec. 6, 1890, 38635/1890 NA CommIA LR.

63. "Bitter Root Lands," *Western News*, Dec. 23, 1890, 4.

64. Carrington to CommIA, July 29, 1891, 28361/1891 NA CommIA LR.

65. Carrington MS, chap. 10.

66. Ibid.

67. *U.S. Statutes at Large*, Mar. 2, 1889, 25:872.

68. Carrington to CommIA, July 11, 1891, 24764/1891 NA CommIA LR. Emphasis in original.

69. CommIA to SecInt, July 16, 1891, land, LB 220, p. 159, NA CommIA LS.

70. Carrington MS, chap. 10.

71. *North West Tribune*, Oct. 30, 1891, 3.

72. *U.S. Statutes at Large*, Mar. 2, 1889, 25:871.

73. Harrison, "Message from the President," 14. See also Carrington MS, chap. 9.

74. Sedgwick to CommIA, Oct. 30, 1890, 34388/1890 NA CommIA LR.

75. "General Carrington Explains," *Missoula Weekly Gazette*, Aug. 5, 1891, 6.

76. Carrington to CommIA, Sept. 29, 1891, 35748/1891 NA CommIA LR.

77. Carrington to CommIA, Oct. 5, 1891, 36551/1891 NA CommIA LR; "A Strange Ruling," *Western News*, Oct. 6, 1891, 2.

78. "Missoula Notes," AS, Oct. 6, 1891, 8; "To the Highest Bidder," AS, Oct. 7, 1891, 1; "The Bitter Root Land Sale," *Missoula Weekly Gazette*, Oct. 7, 1891, 3.

79. Carrington to CommIA, July 29, 1891, 28361/1891 NA CommIA LR.

80. Carrington to CommIA, July 29, 1891, 28656/1891 NA CommIA LR.

81. Carrington to CommIA, Aug. 17. 1891, 30745/1891 NA CommIA LR. Emphasis in original.

82. Carrington to CommIA, Aug. 25, 1891, 31714/1891 NA CommIA LR.

83. CommIA to Carrington, Aug. 26, 1891, land, LB 222, p. 90, NA CommIA LS.

84. Carrington to CommIA, Sept. 29, 1891, 35748/1891 NA CommIA LR.

85. Carrington to CommIA, Oct. 11, 1891, 37294/1891 NA CommIA LR; Carrington MS, chap. 10.

86. Carrington MS, chap. 10.

87. Ibid.

88. Ibid.

89. Carrington MS, chap. 3.

90. Ibid., chap. 11.

91. Fort Missoula, Montana, Records of the United States Army Commands (Army Posts), RG 98, NA; Fort Missoula, Montana, Post Returns, Records of the Office of the Adjutant General, RG 94, NA. Microfilm copies available at Mansfield Library, University of Montana, as "Book Records of Fort Missoula" and "Post Returns, Fort Missoula, Mont., 1877–1916."

92. See, for example, "Stevensville Items," *Light of the Valley*, Oct. 1891, 5; "On the March," *Missoula Gazette* (daily), Oct. 16, 1891, 1; "The Natives Gone," *Western News*, Oct. 20, 1891, 1; "The Indian Exodus," *WM*, Oct. 21, 1891, 4; "Charles Amos Buck," BRVPS, folder 1, MHS; McCormick, *Colors From an Old Montana Sluice Box*, 18; Stone, *Following Old Trails*, 83–90; Matt, "Mary Ann Topsseh Coombs," 8–9; Malouf, "The Life of Ellen (Pierre) Bigsam," box 15, folder 6, Carling I. Malouf Papers, UM, 14; Malouf, "Flathead and Pend d'Oreille," 309, fig. 9.

93. "The Catholic Flathead Indians," *Pilot*, Apr. 23, 1892, 1.

94. Thompson Smith, Salish Pend d'Oreille Culture Committee, to Bigart, personal communication, Mar. 23, 2006.

95. Salish Culture Committee, "Exodus of the Bitterroot Salish."

96. Carrington MS, chap. 11.

97. "Stevensville Items," *Light of the Valley*, Oct. 1891, 5.

98. McCormick, *Colors*, 18.

99. "Charles Amos Buck," BRVPS, folder 1, MHS.

100. Matt, "Mary Ann Topsseh Coombs."

101. Carrington MS, chap. 11; "Obituary," *WM*, Nov. 23, 1892, 1.

102. Ibid., and chap. 12.

103. Malouf, "The Life of Ellen (Pierre) Bigsam," box 15, folder 6, Carling I. Malouf Papers, UM, 14.

104. Sanborn–Perris Map Co. Ltd., "Missoula, Missoula Co., Mont., June 1891."

105. "The Indian Exodus," *WM*, Oct. 21, 1891, 4.

106. Carrington MS, chap. 12.

107. Mary Ronan, *Frontier Woman*, 150–51; Palladino, *Indian and White*, 77–78.

108. Carrington MS, chap. 12.

109. Carrington to CommIA, Nov. 19, 1891, 41847/1891 NA CommIA LR; Carrington to CommIA, Nov. 18, 1891, 41846/1891 NA CommIA LR.

110. Carrington to CommIA, Nov. 17, 1891, 41622/1891 NA CommIA LR.

111. CommIA to Carrington, Sept. 5, 1891, land, LB 222, p. 274, NA CommIA LS; Carrington to CommIA, Nov. 17, 1891, 41622/1891 NA CommIA LR.

112. *U.S. Statutes at Large*, July 28, 1892, 27:294.

113. Whealdon et al., *"I Will Be Meat for My Salish,"* 245; Ronan to CommIA, Dec. 14, 1891, 45331/1891 NA CommIA LR.

114. Ronan to CommIA, Mar. 10, 1892, 9857/1892 NA CommIA LR.

115. Ronan to CommIA, Dec. 14, 1891, 45331/1891 NA CommIA LR; Miller to SecInt, Dec. 15, 1891, NAmf M1070, r. 11, fr. 751.

116. Harrison, "Message from the President," 13.

117. Ronan to CommIA, Jan. 23, 1892, 3815/1892 NA CommIA LR.

118. Ibid.

119. Ronan to CommIA, Apr. 2, 1892, 12943/1892 NA CommIA LR.

120. Ronan to CommIA, Jan. 11, 1893, 2127/1893 NA CommIA LR; "At the Reservation," *AS*, Nov. 1, 1893, 6.

121. Ronan to CommIA, Jan. 23, 1892, 3815/1892 NA CommIA LR.

122. Carter to CommIA, Dec. 2, 1897, 51868/1897 NA CommIA LR.

123. Dusenberry, "Samples of Pend d'Oreille Oral Literature," 119.

124. Ronan to CommIA, Feb. 1, 1893, 5182/1893 NA CommIA LR.

125. Ronan to CommIA, Mar. 4, 1892, NA CommIA LR 9286/1892; Ronan to CommIA, telegram, July 4, 1892, NA CommIA LR 23575/1892.

126. Quoted in *WM*, Feb. 24, 1892, 3.

127. *Western News*, Sept. 13, 1892, 6; June 27, 1893, 5.

128. Ronan to CommIA, June 1, 1892, NA CommIA LR 20878/1892.

129. Dusenberry, "Samples of Pend d'Oreille Oral Literature," 119.

130. Ronan to CommIA, Nov. 30, 1892, NA CommIA LR 43536/1892.

131. CommIA to SecInt, Jan. 14, 1893, NA CommIA LS, land, LB 250, p. 393.

132. *Western News*, June 27, 1893, 5.

133. Ronan to CommIA, Aug. 5, 1893, ARCIA (1893): 183.

134. "Lo the Poor Indian," *AS*, Mar. 14, 1894, 6.

135. "It Was a Red Picnic," *AS*, Apr. 7, 1894, 6.

136. "Lessons for Some Whites," *AS*, Apr. 9, 1894, 6.

137. Ronan to CommIA, Feb. 1, 1893, NA CommIA LR 5182/1893.

138. "One Honest Indian," *AS*, Jan. 15, 1896, 10.

139. "Old Mrs. Ninepipes," *AS*, Jan. 17, 1896, 10.

140. "An Important Decision," *WM*, Jan. 20, 1892, 4.

141. Ronan to CommIA, Aug. 5, 1893, ARCIA (1893): 183.

142. Ronan to CommIA, Jan. 11, 1893, NA CommIA LR 2127/1893.

143. "About Those Indian Lands," *AS*, June 20, 1894, 6.

144. Duncan to SecInt, Oct. 10, 1896, NAmf M1070, r. 11, fr. 796.

145. CommIA to SecInt, Oct. 29, 1896, NA CommIA LS, land, LB 342, p. 35.

146. Smead to CommIA, July 20, 1898, NA CommIA LR 33601/1898; Beede to SecInt, July 25, 1899, NA CommIA LR 37418/1899.

147. Beede to SecInt, Sept. 12, 1900, NAmf M1070, r. 11, fr. 1062.

148. Ibid.

149. CommIA to SecInt, Apr. 11, 1901, NA CommIA LS, land, LB 476, p. 387.

150. "Bitter Root Lands," *Missoulian* (daily), Feb. 4, 1901, 3.

151. Carter to CommIA, Mar. 27, 1896, NA CommIA LR 13456/1896; Carter to CommIA, June 24, 1896, NA CommIA LR 24171/1896; CommIA to Carter, July 1, 1896, NA CommIA LS, land, LB 335, p. 470; Beede to SecInt, Sept. 12, 1900, NAmf M1070, r. 11, fr. 1062; CommIA to SecInt, Oct. 2, 1900, NA CommIA LS, land, LB 453, p. 229.

152. "Charlot's Grievance," *AS*, Jan. 25, 1896, 10.

# Bibliography

## Manuscript Collections


Eastern Washington State Historical Society, Spokane, Wash.
MONAC Collection, MS 184.
Glacier National Park Archives, Glacier National Park, West Glacier, Mont.
GLAC 9813, two untitled typescript manuscripts of Blackfeet war experiences.
Glenbow-Alberta Foundation, Calgary, Alberta
Claude Schaeffer Papers.
Library of Congress, Washington, D.C.
James A. Garfield Papers, "Removal of Flathead Indians, 1871–72," vol. 9, series 11, reel 131.
Marquette University Archives, Milwaukee, Wis.
Bureau of Catholic Indian Missions Papers, St. Ignatius Mission, Mont., files.
Missoula County Courthouse, Missoula, Mont.
Missoula District Court Records.
"Tax Sale Book, 1871–1889."
Missouri Historical Society, St. Louis, Mo.
Meriwether Lewis Collection.
Montana Historical Society Archives, Helena, Mont.
"Charles Allard, Sr.," vertical file.
Bitterroot Valley Pioneer Society Papers, SC 1053.
Lula Wood Brooks Reminiscences, SC 472.
Henry Buck Reminiscence, SC 492.
Thomas W. Harris, Journals, 1860–1870, SC 231.
Samuel Hauser Papers, MC 37.

Charles Hutchins Letters, SC 759.
Hiram Knowles Papers, MS 2.
Martin Maginnis Papers, MC 50.
John P. Martens, Journal, Mar. 1, 1877–June 23, 1878, MF 77, pt. c.
Montana Governors' Papers, MC 35, vol. 1
Montana Pioneers Collection, MC 64.
Montana Secretary [Territorial and State] Records, SMF 30, reel 6.
Montana State Prison Records, SMF 36.
John Owen Papers, MS 44.
Benjamin F. Potts Papers, SC 221.

National Archives, Washington, D.C.
RG 75, Records of the Commissioner of Indian Affairs.
RG 75, Records of the Board of Indian Commissioners.
RG 94, Records of the Office of the Adjutant General.
RG 98, Records of the United States Army Commands (Army Posts).
RG 123, Records of the Court of Claims.
RG 205, Records of the Justice Department (Claims Section).
RG 279, Records of the Indian Claims Commission.
RG 393, Records of the United States Army Continental Commands.

National Archives Microfilm Publications, National Archives, Washington, D.C.
M5, Washington Superintendency of Indian Affairs, "Records of the Washington Superintendency of Indian Affairs, 1853–1874," reels 1 and 22.
M234, U.S. Office of Indian Affairs, "Letters Received by the Office of Indian Affairs, 1874–81," reels 339, 488–518, 612, and 907–908.
M593, U.S. Bureau of the Census, "Population Schedules of the Ninth Census of the United States, 1870," reel 827.
M595, U.S. Bureau of Indian Affairs, "Indian Census Rolls, 1885–1940," reel 107.
M666, U.S. Adjutant General, "Letters Received by the Office of the Adjutant General, Main Series, 1871–1880," reels 405 and 415.
M833, Montana Superintendency of Indian Affairs, "Records of the Montana Superintendency of Indian Affairs, 1867–1873," reels 2–3.
M1070, U.S. Department of the Interior, "Reports of Inspections of the Field Jurisdictions of the Office of Indian Affairs, 1873–1900," reel 11.
M1350, U.S. Bureau of Indian Affairs, "Selected Records of the Bureau of Indian Affairs Relating to the Enrollment of Indians on the Flathead Reservation, 1903–08," reel 1.
M1495, "Special Files of Headquarters, Division of the Missouri, Relating to Military Operations and Administration, 1863–1885," "Post at Hell Gate, Montana Territory, Mar. 1875-May 1877," reel 2.
M1794, U.S. Census Office, "Nonpopulation Census Schedules for the District of Columbia, Montana Territory, Nevada, and Wyoming Territory, 1880: Agriculture."

T9, U.S. Bureau of the Census, "Tenth Census of Population, 1880," reel 742.
Smithsonian Institution, Natural History Library, Washington, D.C.
George Suckley, "Journal—containing the daily proceedings of the U.S. Exploring Expedition under the command of Gov. Isaac I. Stevens" [1853], manuscript.
University of Montana, Toole Archives, Mansfield Library, Missoula
Bass Family Papers, MS 71.
Fort Missoula, Montana, "Letters Sent, July 1, 1877–June 30, 1878," SC 45, reel 1.
Charles M. Lee, Journals, SC 261.
Carling I. Malouf Papers, MS 640.
Missoula County Records, MS 310, series II.
Carrie May Warren, Reminiscences, MS 269.
Francis L. Worden Papers, MS 21, subgroup 2, Worden and Company, series 7, subseries 2.
University of Montana, Mansfield Library, Missoula
Fort Missoula Correspondence, "Letters Sent, 1879–1881," photocopy.
University of Oklahoma, Western History Collections, University Libraries, Norman
Walter S. Campbell Collection.
Yale University, Beinecke Library, New Haven, Conn.
Frederick H. Burr, Diary, Jan. 1, 1857–Jan. 4, 1858, Western Americana Collection, WA MSS 451.
F. H. Burr, Diary, 1858, Western Americana Collection, WA MSS S-1748.
Elwood Evans, journal of 1853 expedition, Western Americana Collection, MS 172.
Yale University, Sterling Library, New Haven, Conn.
Henry B. Carrington, "The Exodus of the Flatheads," unpublished manuscript, Carrington Family Papers.

## Newspapers

*Anaconda (Mont.) Standard*, 1891–96, 1900, 1904, 1908
*Benton Weekly Record* (Fort Benton, Mont.), 1882
*Bitter Root Bugle* (Gantsdale, Mont.), 1889
*Bozeman (Mont.) Avant Courier*, 1873–81
*Bozeman (Mont.) Weekly Chronicle*, 1883–84
*Daily Enterprise* (Livingston, Mont.), 1883
*Daily Independent* (Helena, Mont.), 1874
*Daily Ravalli Republican* (Hamilton, Mont.), 1967
*Evening Star* (Washington, D.C.), 1884
*Garrettsville (Ohio) Journal*, 1872
*Daily Missoulian* (Missoula, Mont.), 1910–51
*Great Falls (Mont.) Tribune*, 1955
*Helena (Mont.) Daily Herald*, 1869–83
*Helena (Mont.) Independent*, 1876–83

*Helena (Mont.) Weekly Herald,* 1868–79
*Independent* (New York, N.Y.), 1872
*Light of the Valley* (Stevensville, Mont.), 1891
*Missoula and Cedar Creek (Mont.) Pioneer,* 1870
*Missoula (Mont.) County Times,* 1883–84
*Missoula (Mont.) Daily Gazette,* 1890
*Missoula (Mont.) Gazette,* 1888–91
*Missoula (Mont.) Pioneer,* 1871
*Missoula (Mont.) Weekly Gazette,* 1891
*Missoulian* (Missoula, Mont.), 1901, 1979
*Montana Post* (Virginia City, Mont.), 1865–66
*New North-West* (Deer Lodge, Mont.), 1869–88
*New York Times,* 1884
*North West Tribune* (Stevensville, Mont.), 1887–91
*Oregon Spectator* (Oregon City), 1853
*Pilot* (Boston, Mass.), 1892
*Pioneer* (Missoula, Mont.), 1871–72
*Rocky Mountain Gazette* (Helena, Mont.), 1872
*Rocky Mountain Husbandman* (Diamond City, Mont., and other locations), 1877–87, 1928–32
*Rocky Mountain Weekly Gazette* (Helena, Mont.), 1870–71
*Ronan Pioneer* (Ronan, Mont.), 1916
*Washington Post,* 1884, 1903
*Weekly Avant Courier* (Bozeman, Mont.), 1883–84
*Weekly Independent* (Deer Lodge and Helena, Mont.), 1871–75
*Weekly Missoulian* (Missoula, Mont.), 1873–92
*Weekly Rocky Mountain Gazette* (Helena, Mont.), 1873
*Western News* (Stevensville and Hamilton, Mont.), 1890–94, 1911

## Books, Articles, and Other Sources

Alter, J. Cecil. *Jim Bridger,* new ed. Norman: University of Oklahoma Press, 1962.

Armstrong, Virginia Irving. *"I Have Spoken": American History through the Voices of the Indians.* Chicago: Swallow Press, 1971.

Baird, Lynn, and Dennis Baird, eds. *In Nez Perce Country: Accounts of the Bitterroots and the Clearwater After Lewis and Clark.* Moscow: University of Idaho Library, 2003.

Barbour, C. "Two Vigilance Committees." *The Overland Monthly* 10 (2nd ser.), no. 57 (Sept. 1887): 285–91.

Barrows, John R. *Ubet.* Caldwell, Idaho: Caxton Printers, Ltd., 1934, 1936.

Bass, Lucille Stewart. *Our Tapestry.* Privately published, n.p., 1973.

Beck, David R. M. *The Struggle for Self-Determination: History of the Menominee Indians Since 1854.* Lincoln: University of Nebraska Press, 2005.

Bigart, Robert J., ed. *Life and Death at St. Mary's Mission, Montana: Births, Marriages, Deaths, and Survival among the Bitterroot Salish Indians, 1866–1891*. Pablo, Mont.: Salish Kootenai College Press, 2004.

Bigart, Robert, and Clarence Woodcock, eds. *In the Name of the Salish and Kootenai Nation: The 1855 Hell Gate Treaty and the Origin of the Flathead Indian Reservation.* Pablo, Mont.: Salish Kootenai College Press, 1996.

Binnema, Theodore. *Common and Contested Ground: A Human and Environmental History of the Northwestern Plains.* Norman: University of Oklahoma Press, 2001.

Bitter Root Valley Historical Society. *Bitterroot Trails.* 4 vols. Darby and Stevensville, Mont.: Bitter Root Valley Historical Society, 1982–2007.

Boyd, Robert T. "The Introduction of Infectious Diseases Among the Indians of the Pacific Northwest, 1774–1874." PhD dissertation, University of Washington, Seattle, 1985, DAI #8521561.

Bradley, James H. "Lieut. James H. Bradley Manuscript." *Contributions to the Historical Society of Montana* 9 (1923): 226–351.

Brown, Ellsworth H. "The History of the Flathead Indians in the Nineteenth Century." PhD dissertation, Michigan State University, East Lansing, 1975, DAI #76-5525.

Brownell, Joan Louise. "The Genesis of Wildlife Conservation in Montana." Master's thesis, Montana State University, Bozeman, 1987.

Brunot, Felix R., Chairman. "Report of the Commission to Negotiate with the Crow Tribe of Indians." U.S. Board of Indian Commissioners, *Annual Report of the Board of Indian Commissioners* (1874): 93–124.

Buckley, Cornelius M., S.J. *Nicolas Point, S.J.: His Life and Northwest Indian Chronicles.* Chicago: Loyola University Press, 1989.

Burns, R. Ignatius, S.J. "A Jesuit at the Hell Gate Treaty of 1855." *Mid-America* 34, no. 2 (Apr. 1952): 87–114.

Carriker, Robert C., and Eleanor R. Carriker, eds. *Microfilm Edition of the Pacific Northwest Tribes Missions Collection of the Oregon Province Archives of the Society of Jesus.* Reels 29–30. Wilmington, Del.: Scholarly Resources, 1987.

Carrington, Henry B. *The Indian Question.* Edited by John M. Carroll. New York: Sol Lewis, 1973. First published in 1884.

Chaffin, Glenn. *The Last Horizon.* Somerset, Calif.: Pine Trail Press, 1971.

Charlo, Clarence. "The Flathead Indians." Student term paper, Arlee High School, Arlee, Mont., 1965. Copy in possession of author.

[Chief Joseph]. "An Indian's Views of Indian Affairs." *North American Review* 128, no. 269 (Apr. 1879): 412–33.

Chittenden, Hiram Martin. *The American Fur Trade of the Far West.* Stanford, Calif.: Academic Reprints, 1954.

Clark, W. P. *The Indian Sign Language.* Lincoln: University of Nebraska Press, 1982.

Coon, Shirley Jay. "The Economic Development of Missoula, Montana." PhD dissertation, University of Chicago, 1926.

Cressman, L. S. *Prehistory of the Far West: Homes of Vanished Peoples.* Salt Lake City: University of Utah Press, 1977.

Culbertson, Joseph. *Joseph Culbertson's Indian Scout Memoirs, 1876–1895.* Edited by M. D. Trout. Anaheim, Calif.: Van-Allen Publishing Co., 1984.

Dary, David. *Red Blood and Black Ink: Journalism in the Old West.* New York: Alfred A. Knopf, 1998.

[D'Aste, Jerome, S.J.] "Rev. and Dear Father." *Woodstock Letters* 7, no. 3 (1878): 179–84.

Davis, E. M. "Miss Woody." *Montana Journal* (Missoula) 3, no. 6 (Nov.–Dec. 1989): 21–22.

Dawes, Marian Elaine. "The Senatorial Career of George Graham Vest." Master's thesis, University of Missouri, Columbia, 1932.

Dempsey, L. James. *Blackfoot War Art: Pictographs of the Reservation Period, 1880–2000.* Norman: University of Oklahoma Press, 2007.

De Smet, Pierre-Jean, S.J. *Life, Letters, and Travels of Father Pierre-Jean De Smet, S.J., 1801–1873.* Edited by Hiram Martin Chittenden and Alfred Talbot Richardson. New York: Francis P. Harper, 1905.

——. *Oregon Missions and Travels Over the Rocky Mountains in 1845–46.* Fairfield, Wash.: Ye Galleon Press, 1978.

Doty, James. "A Visit to the Blackfoot Camp." Edited by Hugh A. Dempsey. *Alberta Historical Review* 14, no. 3 (Summer 1966): 17–26.

Dusenberry, J. Verne. "Samples of Pend d'Oreille Oral Literature and Salish Narratives." In *Lifeways of Intermontane and Plains Montana Indians,* edited by Leslie B. Davis. Bozeman: Museum of the Rockies, Montana State University, 1979, 109–20.

Eagle Calf and Heavy Breast, interpretations. *Picture Writing by the Blackfeet Indians of Glacier National Park, Montana.* Glacier Park, Mont.: Glacier Park Hotel Co., c. 1920.

Ewers, John C. *The Blackfeet: Raiders on the Northwestern Plains.* Norman: University of Oklahoma Press, 1958.

——. "Identification and History of the Small Robes Band of the Piegan Indians." *Journal of the Washington Academy of Sciences* 36, no. 12 (Dec. 15, 1946): 397–401.

——. "Iroquois Indians in the Far West." *Montana: The Magazine of Western History* 13, no. 2 (Apr. 1963): 2–10.

——. "The Nicholas Point Drawings: A Pictorial Record of Plains and Rocky Mountain Indian Life 150 Years Ago." *Columbia: The Magazine of Northwest History* 10, no. 3 (Fall 1996): 24–30.

——. "Were the Blackfoot Rich in Horses?" *American Anthropologist* 45, no. 4 (Oct. 1943): 602–10.

Fahey, John. *The Flathead Indians.* Norman: University of Oklahoma Press, 1974.

Farr, William E. "Going to Buffalo: Indian Hunting Migrations Across the Rocky Mountains: Part 2, Civilian Permits, Army Escorts." *Montana: The Magazine of Western History* 54, no. 1 (Spring 2004): 26–43.

"Father Mengarini." *Woodstock Letters* 16, no. 1 (1887): 93–97.

Foster, Morris W. *Being Comanche: A Social History of an American Indian Community.* Tucson: University of Arizona Press, 1991.

Fowler, Loretta. *Tribal Sovereignty and the Historical Imagination: Cheyenne-Arapaho Politics.* Lincoln: University of Nebraska Press, 2002.

Garcia, Andrew. *Tough Trip Through Paradise, 1878–1879.* Boston: Houghton Mifflin Company, 1967.

Garfield, James A. "Conference of Hon. James A. Garfield, Special Commissioner, with the Indians of the Bitter Root Valley, Montana." *Annual Report of the Board of Indian Commissioners* (1872): 171–74.

———. *The Diary of James A. Garfield.* Edited by Harry James Brown and Frederick D. Williams. East Lansing: Michigan State University Press, 1967.

Gibbon, John. *Adventures on the Western Frontier.* Bloomington: Indiana University Press, 1994.

Hansen, Bert B. and C. C. Wright, leaders. "Full Blood Flathead Indian Montana Study Group, Arlee, Montana: Minutes of Meetings." Mimeo. Missoula: The Montana Study, Montana State University, 1947.

Harmon, Alexandra. *Indians in the Making: Ethnic Relations and Indian Identities around Puget Sound.* Berkeley: University of California Press, 1998.

Harrison, Benjamin. "Message from the President of the United States, Transmitting a Report Relative to the Compensation of Henry B. Carrington, a Special Agent for the Sale of Certain Indian Lands." *Senate Exec. Doc.*, no. 70, 51st Cong., 1st Sess. (1890), serial 2686.

Harrison, Michael. "Chief Charlot's Battle with Bureaucracy." *Montana, the Magazine of Western History* 10, no. 4 (Oct. 1960): 27–33.

Hart, Jeff. *Montana--Native Plants and Early Peoples.* Helena: Montana Historical Society, 1976.

Henry, Alexander. *The Journal of Alexander Henry the Younger, 1799–1814.* Edited by Barry M. Gough. Toronto: Champlain Society, 1988–92.

Honig, Louis O. *James Bridger: The Pathfinder of the West.* Kansas City, Mo.: Brown-White-Lowell Press, 1951.

Howard, Helen Addison. *Northwest Trail Blazers.* Caldwell, Idaho: Caxton Printers, Ltd., 1963.

Howard, O. O. *Nez Perce Joseph: An Account of His Ancestors, His Lands, His Confederates, His Enemies, His Murders, His War, His Pursuit and Capture.* Boston: Lee and Shepard Pubs., 1881.

Hoxie, Frederick E. *Parading Through History: The Making of the Crow Nation in America, 1805–1935.* Cambridge, United Kingdom: Cambridge University Press, 1995.

Humphrey, Seth K. *The Indian Dispossessed*, rev. ed. Boston: Little, Brown, and Company, c. 1905, 1906.

Jackson, Donald, ed. *Letters of the Lewis and Clark Expedition with Related Documents, 1783–1854*, 2nd ed. Urbana: University of Illinois Press, 1978.

James, Elizabeth Jean. "Forging an Indigenous Future: The Nez Perces, 1893–1934." PhD dissertation, Arizona State University, Tempe, 2002, DAI #3069811.

Josephy, Alvin M., Jr. *The Nez Perce Indians and the Opening of the Northwest.* New Haven, Conn.: Yale University Press, 1965.

Kappler, Charles J., ed. *Indian Affairs: Laws and Treaties.* Washington, D.C.: U.S. Government Printing Office, 1904.

Keyser, James D. *The Five Crows Ledger: Biographic Warrior Art of the Flathead Indians.* Salt Lake City: University of Utah Press, 2000.

Koch, Elers. "Big Game in Montana from Early Historical Records." *The Journal of Wildlife Management* 5, no. 4 (Oct. 1941): 357–70.

Lancaster, Richard. *Piegan: A Look from Within at the Life, Times, and Legacy of an American Indian Tribe.* Garden City, N.Y.: Doubleday & Co., 1966.

Larpenteur, Charles. *Forty Years a Fur Trader on the Upper Missouri: The Personal Narrative of Charles Larpenteur, 1833–1872.* Edited by Elliot Coues. New York: Francis P. Harper, 1898.

[Leeson, Michael A., ed.] *History of Montana, 1739–1885.* Chicago: Warner, Beers & Company, 1885.

Leforge, Thomas H. *Memoirs of a White Crow Indian.* As told by Thomas B. Marquis. 1928. Reprint, Lincoln: University of Nebraska Press, 1974.

Lippincott, Joseph Barlow. "Grandeur in an American Forest." *The Forester* 6, no. 2 (Feb. 1900): 24–28.

Lolo History Committee. *Lolo Creek Reflections.* Missoula, Mont.: Economy Publishers, 1976.

Maerdian, Otto. "Pioneer Ranching in Central Montana." In *Frontier Omnibus,* edited by John W. Hakola. Missoula and Helena: Montana State University Press and Historical Society of Montana, 1962, 399–416.

McCormick, Washington J. *Colors From an Old Montana Sluice Box.* Missoula, Mont.: Friends of the University of Montana Library, 1980.

MacDonald, Duncan. "The Nez Perces: The History of Their Troubles and the Campaign of 1877." *Idaho Yesterdays* 21, no. 1 (Spring 1977): 2–15, 26–30; and vol. 21, no. 4 (Winter 1978): 2–10, 18–28.

McGinnis, Anthony. *Counting Coup and Cutting Horses: Intertribal Warfare on the Northern Plains, 1738–1889.* Evergreen, Colo.: Cordillera Press, 1990.

McKeen, Catherine. "Henry Beebee Carrington: A Soldier's Tale." PhD dissertation, State University of New York at Stony Brook, 1998, DAI #9912592.

McWhorter, L. V. *Hear Me, My Chiefs! Nez Perce History and Legend.* Caldwell, Idaho: Caxton Printers, Ltd., 1952.

Malouf, Carling [I.]. *Economy and Land Use by the Indians of Western Montana, U.S.A.* Mimeo. Missoula, Mont.: n.p., 1952.

———. "Flathead and Pend d'Oreille." *Handbook of North American Indians* 12:297–312. Washington, D.C.: Smithsonian Institution, 1998.

Marquis, Thomas B. *Wooden Leg: A Warrior Who Fought Custer.* 1931. Reprint, Lincoln: University of Nebraska Press, 1962.

Matt, Don. "Mary Ann Topsseh Coombs." *Char-Koosta* 5, no. 14 (Nov. 15, 1975): 8–9.

[Menetrey, Joseph, S.J.]. "Extract from a Letter of Father Manetrey [*sic*], of the Society of Jesus, to the Father Superior of the Missions of the Same Society in California and at the Rocky Mountains." *Annals of the Propagation of the Faith* (London) 19, no. 9 (Sept. 1858): 300–302.

Mengarini, Gregory, S.J. *Recollections of the Flathead Mission*. Edited by Gloria Ricci Lothrop. Glendale, Calif.: Arthur H. Clark Co., 1977.

———. "The Rocky Mountains." *Woodstock Letters* 17 (1888): 298–309, and vol. 18 (1889): 25–43, 147–52.

Meredith, Emily R. "Bannack and Gallatin City in 1862–1863." In *Frontier Omnibus*, edited by John W. Hakola. Missoula and Helena: Montana State University Press and Historical Society of Montana, 1962, 243–53.

Meyer, Melissa L. *The White Earth Tragedy: Ethnicity and Dispossession at a Minnesota Anishinaabe Reservation, 1889<n<1920*. Lincoln: University of Nebraska Press, 1994.

Meyer, Roy W. *History of the Santee Sioux: United States Indian Policy on Trial*. Lincoln: University of Nebraska Press, 1967.

Montana Historical Society. *Not in Precious Metals Alone: A Manuscript History of Montana*. Helena: Montana Historical Society Press, 1976.

Moore, Albert Thomas. *Pi-Lu'-Ye-Kin: The Life History of a Nez Perce Indian*. Edited by Anthony E. Thomas. Washington, D.C.: American Anthropological Association, 1970.

Moulton, Gary E., ed. *The Journals of the Lewis & Clark Expedition*. Lincoln: University of Nebraska Press, 1983–2001.

Mullins, John. "Report of First Lieutenant John Mullins, 2nd dragoons, on Route from Fort Benton to Fort Union, between the Missouri and Yellowstone Rivers, 1860." In U.S. Secretary of War, *Report of the Secretary of War, Communicating,...the Report of Brevet Brigadier General W. F. Raynolds, on the Exploration of the Yellowstone and the Country Drained by that River*, Senate Executive Document No. 77, 40th Cong., 2nd Sess. (1868), serial 1317, 161–70.

O'Neil, Carle F. *Two Men of Demersville*. Privately printed, n.p., 1990.

Overholser, J. F. "Livestock Growers Threatened by Indians." *Frontier* 13, no. 1 (Nov. 1932): 68–70.

Owen, John. *The Journals and Letters of Major John Owen, Pioneer of the Northwest, 1850–1871*. Edited by Seymour Dunbar and Paul C. Phillips. New York: Edward Eberstadt, 1927.

Palladino, Lawrence B., S.J. *Indian and White in the Northwest: A History of Catholicity in Montana, 1831 to 1891*, 2nd ed. Lancaster, Penn.: Wickersham Publishing Company, 1922.

Patterson, Ida S. *Montana Memories: The Life of Emma Magee in the Rocky Mountain West, 1866–1950*. Pablo, Mont.: The Steve Matt, Sr., Memorial Fund, Salish Kootenai Community College, 1981.

Point, Nicolas, S.J. *Wilderness Kingdom: Indian Life in the Rocky Mountains, 1840–1847*. Translated by Joseph P. Donnelly, S.J. New York: Holt, Rinehart and Winston, 1967.

Rappagliosi, Philip, S.J. *Letters from the Rocky Mountain Indian Missions.* Edited by Robert Bigart. Lincoln: University of Nebraska Press, 2003.

Richards, Kent D. *Isaac I. Stevens: Young Man in a Hurry.* Provo, Utah: Brigham Young University Press, 1979.

"Rocky Mountain Correspondence." *McGee's Illustrated Weekly* 3, no. 1 (Nov. 24, 1877): 3.

Ronan, Margaret. "Memoirs of a Frontiers Woman: Mary C. Ronan." Master's thesis, State University of Montana, Missoula, 1932.

Ronan, Mary. *Frontier Woman: The Story of Mary Ronan as Told to Margaret Ronan.* Edited by H. G. Merriam. Missoula: University of Montana Publications in History, 1973.

Ronan, Peter. *Historical Sketch of the Flathead Indian Nation* Minneapolis: Ross & Haines, 1965.

Salish Culture Committee. "The Exodus of the Bitterroot Salish." Booklet. St. Ignatius, Mont.: Salish Culture Committee, 1998.

Sanborn-Perris Map Co. Ltd. "Missoula, Missoula Co., Mont., June 1891." Map. New York: Sanborn-Perris Map Co. Ltd., 1891.

Schaeffer, Claude. "The First Jesuit Mission to the Flathead, 1840–1850: A Study in Culture Conflicts." *Pacific Northwest Quarterly* 28, no. 3 (July 1937): 227–>50.

Schafft, Charles. "Sketch of a Life: Chas. Schafft." Edited by Vivian Paladin. *Montana, the Magazine of Western History* 26, no. 1 (Jan. 1976): 26–37.

——. *See also* Shafft, Charley.

Schultz, James Willard. *Why Gone Those Times? Blackfoot Tales.* Norman: University of Oklahoma Press, 1974.

Secoy, Frank Raymond. *Changing Military Patterns on the Great Plains: 17th Century Through Early 19th Century.* Seattle: University of Washington Press, 1953.

Seifried, Richard Dwight. "Early Administration of the Flathead Indian Reservation, 1855 to 1893." Master's thesis, University of Montana, Missoula, 1968.

Shafft, Charley. "General Garfield and the Flatheads." *The Council Fire and Arbitrator* (Washington, D.C.) 5, no. 1 (Jan. 1882): 19–21.

——. *See also* Schafft, Charles.

Smith, Thompson, of the Salish Pend d'Oreille Culture Committee, to Bigart, personal communication, Mar. 23, 2006.

S.O.S. Writers' Club. *Montana's Little Legends.* Hamilton, Mont.: Daily Ravalli Republican, 1963.

*Some Bitterroot Memories, 1860–1930: A Homey Account of the Florence Community.* Missoula, Mont.: Gateway Printing & Litho, n.d.

Spence, Clark C. *Territorial Politics and Government in Montana, 1864–89.* Urbana: University of Illinois Press, 1975.

Spier, Leslie. *The Prophet Dance of the Northwest and Its Derivatives: The Source of the Ghost Dance.* Menasha, Wis.: George Banta Publishing Company, 1935.

Stanley, Rev. E. J. *Life of Rev. L. B. Stateler or Sixty-Five Years on the Frontier.* Nashville, Tenn.: Publishing House of the M. E. Church, South, 1907.

Stevens, Isaac I. "Narrative and Final Report of Explorations for a Route for a Pacific Railroad from St. Paul to Puget Sound, 1855." In vol. 12, bk. 1 of *Reports of Explorations and Surveys to Ascertain the Most Practicable and Economical Route for a Railroad from the Mississippi River to the Pacific Ocean, 1853–5*. Washington, D.C.: Thomas H. Ford, Printer, 1860, 1–358.

——. "Report of Explorations for a Route for the Pacific Railroad, from St. Paul to Puget Sound." In vol. 1 of *Reports of Explorations and Surveys to Ascertain the Most Practicable and Economical Route for a Railroad from the Mississippi River to the Pacific Ocean, 1853–4*. Washington, D.C.: Beverley Tucker, Printer, 1855, 1–651.

Stevensville Historical Society. *Montana Genesis: A History of the Stevensville Area of the Bitterroot Valley*. Missoula, Mont.: Mountain Press Publishing Company, 1971.

Stone, Arthur L. *Following Old Trails*. Missoula, Mont.: Morton John Elrod, 1913.

Strahorn, Carrie Adell. *Fifteen Thousand Miles by Stage*. Lincoln: University of Nebraska Press, 1988.

Strickland, Rennard, ed. *Felix S. Cohen's Handbook of Federal Indian Law: 1982 Edition*. Charlottesville, Va.: Michie Bobbs-Merrill, 1982.

Stuart, Granville. *Forty Years on the Frontier*. Cleveland, Ohio: Arthur H. Clark Company, 1925.

Teit, James A. "The Salishan Tribes of the Western Plateaus." Edited by Franz Boas. *Annual Report of the Bureau of American Ethnology*, no. 45 (1927–28): 23–396.

Thompson, David. *David Thompson's Narrative, 1784–1812*. Edited by Richard Glover. Toronto: Champlain Society, 1962.

Topping, E. S. *The Chronicles of the Yellowstone*. Edited by Robert A. Murray. Minneapolis, Minn.: Ross & Haines, Inc., 1968.

Tracy, Gordon A. *Uncle Jack's Fiddlin Around*. Santa Margarita, Calif.: Tracy Management Agency, 1992.

Tunison, George M. "Before the Indian Claims Commission." Doc. 61, Depositions Oct. 27–31, 1952, typescript, Exhibit A, RG 279, NA.

Turney-High, Harry Holbert. "The Diffusion of the Horse to the Flatheads." *Man* 35, no. 12 (Dec. 1935): 183–85.

——. *The Flathead Indians of Montana*. Memoirs of the American Anthropological Association, no. 48 (1937).

Two Leggings. *Two Leggings: The Making of a Crow Warrior*. Edited by Peter Nabokov. 1967. Reprint, Lincoln: University of Nebraska Press, 1982.

Uhlenbeck-Melchior, Wilhelmina Maria, and C. C. Uhlenbeck. *Montana 1911: A Professor and His Wife Among the Blackfeet*. Calgary, Alberta: University of Calgary Press, 2005.

U.S. Bureau of the Census. *Historical Statistics of the United States: Colonial Times to 1970*. Washington, D.C.: U.S. Government Printing Office, 1975.

U.S. Census Bureau. *Statistical Abstract of the United States*, 1987, 2008, and 2010.

U.S. Census Division. *Abstract of the Eleventh Census, 1890*, 2nd ed. Washington, D.C.: U.S. Government Printing Office, 1896.

U.S. Census Office. *Compendium of the Eleventh Census: 1890: Part I. Population.* Washington, D.C.: U.S. Government Printing Office, 1892.

U.S. Commissioner of Indian Affairs. *Annual Report.* Washington, D.C.: U.S. Government Printing Office, 1859–1893.

U.S. Congress, House of Representatives. "Sale of Lands of Flathead Indians." *House of Representatives Report,* no. 2249, 50th Cong., 1st Sess. (1888), serial 2603.

*U.S. Congressional Record,* 45th Cong., 2nd Sess., vol. 7, pt. 3 (Apr. 27, 1878).

*U.S. Congressional Record,* 50th Cong. 1st Sess., vol. 19, pt. 2 (Feb. 27, 1888).

*U.S. Congressional Record*, 50th Cong., 2d Sess., vol. 20, pt. 2 (Feb. 6, 1889).

*U.S. Congressional Record*, 50th Cong, 2d Sess., vol. 20, pt. 3 (Feb. 26, 1889).

U.S. Department of Agriculture. *Climate and Man: Yearbook of Agriculture.* Washington, D.C.: U.S. Government Printing Office, 1941.

———, Weather Bureau. *Summaries of Climatological Data by Sections: Bulletin W*, 2nd ed. Washington, D.C.: Weather Bureau, 1926, section 28: Western Montana.

U.S. Department of the Interior. *Register of Officers and Agents, Civil, Military, and Naval, in the Service of the United States.* Washington, D.C.: U.S. Government Printing Office, 1870–1878.

U.S. Secretary of the Interior. *Annual Report.* Washington, D.C.: U.S. Government Printing Office, 1854–1877.

*U.S. Statutes at Large*, vol. 17 (1872), vol. 23 (1884–85), vol. 25 (1889), vol. 26 (1891), vol. 27 (1892).

Utley, Robert M. *The Lance and the Shield: The Life and Times of Sitting Bull.* New York: Henry Holt and Company, 1993.

Vaughn, Robert. *Then and Now: or Thirty-Six Years in the Rockies: Personal Reminiscences of Some of the First Pioneers of the State of Montana, 1864–1900.* Minneapolis, Minn.: Tribune Printing Company, 1900.

Vest, G. G., and Martin Maginnis. "Report of the Subcommittee of the Special Committee of the United States Senate, Appointed to Visit the Indian Tribes in Northern Montana." *Senate Report,* no. 283, 48th Cong., 1st Sess. (1884), serial 2174.

Vestal, Stanley. *Sitting Bull: Champion of the Sioux.* Norman: University of Oklahoma Press, 1957.

Walcheck, Ken. "Montana Wildlife 170 Years Ago As Lewis and Clark Saw It." *Montana Outdoors* 7, no. 4 (July/Aug. 1976): 15–30.

Weisel, George F., ed. *Men and Trade on the Northwest Frontier as Shown by the Fort Owen Ledger.* Missoula: Montana State University Press, 1955.

Whealdon, Bon I., et al. *"I Will Be Meat for My Salish": The Buffalo and the Montana Writers Project Interviews on the Flathead Indian Reservation.* Edited by Robert Bigart. Pablo and Helena, Mont.: Salish Kootenai College Press and Montana Historical Society Press, 2001.

Wheeler, Wm. F. "Judge Caleb E. Irvine, Soldier, Pioneer and Jurist." *Contributions to the Historical Society of Montana* 6 (1907): 475–78.

White Bull, Chief Joseph. *The Warrior Who Killed Custer: The Personal Narrative of Chief Joseph White Bull.* Translated and edited by James H. Howard. Lincoln: University of Nebraska Press, 1968.

Wissler, Clark. "The Social Life of the Blackfoot Indians." *Anthropological Papers of the American Museum of Natural History* 7, pt. 1 (1912): 1–64.

Woody, F. H. "A Sketch of the Early History of Western Montana." *Contributions to the Historical Society of Montana* 2 (1896): 88–106.

Wyeth, Nathaniel J. "The Correspondence and Journals of Captain Nathaniel J. Wyeth, 1831–6." Edited by F. G. Young. *Sources of the History of Oregon* 1 (1899): 1–262.

Zimmer, William F. *Frontier Soldier: An Enlisted Man's Journal of the Sioux and Nez Perce Campaigns, 1877.* Helena: Montana Historical Society Press, 1998.

# Index

Note: During the nineteenth century many Salish people were known by a Christian or first name and an Indian name. Individuals in this index may be listed under either a Christian name or a family or surname.